T0369629

THE POLITICS OF HUMILIATION

THE POLITICS OF HUMILIATION

A Modern History

UTE FREVERT

Translated by Adam Bresnahan

OXFORD
UNIVERSITY PRESS

OXFORD
UNIVERSITY PRESS

Great Clarendon Street, Oxford, OX2 6DP,
United Kingdom

Oxford University Press is a department of the University of Oxford.
It furthers the University's objective of excellence in research, scholarship,
and education by publishing worldwide. Oxford is a registered trade mark of
Oxford University Press in the UK and in certain other countries

© Ute Frevert 2020

The moral rights of the author have been asserted

First Edition published in 2020

Impression: 1

Published in the United States of America by Oxford University Press
198 Madison Avenue, New York, NY 10016, United States of America

British Library Cataloguing in Publication Data

Data available

Library of Congress Control Number: 2019949404

ISBN 978-0-19-882031-4

Printed and bound in Great Britain by
Clays Ltd, Elcograf S.p.A.

CONTENTS

CONTENTS

LIST OF ILLUSTRATIONS

INTRODUCTION

The Power of Shame

Sidi Bouzid, Tunisia, December 2010: 26-year-old vegetable merchant Mohamed Bouazizi douses himself with gasoline and sets his body on fire in front of the mayor's mansion. After years of police harassment, a female officer who confiscated his wares and slapped him finally drove him over the edge. A journalist later explained Bouazizi's self-immolation as demonstrating that he 'would no longer take the debasement and humiliation'. His desperate act of protest then triggered the 'revolt of dignity' that went down in history as the Arab Spring.[1] In many North African and Middle Eastern countries, men and women organized against authoritarian regimes, occupied central city squares, and disobeyed police commands. Posters, graffiti, and Facebook posts made frequent use of the word 'dignity'. When asked why they were demonstrating and what their goals were, many activists answered that they felt humiliated by the way their governments were treating them. This occasioned *New York Times* reporter Thomas Friedman to claim that humiliation was the 'single most underestimated force in politics'.[2]

In November 2012, Shena Hardin of Cleveland, Ohio was subjected to something more akin to shame and less to humiliation. She stood at the corner of a busy intersection holding a sign that read: 'Only an idiot would drive on the sidewalk to avoid a school bus.' Hardin, indeed, had done it a few times. As if being fined and having her licence suspended was not enough, the judge sentenced Hardin to a so-called shame sanction: a form of public shaming that clearly

1

Fig. 1. Shena Hardin, Cleveland, Ohio, November 2012

marked Hardin as an idiot. Such sentences are intended not only to discipline and punish, but also to educate and improve. On Hardin, the effect was one of ambivalence. First, she demonstrated coolness and nonchalance, despite being visibly aggravated by the media attention. After the judge had her lift the sign up higher, she conceded that she had learned her lesson. But the experience, she added, would not 'break' her.[3]

This distinguishes her case from that of 13-year-old Izabel Laxamana. Angered at finding pictures of her on the internet in a sports bra and leggings, the teenager's father filmed himself cutting off her long hair. Shortly afterwards, he put the video online and it went viral. Unable to bear the humiliation in front of her schoolmates, the girl from Tacoma, Washington committed suicide by jumping off a bridge in May 2015.

The case sounded patently medieval to US journalist Amanda Hess. She notes that while ritual public shaming has become obsolescent as a form of criminal punishment, some parents have started using social media to embarrass and shame children in front of their peers. The publicity afforded by Facebook and YouTube make them perfect venues for castigating those who break the rules, with often tragic consequences for the punished. Teenagers with low self-esteem are helpless in the face of such humiliation: they are 'broken' by their ridiculers as much as by the gaze of the public and its often stinging comments.[4]

Why do people feel the need to embarrass others in public—even their own children—and where does this need come from? What is the point of shaming someone, and what effects does it have? Why is shaming widespread even in societies that value dignity, recognition, and respect highly? Is it proof that 'medieval attitudes' are still with us? Or has the 'enlightened' modern era set loose its own desire to shame and humiliate with new forms and targets?

Public shaming puts power on display. By bringing people to their knees in front of others, social actors emphatically assert their superior, more powerful position. According to sociologist Max Weber, power 'is the probability that one actor within a social relationship will be in a position to carry out his own will despite resistance, regardless of the basis on which this probability rests'.[5] Thus, Izabel Laxamana's father exerted power over her. He forbade her from putting selfies on the internet, and when she did it anyway, he humiliated her and, on top of that, made the act of humiliation public. In doing so, he underscored his own power and Izabel's inability to defend herself. This humiliation made her bow her head in shame: she wanted to become invisible and saw no other option than to kill herself.

The awareness that shame is a frighteningly powerful emotion stretches all the way back to ancient times in places as far apart as Greece and Iceland.[6] Shame can be deadly and, even if it does not go that far, can still have a lasting effect on the living. Anyone who has ever been deeply shamed knows that shaking the feeling off is not easy. The presence and witness of others is a crucial aspect of it, although we might also secretly feel ashamed of ourselves for doing or thinking something that contradicts our sense of self or common notions of morality and propriety. We might, for instance, feel ashamed for envying a colleague who just got promoted, or for taking joy in watching the boss tear into a colleague in front of the whole office. Acts of public humiliation are generally seen as intolerable displays of disregard for human dignity, or even as attacks on it; thus, if we openly or tacitly approve of them, we might experience shame.

But what makes such acts so despicable? Is it because we know about the power of the public gaze, a gaze that cannot be avoided, that gets beneath our skin and marks the body of the humiliated? When others witness our individual faults or transgressions, this triggers a feeling of shame, which is all the more intense the more we want to be held in high esteem. A child who steals a candy bar from the store and knows that doing so is not allowed might secretly feel ashamed but not show it. However, if the child gets caught and her parents find out about it, she does not need to be told 'shame on you!' to feel it. Being publicly humiliated makes her blush, and she has just one wish: to get away from the others' stares as soon as possible.

For these reasons, psychologists call shame a social or interpersonal emotion. It is generally experienced in the presence of others—indeed, only one out of six respondents say that they think of shame as a private, 'solitary' feeling.[7] The social embeddedness of shame can be both powerful and dangerous. The fear of being shamed sometimes even drives people to risk life and limb. In Erich Kästner's classic children's book *The Flying Classroom*, little Uli's fellow classmates are constantly teasing him for his lack of courage, which makes his face turn 'red as a turkey-cock'. In order to prove that he is not a coward, he finally leaps from the top rung of a tall ladder. This act of defiance does indeed cost him some serious injuries and a trip to the hospital, but at least it shuts up the bullies.[8]

Kästner's Uli (the book was first published in 1933) grows up in a youth culture that treats cowardice as one of the worst weaknesses. Boys have to be brave and prove it. If they fail to do so, they might be disliked, despised, and even cast out of the group. Uli accepts and internalizes these norms and the only thing he can think of to beat the bullies is to do something stunningly daring. Izabel Laxamana's case was different. She probably was not ashamed for ignoring her father's commands and posing in a sports bra on the internet, and she did not necessarily share his ideas of what constitutes morality and decency. She was ashamed of being punished and having a video of it spread around school. If the father had not filmed the episode, the daughter might have been able to pull off her short hair as a self-conscious, trendsetting style decision. The video, however, made her humiliation public.

These and many other examples demonstrate the impact that public humiliation can have on people. On the one hand, they show the power of perpetrators to chastise and publicize acts they view as violations of norm or convention. On the other, they testify to the power of witnesses, whether real or imaginary. The play of power and powerlessness, shame and disgrace, perpetrator and victim always takes place in public spaces. Witnesses can approve of acts of shaming and intensify them. But they can also disapprove. Power relations can be turned on their head, shaming those who shame. Modern history gives us vivid examples that span from people gradually distancing themselves from someone who shames to broad criticism of that person, from individual acts of protest to communal revolt.

History and Its Interpretation

It seems that collective memory has in its stores quite a bit of more or less concrete knowledge of earlier practices of shaming that can be called up at will. When Izabel's public humiliation reminded journalist Amanda Hess of medieval times, she might have thought of people being pilloried. She also knew that a shaved head, particularly for women, has historically come to be an almost archetypical symbol of social debasement.

This book deals with such symbols and practices. It traces their development from the eighteenth century to today, and while it focuses on Europe, it also offers a look at other parts of the world. It seeks to identify continuities and discontinuities and analyses striking trends and controversies. That repertoires of shaming and humiliation have been around for a long time in places near and far does not necessarily mean that they always take the same shape or appear in the same contexts. Who uses them when against whom and to what end depends on particular political opportunities, social conditions, and moral economies. Women are not always punished by having their heads shaven; citizens not always robbed of their dignity by their government; criminals not always humiliated in public.

What characterizes societies that accept—or even encourage—such practices? What kind of political regimes use humiliation, and which seek to prevent it? Should we read the history of humiliation as a story of Western progress peopled by bourgeois-liberal heroes waving the banner of human dignity? Or has modernity brought with it new methods of and occasions for humiliation and new ways of justifying or understanding it?

The idea that the experience of the Second World War made us place greater value on civility, respect, and recognition is commonplace. Indeed, the preamble to the Charter of the United Nations, signed in 1945, professes a belief 'in the dignity and worth of the human person'. Article 1 of the Universal Declaration of Human Rights, proclaimed in 1948, states: 'All human beings are born free and equal in dignity and rights.'[9] The Basic Law of the Federal Republic of Germany, ratified in 1949, counts human dignity as the highest inviolable right and makes it the duty of the state to 'respect and protect it'.[10] Yet human dignity and the individual rights associated with it have a much longer history. As early as the eighteenth century, they were used as an argument against 'dishonourable' forms of punishment and their consecration in law.[11]

In his famous study on the birth of the prison, Michel Foucault ironically called this argument the 'discourse of the heart'. He claimed that all the talk about the 'humanity' of some forms of punishment was little more than a strategy to justify the 'refinement of punitive practices', deployed by the state for the purpose of guaranteeing more omnipresent surveillance of the 'social body'. But why did people who allegedly wanted to exert maximum control choose the language of the heart and 'sensibility' to promote it? Why did judges express moral disgust with corporal punishment and sympathy with men and women whom they sentenced to floggings, branding, and public exposure? What changes did their hearts have to undergo to open them up to the new discourse of humanity? Why did human dignity become an emotionally invested topic in the late eighteenth and early nineteenth century, and why has it remained important ever since? Despite Foucault's contention, the recourse to emotions does not simply follow 'a principle of calculation', but has its own historical logic. Writing it off as an opportunistic trick passes up the chance to determine its proper place in modern culture and society.[12]

In contrast to Foucault, Israeli philosopher Avishai Margalit maintains that decency, dignity, and honour have a crucial function in social structures. For Margalit, a decent society is 'one whose institutions do not humiliate people' and do respect their dignity.[13] This is very similar to ideas that became prominent around 1800. Enlightenment-era jurists were already grappling with the notions of honour and dignity when they sought to replace the traditional system of corporal punishment and public shaming. From this perspective, the modern world seems dedicated to working against the destructive power of social and political humiliation by opposing it with equally powerful instruments designed to foster interpersonal respect and protect the feeling of self-worth.

Humiliation as Strategy and Stigma

At the same time, contemporary societies still use shaming and humiliation to exert social and political power. This goes beyond all the petty everyday debasements that occur between two people and rarely get out to the public. It is certainly an insult that can occasion a visit to the courthouse when one neighbour calls another an idiot in

Fig. 2. Punishment of a female French collaborator, Marseilles, 1944

an argument over the height of his bushes. But true humiliation or shaming takes place in a public space in front of witnesses who play an indispensable, active role. Moreover, public humiliation is not used in conflicts over trivial matters that only affect the two parties involved. There must be more at stake: above all, the violation of a norm that is important for a larger collective, which has an interest in ensuring that it remains sacrosanct. Punishing someone in public symbolically excludes that person from the group. If they are allowed back in afterwards, social scientists speak of 'reintegrative shaming'.[14]

The opposite is stigmatizing humiliation, which seeks to exclude categorically. It was a matter neither of punishment nor of integration when German soldiers shaved the beards of Jewish men in occupied Poland in 1939/40,[15] or when Serbian soldiers and militiamen systematically raped Muslim women during the Bosnian War of the 1990s. Rather, the goal was to assert power and degrade the members of another group in order to permanently damage or even destroy their moral and social integrity.

Both reintegrative shaming and stigmatizing humiliation are planned, coordinated, and public. They are neither spur-of-the-moment nor wholly contingent upon each individual situation. Rather, they follow well-thought-out scripts and have a ritualized structure. Repeated over time and easily recognizable, they can be tailored to fulfil either function. In the end, both have the aim of stabilizing existing power relations or establishing new ones by showcasing the powerlessness of others. In this sense, one might speak of humiliation as politics, as an intentional strategy of asserting power that involves different actors and occurs in different places.

The ubiquity of such strategies, practices, and places testifies to their appeal for those in power, those seeking power, and those fighting for power. At the same time, it demonstrates the great reservations and resistance—both past and present—towards 'decent' and civil interaction. Even in liberal societies, old forms of stigmatization have been preserved and new ones invented, practices that have little to do with decency and dignity. In the German-speaking world, the concept of 'pillory by media' (roughly the equivalent of the English 'trial by media') has been around since the late nineteenth century and has even more relevance today. In October 2015, the German tabloid *Bild* published a double spread with the names and faces of people who had made racist and xenophobic statements on social media. One of them took the paper to court for libel for publishing her face in this 'pillory of shame'. She won the case on appeal.[16] Shaming penalties are also popular, as mentioned before, among US judges (mostly in local courts), even if there is no shortage of critics. And when the BBC did a documentary on official practices of shaming in Chinese elementary schools in 2008, the British audience was split: while some saw the 'dark' European Middle Ages playing out before their eyes and hoped China would soon be struck by the light of reason, others thought that the rituals, which ended with the return of the shamed child into the class group, were not such a bad idea at all.[17]

International Relations

Like the old Christian practices of religious penitence, such rituals seek to embarrass and exclude the transgressor in order to better them and reintegrate them into the community. Shame is ideally followed by regret, which is a precondition for forgiveness and reconciliation. Humiliation among political leaders is not much different, even though it puts power and honour on display far more directly and dramatically. A state doing injury to the honour of another without apologizing can incite a war, as was the case in 1870 between France and Prussia. Ending war with peace treaties that humiliate one or more of the warring parties makes new conflicts more likely, a fact that is well known from the 1919 Paris Treaties, which embarrassed Germany, Austria, and Hungary. In such cases, politicians and diplomats might proceed with caution and avoid humiliating their counterparts. But they also have the option of deliberately using humiliation as a tactic to improve their position in national and international power struggles.

How this works could be observed up close in 2010. When a Turkish television channel broadcast a series that depicted Israeli soldiers as child murderers, Israel's deputy foreign minister, Danny Ayalon, summoned Turkey's ambassador to Israel. Before the meeting, he told journalists that they were about to witness an act of symbolic humiliation: the Turkish ambassador had to sit on a lower sofa, the Turkish flag was missing, and the Israelis refused to smile. This was all in line with the government's right-wing foreign policy, which was more concerned with showing strength and pride than with polite exchange. The intentions were, of course, not lost on the Turkish government. They reacted with sharply worded protest, fuelling the flames by claiming that the entire Turkish people saw themselves humiliated. President Abdullah Gül demanded that Ayalon publicly apologize, which he refused to do. Fearing the damage the incident might do to the then good relations with his country's most important military ally in the region, Israeli president Shimon Peres intervened. He got Ayalon to say that it was 'not [his] way to insult foreign ambassadors'. That, however, did not go far enough for the Turkish side. After another hectic day of diplomatic back-and-forth, Ankara's ambassador finally received a letter that said: 'I had no intention to humiliate you personally and apologize for the way the démarche was handled and perceived. Please convey this to the Turkish people for whom we have great respect.'[18]

Ayalon's statement was carefully worded, applying a diplomatic vocabulary that had been developing since the early modern period. But only during the nineteenth century did politicians begin referring to the 'people', who had to be informed of the apology and be respected by others. This reflected the historically new role that the nation and national citizens had taken on. After the French Revolution, the state came to be seen as an institution of the nation (comprising all citizens) that represented its sovereignty. The honour of the state, which had previously been the honour of the prince, was thus transferred to the honour of the nation. As a consequence, insulting the state affected every citizen, male and female, young and old. This goes a long way towards explaining why the Turkish government claimed that in offending their diplomat, Israel's minister had hurt the Turkish people, and why Ayalon then apologized not only to the ambassador, but also to the Turks as a whole. Thus, in modern times, international relations are often played out in front of a large audience and are, as such, dramatized. When cameras capture every minute detail of diplomatic communication, humiliating gestures and statements take on a force that would have been unthinkable in times of secretive aristocratic politics.

The media are just as important for the politics of humiliation on the international stage as are nationalization and democratization. Indeed, journalists have not come to be known as representing the fourth branch of government for nothing: they can write about violations of norms, report on alleged acts of humiliation, and demand sanctions. And they themselves can humiliate by lampooning politicians both foreign and domestic and dragging them through the mud. In 2016, German television show host Jan Böhmermann's satirical poem about Turkish president Erdoğan made waves, causing the Turkish vice president to charge that the poem had insulted the president and along with him all 78 million Turks. Erdoğan not only took the satirist to court for libel, he also wanted to see him tried under an obscure German law that forbids insulting foreign representatives and heads of state (§103 StGB).[19]

Semantic Distinctions

In his lawsuit, Erdoğan accused Böhmermann of violating Article 185 of the German penal code, which does indeed speak of insult, but does not define what it is. In 1989, the Federal Court of Justice suggested a definition:

> The laws should provide protection against attacks on a person's honour ... An attack on a person's honour occurs when a perpetrator makes false defamatory claims about another's alleged demerits, which, if they did indeed exist, would diminish the person's prestige. Only through such 'defamation' (which can be a deprecating value judgement or a dishonouring accusation) does one do injury to another person's right to be respected, which follows out of his or her honour. It expresses contempt, disdain, and disrespect, which legal practice has defined as the elements of this crime.[20]

So, what distinguishes insult from shaming and humiliation? After all, shaming too expresses disdain and contempt, and acts of humiliation can be seen as acts of profound disrespect. Shaming and humiliating always involve an attack on the victim's honour. Even more, they explicitly aim to undermine the respect others have for that person, and his or her own sense of self-worth. Whoever is humiliated or shamed in public will have a difficult time restoring their 'prestige' and realizing their 'right to be respected'. In contrast, insults have less weight because they follow a logic of provocation and response, and it is only in the response that the insult gains any significance. While the shamed and humiliated person is passive and suffering, the insulted person is not: they must decide whether or not they want to reply to the provocation or simply ignore it. They can argue, insult back, file suit. But they can also laugh it off, shrug their shoulders, or, like in Erich Maria Remarque's novel *Three Comrades*, try to one-up the other.[21] After all, insults have no foundation in reality: the insulted has no real 'demerits' and has not done anything wrong. As the Federal Court of Justice stated, insulting someone is per definition libel. If an insult were to be based in truth, it would no longer be an insult, but a valid piece of criticism and disapproval.

In addition, insults lack both the dimension of power (and power-lessness) and the sanctioning force that have traditionally been associated with shaming. Shaming another person is a reaction to the violation of a norm adhered to by a collective. In contrast, insults function without appeal to social norms and conventions. This is why they are generally handled as civil cases if and when they make it to court. The public only has an interest in treating them as criminal cases in exceptional circumstances, such as when racial slurs are used.[22]

The example of racism elucidates what distinguishes shaming from humiliation. Shaming is used to punish behaviour that runs contrary to what holds weight for a social group or organization, and it is carried out within that very group. In contrast, humiliation works by distinguishing radically between those who are in and those who are out: we are us, you are different and count for less. Whoever degrades, disrespects, or attacks someone because of their ethnicity aims to exclude them from his own community and demonstrate his superior status. The more humiliated the victim, the greater the perpetrator's feeling of power, a fact demonstrated in 1938 Vienna, when anti-Semites forced Jewish citizens to scrub the sidewalk on their knees.[23]

Power is also clearly at stake whenever shaming occurs. The shamed person has little means of defending herself, and she suffers a loss of honour and respect even after she has been reintegrated into the group. But the relation between the person who shames and those who are shamed is not truly hierarchical and asymmetrical. Strictly

13

speaking, the victim is responsible for their temporary exclusion by having acted against collective rules. The situation of the Viennese Jews, though, was altogether different: they were simply told that they were no longer part of the German-Austrian community. They were made into outsiders not for what they did, but for who they were— Jews—and as such suffered public humiliation.

Despite these differences, everyday language does not neatly distinguish between shaming and humiliation.[24] In part, this might have to do with the ever-increasing number of new and mixed types of castigation that straddle the analytical line between the two. When, as in the modern era, the cohesive power of social bonds begins to falter and people can choose to belong to a number of different groups, the classic forms of shaming lose their efficacy because they no longer have a clearly defined audience. At the same time, new institutions and organizations invent their own practices of debasement and denunciation, which often serve as rites of passage. It is not always obvious whether these new forms serve a normative, integrating function or aim to expel a person categorically from the group. For instance, treatment of homosexuals can be shaming when homosexuality is seen as an illness to be cured, an archaic view that still has many adherents in countries around the world. But it can also take on a humiliating, radically stigmatizing and excluding character. In both cases, homosexual men and women might feel the same sense of rejection and degradation, even though the political consequences might be vastly different.[25]

Conflating shaming and humiliation also reflects shifts in language and philosophical-legal concepts over the course of the nineteenth and twentieth centuries. As the notion of dignity acquired a more important position in social and political discourse, the significance of honour began to dissipate. Correlatively, 'humiliation' came increasingly into common parlance and 'shaming' faded in use.[26] But drawing a clear distinction between the meanings of honour and dignity is also tough, and philosophers and legal scholars have a hard time separating one from the other. Sometimes, honour and honourability are regarded as elements of personal dignity; other authors apply the terms interchangeably. This goes back to the nineteenth century, when human or 'general' honour and dignity became treated as quasi-synonyms.[27] In any event, such merging of concepts makes it even more difficult to distinguish neatly between the related practices of shaming and humiliation.[28]

People, Places, Times

This book studies both types of power relations. It considers a wide array of different people, groups, situations, and institutions: legal scholars and practitioners debating the pros and cons of public corporal punishment; teachers and school administrators arguing over whether it is permissible to hit pupils or send them to the corner; soldiers, officers, and legislators quarrelling about abuses in the military; mothers and fathers wondering whether they should or are allowed to shame a disobedient child; parents' guides and children's books that take a position on the shaming debate; youth groups, fraternities, and sororities that force newcomers to undergo demeaning initiation rituals; ordinary citizens publicly shaving the heads of women who acted against the conventions of femininity or national honour; a mother who believes that school sports debase her children; diplomats and politicians who either humiliate others or claim to have been humiliated in order to legitimize their own actions and strategies.

Most of the people and cases discussed here come from Europe, a continent that has a long tradition of public shaming and humiliation and a far shorter history of criticizing those practices. But shaming and humiliation are practised the world over. During China's Cultural Revolution, students systematically insulted and abused their teachers and professors in public. In 2016, members of the teachers' union in Mexico cut the hair of six other teachers who refused to support a strike. They had them walk barefoot through the streets wearing signs that read 'traitor'.[29] In the same year, religious militants in northern India kidnapped a young Christian accused of trying to convert Hindus.

They shamed him by shaving his head and forcing him to ride around town on a donkey for four hours.[30] These and other countries have their own traditions of shaming and humiliation. At the same time, they draw from a set of practices and symbols that seems astonishingly similar all over the globe.

Shame, Humility, and the History of Emotions

Nevertheless, shaming and humiliation are not anthropological constants that have simply undergone slight changes across space and time. Nor are the feelings of shame and humiliation that they might cause universal and uniform.

Over the course of history, humiliation has been experienced, described, and evaluated in different ways. Both Old and New Testaments tell us that man should act with humility and reverence in order to receive God's grace. 'When they cast you down, and you say, "Exaltation will come!" Then He will save the humble person' (Job 22:29). God's anger at Israel's faithlessness and disobedience could usually be pacified by the people acknowledging their guilt. Remorse and humility were thus among the highest values in Judaism and Christianity. Priests and laypeople alike had no qualms with submitting themselves to God's will, in both word and gesture.[31] In contrast, the Greeks and Romans associated humility with the subservience of slaves. Drawing inspiration from them two millennia later, Friedrich Nietzsche equated humility with cowardice and weakness, dismissing it as an element of 'slave morality'. Late eighteenth-century Europeans held a similar opinion of what they viewed as the extreme 'debasement' and 'humiliation' of 'Oriental' people at the will of their godlike rulers.[32] Such forms of 'subjugation' were hardly reconcilable with the new ideals and values spurred by the Enlightenment and the development of civil societies. For proud and self-confident citizens of the 'Occident', they served as further justification for their feeling of superiority over other countries and cultures.

Like humility, shame is a socio-cultural convention. Children learn to feel shame from parents, teachers, and other adults, either through simple observation and imitation or through being chided for breaking the rules. Therefore, the feeling only kicks in at a certain age. While some societies make heavy use of shame and shaming, others employ it less or tend to dispense with it as a means of educational and social discipline. The amount to which a given society avails itself of shame is largely dependent on its degree of social differentiation and on the value attributed to notions of individuality, freedom, and autonomy. Traditional societies with well-defined social divisions and internal bonding mechanisms generally cultivate a multitude of shaming practices, which, in turn, generate nuanced feelings of shame and embarrassment. For women, shame means something different than for men; the lower classes experience it in other ways than the upper classes. Such differences by no means end with the advent of modernity. In theory, citizens are now supposed to act as free and autonomous individuals, liberated from the fetters of old regime discipline and social surveillance. In practice, however, people continue living as social beings and thus remain dependent on the recognition and appreciation of others. This renders them susceptible to shame and shaming.

One might even join sociologist Norbert Elias and claim that in modern societies, people's sensitivity towards shame increases rather than decreases. Elias views shame as the standard reaction to the 'fear of social degradation' and 'other people's gestures of superiority' in the face of one's own 'defencelessness' and vulnerability. If we agree with him that the 'shame-threshold' weakens with the process of civilization, then nineteenth- and twentieth-century Europeans might have felt a more intense form of shame with more frequency than their sixteenth- and seventeenth-century counterparts.[33] Philosopher Georg Simmel made a similar argument around 1900 when he claimed that modernity's emphasis on the 'consciousness of self' (*Ichbewußtsein*) was the 'main station' of the feeling of shame. But such a heightened sense of self could lead in two directions: it could help people live an autonomous, self-determined life protected by strong institutions. Above all, the rule of law is supposed to keep 'degradations' at bay and strengthen our capability to fend off 'gestures of superiority'.[34]

On the other hand, the modern sense of self could also motivate people to view themselves constantly in the eyes of others and to be on the lookout anxiously for signals of disrespect and debasement. Narcissism and shame are thus closely related, as contemporary psychologists and psychotherapists confirm. Moreover, narcissism is not primarily a 'defence' against shame; instead, shame figures, in Léon Wurmser's words, as 'the veiled companion of narcissism'. Self-love and self-admiration tend to go along with public exposure, and shame is a 'response to exposure'.[35]

While psychological diagnoses and sociological theories of shame and shaming can help us take a more nuanced, broader perspective, they do not tell us much about the historical events and developments that ultimately led some societies to bid farewell to shame-inducing practices. Similarly, they cannot explain why ancient forms of shaming (like head-shaving) have been repeatedly brought back to life, in the past as well as in the present. For these reasons, this book focuses neither on individual trauma and sensitivities nor on macrostructural processes of transformation. Instead, it sets its sights on concrete, corporeal actors and their relations to shifting sites of public shaming and humiliation. It deals with perpetrators, victims, and witnesses, with claims to power and resistance, with approval and critique. Those claims and contestations take place in an environment that either enables and invites or prohibits and complicates them. Different societies and historical moments offer different opportunities to shame and humiliate, and provide citizens with different justifications to engage in or refrain from degrading others.

The exploration of the modern politics of humiliation therefore follows a famous maxim of Karl Marx: 'Men make their own history, but they do not make it just as they please; they do not make it under circumstances chosen by themselves, but under circumstances directly encountered, given and transmitted from the past.'[36] People grapple with their 'circumstances', are motivated by them, and look for alternatives. Ideas of honour and dignity play a decisive, albeit often overlooked and underestimated role. How people conceive of what honour and dignity mean in social life changes over time and according to 'circumstances'. The polysemy of the concept of honour and the egalitarian tenor of modern Western societies have helped crown human dignity as one of the highest values, while practices of public shaming and strategies of humiliation have come to lose their credibility—without, however, completely going out of fashion.

The process began in state institutions, primarily in punitive law (Chapter 1) and how it was exercised and performed. It continued to develop, although with considerable delay, in schools and families, where sensitivity towards attacks on human dignity has considerably increased over the last few decades. At the same time, new media, and in particular the internet, have become powerful forums for public humiliation, and peer groups have come to play an active, often inglorious role (Chapter 2). The politics of humiliation in international relations has survived the longest (Chapter 3). When national honour rears its ugly head, touchiness and suspicions of plots to humiliate will quickly follow, shared and supported by national publics that are only too keen to assert their sense of sovereign power and, frequently, superiority. It is questionable whether the 'politics of apology' that has been on the rise since the 1990s can effect any lasting change. Crosscurrents are massive and in the ascendant as right-wing populism seizes power. Under Donald Trump's US presidency, the politics of humiliation have climaxed, both in domestic and in foreign relations. Decency, or the right not to be humiliated, is an alien concept to a political leader who is loved by millions for his bullying strength and insulting speech. Others turn away with shame and hope for better days.

1

PILLORIES AND PUBLIC BEATINGS

State Punishments under Fire

When Carl Gottlieb Svarez lectured the Prussian prince and future king Friedrich Wilhelm III on jurisprudence in the early 1790s, the pillory was still being used on a regular basis. Pillories could be found all over Europe in market and church squares; made of wood or stone, most featured iron rings to keep the punished person's neck in place. Sometimes, the iron collar was anchored onto the wall of a town hall or church. Another common form of public shaming was the stocks, which consisted of two boards with holes for hands and neck connected with a hinge on one end. At London's central market in Cornhill, there were two types of pillory: the *stokkes* for men and the *thewe* (chair) for women.[1]

Svarez did not mention any of this in his talks. He gave his royal student an introductory lesson on the principles of criminal law and explained various types of punishment. He laid out the difference between the prison and the penitentiary, discussed the advantages and disadvantages of fines, and inquired into whether the death penalty was fair and just. But he did not say a word about the pillory.

While this might be surprising at first glance, it is indicative of Svarez's conviction that to all intents and purposes, the pillory should be relegated to the past. The new Prussian General Law Code of 1794 (ALR), which was co-authored by the enlightened jurist, only made some cursory remarks about public exposure, reserving it for a small number of crimes. As a point of comparison, the Tuscan penal law of

November 1786 detailed meticulous rules for how to conduct public shaming, and so did the penal code approved by Joseph II for the Habsburg Empire a few weeks later. It proclaimed that the convicted should be shown at a central gathering place one hour a day for three successive days. He was to be 'held in iron' with a 'sign hanging before his chest' informing townspeople about the crime he had committed.[2]

Public Shaming in the Early Modern Period

This was fully in line with the way shame sanctions had been conducted in the past. The pillory begins appearing in European legal documents during the late Middle Ages, when it was primarily used to punish theft and sex crimes. Around the year 1600, people sentenced in Munich had to stand in the pillory for two hours a day on three successive Sundays or holidays, thus directly subjecting them to the public eye and judgement.[3] In fact, passers-by did not spare them expressions of condemnation and disapproval. Depending on the crime, people spat or pelted them with rotten food and faeces.[4] In 1780, two men put on the stocks in London for 'acts of sodomy'—a code word for homosexuality—were seriously injured by the stones thrown at them. Twenty thousand people reportedly showed up to take part in the event and express their outrage over the 'disgusting', 'unspeakable' crime. Although the conservative MP Edmund Burke also thought the men's acts worthy of moral sanction, the violence went too far for him: he spoke out in Parliament, condemning the perverse transformation of the pillory from an 'instrument of reproach and shame' into a murder weapon.[5]

Punishing people in front of large crowds was nothing unusual at the time. Long into the nineteenth century, executions were public events. Prussia's penal law took until 1851 to finally move them behind prison walls; Great Britain followed in 1868, the Netherlands in 1870. In France, the last public beheading occurred in 1939. The traditional argument was that because criminals had acted against social order and public peace, it was only right to punish them where all could see. Those who watched functioned as both spectators and participants, because their physical presence, emotional involvement, and moral assent ultimately served to affirm the judge's ruling. Moreover, it was hoped that public exposure would act as a deterrent. The fear of being publicly sanctioned would keep people, at least this was the belief, from committing similar transgressions.[6]

There is much evidence to support the claim that public punishments were intended as a form of shaming, and Burke was not the only one of his time to call the pillory a 'punishment of shame'. Since the Middle Ages, low and high courts alike had been sentencing people to penalties that, according to the Augsburg city annalist in 1462, aimed to burden the castigated with 'great shame and disgrace'.[7] In the early modern period, it became increasingly common for the executioner to be the one tasked with putting people on the pillory, and his touch alone was enough to rob a man of his honour. But the milder forms of shame sanctions carried out by bailiffs and constables also had a dishonouring effect.[8]

In this respect, they were similar to religious, church-based acts of public repentance that were initially practised as part of Maundy Thursday liturgies and later on normal Sundays and holidays. Well into the sixteenth century, sinners, male and female alike, would beg for forgiveness by kneeling at the altar in rough cloth and bare feet. As these forms of self-chastisement gradually faded into the past, new public forms of repentance were invented to replace them. As punishment for crimes like manslaughter, usury, blasphemy, arson, adultery, sodomy, and others, transgressors were forced to walk ahead of the Sunday procession with a candle in their hand or stand in front of the church wearing a special outfit while the congregation entered the service. In church, they were assigned designated seats. At the end of it all, the person repenting was deemed 'amended' of their sins and could be reintegrated into the community of believers.[9]

The secular courts of early modern states took a cue from such religious rituals. They too wanted to punish culprits in a way that

Fig. 3. A 'skimmington ride', eighteenth century (William Hogarth)

validated the force of the broken norm for all to see. Local customs of reprimand common throughout Europe had a similar function by ridiculing people who acted against social conventions. In England, women who mistreated their husbands were forced to go on so-called skimmington rides: they (and sometimes their husbands too) sat backwards on a donkey and were paraded around, all the while being mocked by their neighbours, who watched and took active part in the spectacle. In 1604, participants of one such event in Suffolk stated that the purpose was not just to shame the woman who had beaten her husband, but to send a warning to other women not 'to offend in like sorts'.[10]

The use of charivaris as an instrument of shaming found enthusiastic adherents in France as well. Young men in particular believed that they had a right to curse rule-breakers publicly. In cities, dominant wives and their humiliated husbands were targeted, and in villages, widows and widowers who took new vows of marriage were subjected to the embarrassing public shaming ritual.[11] Women who did not marry after their husband's death but remained sexually active were likewise candidates for public scorn. In 1721, local church officials and community leaders of the Scottish town of Dumfriesshire ordered the recently widowed Jenny Forsyth 'to be branked' because her relationship with another man had brought shame upon her family and neighbours. Women from the parish then got together and banged on pots and pans in front of Jenny's house, forced the young widow from her home against her will, put the scold's bridle on her head, and paraded her through the streets, only stopping after their victim promised to start behaving like a 'decent, god-fearing person'.[12]

Although such shaming was being meted out 'from above' like a government-sanctioned punishment, it still had many elements that recalled classic customs of reprimand 'from below'. Even in official punishments carried out by constables in accordance with a judge's sentence, locals always took an active part. Indeed, it could not have functioned without them, because the presence of a third party was constitutive of public shaming. Being excoriated in front of one's peers and neighbours with 'public derision and retribution', as a convicted man put it in 1728, proved more than embarrassing:[13] it lessened his honour and reputation and made him sense, alongside the pain inflicted on his skin, the degree of social contempt and condemnation expressed against him.

Being despised and looked down on was a serious matter in societies that primarily viewed and treated people as members of social groups, corporations, and estates. Whoever violated the respective norms and morals was made susceptible to the collective's sanctioning power. Defending oneself or changing group and corporation membership was hardly ever possible, so that people who had been subjected to public shaming and could not bear the blame were left with only one choice: to leave their home and move somewhere else. Indeed, this was often part of the punishment itself. People put in the stocks were frequently banished from the town or county and chased out with canes. But news of shame sanctions sometimes travelled faster than their victims. In the late eighteenth century, a female fruit seller went to the Parisian police to complain about a competitor who was spreading rumours that she had been whipped and branded in the province she came from. The stigma of a loss of honour thus remained even after one had left the site of shaming.[14]

Public shaming had material consequences for more people than the vendor who feared losing customers. Women who were pilloried for bearing children out of wedlock lost their jobs—not because of the illegitimate child, but because they had been publicly rebuked and humiliated.[15] Exposing a culprit to the eye of the people, according to an English source from 1730, aimed at 'marking him out to the public as a person not fit to be trusted, but to be shunned and avoided by all creditable and honest men'.[16] Such 'disgrace' would hardly be forgotten, as Samuel Johnson remarked in 1778: 'People are not very willing to ask a man to their tables who has stood in the pillory.'[17] Continental guilds that only allowed honourable men into their ranks made sure to bar entry to those who had been publicly shamed. As a consequence, judges in eighteenth-century Salzburg stopped sentencing craftsmen to the pillory after they realized that everyone who had been set in the stocks had been expelled from his guild and abandoned to a life of poverty.[18]

At any rate, the courts generally used shaming sanctions cautiously. In sixteenth-century Cologne, they had a culprit sit in the 'Kax' about once every five years. In Norwich, the stocks pretty much disappeared after 1660, and in Surrey, pillory sentences occurred once every eighteen months between 1660 and 1800. In the far more populous city of London, reports of men and women standing on the pillory were more frequent. Here, a maximum of ten people per year were pilloried during the eighteenth century. Still, only a tiny minority of all sentences involved being exposed to the public. In the north German county of Lippe, lower courts applied the punishment in less than 2 per cent of all verdicts delivered between 1650 and 1800.[19]

Those who did end up on the pillory had a hard fate, though. In 1773, a farmer from Lippe asked the government to grant him and his father clemency after being sentenced to the stocks for assaulting a shepherd. The son found it completely inappropriate that his 'old father who had lived honourably in this world for 75 years' should be 'tied to a post where he is to be put on display for three hours on Sunday and thus must worry himself half to death'. Confronted with public reprimand in 1778 for defaming the character of a deceased councillor, a woman complained: 'To be submitted to such reviling punishment in front of the whole town at my age of some 60 years is too harsh and offends my nearest relatives too.' Her husband agreed, claiming that putting her on the pillory was a 'disreputable form of public corporal punishment' that 'caused the whole family to suffer'.[20] Whoever had the means paid a fine in order to get out of it. In 1793, a north German farmer was reported to say that 'he would rather lose his best cow than stand in the pillory'.[21]

The Pillory's Final Days

The pillory was not only feared and disliked by those who had to suffer it. Liberals without any personal experience also looked at it with disapproval. Johann Adam Bergk, who had translated Cesare Beccaria's Dei delitti e delle pene into German in 1798, fiercely opposed all 'punishments that destroy respect for the person'. Informed by Kantian notions of dignity, he claimed that whoever 'robbed a moral person of her worth and denied her respect' acted not only against 'moral law', but also 'without purpose, because such punishments do not improve'. Shaming and other immoderate sanctions, Bergk warned, might even cause people to sympathize with or pity the person punished, thus undermining the 'rule of law'.[22]

In the run of the eighteenth century, public opinion and penal practice increasingly clashed. Of particular fame was the case of writer Daniel Defoe. In 1702, he anonymously published a satirical pamphlet that offended both the heads of the Anglican Church and many Members of Parliament. After it was publicly burnt by the executioner, a court convicted its author (whose identity had been revealed) of seditious libel and punished him with a hefty fine and lengthy stay in prison. In addition, he had to while away in the pillory for three days in July 1703. But his friends and supporters were able to turn the act of

DANIEL DE FOE AU PILORI. — Page 123.

Fig. 4. Daniel Defoe in the pillory, London, 1703

public shaming into a personal triumph for Defoe by selling to those
present copies of the pamphlet as well as Defoe's satirical poem
'Hymn to the Pillory', which had been composed just for the occasion.
Spectators' attitudes changed, and rather than pelting Defoe with eggs,
faeces, and stones, they drank to his health and adorned the pillory
with flowers.[23]

In 1727, the government of Saxony feared a similar turnaround, and
thus advised that Anna Sophia Mittwoch be sent to the new penitentiary for two years of 'hard labour' instead of sentencing her to the
pillory. Mittwoch had been convicted of stealing watches and silver
from a Catholic home during the latest confessional riots in Dresden.
But as she had returned the stolen goods, officials warned that 'residents and in particular the common people' might react negatively
towards the court's harsh verdict. Putting her on the pillory might lead

to further tumult, and so it seemed preferable to move the punishment away from the public gaze.[24]

This case clearly supports Foucault's argument that the invention of the prison in the eighteenth century signalled the discovery of a new technology of power and discipline. While the enclosed structures hid the punished from the public eye, they subjected them to more intense surveillance and control. Prisons' very architecture ensured that commoners no longer took part in the process of punishment, thus keeping them from developing emotional and moral investment in individual cases.[25] Whether that investment went in favour of the government's decision could quite obviously no longer be taken for granted, and it was near impossible to predict in which instances people would refuse to shame the castigated, out of either compassion or outright identification with their plight. In 1812, Daniel Eaton, who had published the third part of Thomas Paine's The Age of Reason, was sentenced to prison and the pillory for blasphemy. But rather than being booed, somewhere between 12,000 and 20,000 people gathered opposite Newgate gaol to cheer and applaud him. They turned his 'punishment of shame' into 'his glory' and 'a triumph' for his cause.[26] Two years later, the British government granted clemency to MP and naval hero Thomas Lord Cochrane, who had been sentenced to an hour on the pillory for his role in the Great Stock Exchange Fraud of 1814. Like the Saxon government in 1727, they too feared riots and expressions of popular sympathy.[27]

In 1815, MP Michael Taylor proposed legislation in the House of Commons to abolish the pillory once and for all. While the House of Commons passed the bill, the House of Lords was split. Although many members were critics of the shame penalty because its effect depended on the cooperation of the 'mob', in the end, the majority sided with the Lord Chancellor, who wanted to retain it for perjury and fraud. Nevertheless, it was rarely used after that and was finally done away with in 1837.[28]

Benjamin Rush, an outspoken critic of the 'barbarity' of the pillory, the stocks, and the 'whipping-post', died before he could witness their end (the founding father and signatory of the Declaration of Independence of the United States passed away in 1813). In 1787, he lectured about the dangers of shameful and humiliating sanctions at Benjamin Franklin's house in Philadelphia and was met with much interest. He argued that 'public punishments, so far from preventing crimes by the terror they excite in the minds of spectators, are directly calculated to produce them', admonishing that they left 'scars, which disfigure the whole character' both on those who suffered them and on those who stood by. As an alternative, he proposed that punishments should be made 'effectual for the reformation of criminals, and beneficial to society'.[29]

Rush referenced others sympathetic to his position, including the French lawyer Charles Dufriche de Valazé, who had dedicated an essay to the brother of Louis XVI in 1784 pleading for milder punishments and the abolishment of shameful mutilations that marked the person as dishonourable for life.[30] In the previous year, Dresden-based jurists Hans Ernst von Globig and Johann Georg Huster, who had won the 1782 Prize of the Economic Society of Bern, Switzerland, for their text on penal law, sharply criticized 'branding as a barbarous disgrace'.[31] Heavily influenced by Beccaria's recommendations, the new French Code Pénal of 1791 finally did away with branding. Working with the principles of improvement (of the convicted) and civilizing (of society), it also placed limitations on the use of the pillory and iron collar (carcan). But even revolutionaries did not want to dispense entirely with public shaming and ostracization.[32]

At the same time, less revolutionary-minded people also found reasons to work against dishonouring penalties. In 1756, Friedrich II appealed to reason and pragmatism when he exhorted Prussian courts not to compound the punishments of those sent to the penitentiary or the workhouse by declaring them infamous. He stated that it was 'very disadvantageous' for the state to strip the convicted of his honour, because this would inevitably condemn him to being 'a useless member of society'. The status of being dishonoured, the Prussian king argued, would make it impossible for him 'to earn his bread in an honest way' after his release.[33] Other minds chose to formulate their pleas in language closer to the enlightened spirit of the times. In 1777, Austrian law professor Joseph von Sonnenfels wrote that the loss of honour 'that can follow from a punishment, mutilation, branding, exposure at the pillory' was contrary to 'the final purpose of the future betterment of the punished'.[34]

The Prussian General Law Code of 1794 (ALR) remained ambiguous on the matter. In many cases, it favoured collective deterrence over individual improvement and resocialization. For instance, it provided that members of robber bands be branded on their shoulder, thus ensuring that they could never return to a normal life. The pillory was reserved for those who had fraudulently declared bankruptcy and were to spend the rest of their days in hard labour. But even lesser prison sentences for crimes like forgery and perjury could be compounded with public shaming.[35] Yet, as Grand Chancellor Johann Heinrich von Carmer confirmed in 1794, the ALR intended 'to gradually, to the greatest extent possible, bring these types of punishment out of practice'. He himself considered them a major obstacle 'to the moral improvement' of the lower classes, because they 'completely stifle and kill their already weak sense of honour and self-respect, which in better organized minds serve as such a powerful deterrent against many crimes'. When provincial courts inquired, however, whether they could still impose sanctions like the barrel or the shrew's fiddle, Carmer generally approved, under the condition that they were administered 'with great caution and as seldom as possible' and only 'so long as there are not enough proper prisons'.[36]

Thus, there was a considerable gap between the aims of the new legal code and the praxis of local courts, and provincial governments often resisted the prescriptions coming from Berlin. Even though the ALR—not unlike the revolutionary French Code—placed limits on public shaming, it did not completely abolish it.[37] Nevertheless, the pillory and related forms of public chastening gradually faded out of use, just as Carmer had intended and predicted. Arguments against shame penalties were made 'so often', and, in the words of the Grand

Chancellor, 'with complete justification', that they met with less and less resistance.

For all that, it still took a long time before European states did away with shame sanctions once and for all. The Napoleonic Code Pénal of 1810 even increased their use under the auspices of deterrence, dictating that those sentenced to prison or hard labour, whether for life or not, had first to be exposed to the eyes of the public (*exposé aux regards du peuple sur la place publique*).[38] In 1832, the *exposition publique* was struck for non-life sentences in order to facilitate reintegration.[39] Yet another revolution was needed before a decree was finally issued banning public shaming. Notably, one argument made by the 1848 ordinance to justify the ban was that the pillory did injury to the 'dignité humaine'.[40]

Human Dignity as a Legal Argument

Drawing on human dignity to bolster positions on penal policy was nothing uncommon in the first half of the nineteenth century. As early as 1818, a judicial committee in Cologne stated that 'one must respect the human dignity of even the guilty and the criminal'. As a consequence, they rejected all forms of punishment that 'injures a person's sense of honour and degrades man to the state of an animal'.[41] In doing so, they revived an idea that Bergk had already developed in his 1798 commentary on Beccaria's text, but which at that time had remained rather uninfluential. Usually, those who criticized demeaning, humiliating sanctions as 'squelching man's striving for honour' and impairing 'a powerful motivator of good behaviour in the state'[42] viewed honour strictly within the confines of state affairs and civil society. Bergk and the Rhenish jurists, in contrast, turned the tables by changing the perspective. Connecting feelings of honour and human dignity, they put the individual person centre stage. They thus initiated a new, modern discourse that continues to frame debates on the protection of personal honour and the (il)legitimacy of shame sanctions to this very day.

The reason the Cologne committee sent its recommendations to Prussia's minister of justice was to prevent the ALR from becoming law in the Rhineland. Having lived under French legislation since the Revolutionary Wars of the late eighteenth century, the Rhine provinces' post-war integration into Prussia was not accompanied by an immediate change in law. French legal institutions and codes were advantageous for many middle-class citizens, who tenaciously fought to keep them in place. Things were different, however, when it came to public shaming. While French soldiers had initially torn down local pillories as symbols of the Ancien Régime, French administrators were quick to reconstruct them, in accordance with both the 1791 and the 1810 penal codes. After Napoleon's defeat in 1813, Prussian governors rushed to get rid of what they called the 'counterproductive shame punishments' of French penal law. Instead, they promised to replace them with a 'mildness that respects the worth of man and conforms to German sensibilities'. They advised courts not to sentence convicted criminals automatically to the pillory, but rather to leave it to the judge's discretion. In cases involving shame penalties, governors even went so far as to demand judges send them 'the judgement with all documents' so that they themselves could have the final word.[43]

In Berlin, they were backed by the Prussian minister of justice, who wanted to limit the use of public humiliation as much as possible. Indeed, he only believed in it as long as it was likely to have a deterring function, as in cases of robbery. When it came to penalizing 'unnatural' and 'abhorrent' crimes like the rape of one's own sister, though, the pillory seemed to him counterproductive, as it drew attention to a crime that, 'in the interest of the public and its moral well-being', should rather be forgotten. In these cases, the state sought to protect citizens' morality by limiting the 'publicity' of punishments.[44] On the other hand, the pillory was far from being the harshest sanction, and for crimes like counterfeiting, which French penal law sentenced with public execution, it looked like child's play. So when, in 1835, the Prussian king ordered Rhenish courts to punish counterfeiting with the pillory, he expressed both a 'mildness' befitting of 'German sensibilities' and a hope in the pillory's deterring effect.[45]

That hope had lingered on in the debates about legal reform that had been taking place in Prussia since the 1820s. Around the mid-1830s, however, the pillory disappeared from discussion and the new penal code of 1851 no longer mentioned it. The notion of deterrence had finally given way to the principle of improvement and the convicted person's reconciliation with society. Human dignity and what Prussian governors had, in 1813, called the 'respect and worth of man' were, it seemed, on the advance.

Corporal Punishment: An Affront to Dignity

But what exactly dignity, respect, and human worth signified was contested, as the heated debates on corporal punishment reveal. During the decades-long work on the revision of Prussian penal law, experts dedicated considerably more energy to beatings, floggings, and whippings than to the pillory, not to mention branding. Indeed, the controversy could be traced all the way back to the late eighteenth century. When Svarez gave his royal student an introductory course on the principles of law, he sharply criticized corporal punishment, claiming that while it might have been customary in the military, it was counterproductive for civilians, 'on the one hand because of its largely arbitrary nature, and on the other, because it degrades the character of the nation', as could be studied in China and Russia.[46] Svarez's liberal views, however, did not become law. His colleague Ernst Ferdinand Klein, who was responsible for drafting the criminal law section of the 1794 code, had far less aversion to corporal punishment. While the code treated the pillory and other forms of public shaming with restraint, it prescribed flogging for all kinds of crimes: theft, rioting, the defacement of monuments, double baptisms, 'concealed pregnancy and birth', and other 'crude transgressions'.[47]

Klein also exerted considerable influence on a royal decree from 1799 that used the occasion of an increase in burglaries 'to make deterring examples'. In order to protect individual property and 'improve the criminals when possible', the decree deemed they should be given a severe beating. This was fully in line with the ALR. Two things, however, had changed. On the one hand, the king, as Svarez's former student, insisted that beatings take the convicted person's 'sex, age, healthy or sickly body, and other individual characteristics' into account. Ultimately, judges exercised discretion over how many lashings a criminal received and over the intervals between them.[48] On the other hand, Friedrich Wilhelm III wanted such lashings to be carried out within prison walls 'by one or two alternating guards, whereby nobody may be present except an officer of the court'. The public, therefore, was to be excluded and no longer played a vital part in this particular type of shame sanction. In Klein's opinion, this served the purpose of social and economic reintegration. Publicly administered whippings would, he argued, amount to 'public defamation and would for this reason hinder the punished in his future endeavours'. The public, too, would benefit from being spared the brutal spectacle, 'for every cultivated nation naturally despises such rituals'.[49]

Although Klein's position might seem to align with Svarez's here, the congruence is but superficial: strictly speaking, they were talking about two different issues. Klein recapitulated the well-known argument against the pillory and drew on the notion that the theatre of public castigation only appealed to a primitive, morally immature audience. In contrast, Svarez focused on the punished person herself as a member of the nation that, as a whole, was demeaned through her humiliating treatment.

Without explicitly mentioning the concept, Svarez thus placed himself on the side of those who believed in human dignity and wanted to make it the standard measure of all legislation. For many contemporaries and, in particular, civil servants, Immanuel Kant's ideas and reasoning proved highly influential in this regard. In 1785, the Königsberg philosopher had defined dignity as a 'holy' asset of humanity, as an 'inner worth' without 'price' or 'equivalent'.[50] Twelve years later, in his *Metaphysics of Morals*, Kant added: 'Humanity itself is a dignity; for a human being cannot be used merely as a means by any human being . . . but must always be used at the same time as an end. It is just in this that his dignity (personality) consists, by which he raises himself above all other beings in the world that are not human beings and yet can be used, and so over all *things*.' Every human being thus 'has a legitimate claim to respect from his fellow human beings and is *in turn* bound to respect every other'.[51] What Kant left unresolved, though, was whether the individual person's legitimate claim was also binding for the state proper. Was the latter obliged to protect the dignity of all citizens? Legal codes and royal ordinances issued during the late eighteenth century evidently did not yet see it this way.

Nevertheless, the Prussian decree from 1799 marked a turning point in two respects. First, it individualized corporal punishment. Second, by ordering that lashings now had to be executed behind closed doors, it put an end to the long tradition of public beatings. Such beatings had targeted women as much as men, in Prussia as much as in other European countries. In England, the common practice had—as in a case from 1731—the convicted 'stript from the middle upwards and whipped at the cart's tail . . . till blood came'. Parishes provided centrally located 'whipping posts'.[52] In 1703, the mayor of Deal, a small town in southern England, noted in his diary:

> I took up a common prostitute, whose conduct was very offensive . . . brought her to the whipping-post—being about mid-market, where was present some hundreds of people—I caused her to have twelve lashes; and at every third lash I parleyed with her and bid her tell all the women of the like calling wheresoever she came that the Mayor of Deal would serve them as he had served her, if they came to Deal and committed such wicked deeds as she had done.[53]

Being treated in this fashion was meant to humiliate, and indeed felt humiliating. When, in 1760, Elanor Steed was sentenced to a public whipping in London for larceny, her son George, a master bricklayer, pleaded for mercy, both for her sake and for his own: 'Publickly Wipt itt Being Shuch a Grate Scandell to Me in My Business & Wood Go Nere to Be My Ruing.' His plea hit on the close link between honour and shame on the one hand and socio-economic well-being on the other. Quite obviously, the bricklayer was concerned less for his mother's honour and more for the loss of his own reputation and the financial consequences this might have. At the same time, mother and son were inextricably bound and his honour depended on hers.[54] In 1838, Prussian ministers took the same view when speaking out against corporal punishment for women: 'the fact that the husband will see his family demeaned by the punishment suffered by his wife' would do 'enduring harm to married life'.[55] The opposite was apparently not the case, or at least it was not seen as grounds for outlawing the beating of married men.

In England, too, protecting men from corporal punishment was not yet a topic of debate. For women, it had been formally abolished in 1817 after its actual use had been tapering off for years. Men, however, were still being whipped, if increasingly behind prison walls or in correction wards. In the first decade of the nineteenth century, only 122 men (and no women) in London were punished by public beating; 471 men and 85 women suffered the rod in prison during the same period.[56] Officially, the public practice of whipping men ended as late as 1862.[57]

On the continent, public opinion also turned against imposing bodily sanctions and carrying them out openly for all to see. Even those who generally approved of corporal punishments were bothered by the 'publicity' and feared its 'corrupting' effect on both the punished and the spectators. Thus, the Prussian decree from 1799 banishing beatings from the public eye was made in the spirit of the times.[58]

Soon after, though, citizens and legal experts began criticizing the very continuation of the demeaning practice itself. This, they said, ran contrary to principles of criminal punishment that respected and protected the convicted person's honour and dignity.[59] Such principles had already gained support in revolutionary France. The 1791 Code Pénal put an end to juridically ordered floggings and whippings, and things stayed that way after Napoleon's ascent to power. Residents of the Rhineland, which was under French control and jurisdiction from 1794/1804 until 1813 and was later incorporated into Prussia, starkly resisted all attempts from Berlin to bring them back. In 1843, the officials charged with revising Prussia's penal code held 'that if this type of punishment is retained, the introduction of the draft into the Rhine provinces will be morally impossible... The aversion to the punishment is so great—even among the calmest and best, even among those who would never entertain the thought of systematic opposition—that one can no longer think of forcing it upon the Rhinelanders.'[60]

So it was not just recalcitrant liberals and revolutionary-minded democrats who railed against state-administered beatings. Conservatives and loyal royalists also rejected what they saw as a regressive form of punishment. As early as 1818, the Rhenish judicial committee applied to have the decree from 1799 suspended for the Rhine provinces.[61] In 1827, the Higher Regional Court of Cologne did give some consideration to the notion that corporal punishment might be preferable to gaol or fines 'for minor crimes committed by members of the lower classes'. But in 1843, the Rhenish legislature outright dismissed such deliberation. The aristocratic, middle-class, and peasant representatives all voted against beatings both as criminal punishment and as a disciplinary measure. Reintroducing them, it was contended, would 'bring back a feeling of utmost humiliation and degradation' and 'violently eliminate the dominant respect of human dignity from people's sentiments'. The Prussian governor also stated his unconditional agreement with the legislature's protest.[62]

Thus, by 1843, human dignity as a regulative idea had evidently gained credence among parliamentary representatives. Motivated by the votes on the Rhine, officials back in Berlin took another look at their drafts. More and more spoke out against the 'bestial treatment of man that is injurious to human dignity', arguing that if the state were nevertheless to keep administering demeaning penalties, it would run the risk of betraying the people's confidence in justice and hurt the 'feeling for human dignity'.[63] Modern penal law, they concluded, could not tolerate corporal punishment.

Human dignity—which was often treated synonymously with human honour—was on the mind of many legal theorists and practitioners, and Kant's definition was widely quoted.[64] Others drew on both religious and secular ideas to express their discontent over how 'a being which, like I and others, so rightfully may say that he is made in God's image, is at the same time . . . treated as an irrational body, thus insulting the nation and humanity as a whole in an utterly debasing fashion'.[65]

But there were also dissenting voices. In 1842, Hamburg senator Martin Hudtwalcker rebutted that completely abolishing corporal punishment would prove counterproductive, fearing that if floggings were replaced by shorter or longer prison sentences, many of the affected sailors and longshoremen in harbour cities like Hamburg would lose their jobs.[66] Similar opinions could be heard in Prussia. Besides the fact that there were simply not enough prisons, some claimed being put in gaol ran counter to the interests of the 'lowest classes'. Imprisoned, they would find it impossible to work and earn a living for their families. By contrast, corporal punishment only interrupted employment for a short time and thus seemed both more practical and more economic.[67]

Still, supporting corporal punishment was gradually becoming a marginal position. In 1845, the Prussian State Council voted seven to two to abolish it, and three years later, a committee of the first Prussian parliament reached a similar decision: tasked with evaluating the decades-long revisions of the penal code, seven were against corporal punishment, four for it. Not long thereafter, a new revolution broke out in France and made its way to Berlin in March 1848. The second parliament, convened by King Friedrich Wilhelm IV, had more pressing matters than addressing the committee's recommendations. It paved the way for a constitutional convention and passed a law that gave the vote to all men over 24 who were not receiving poor relief.

This radically changed the political situation and promised to turn power relations on their head. The most 'contested partisan question of the day' that so many had fought over was now finally resolved by royal decree. On 6 May 1848, the Prussian king abolished corporal punishment out of respect for the 'equal political rights given to all My subjects by the new laws'.[68] In doing so, he was following a motion of the Ministry of State, where Rhenish liberals had become the dominant voice. They took sides with Heidelberg professor Carl Mittermaier, who considered corporal punishment injurious not only to 'human dignity', but also to the 'nation', particularly when it was imposed solely on the lower classes.[69]

The Social Pyramid of Shame

As was well known, social class played an important role in punitive practice. 'You are all aware', young liberal law professor Theodor Mommsen wrote in 1849, 'how it has gone up until now, especially in the police courts: he who could pay, paid, and he who could not pay took his beatings.' To the extent to which members of well-to-do classes were ever even sentenced to corporal punishment, they did all they could to have their sentence substituted with a fine. This was not written in any law, 'but it was as certain as prayer in a church'.[70]

In matters of honour, the Prussian penal code privileged some classes over others up until 1848. The ALR condoned a clear-cut pyramid of honour based on the common opinion that honour was unequally distributed and held different meanings for people of different social status. Members of the nobility were attributed with the greatest honour and the most sensitive feelings about it; the 1732 edition of *Zedler's Universal Lexicon* called them the 'honour estate' *par excellence*.[71] Members of the urban middle classes and the peasantry possessed less honour, which was codified in the fact that insulting them carried a lesser penalty than insulting an aristocrat. The severity of the punishment rose with the estate of the person insulted. Moreover, insulting those 'below' one's own estate was seen as less injurious than insulting those 'above'.[72]

Consequently, public humiliation was perceived differently when it was meted out to a nobleman than when it was suffered by a peasant.

In their prize-winning essay from 1783, Globig and Huster wrote that shame punishments were 'far more effective' when used against the 'distinguished and noble' than against 'the rabble'.[73] But the former, British gentlemen no less than members of the Prussian 'honour estate', were almost never subjected to these kinds of penalties, precisely because they destroyed one's good name and devalued the currency on which these classes based their very existence.[74] Being whipped and beaten in public was, in the end, reserved for the 'lowly', as the Dresden jurists called them; in 1799, Klein spoke of 'people who can only be reasoned with through their skin'.[75]

But even for the 'lowly', honour was in no way unimportant, a fact demonstrated by the appeals for clemency from those who saw an unbearable 'insult' in having been sentenced to corporal punishment. The numerous libel suits filed in both rural and urban areas also speak against the assumption that ordinary men and women took less interest in their honour than those on top of the social pyramid.[76] In the eighteenth century, the Parisian police received numerous complaints, mostly for defamation. They almost always came from people who felt that a neighbour or colleague had insulted them. The majority of complaints were made by tradespeople and shopkeepers, who valued their honour so greatly that they were willing to pay the not inconsiderable fee for filing a charge against the offending party.[77]

Things were not much different in the countryside. Two out of every three libel cases that went to court between 1685 and 1795 in northern Germany were from men and women of the lower strata. They too did not shy from making their case in order to disclaim accusations of being a thief, rascal, whore, adulterer, syphilitic, witch, wizard, dog, flea, or wacko, force the name-caller to take it back in public, and thus get 'satisfaction'.[78] Newspaper ads in which people apologized for insulting someone served the same purpose. In London, this method of settling an honour-related conflict became fashionable in the 1740s, especially for craftspeople, small traders, and transport workers who retracted, in print, their 'scandalous words'.

In a number of cases, though, they still had to ask personally for forgiveness on their knees and in front of witnesses.[79]

Lower-class men and women also demanded satisfaction when they felt offended by someone of higher social status. In 1824, a maid from Göttingen filed suit against her employer, a Catholic priest, for repeatedly insulting her with words that 'as everyone knows are among the most insulting terms for poor women'. She refused to stand for such offensive behaviour and sued for an apology, honourable amends, and a fine. The very fact that the 1810 Prussian law for servants expressly prohibited those who had been 'handled by their employers with insulting words or lowly actions' from filing suit demonstrates *ex negativo* how sensitive this group's feelings of honour could be. If there had been no need to fear that servants would actually defend themselves against being hit and maligned by their masters, there would have been no need to pass such laws in the first place.[80]

Thus, the 'lowly' also treated their honour like capital whose value had to be protected, and they too feared public shaming. This makes contemporaries' laments that the underclasses' feelings of honour were undeveloped appear rather curious. The opposite, it seems, was closer to the truth. In traditional societies, every person placed great worth on their honour, which is the reason why insults and shame sanctions could have such a powerful effect.

The claim that the underclasses lacked feelings of honour primarily served a strategic purpose: it legitimized the practice of treating them more roughly than others. 'I would be very happy', complained the Royal Master of the Horse Carl Heinrich August von Lindenau in 1791, 'if it was somehow possible to get by without giving those stablehands a beating, but even with the best intentions it simply cannot be done.' They were, according to Lindenau, 'a bunch of rough-hewn, immoral, mostly very young men' whose 'insolent behaviour' demanded harsh treatment. 'Unfortunately!' corporal punishment was indispensable for such 'brash lads'. Even Grand Chancellor Carmer showed understanding for these views, claiming that 'for this class of people', beatings could not be avoided; nevertheless, he qualified that they should not threaten the health or life of the chastised.[81]

From time to time, the discriminatory treatment of the lower classes did become the object of criticism. In 1799, Ernst Ferdinand Klein warned that if the state reserved corporal punishment for certain estates only, the latter would ultimately be 'degraded'.[82] Still, the Prussian king reinforced such prejudices, stating, in 1812, that beatings were really only appropriate for criminals from the 'lowest class'.[83] The opinion that 'corporal punishment could not be dispensed with because of the low level of culture' persisted, and not only in rural parts of eastern Prussia. In the 1840s, the majority of provincial legislatures agreed that for beggars, vagrants, journeymen, servants, and maids, prison sentences, as an alternative to public floggings, would do no good.[84]

Gender

It is rather remarkable that representatives named servants and maids in the same sentence. After all, the nineteenth century generally took great care to draw strong distinctions between men and women in all aspects of social life, including in matters of honour. The idea was that all women possessed a specific kind of gendered honour that con- sisted in what was then called 'virtue and chastity'. Women were only supposed to have sexual relations with their husbands—pre-marital and extra-marital sex were, at least in theory, taboo. Gender norms prescribed that they wear decent clothes, avoid vulgar language and gestures, and lower their eyes rather than risk a bold gaze.[85]

Such rules had been around long before the nineteenth century. In the Middle Ages, shame was already valued as a primarily feminine virtue, and it was given an openly sexual connotation.[86] According to a law professor writing in the late eighteenth century, it was like being slapped in the face 'when someone kissed a woman against her will'. It was equally 'abusive' 'when someone falsely claimed that a woman had allowed him lecherous freedoms'.[87] Women rumoured to have done such things were called 'whores' and 'women of easy virtue', both in the countryside and in the cities. In eighteenth-century Paris, sexual insults were almost exclusively aimed at women and were usually about promiscuity, prostitution, and venereal disease.[88]

The courts had also long treated women differently than men. The common early modern custom of punishing lecherous behaviour by chaining stones to the offender's legs was reserved for women. Shaving the transgressor's head, which had been around since Antiquity, targeted women only and was held to be particularly shameful, as songs from the eighteenth century reveal.[89] Religious institutions imposed public penance on women who had born children out of wedlock. In 1777, a young unmarried mother had to 'stand before the

Fig. 5. Shackle stones from Bitterfeld, Germany, sixteenth to seventeenth century

church with a straw-crown' every Sunday at early Mass.[90] Shaming here functioned as a means of enforcing a moral economy that was particularly fixated on women and their sexuality.

During the nineteenth century, such fixation grew ever more obsessive. Expectations of female 'purity' and 'chastity' became stricter, and exceptions were no longer granted. At the same time, the widely held notion of women's natural frailty and delicacy invited legal experts and commentators to consider different forms of punishment according to gender. Women, they argued, should be protected from the public gaze and spared the shame of being openly humiliated. By the 1830s, it was no longer seen as acceptable to pillory female offenders, not only because of their physical and emotional tenderness, but also to avoid the 'excesses' often occasioned by its use.[91] Officials obviously anticipated greater crowds and more immoral transgressions when a woman was reprimanded in public. In a similar vein, a royal decree from 1833 stated that in Prussia, 'no women over the age of ten shall be sentenced to corporal punishment, but shall instead be given a proportional prison sentence'. To beat women, even 'depraved' women, the king said, did injury to their 'shame' and was thus impermissible.[92] For men, whose nature was not seen as being particularly affected by shame, different standards applied.[93] Five years later, the Prussian State Council accordingly voted to sentence only men with floggings, 'because when carried out against women, the punishment gives occasion to filthy, despicable acts that degrade its dignity'. The 1845 draft of the new penal code finally did away with whipping women on the grounds of its 'indecency'.[94]

Civic Honour

In 1848, Prussia did more than abolish corporal punishment altogether. The king also ordered that social status should no longer play a role in sentencing for insults and other offences. Following the principle of equal political rights promoted by the revolution, the honour of citizens was now to be measured equally.[95]

Since the beginning of the nineteenth century, liberal jurists and politicians had been working towards recognition of citizens' universal honour. The more they came to view the state as an institution of the nation and not just of the ruler, the more they came to believe that the members of the nation could and should share in the state's honour. Thus, independent of their social status and the specific type of honour associated with it, every male member of the nation was to be the bearer of civic honour. It served as the foundation of political and social rights, such as the right to vote and hold public office; the right to sit on a jury; the right to bear arms and serve in the military; and the right to open a business and wear badges of honour. These 'civil privileges' were considered an 'invention of the modern era'. Writing in the 1850s, law professor Reinhold Köstlin praised them as a matter of pride for every citizen, whose 'personality' brought together 'human dignity, legal equality, and state citizenship'. While dignity—which Köstlin used synonymously with 'universal human honour'—was 'innate', legal equality and state citizenship were given and guaranteed by the state. As a consequence, civic honour and civil privileges, which 'only existed through the state', could 'also only be infringed upon by the state through judgements and laws'.[96]

However, not everyone shared this opinion, just as not everyone agreed with the abolition of 'shaming', 'demeaning', and 'humiliating' punishments.[97] Not long after the revolution was crushed, proponents of corporal punishment began making their voices heard once again. In 1852, a provincial parliament asked the Prussian king for a new law that would punish the 'misdeeds of farmhands and servants against their lords and their representatives' just as harshly as it would labourers who caused damage to agriculture 'by striking, disobedience, and contumacy'. In such cases, they recommended moderate whipping as an urgent necessity.[98]

Most of the petition's signatories were conservative landowners from rural areas. But they were backed by urbanites, too. In a polemic from 1879, Otto Mittelstädt, a Hamburg judge, member of the city parliament and expert on prison administration, sharply criticized 'the notions of humanity and human dignity' that had come into favour in 'common liberalism'. He took jabs at the 'well-meaning pedagogues and friends of humanity' whose trust in the 'limitless perfectability of the individual' he deemed a 'superstition'. Trying to 'educate the people' by sentencing them to prison was but a 'fatal error'. In Mittelstädt's opinion, criminal statistics proved how 'bankrupt' this system really was and how little it did to put a damper on the massive growth of 'shamelessness and nefariousness' in society. Instead, the shameless and nefarious should seriously be deterred through 'reinstitution of corporal punishment' and increased use of it. For particularly 'insolent crimes, for malicious destruction of property, assault and similar base actions of adolescents', 'an appropriate quantity of beatings' was bound to be far more effective than a stay in prison.[99]

Mittelstädt's ideas found both supporters and critics. But even those who wholeheartedly accepted beatings as a form of discipline tended to reject them as a legally administered penalty. Bringing back traditional punishments of shaming in a new garb seemed a 'dubious joke'.[100] For his part, Mittelstädt was actually willing to pay some respect to 'modern sensibilities'. Offenders, he proposed, should not be pilloried in person. Only their name and picture needed to be nailed to the pillory in order to 'impress upon them the stamp of infamy for the whole world to see'.[101] The Hamburg judge thus took aim at the core of liberal punitive and legal theory. He argued against its concept of universal human dignity, and, by pleading for the reinstitution of humiliating punishments, also attacked the notion of civic honour. By then, however, such pleas no longer enjoyed broad political support.

At the same time, civic honour was not believed to be sacrosanct. In contrast to human honour or dignity, the state was, in principle, allowed to strip its citizens of their honour and the rights associated with it. The only matter of contention was under which circumstances and for how long. The German Empire's penal code of 1871 prescribed two general forms: for prison sentences over three months, the temporary loss of civil privileges was an optional supplementary sentence ordered on the judge's discretion; for penitentiary sentences, it was part of the sentence itself.[102]

Yet particular shame sanctions that impinged upon both civic and human honour or dignity remained taboo. The Prussian penal code from 1851 had got rid of them, with a single exception: the publication of sentences. And this too was long and controversially debated. While some jurists supported it as an intensification of the punishment and an effective deterrent, others countered that it did injury to the 'innocent family of the offender'. In the penal code's final version, its proponents ultimately came out on top, but not without qualifications. The publication of sentences, they argued, had basically lost its character of aggravating the penalty due to the fact that criminal trials had been held in public since 1849. Its true purpose was to inform an even broader audience about those who had committed serious crimes and, as a consequence, had lost their civic honour and were to spend years in prison.[103]

Forced Publicity

In the early nineteenth century, public trials were still an object of contention. In 1818, the Rhenish judicial committee promoted them on the grounds that they would help 'spread more correct ideas about honour and shame'. In contrast, the Prussian minister of justice raised concerns that public trials would make people aware of the offence, which would then 'place the entire civic existence of the convicted in danger of being destroyed forever'. Anselm von Feuerbach, the author of Bavaria's exemplary penal code of 1813, admitted that public trials were more conducive to making the defendant feel ashamed. Nevertheless, he supported this 'thorn of shame' as a 'new, powerful means of enhancing and retaining honourability and honesty'. His colleague Heinrich Benedikt von Weber, high court judge in Württemberg and author of a new code of criminal procedure, had some reservations. He reasoned it was improper to 'allow full publicity for misdemeanours' because 'the public appearance of the accused and the concomitant injury to his feeling of honour would not be proportional to his guilt'. During debates held by the Saxon parliament in 1843, representatives criticized public trials as a new 'kind of pillory' that, especially for women, might prove worse than the sentence itself.[104]

The liberal politician and historian Carl Theodor Welcker held the same opinion, but like Feuerbach, he drew different conclusions from it. Writing in 1847, he viewed the British 'representative constitution' as a model because it allowed the 'voice of honour and morality' to speak 'in common public assemblies' and served to 'publicly shame wrong-doing'. Public jury trials, he thought, were 'true courts of honour and morality' in which everyone present was called upon 'to speak their highest feelings and thoughts and suppress their basest'. At the end, he who had been judged guilty stood 'publicly branded', an idea that was clearly to the liking of the author who, at the same time, was well known for his fiery criticism of degrading corporal punishments. The 'denunciation' of the offender by honourable citizens in an open trial had, as Welcker saw it, a healing effect in multiple respects: it directed 'the feeling of honour of the convicted and of all others towards what was right', condemned the bad action, and showed the punished the path to a decent, moral life.[105]

Even if the professor's view was highly idealized, the proponents of public trials eventually got their way and celebrated their win as a triumph of the rule of law.[106] After being made into standard procedure, public trials would have largely lost their initial shaming function if it were not for the burgeoning press reports. Journalists who regularly reported on trials took active part in the construction of a moral order that was negotiated in the courtroom and commented upon outside.[107] This was true for sensational cases that entertained the public 'in a manner that vigorously affected their nerves'.[108] But it also held for everyday cases, like that of a businessman who had, in 1902, published an advertisement offering to sell a debt that contained the debtor's full name. Rather than pay the debt, the debtor sued the man for libel and the jury sided with him. On appeal, though, the

Berlin District Court did not think that the ad intentionally maligned the man's honour and concluded that the creditor had meant the public auction of the debt 'in earnest': he just wanted to get his money back, the judges said, not embarrass the debtor.[109]

When newspapers covered such trials, they evinced the public's interest in all kinds of legal proceedings. Furthermore, the article shed light on the continuing significance of honour and libel. The debtor obviously did not care if the trials further shamed and 'branded' him, as some had hoped and others had feared. He felt that the publication of his debts had insulted him and blemished his honour. As the judges explicated, honour was equivalent with 'reputation' here, which was then defined as 'public confidence in the moral worth and competence of a person'.[110]

Undermining the public confidence in him, as the plaintiff in the 1902 case accused his creditor of doing, could be seen as libel or even intentional shaming. German penal law was relatively sensitive to such cases.[111] In contrast to Great Britain, where plaintiffs had to prove that they had suffered material damages, it placed more weight on the 'subjectivity' of honour and the feelings of the insulted person.[112] But in order to rein in the 'epidemic of libel cases'—in 1903, libel was the third most common crime after assault and theft— lawmakers imposed some conditions on filing suit.[113] They forced plaintiffs to pursue the case privately, which meant they risked having to pay for the trial costs. In fact, most cases were settled before ever making it to court, a likely consequence of mandatory pre-trial mediation. Many accusers actually preferred civil suits since the sanctions were more tangible: the defendant had to recant the insult, apologize, and pay a fine. On the other hand, success in a criminal case also promised a sweet reward: according to Article 200 of the penal code, the plaintiff could make the judgement public at the defendant's expense.[114]

Imperial Germany had adopted this article from Prussian law. It did not, however, go as far as automatically publishing all penitentiary and lengthy prison sentences. Such extensive information, it was claimed, would seriously impede the offender's reintegration into society and harm the reputation of his or her family. Why then, one might ask, did cases of libel retain their special status? The answer lies in the high premium legislators placed on honour and the role the public played in validating it. According to legal commentaries, publicly humiliating the libellous party was, for the person insulted, an 'ideal compensation on a level with repentance' that served to 'repair her reputation' in front of a larger audience.[115]

From a historical standpoint, the publication of sentences seemed like a relic of older forms of 'private' penalties aimed at satisfying the victim's desire for retribution. Since the early nineteenth century, the state had generally been turning punishments into a public matter. Fines were paid to the treasury, not to the person injured, who could at most sue the offender in civil court for compensation and satisfaction. While Prussia's ALR still prescribed retraction, apology, or a declaration of respect as reparation for attacks on another's honour, the king abolished such practices in 1811 in order to limit the 'uncountable number of useless libel cases'. Moreover, as high officials argued, formal apologies always had something demeaning about them. Defamation, however, ran contrary to the aim of law, which was by no means supposed to 'feed and promote the feeling of revenge enjoyed by the insulted after the humiliation of his insulter'.[116] Later, those seeking to justify the publication of sentences drew on the same principles, making explicit that the point was not to 'humiliate' the offender, but rather to restore the 'injured honour of the insulted'.[117]

Nevertheless, the publication of sentences had its critics. In 1882, the Imperial Court of Justice stated that publicity was undoubtedly 'suited to increase the suffering caused by the primary sentence and shame the convicted within his familiar circle'. Dismissing it as part of an older tradition geared towards 'humiliating the offender', the judges found it no longer compatible with liberal penal law. In their view, the punishment proper was meant to give the injured sufficient 'satisfaction'.[118]

Whether a man who had been convicted of lèse-majesté and insulting the German chancellor by a district court ever 'suffered' from his sentence is unknown. If his invectives were politically motivated, he might very well have shrugged his shoulders at it. The notion that every punishment carried 'the nature of an injury to honour' and the 'effect of a humiliating act' probably found little resonance with someone who could justify his actions to himself and his peers.[119] His self-respect and reputation were likely unscathed, especially if he was part of a social and political milieu that shared his convictions. In such circumstances, even the publication of the sentence would hardly have caused him any humiliation or shame.

Even if it did not matter much to this individual person, the Imperial Court's decision was significant because of the legal opinion it conveyed. The state, as the judges saw it, had no genuine stake in publicizing a libel verdict. As they clarified five years later, legislators did 'not view the public interest as having a part in the publication' of sentences and therefore left it to the injured party.[120] As a matter of fact, the state—or the general public it sought to represent—was not at all eager to humiliate the convicted person publicly, which the Imperial Court, among others, saw as the true—if only implicit— function of publication.[121] Simply put, from the perspective of legal policy, coupling punishments with public shaming had definitely fallen out of favour by the late nineteenth century.

Popular Justice

Despite criticism from all sides, though, Article 200 was not stricken from the German penal code. Even during the Weimar Republic, when liberal politicians tried to reform the code and strip it of its conservative elements, they did not touch the article's basic tenets. Although the minister of justice Gustav Radbruch was fiercely opposed to all forms of shaming, which he denounced as 'moral lynch justice', he was not bothered by publishing sentences. On the contrary, he wanted to follow the Prussian model of making it a mandatory part of all serious sentences, justifying it as a measure that would both help protect society and improve the convicted.[122] The Weimar Republic did not last long enough for this to happen, but National Socialism made it a reality.[123]

After 1945, West Germany returned to the imperial practice of informing the public about libel sentences whenever the victim wanted it. As late as the 1980s, newspapers still printed such notices, mostly about sentences against people who had insulted police officers. In these cases, the public prosecutor insisted on making the sentences known to the public, including the full name and address of the culprit. Some later reported that their colleagues at work had talked to them about it. A judge of the Berlin District Court viewed this as a 'renaissance of the pillory', going so far as to speak of 'stigmatization'.[124]

The East German justice system took a less critical approach to the law. Following the road paved by Radbruch and the 'Third Reich', the GDR parliament passed a law in 1957 that expanded the publication of sentences to cover all crimes under the condition that 'it bolsters the corrective impact, has an effect on other citizens, and educates and informs the populace'.[125] It was conceived of as a 'supplementary penalty' that would increase 'the public criticism exercised against the behaviour of the convicted' and create 'a general atmosphere of unforgiveness towards transgressions of the law'. Nevertheless, the legislation required that the punishment be used with restraint, as the Supreme Court confirmed in 1960. It threw out a sentence handed down by a lower court against five men who had produced and distributed 'lewd images'. The high court deemed the order to announce prison sentences in a regional newspaper 'erroneous', reasoning that because the convicted were 'good workers', had shown regret, and asserted that they would 'in the future follow the commandments of socialist morality', the sentence should not be made public. According to the judges, doing so would only 'pillory' and 'boycott' the men and isolate them from the collective, which was not in line with the 'function of punishment in our workers' and peasants' state'.[126]

Two years later, the Magdeburg district court ruled against publishing a conviction for a different reason. The court had given a man a fine for libel but rejected the petition of the woman he insulted that the judgement be released. This would, as the judges observed, 'not help the honour of the plaintiff, but rather would widely disseminate the insult'. But the woman stuck to her guns and demanded that the judgement be printed in the regional daily. The appeals court rejected her petition and held up the district court's argument. At this point, chief instructor Georg Knecht at the East Berlin Ministry of Justice intervened. He chastised the Magdeburg judges for acting on the notion 'that bourgeois ideas of morality are expressed in the Penal Code's §200 and that the restitution of honour according to the principles "eye for an eye, tooth for a tooth" is contrary to socialist conceptions of ethics and morality'. In Knecht's opinion, those assumptions were false, since the principles of 'redress, satisfaction, and the rehabilitation of the injured party' applied in the German Democratic Republic too. Indeed, protecting the honour of its citizens was, he claimed, a serious matter for the socialist state, and publishing the sentence was one way of achieving that very end. It was not meant, Knecht added, to 'defame' the convicted or 'isolate and pillory' him, but rather to 'educate' him.[127]

'Education' was the code word that replaced 'improvement' in East German socialism. Educating lawbreakers so that they both understood and regretted what they had done took multiple forms, from publishing sentences to the public reprimands that were added to the Penal Code in 1957. Judges, though, were not the only ones to educate transgressors. In due course, people themselves were supposed to be put in charge and 'carry out the social education' of criminals. Neighbours, colleagues, and superiors were given the chance to speak up during trials and report on 'the consequences of the crime, the behaviour of the defendant, and the possibility of his further education'.[128] 'Social forces' in the shape of local associations and work brigades were supposed to take on both 'punitive' and 'educational' functions: they censured, criticized, and expressed their contempt, but they also supported the convicted 'in his further professional and cultural development'.[129]

In matters of education and support, the so-called conflict committees were in high demand. First instituted in 1952, their initial purpose was to settle differences and organize arbitration at the workplace. In 1963, similar committees were set up in residential areas in order to get housewives and retired seniors involved in this local form of atonement. Over half of the cases they dealt with were instances of libel between neighbours. The mediation generally ended with the accused apologizing to the plaintiff and committee members; sometimes, their apologies were publicly posted.[130] Arbitration committees also worked in rural areas, with large numbers of people participating. After two youngsters in Saxony had, under the influence of alcohol, destroyed some fruit trees, over eighty people took part in the arbitration, which apparently had a 'very educational' effect on the censured men. At the very least, 'such lapses' were not repeated. The 'educational counselling' given to a drunken dairy farmer in the presence of about seventy members of an agricultural cooperative in Mecklenburg seems to have led to a 'noticeable change in his behaviour'.[131]

Such strategies of public shaming displayed the typical ambivalence between 'unforgiving' exclusion and disciplinary inclusion.[132] There is much evidence that they were less well received by the person shamed than by those doing the shaming. Workers who were accused of breaking the law frequently stated that it was 'more uncomfortable' to have their act handled by the conflict committee than by a court. Some felt incapable of 'taking a position on their problem in public'. Thus, while the committees were officially praised as executing the 'power of the workers' morals', those subjected to them viewed them as forms of collective humiliation.[133]

'Symbolic Pillories' during National Socialism

As direct predecessors and models of such social courts, the GDR named the early comrades' courts of the Soviet Union, which were also copied in communist China.[134] It would be equally appropriate to refer here to the far longer tradition of informal village courts and practices of humiliation, in which local communities bolstered their moral economy and defended themselves against those who violated social norms. When some states deliberately revived this tradition in the twentieth century, they signalled their departure from liberal notions of society based on human dignity and personal freedom. Instead, they favoured collectivist ideas that placed the community above the rights and interests of the individual. In such regimes, public shaming was just one of many techniques of domination.

During National Socialism, public shaming enjoyed particularly high esteem. Beginning in 1934, the regime implemented social courts of honour where 'labour comrades' would 'repent' for insults and other transgressions of duty. Public denunciation and stigmatization played a central role as hearings took place in public and usually ended with a warning, censure, fine, or dismissal.[135] For Roland Freisler, then state secretary of the Ministry of Justice, such procedures would sensibly resolve affairs of honour among colleagues while at the same time protecting the sense and feeling of honour deemed crucial for society at large. In a similar vein, law professor Friedrich Schaffstein emphasized the 'integrative effect' of honour courts and the power of humiliating punishments to forge 'feelings of community'.[136]

The alpha and omega of National Socialism was the people's community and its interests were held above everything else. As a consequence, honour was not seen as a 'personal right', a reading rejected by jurists loyal to the regime as the 'individualist interpretation'. They also had no patience for the 'overly emotional prioritization of human dignity and human rights'. Instead, they valued the 'protection of the honour of the community'. This included the honour of the family, the party, and, last but not least, the racially defined *Volksgemeinschaft*. The latter was enabled and encouraged to make 'moral judgements of unworthiness' about its members and strip them of their honour. According to Schaffstein, every punishment was 'at once and primarily an honour punishment'. The same thing could be read in a 1935 report on 'the future German penal law'.[137]

Some jurists and politicians had even bigger plans. In 1934, Freisler expressed his emphatic support for reintroducing the pillory. In an official paper for the Academy for German Law, he proposed that a person 'who has behaved in a particularly unsocial manner that constitutes a punishable offence might be put on public display'. Most of his fellow jurists refused to follow Freisler here, arguing that a return to 'medieval' practices fitted 'neither the people's sensibilities nor modern thinking about the practical tasks of penal law'. The 1935 committee led by the minister of justice Franz Gürtner also rejected the idea. But it did recommend the publication of all sentences in newspapers as well as 'on advertising columns, on the radio, and in films' as a form of 'symbolic pillory'.[138]

In doing so, the committee went well beyond standing custom. After 1871, only sentences for libel were published in the German Empire, and then only when the libelled person insisted on it. For the committee, though, it was the state that should take action, and it did. In 1935, the Ministry of Justice ordered court press offices to release the full names of people sentenced to long prison terms. As a measure of deterrence, the publication was given 'priority over the consideration of the individual, who has committed a grave transgression against the people's community'. 'Expiation', retribution, and the public 'stigmatization of the convicted' counted far more than individual rights and human dignity.[139]

Not surprisingly, then, there was a sharp rise in public shamings during the 'Third Reich', most of which were by no means occasioned by a punishable offence or court judgement. As early as 1933, some local newspapers inserted a column titled 'On the pillory' that printed the names and addresses of women who entertained intimate relations with Jewish men. While not a crime, it was viewed as a racial 'disgrace' and correspondingly condemned. The so-called pillory parades conducted by stormtroopers in many German cities were even more drastic and violent. In Breslau, 'racially defiled' couples were led through the streets on Sundays in the summer of 1935, often accompanied by marching bands and a crowd that grew larger by the week.[140] Not everyone was enthusiastic about the performance, though. As early as 19 August 1933, the *New York Times* reported on 'the brutal treatment of a non-Jewish girl of 19 who had been found in the company of a Jew'. A group of British tourists who had witnessed the incident wrote a letter to the Nuremberg authorities and pointed out that such occurrences 'must inevitably disgust all foreign visitors to the city'.[141]

This even held true for 24-year-old Martha Dodd, the daughter of the newly appointed US ambassador in Berlin. She had come to Germany full of enthusiasm for the National Socialist regime and its promises to the German people. Public excitement felt 'contagious, and I "Heiled" as vigorously as any Nazi'. The Nuremberg incident, however, which she observed from close-up, made her feel 'nervous and cold, the mood of exhilaration vanished completely': The young girl

> looked ghastly. Her head had been shaved clean of hair and she was wearing a placard across her breast. We followed her for a moment, watching the crowd insult and jibe and drive her. Quentin and my brother asked several people around us, what was the matter. We understood from their German that she was a Gentile who had been consorting with a Jew. The placard said: 'I have Offered Myself to a Jew'.

Witnessing such 'ugly, bare brutality' darkened Martha's picture 'of a happy, carefree Germany'. Still, she urged the journalist who accompanied her not to write about it since it would 'create a bad impression'.[142]

The *New York Times*, however, chose not to show such restraint, and its headline read 'Nazis Use Penalty of Medieval Days'. Foreigners were not the only ones who reacted with disgust and bewilderment. A German businessman who had witnessed the Breslau 'processions' in 1935 complained to the local authorities: as a 'full Aryan', he found it shameful 'to see such a thing' and felt himself 'set back at least a century'.[143] Whether consciously or not, the parades did indeed

Fig. 6. Traditional whipping post in Breslau, before 1945

adapt earlier elements of public shaming. During the Breslau episode, participants met in front of the old whipping post, which, like in many European cities, was not stored away in the local museum, but still found its place in the main square. The accused's heads were shaven, a form of humiliation that, as mentioned above, had been popular in the late Middle Ages, primarily against women.[144]

As in pre-modern times, the shamers needed an audience, which, despite dissent from some quarters, was not lacking. There were always enough men, women, and children willing to join the parade or stand by and watch and cheer. In Breslau, the crowd counted several hundreds of people who actively participated in the spectacle. In March 1938, when Viennese Jews were forced to scrub anti-Nazi graffiti from the pavements, well-dressed men and women of all ages came and mocked them. These people were certainly not members of the 'mob' who were later accused of orchestrating the whole thing. Photographs show laughing, smirking faces; they do not show anyone turned away in disgust. Clearly, citizens enjoyed the degrading show.

Similar acts of public humiliation had been performed in Austria before the 'Anschluss'. Under the authoritarian rule of chancellors Engelbert Dollfuss and Kurt Schuschnigg, communist and National Socialist activists were often forced to scrub their party members' graffiti from walls, houses, and pavements.[145] But the degradation of Jews in 1938 was unusual in three respects: first, even women and old men were forced to their knees; second, the shaming was not organized by the local police, but by Nazi militia men acting on their own initiative; and third, the Viennese Jews bore no personal or political relationship to the graffiti they were forced to scrub. Choosing them to do it was an act of racist bullying, an expression of sheer anti-Semitism that revelled in the crude humiliation of its victims.

In pre-Nazi Germany, too, there was a tradition of public shaming carried out by individuals rather than by state officials. It dated from the 1920s, when the area west of the river Rhine was occupied by French, Belgian, British, and American troops in accordance with the Treaty of Versailles. The presence of French colonial soldiers in particular was met with resistance by the German population and was defamed as the 'black scandal'.[146] Its counterpart in the derogatory imagination was the 'white scandal', a term used to condemn women who had sexual relations with occupying forces—and above all soldiers from the colonies—as disgraceful, shameless, and unworthy. There was hardly a single German press institution that did not report on the 'scandals' with indignation, and (illegal) newspapers ran columns featuring titles like 'On the pillory'.[147] In many towns, this was taken literally. 'Shameless' women were forced to sweep the marketplace in order to be 'ridiculed by the people', and their names were displayed on signs. In Mainz, young men cut off the hair of 'French girls'. In the Ruhr Valley, which had been occupied by French and Belgian troops in 1923, a woman was tied to an advertising column with an insulting poem hanging from her neck while people poured paint into her hair. It is possible that the assaulters belonged to a so-called 'barbers' club' whose members—men between 15 and

31—were taken to court in 1924 for 'publicly demeaning women who supposedly had relations with the French'. A general amnesty set them all free.[148]

A decade later, National Socialists were consciously drawing on these practices of shaming. But the parades and 'processions' they organized were not shows of resistance against an occupying power or against women who supposedly collaborated with them. Storm-troopers acted with full knowledge of their own power, arrogating the right to embarrass and humiliate people without direct orders from above. Nor could they accuse their victims of having broken the law or any other relevant rule of conduct, as earlier forms of 'people's justice' or communal forms of shaming had done. Their point was not to strengthen and defend traditional behavioural norms, but to establish a new normative order.[149] Intimate relationships and marriages between Jews and non-Jews had been an everyday affair in Germany since the nineteenth century, despite the presence of social anti-Semitism. By scandalizing such relations, a new racial state was to emerge that touted 'racial purity' as the signature of national identity and greatness.[150] Public shaming turned this claim into a social practice that sought to affect and enlist every member of the 'people's community'.

Jews and their non-Jewish partners were not the only ones who fell victim to such forms of humiliation. In September 1933, Nazi thugs forced the Catholic politician and former minister Heinrich Hirtsiefer

Fig. 7. Pictures from *National-Zeitung* (Essen, Germany), 12 September 1933

to 'march' through the streets of Essen with a sign around his neck that read: 'I am the starving Hirtsiefer'. It played on the fact that the corpulent 57-year-old father of four had filed a claim to have his pension and related benefits (which the new regime had suspended) paid out in order to feed his family.[151] Hirtsiefer's fate was shared by many other representatives of the Weimar Republic who were made to suffer public humiliation and ridicule before being locked up in concentration camps.

High party officials knew about this and harboured mixed feelings. In March 1933, Adolf Hitler was outraged when he saw a photo of an act of public shaming printed on the front page of the *Washington Times*. Later, the party's press division dismissed the image as a fake—which it was not. In fact, the SS men who had forced the Jewish lawyer Michael Siegel to walk barefoot with cut-off trousers through the centre of Munich had been so proud of their humiliating behaviour that they had asked press photographers for prints. The Nazi leadership, though, believed—not without cause—that the international circulation of such images shone a bad light on the new Germany.[152]

Even State Secretary Freisler, who generally looked favourably on public exposure, distanced himself from these practices. 'The pillory in general', he stated in 1934, 'has, over the last year, become naturalized in an exceptional fashion' thanks to the 'service of our people's organization the SA'. But he also saw its 'dark side' in its 'extremely raw forms' and in the 'danger that it will become a source of pleasure for parts of the population'. Thus, in order to bring the chaos under control and avoid 'uncomfortable side effects', he pleaded that National Socialist formations should behave in a more 'disciplined manner'.[153] In 1935, the minister of economics Hjalmar Schacht urged leaders to replace the 'prevailing lawless condition and illegal activity' with a systematic approach. This was achieved by the 'Law for the Protection of German Blood and German Honour', better known as the Nuremberg Laws, which were presented at the 1935 Party Rally in Nuremberg. The law forbade marriages and 'extra-marital intercourse between Jews and citizens of German and kindred blood'. Afterwards, the acts of public shaming did actually decrease; at the same time, the police departments received an unprecedented flood of denunciations.[154]

The history of public humiliation in National Socialism does not stop there. Police and SS perfected their methods of torture, going beyond inflicting physical pain by subjecting their victims to demeaning acts. During an interrogation of Officer Fabian von Schlabrendorff in Berlin in 1944, criminal commissioner Walter Habecker punched the prisoner 'in the face', a gesture that was meant to dishonour Schlabrendorff and was perceived as such. Schlabrendorff found it 'particularly demeaning' 'that even the female secretary slapped me on Habecker's order'. He was chained and forced to squat while being hit with a bar so hard 'that I lost my balance and fell forward onto my unprotected face'.[155]

Especially in concentration camps, the humiliation inflicted on prisoners knew no limits. When Hirtsiefer arrived at the Börgermoor camp in 1933, the SS guards gave him, as a fellow prisoner recalled,

> a pair of trousers, much too short and tight, which gaped in front and had to be fastened across the belly with a piece of string. They pulled out the tail of his shirt in front. Then they gave him a coat which he had to put on inside out. On his head they placed a tiny soldier's cap. He had to press his feet into clogs with rubber leggings in which he could scarcely walk. With roars of laughter they led him in this outfit from one hut to the other . . . The S.S.-man in the cooking-hut had prepared his welcome for him. He had dirtied his hands with soot and hit him on the face.[156]

After the onset of the war, another wave of public humiliation began that primarily targeted German women who maintained intimate relations with foreign men, whether they be French prisoners of war or forced labourers from Poland and the Soviet Union. Such relations were strictly forbidden, and Heinrich Himmler, leader of the SS and head of the police, ordered that anyone caught breaking the rule be immediately arrested. But by no means did Himmler want to

> hinder the consequences of the German population's justified rage over such scandalous behaviour. To the contrary, I hold the effect of public defamation to be exceptionally deterring and would have no reservations

Fig. 8. The humiliation of Martha Vollrath in Altenburg, February 1941

if one, for instance, were to cut off German women's hair in the presence of the female youth of a village [as punishment] for their dishonourable behaviour or if one were to parade her through the village with a sign stating the transgression.[157]

The Stuttgart police acted in line when they informed district administrators and police chiefs in June 1941 that 'nothing stands in the way of publicly humiliating dishonourable women'. Local party bosses lost no time. The same ritual was repeated all over the country: the woman's hair was cut off in public, then she was paraded through the streets on a wagon or on foot while people gathered and loudly expressed their 'disgust'. SA men and party members were always in the front row.[158]

But it took only six months before the police changed their minds and ordered an end to these practices. What had happened? Evidently, local villagers and townspeople were not overly enthusiastic about seeing their female friends and relatives so demeaned in public. Many failed to understand why going with men from Spain, France, Hungary, or Romania—official allies or friends of Germany—was looked down upon and punished. Women often reacted with more outrage than men. In 1940, even the wife and daughter of a high Nazi Party official in the city of Ulm protested against his publicly shaming a 'disreputable' woman. Some were bothered by the double standard that left German men who had intimate relations with foreign women unscathed.[159] In the face of such widespread criticism, Hitler, in October 1941, forbade 'in the future all public denunciation and humiliation of those Germans who behave dishonourably in relations with foreigners'. All party officials were told 'that pillorying in the press, cutting of hair, public exposure, the parading around with signs etc.' would have to cease.[160]

Instead, pillorying found its way into the courtroom, where Roland Freisler got his second chance. Although he had failed to attract support for his proposal to bring back the pillory officially, becoming president of the People's Court (*Volksgerichtshof*) in 1942 enabled Freisler to shame, humiliate, and demean people as he pleased. His trials were extremely emotional and made him into a crowd-puller. Hundreds of people 'from all classes, invited and not invited', often crammed into the courtroom as if they were going 'to the cinema' or a sports event.[161]

But the public did not always have unlimited access to trials. Those accused of treason for the 20 July 1944 plot to assassinate Hitler were only allowed to speak before a select group of ministers, party officials, and officers from the military, SS, SA, and Gestapo. Journalists were told to follow prescribed language rules and not to write anything that might stir up sympathy for the 'traitors' or their motives. At the same time, minister of propaganda Joseph Goebbels had the proceedings filmed and photographed, so that Freisler's abrasive, derisive style of interrogating the already doomed defendants can still be viewed today.[162]

The men's appearance in itself was enough to make them look like clowns. They wore raggedy civilian clothes, and General Field Marshal

Erwin von Witzleben's trousers were so large that he had to hold them up. Erich Hoepner, a highly decorated general, sat there in a sweater without tie. They were subjected to tirades of difficult-to-translate insults, 'long-drawn-out, cheap propaganda harangues' delivered 'in a voice which would easily have carried through several large court rooms'. Freisler went all out in using his oratory abilities and did not miss a chance to embarrass and humiliate his victims.[163]

Yet not all National Socialists were pleased with Freisler's condescending, denunciatory style and criticized it for detracting from the 'seriousness' of the court. Justice minister Otto Thierack complained to Goebbels that Freisler staged the trials 'too publicly and too dramatically' and feared that this would have 'unpleasant effects' on the audience. For his part, the minister of propaganda laced his 'statement of facts' that was broadcast over the radio on 26 July 1944 with invective. He gave Freisler clear instructions on how to conduct the trial and stated that he was certain that the judge would 'find the right tone to deal with them'. Hitler agreed: 'Freisler will see to that. That's our Vyshinsky.'[164]

Other Countries, Same Customs

Andrey Vyshinsky was procurator general of the Soviet Union and headed up the Moscow trials during the Great Purge in the late 1930s. In court, he was known for demeaning and insulting defendants, some of whom were high-ranking military officers and old members of the Communist Party. As in Nazi Germany, the Soviet Union rushed alleged enemies and traitors through the courts, where public humiliation played a considerable role. Mao Zedong's China later put on similar show trials.[165]

After the Second World War, this kind of state-sanctioned repression was followed by countless incidents of locally orchestrated, unofficial shaming. In countries that had been occupied by Germany, people began taking revenge on collaborators, and women who had engaged in relations with occupying soldiers were made to feel the

Fig. 9. Chartres, France, August 1944 (Robert Capa)

contempt of their fellow citizens. Collective acts of public humiliation took place in France, Belgium, the Netherlands, Norway, Denmark, Italy, Czechoslovakia, and Greece.[166] Robert Capa's August 1944 photograph of a young woman with a child in her arms being chased through the streets of Chartres became famous. Twenty-three years old, Simone Touseau had worked for the Germans as a translator and had had a child with a German soldier. She was now publicly humiliated for this *'collaboration horizontale'*.[167]

The same pattern played out with slight variations in other cities in France and across Europe: a woman was dragged across a public square and placed high up where many could see her head being shaved. After that, she was paraded through the streets. The prevalence of this ritual over the entire continent attests to the fact that the repertoire of shaming was well known and could be made reality at any time. Nazi Germany, which took the politics of 'racial purity' to its extreme, was not the only country where protecting national honour was fused with the protection of 'blood' and the female body. In the occupied nations, too, women who had relations with the enemy were viewed as having insulted the honour of their country. A few months after Germany invaded Poland in 1939, a placard was posted that stated: 'The pride of Polish women must be the holiest thing for you, you must defend your honour. Women who behave shamelessly towards the murderers of our sons, fathers, and brothers blemish us with a terrible disgrace.' Members of local resistance groups hunted down such 'shameless' women, shaved their heads, and beat them up.[168]

Men's dominance in positions of power goes a long way in explaining why it was usually male perpetrators who shamed women in public. At the same time, it was part of sexual politics: men took revenge, both symbolic and real, on women who chose foreigners and enemies as intimate partners and thereby rejected their own people.

As with the British tourists and Martha Dodd in Nuremberg 1933, these shaming rituals did not leave a good impression on outside observers. In 1944, American poet Gertrude Stein, who had been living in France since 1903 and who had sympathies for the Vichy regime, stated that she felt thrown back to the Middle Ages. For their part, British and American soldiers showed a range of reactions, from irritation to disgust. But as a rule, they did not involve themselves in the internal conflicts of the liberated countries, instead electing to enjoy the pleasures of erotic collaboration for themselves.[169]

In occupied Germany and Austria, too, Allied soldiers had 'relations' with local 'Fräuleins', despite initial prohibitions against fraternization. As after the First World War in the Rhineland, scornful statements and deprecating gestures followed. In October 1945, young men from the city of Linz formed a 'head shaving commando' with the aim of punishing 'shameless' young women who were 'all too free in their contact with American soldiers'. The men were motivated by a mixture of personal slight and nationalist pride:

> I was drafted as a young man and I was there at the fight for Vienna . . .
> And then I was in a POW camp . . . I returned to Linz totally exhausted
> and half starving . . . And then, the girls don't even look at me, but are
> only interested in the Americans. They ridiculed us. And it wasn't just one

guy's girlfriend ... who ran off. It was quite a few, a lot ... But whatever, the Americans were the winners![170]

Post-war Shame and Shaming

After the war that National Socialism had fashioned as a fight for the life or death of the German people and the 'Aryan race', the Allied occupation seemed to many Germans the absolute height of humiliation. The prohibition on fraternization underscored the moral distance between occupiers and occupied. Furthermore, Germans were made to confront the crimes that had been committed, in their very name, before and during the war. Footage of the liberation of concentration and extermination camps was shown to them in theatres and prisoner-of-war camps. But whether the shocking images produced the shaming effect that American and British officials had hoped for was difficult to assess. Shame had many faces and sometimes only found expression in helpless silence. Even though it might have been felt, it could quickly be suppressed, especially when those overcome by the emotion were being watched by others or experienced it in groups in which they did not want to suffer the sense of being exposed.[171]

At the same time, shame and shaming were constants in the political rhetoric of post-war Germany. The 1945 founding statement of the Communist Party admonished that 'in every German' there must exist 'the consciousness and shame that the German people has a significant share of guilt' to bear. After returning from exile in Moscow, party functionary Walter Ulbricht exhorted: 'Only when our people are fully engrossed with the crimes of Hitlerism, only when they are engrossed by deep shame in the fact that they permitted these barbaric crimes to occur, only then will they summon up the inner power to take a new path.' For prominent East German intellectuals like Anna Seghers, Arnold Zweig, Johannes R. Becher, and Stefan Hermlin, shame was the emotion that would enable repentance, catharsis, and a new beginning. In September 1945, Becher modified a quote from Karl Marx: 'Shame is a revolutionary feeling, which—felt deeply—makes the whole person red hot and burns out the waste of the rotten old stuff in us.'[172]

The first president of West Germany, Theodor Heuss, dispensed with such pathos in his December 1949 speech at the Society for Christian-Jewish Cooperation, in which he coined the concept 'collective shame'. 'The worst that Hitler has done to us—and he has violated us in many ways—is that that he forced us into the shameful condition of having to share the name "German" with him and his henchmen.' Six years later, Heuss explained that this shame was not something one could 'shake off—it will follow us—but one can and must try to overcome it with counteraction, counteraction, not just counterassertions'.[173] Heuss was interested not in a silent shame, but in a vocal, active shame. Without using Becher's revolutionary rhetoric, he also subscribed to shame as an impulse for inducing radical, sustained behavioural changes.

Seen in this way, shame was not simply a negation of guilt or a defence against moral condemnations, but a way of assuming personal and political responsibility. This contradicts the widespread assumption that post-war Germans were inhibited by shame to speak about their past, that they tried to save face, and that they rejected the necessity of 'complete self-analysis' and 'purification', as philosopher Karl Jaspers put it in 1946. Indeed, one of the most common modifiers used to qualify shame, 'deep', indicates that shame goes under one's skin and causes immense displeasure. As such, it had the potential, as Ulbricht put it, to forge new paths.[174]

Yet not everybody was ready to answer the call to shame and accept an explicit politics of shaming. In the Federal Republic of Germany, Nazi elites often retained their positions in private business and public administration, whereas resistance fighters came away empty-handed and lacked sufficient power to point fingers. The GDR, in contrast, wielded shame as an instrument of propaganda and education. The 1950s in particular were characterized by a micropolitics that shamed everyone who had not belonged to the communist resistance. By turning anti-fascism into its founding myth, the socialist state accused the majority of its populace of having been complicit with fascism. As the writer Erwin Strittmatter ironically noted in his diary in 1968, such shaming exerted a subcutaneous force:

> You taught us to understand the inhumanity of fascism. You showed us the cruelty in the concentration camps and the murder and torture of political opponents that we tolerated with our silence and lack of protest. We understood and were grateful to the teachers you sent to us to make us see and have insights. After that, we did as it suited you.

Born in 1912, Strittmatter had fought in a police mountain trooper regiment during the war. After 1945, he 'converted' to Marxism, but not without critically reflecting on the conflation of individual shame and official shaming.[175] Such shaming played out differently than the sanctions of the social courts in work brigades, rural cooperatives, and neighbourhoods or the campaigns against slackers in schools and factories. It did not lambast individual misdemeanours, but designed a moral-political map with clear demarcations of good and evil. By emphasizing who the heroes were, the regime crafted them into standards for everyone else. Comparing oneself to this standard was supposed to lead to what Strittmatter called 'insight', which would in turn motivate moral submission and political cooperation. This kind of moral shaming dispensed with public acts of castigation; instead, it set up a symbolic pillory that was of inestimable importance for the social and moral integration of those who found it hard to adjust to the new socialist state.

Civility versus Barbarism

One of the few things the GDR had in common with the Federal Republic was that it largely eschewed more expressive methods to stigmatize former political opponents officially. Such methods, though, became extremely popular in communist China. During the Cultural Revolution, mostly young men and women participated in excessive acts of humiliation against members of the older generation of functionaries, teachers, and intellectuals. In 1966, students at a girls' school in Beijing shaved their principal's head, forced her to scrub the toilets, and beat her so brutally that she died of the injuries. In 1968, a man who sent an anonymous letter to the local revolutionary committee in defence of his father, a former party secretary, was paraded through the streets with a sign around his neck. The methods used were similar to those known in Europe, all the way up to the dunce's cap. They found more or less silent approval from the central party authorities. At least initially, Chairman Mao Zedong did nothing to stop the brutal violence of the militant Red Guards, who sought to 'purify' society of 'counterrevolutionary' enemies.[176]

In the end, it was this unhinged violence that spurred Chinese political and military leaders to put an end to the chaotic scenes of retribution. But it took half a century until people were able to speak somewhat openly about it. Since 2013, those who actively participated in the Cultural Revolution have increasingly been publishing apologies for the suffering they caused. These apologies stirred up debates in blogs and underground publications that were quickly suppressed by the government. One person stated that he regretted his behaviour in the 1960s because he saw the same patterns re-emerging and was concerned about the civility of his country.[177]

Since the 1990s, similar concerns have motivated American intellectuals' criticism of 'shame sanctions' as legal punishment. In the USA, numerous judges at lower-level courts have started—or returned to—sentencing people to some form of public shaming for traffic violations and petty crimes. Yet many see this policy as a sign of regression. According to the philosopher Martha Nussbaum, states that seek to promote principles of equality and human dignity must prohibit the use of shame sanctions. Such penalties, she argues, not only violate liberal principles. They also draw too stark a line between those who see themselves as law-abiding citizens and those who break the laws and are subject to collective stigmatization. In contrast, supporters of shame sanctions claim that they are a better alternative to sentences in overfull prisons and a more efficient means of countering the erosion of moral standards in society.[178]

On the other side of the Atlantic, these kinds of argument have been around since the eighteenth century and are well remembered. This does not mean that 'Old Europe' is a stranger to contemporary criticisms of the loss of civil virtues like respect, tact, and mindfulness. Many people keep their distance from the recent brand of narcissistic individualism that encourages a no-holds-barred approach to self-actualization. At the same time, liberal Europeans know that, in the hands of the powerful, shaming can be a double-edged sword. They recall how long it took to separate morality from law and how much energy was spent fighting for their separation. Finally, they recollect those instances in which the state projected itself as the bastion of morality and enlisted the law to serve its ends. This was the case during National Socialism and fascism, but also, to varying degrees, in state socialist countries and, among others, in post-war Greece. In 1958, the Athens parliament passed a law that criminalized certain forms of protest favoured by young 'agitators'. At the hands of the local police, such 'agitators' were then publicly humiliated—with their heads shaven and their trousers shortened.[179]

The notion that similar practices of state-sanctioned shaming were used in the conservative Greece of the 1950s, the communist China of the 1960s, and the democratic USA of the 1990s might seem bewildering. Obviously, political regimes around the world have rushed to pick up methods of public pillorying when there are transgressions to be punished. In contrast to the practice of exposing people to the public gaze in eighteenth- and nineteenth-century Europe, modern shaming has—with the exception of China's Red Guards—generally dispensed with direct physical violence; otherwise, things have largely remained the same. The shamed have always had to wear signs that tell of the transgression committed, and the dunce cap humiliating a 'revisionist' Chinese party official was reminiscent of similar hats that have long been part of the European culture of shaming.[180] Finally, the shaved heads of the Greek 'teddy boys' referenced the shaved heads of those pilloried in the early modern period and those denounced for defaming national honour in the twentieth century.[181]

How can the spatial and temporal reach of such practices be explained? There is little evidence to suggest that it is all a matter of a large-scale European export, which might at best be true for North America, where British and French settler colonies had first-hand knowledge of common European forms of shame punishment. Such transfers definitely did not take place in China, which sought to avoid European influences until the late nineteenth century. In the 1870s, Chinese travellers to Europe noted with surprise that criminals were kept in prisons under comfortable conditions with adequate nourishment rather than flogged in the streets—as was normal at home.[182] This attests to the hypothesis that degrading practices were 'home-made' and drew on local traditions. The recitation of similar signs and scripts might then be explained by the performative effectiveness and expressivity that made them attractive enough to rule out alternatives. This is true of east Asia no less than of North America, western and eastern Europe, or the Mediterranean, despite minor regional differences.

What Europe and North America had in common, though, was that public shaming and corporal punishment had been contested since the eighteenth century. Dissenting voices became increasingly frequent and louder in the first half of the nineteenth century until these practices were finally abolished. Critics argued that publicly humiliating criminals did nothing to reintegrate them and had no deterrent effect for others. The notion that they bolstered the collective sense of law and order was also questioned on the grounds that it was increasingly a matter of uncertainty whether the population would support and participate in any particular act of punishment. Indeed, penalties carried out in public often gave rise to expressions of solidarity with the exposed person, which ultimately served to undermine state authority.

Above all, however, liberal-minded contemporaries claimed that corporal punishment and public shaming were irreconcilable with the concept of human dignity. The definition of human dignity was not identical with the notion of humanity as such.[183] That cruel forms of corporal punishment like branding and whipping violated the principles of humanity was one argument, and that they violated the dignity of their victims was another. Humanity demanded that those who administered or witnessed punishment feel compassion with the punished rather than satisfy the need for revenge and retribution. Moreover, the principles of humanity dictated seeing even in the most brutal criminal a person who had been pushed to commit a dreadful crime by factors often outside of his control and who was thus deserving of empathy rather than contempt.

Even those individuals were attributed with dignity. Unlike honour, which was ascribed to people based on their social position and personal behaviour, dignity was seen as a constituent part of being human. This distinguished the criminal from animality as it was conceived during the nineteenth century. Indeed, the frequency with which contemporaries implicitly or explicitly used comparisons between man and animal to highlight dignity as a special feature of man is striking. Whenever they attempted to delegitimize public shaming or corporal punishment, they stated that it was impermissible to treat people like animals, which is to say, as mere bodies. Slavery, branding, beatings, and exposure to the public gaze were all considered to stand in conflict with human dignity, while animals only seemed to understand the language of force and domination.[184]

Important to note in this context is that it was not the causation of suffering and the feeling of pain which were thought to be unbearable for humans. Rather, penalties that visibly injured the body drew criticism because they acted upon man as if he were a being without sensitivity, free will, and reason. Such treatment was perceived as utterly degrading, although class differences were tacitly condoned and approved of, even by those who otherwise vehemently supported equality before the law. Nevertheless, the abolition of corporal punishment remained a key liberal demand, and the argument that it violated human dignity (which was often equated with honour) gained in prominence. Administering it in public was intolerable even for conservatives, who supported it if only it were carried out behind closed doors. But there were also counter-movements that deliberately used communitarian rhetoric to brush aside such 'individualist' tendencies. During National Socialism and fascism, public pillorying gained a new face. Under the guise of democratic participation and education, state socialism later sought to enforce its particular morality with practices of shaming, thus encouraging citizens to make its illiberal moral policies a reality.

Looking back on the historical record, there is an evident trend: the more liberal the state and its officials, the greater the aversion towards mixing law and morality and publicly shaming citizens. At the same time, liberal states tend to act with stronger determination and protect citizens from being demeaned by others. After all, states and criminal justice systems are not the only institutions that adopt as their own a politics of humiliation. Degrading, ridiculing, and embarrassing others also finds its place in the family, at school, in the military, among peers, and in the media.

2

SOCIAL SITES OF PUBLIC SHAMING

From the Classroom to Online Bullying

In 1989, the artist Martin Kippenberger, then 36 years old, made a number of life-size sculptures of a grown man in a button-up shirt and dress trousers standing in a corner, his head bowed and his hands behind his back. The title, 'Martin, into the Corner, You Should Be Ashamed of Yourself', was almost superfluous, as every European of Kippenberger's age (not to speak of those older) was familiar with the situation: someone is singled out, marginalized, and shamed in front of others.

The fact that the man had his back turned to viewers might at first seem remarkable. After all, shaming usually occurs face-to-face, so that the person shamed can see the other's contempt. But Kippenberger's installation was modelled on the common method of classroom discipline by which teachers send disobedient pupils to the corner with their backs turned to the class. So even though the pupil might not be able to be shamed through direct eye contact with the others, she also cannot communicate with them or subvert the punishment by making faces or otherwise showing a lack of concern.

This kind of classroom discipline vaguely recalls the classic pillory. There, too, people were subjected to the gaze of others, and it too was used to punish rule-breakers, if with more cruelty, pain, and consequence than its classroom counterpart. Finally, its effectiveness also

Fig. 10. *Martin, ab in die Ecke und schäm dich (Martin, into the Corner, You Should Be Ashamed of Yourself)*, sculpture by Martin Kippenberger, 1989/90.

depended largely on the audience: did they approve of the punishment and participate by actively deriding or cursing the culprit? Or did they remain silent, show signs of sympathy, or even try to free her from her predicament? In short, the complicity of others has always been decisive for whether or not such public punishments have the intended effect of shaming the transgressor. On the same note, the castigated could read from the others' words and body language whether she should really feel ashamed. If she did not share their feelings or norms, she could spare herself the shame altogether. Nevertheless, in doing so, she might run the risk of being permanently ostracized by the collective.

Things were not all that different in the classroom. Although teachers administered their shame sanctions 'from above', the reactions of other pupils were in no way insignificant for the pupil standing in the corner. If they found the action that had led to the punishment good, just, or courageous, the attempt at shaming would fail and the cornered pupil would become the hero of the class. The same thing could happen if the teacher was generally hated. If,

Fig. 11. Pupil wearing a dunce's hat, detail from a model of a classroom, France c.1830

however, an unpopular pupil was reprimanded, their classmates might join in on the shaming with *schadenfreude*.[1]

The example from the schoolhouse shows that shaming has historically been a matter of routine beyond state-sanctioned punishments. Indeed, it remains as present as ever in other places and in other media. Carried out by different people on different occasions in front of different audiences, shaming always pursues similar aims and ends: to exclude the shamed, display the power of those shaming, and gain the complicity of the audience. The more the state ceases to use shame sanctions, the more dominant and conspicuous social practices of shaming become. At the same time, they increasingly attract disdain and critique, as in Kippenberger's ironic installation.

Schools as Laboratories of Shaming

Kippenberger was no stranger to situations of shaming, either as a child or as an artist.[2] When he went to school in the 1960s, spankings, detention, and standing in the corner were all everyday events, carried out by teachers who expected that the rest of the class would go along with them or at least stand by and watch. In order to be sure their authoritarian act would not backfire on them, they had to be able to evaluate whether classmates would sympathize with their classmate or not.

In the nineteenth and early twentieth centuries, when teachers' power and authority was unquestioned, they could spare themselves such calculations. In the exceptional case that an individual or group protested against a teacher's actions, the principal would step in and restore the status quo. The silent assent of parents was taken for granted, as they would rarely defend their chastised children against the school's measures. Even when teachers hit children, most parents did not speak up, either because they felt unable to challenge the teacher's authority or because they believed that their child had probably deserved it, or at least that it would not do her any harm.

Alongside the cane and the corner, teachers had an arsenal of other punishments. In the nineteenth century, they literally forced pupils onto their knees—in extreme cases on a piece of 'sharpened wood'. Even though the 1789 *Manual for German School Principals* had already declared this punishment 'irrational', Bavarian schools were still using it a century later.[3] British public schools, too, had pupils kneel down before being officially flogged in order to increase the pain and the shaming effect.[4] Kneeling, of course, had a special significance: it was originally viewed as 'a sign of humility before God'. This is why it was seen as 'foolish' or 'irrational' to convert it into a secular practice of public degradation. Accordingly, late eighteenth-century reformers pushed for its 'total abolishment' in schools, albeit with limited success.[5]

Over the course of the nineteenth century, blatant forms of shaming like the dunce cap, donkey ears, or having a wooden donkey hung around one's neck disappeared from everyday school life, and children were no longer forced into 'holes of shame'.[6] But milder instruments of shaming remained, including making pupils stand at their desks or at the door or write their names in a 'book of shame'. Spanking, in 'moderate' form, was officially permissible as a 'last resort' after 'other means of control have been tried' or when the pupil had committed 'grave moral offences'.[7] Still, teachers gradually lost their freedom to choose how to hit whom: 'Blows with the hand, cuff, boxing ears, shaking' were, in 1910 London, considered 'irregular ways of inflicting corporal punishment' and 'strictly forbidden'. Girls might only be struck on their hands, boys on their bottoms. Administered in front of the whole class, such beatings were doubly shaming.[8]

While state schools were increasingly monitored for 'irregular' punishments, British prep and private schools stood out for their unmitigated power to exert physical violence against their pupils. The cane and the birch figured prominently in personal accounts of boarding school life, with famous elite institutions like Harrow, Charterhouse, and Eton proudly and self-confidently defending such education through shame and discipline.[9] It took until the 1990s for private schools in Britain to lose the legal right to use corporal punishment. State schools had been ordered to give it up in 1986.[10] Many states in the USA, mostly in the South and the so-called Bible Belt, still tolerate spanking, notwithstanding the century-old appeals of American pedagogues that schools should not humiliate pupils, but should seek to boost their self-confidence.[11]

Aside from physical violence, non-codified practices of shaming have continued to exist in classrooms below the legal radar. As many a reader might remember, calling on a weaker student to solve a complex maths problem in front of the whole class has never been about the process of learning. In a large survey conducted in Germany in 2009, one in every four ninth-graders said they had been 'humiliated by teachers in front of other pupils' or 'treated cruelly', boys more than girls.[12] Subjects like music, where students would be asked to sing alone, and gym class could be exploited for this purpose just as well as maths could. Even more than cognitive weaknesses, physical ones seemed to predestine pupils to be shamed. Having one's grades read aloud to classmates was often seen as less shameful than falling off the balancing beam or tripping over a hurdle with everybody watching.

In 2015, a German mother took it upon herself to put an end to such 'humiliating' practices in school sports. In a petition addressed to the Ministry of Education, she told the story of her youngest son, who had come home crying. In a nation-wide competition, he had only received a certificate of participation rather than a winner's medal because he could not throw, run, and leap well enough. This had caused him terrible shame and despair, which was why the worried mother wanted such public scenes of failure to stop. Her petition made headlines and within a few days had been signed by 20,000 people.[13]

Everybody knows that athletic competitions are no fun for less capable students, and the comments on the petition spoke volumes.[14] Many adults recalled the shame they themselves had felt when they had done poorly in sports. But back then, no mother, not to mention father, would ever have thought of decrying such events as ritualized forms of humiliation or of demanding that they be ended. Clearly, tolerance is far lower today, and what used to be uncomfortable but accepted now has the potential to become a scandal.

Looking back in history, one can distinguish between three consecutive attitudes towards shaming in educational contexts: first there was indifference, followed by progressively stronger condemnation, and capped off by robust resistance. While people barely took the issue seriously around 1800, a wave of criticism began in the later nineteenth century and continued into the twentieth. It sought to put limits on public shaming and protect pupils from its negative social and psychological effects. The end of this process is marked by the demand that shaming—now viewed more and more as a form of humiliation—should disappear altogether. What is viewed as shaming or humiliation, though, has differed over time. Still, history has witnessed a notable tendency to expand what counts as one or the other.

Do Children Have Honour?

In 1798, the recently enthroned Prussian king Friedrich Wilhelm III decreed that students could be sentenced to corporal punishment for excessively crude behaviour. In doing so, he was attacking their honour. After all, university students maintained a culture of academic freedom. Instead of being subject to the policeman's baton, they benefited from a much milder system of academic discipline. Moreover, most of them were aristocrats or sons of (upper) middle-class

Fig. 12. Corporal punishment in school. Etching, Germany, *c*.1820

families for whom beatings, and public beatings at that, were seen as highly dishonouring.

The king tried to make the bitter pill easier to swallow by asking students to see such disciplinary measures as a form of 'paternal betterment'. 'Executed in the presence of superiors and accompanied by their necessary condemnations', he claimed, they were continuous with familial discipline. Accordingly, 'it must be ensured that the sound feeling of honour of the punished is not harmed, but that he is so treated as if he were still at a lower school and of an age when beatings carried out by parents or teachers do not occasion complaint'.[15]

In truth, however, this well-meaning explanation further humiliated students, as it likened them to immature children and subordinate adolescents. Sons hit by their fathers, pupils hit by their teachers, apprentices hit by their masters all had to tolerate physical violence and were not allowed to complain or put up resistance. In relations between servants and masters, the latter's 'scolding and small acts of violence' were judged legitimate and not punishable by law, especially when the servant had 'enraged' his master 'through improper behaviour'.[16] Such 'improper behaviour' was a necessary condition for corporal punishment, even if the definition often changed and could be expanded at will.

By speaking of students' 'sound feeling of honour' that must not be 'harmed', the royal decree drew attention to something else, too. It implied that if the young men were treated like children or pupils, they had no reason to feel hurt or harmed. But if being castigated by one's father or teacher did not violate a young person's feeling of honour, did this mean that they had no feeling of honour in the first place?

Many authors who wrote about education following the 'pedagogical' eighteenth century were interested in this topic. On the whole, hardly anybody believed that children were born with feelings of honour and shame. 'In the first years of childhood', stated a pedagogical encyclopaedia from 1860, 'the human is nearly on the level of an animal.'[17] The dominant view was that honour and shame developed over time and thus had to be carefully cultivated.[18] It was believed that children were just as little familiar with these feelings as the 'savages' encountered in Africa: they shared their 'uncivilized' state, and neither could feel dishonoured when they were beaten by persons of authority. But in contrast to Africans, 'who can never go beyond their current level', European children, so it was said, could and should be educated.[19]

Consequently, educators were advised to 'stimulate' the 'honour drive' of their pupils. At the same time, they were supposed to make sure that children 'learn to *feel ashamed*' when they did something wrong. Mothers, alongside teachers, were considered the most crucial 'civilizing' agents who, from early on, had to prepare their offspring for the complexities of modern life. According to Hermann Klencke's 'practical book for German women', the feeling of honour would serve as a 'compass' in their child's life and 'thus must be strongly developed in the child by the mother'.[20]

Expert Advice

Klencke, a medical doctor, first published his advice book in 1870. It was a bestseller, new editions quickly followed, and, over many decades, influenced how middle-class families raised their children.[21] The author's medical expertise gave his recommendations an authority that made mere experience seem insignificant in comparison, even if it had been passed down from generation to generation of mothers. Having redefined itself as a natural science, medicine was highly revered during the nineteenth (and twentieth) century. Fittingly, the advice of doctors carried weight even when they coloured the facts with moral judgements, as Klencke did freely and extensively.

Honour and feelings of honour had a particularly significant role to play in the upbringing of young boys. After all, 'the source of all *masculine* courage' is, the author claimed, derived from the 'drive to honour'. Even if 'in our current times of civilization' boys were no longer primarily raised to become warriors and heroes, but men 'of peaceful occupation', the 'moral courage' requisite for those occupations could only be attained with the help of this so-called drive to honour. Klencke believed that it took a different shape in girls, whose lives had another purpose: they were supposed to 'allow their beauty and virtues to shine gently in the silent shadows of domestic life' and avoid vanity, craving for admiration, affectation, and hypocrisy. Klencke agreed with his contemporaries that a girl's most beautiful virtue was her 'shame'.[22]

This was why he advised that girls be disciplined with 'emotional' rather than physical intervention. Whereas disobedient boys needed a good beating, gentle girls were 'sensitive towards every form of shame', which had a 'deeper effect on idleness and foolishness than reprimands, exhortation, threats, and corporal punishment'. A mother could shame her daughter in private conversation just as well as in front of siblings or friends. What always worked was 'shaming isolation', exclusion from the group.[23]

Klencke's constant talk of humiliation and shaming was nothing uncommon for nineteenth-century advice literature, nor was it a German peculiarity. American manuals and journals also recommended that the child's will had to be 'broken' and that children were to be made to follow social norms, even if doing so required some violence.[24] In 1853, Pastor Heman Humphrey urged mothers to use the cane before their child was 18 months old. He was following in the footsteps of Swiss educator Johann Georg Sulzer, who had popularized the notion a century earlier. Sulzer, who viewed himself as an Enlightenment thinker, believed that parents had to beat out 'obstinacy' with 'serious chiding and the rod' in the child's first year of life, because only then would they become 'obedient, malleable, and good'. In the 1740s, when Sulzer gave private lessons to the children of a wealthy German merchant, he had no reservations about meting out corporal punishments that would leave 'an almost permanent impression'. For an ambitious child, though, he suggested other forms of 'shaming'. She was to be reprimanded in front of all 'housemates' while everyone 'showed her their contempt' and 'acted as if they no longer wanted to have anything to do with her'.[25]

In the mid-eighteenth century, there was no shortage of 'housemates', as parents and siblings shared their middle-class homes with single aunts and cousins, apprentices, and servants. Such an audience, according to Sulzer, was crucial if the act of shaming was to sink in. Carried out 'with a sort of solemnity', it would not fail to influence the child's future behaviour.[26]

Later experts, however, took issue with this advice. Adolf Matthias, author of a bestselling 1897 manual on raising children that remained in press until the 1920s, pleaded with parents to punish their children in private. Especially when admonishing 'acts against honesty, truthfulness, and modesty', he cautioned that they should avoid public shaming.[27] In 1908, Protestant pastor Heinrich Lhotzky considered it an 'unpleasant trick' when parents 'put their children to shame before strangers by making fun of them or recounting all their faults and failings'.[28] A few years later, school inspector Richard Kabisch went so far as to warn fathers and teachers against 'all swearing and scolding' on the grounds that such abuses would do injury to the child's honour. Kabisch was in step with his contemporaries when he held up honour as being indispensable for people who wanted to 'walk upright'.[29]

Walking upright stood in stark contrast to kneeling, which was increasingly equated with humiliation and criticized for that very reason.[30] At the same time, though, experts wanted children to be raised with feelings of 'self-humiliation'. For Klencke, self-humiliation meant that children should apologize for their wrongdoings; and if they failed to do so, they had to be actively 'shamed'.[31] Self-humiliation thus preceded external shaming and possibly made it unnecessary. Moreover, it was held to be an act of courtesy and politeness.

But what, today's readers might ask, made an apology into something degrading and humiliating for the person who was apologizing? This can only be understood by emphasizing the centrality of honour in conceptions of self-identity dominant at the time. In a society that placed honour higher than all other emotions, an apology could be seen as lowering one's honour, a view that children quickly internalized. In Mark Twain's 1884 novel *Adventures of Huckleberry Finn*, Huck, who grew up in the honour-based society of the American South, fights with himself over whether to say sorry to his friend Jim, a fugitive slave, for playing shameful tricks on him. 'It was fifteen minutes before I could work myself up to go and humble myself to a nigger—but I done it and I warn't ever sorry for it afterwards, neither.'[32] In 1904, Friedrich Wilhelm Foerster, who taught classes on moral education in Zurich, Switzerland, observed that no 'boys and girls' between 11 and 15 years of age 'wanted to be the first to ask for forgiveness' and that they 'believed he who says the first nice thing is demeaned'.[33]

Adults likewise found it difficult to apologize. Foerster quoted the Scottish writer Robert Louis Stevenson, who took four days before he finally begged pardon from his handmaid for his crude behaviour, and, when he did, became 'as red and ashamed as could be'. For his part, Stevenson considered his hesitation and shame as expressions of cowardice, since he was not so much ashamed of his behaviour as he was about having to apologize for it. He felt shame about his apology 'because I was doing a thing that would be called ridiculous', reflecting that 'I did not know I had so much respect of middle-class notions before'.[34] A true Victorian, Stevenson had been weaned on class privilege and thus had a tough time admitting his mistake to his servant. Apologizing to someone of a lower status, and thereby literally lowering oneself, was indeed something that happened rather seldom: parents rarely said sorry to their children, teachers rarely to their pupils. It was much easier to demand apologies from those of lower status, who did not, in the common opinion, have much honour to lose anyway.

Only generations later did conventions start to change and good manners demand that one not only admit, but also apologize for misconduct, even if it meant to one's own children. In Christine

Nöstlinger's 1972 prize-winning children's book *The Cucumber King*, the main character's father fails to apologize to his family for making a grave mistake, instead unconvincingly pretending that he had entirely forgotten about it. This pains 12-year-old Wolfgang, who finds his father's behaviour both childish and shameful. The moral, of course, is that Wolfgang will act differently from his father.[35] This shift in mores was only made possible when honour lost some of its social significance. The ongoing democratization and de-hierarchization of social relations also put an end to the idea that apologizing implied a loss of status and an act of self-humiliation.

The Pedagogical Turn

At the same time, the notion of honour was coming closer to being identified with the general concept of human dignity. In the late nineteenth and early twentieth centuries, more and more pedagogues joined in the chorus condemning 'undignified' punishments that violated children's and adolescents' 'feelings of honour'. School superintendent Wilhelm Lüngen let out a sigh of relief in 1907 at the fact that corporal punishment 'no longer plays the dominant role today that it did fifty years ago', but regretted that it 'unfortunately still plays all too great a role'.[36] Indeed, most teachers were not yet prepared to dispense with it completely. Even though it had become general consensus that corporal punishment for adults was irreconcilable with modern notions of human dignity, the norms for children were different. According to Adolf Matthias, the bestselling author on childrearing, the belief that one would 'violate a child's human dignity with one stroke' confused the 'self-conscious adult with the child'. In his opinion, such 'sensitivity' was false and vastly exaggerated.[37]

Matthias' comments give powerful insight into why educators parted ways with corporal punishment and shaming much later than judges and prosecutors did: by denying that children had a sense of honour and shame, they could feel justified in swinging the paddle. Human dignity and honour were not yet conceived of as absolute normative standards, but were seen as having gradations that varied according to age and gender. While many found it perfectly 'rational' to give 'bratty' boys a few 'moderate beatings', hardly anyone spoke of spanking misbehaving girls.[38]

But experts also recommended that beatings for boys only be used in exceptional cases and remain just that—moderate. In 1914, a high school teacher maintained that the 'ruler and hand' were not 'among the father's means of punishment'. Instead, he should verbally casti-gate his sons, but not too harshly and too frequently. Constant tirades 'make boys thick-skinned and demean the father himself'.[39] In other words, they would fail to produce shame as an internal corrective to bad behaviour. In 1919, social democrat and former teacher Heinrich Schulz stated that children should be shamed or demeaned before others as little as possible, and that a sharp glare would have a greater effect than words, especially when the child already regretted her 'wrong'. Addressing proletarian mothers, he wrote that a mere rep-rimanding gaze would make their children 'thankful that you spared them further shaming in words'.[40]

Shaming in familial contexts, advice authors seemed to agree, should thus be less loudly vocal, less corporal, and less public. In fact, shaming found a smaller audience anyway because families and, with them, households were shrinking and turning more private. Not only were there fewer siblings and relatives living in the same house, but fewer servants and apprentices (or none at all). Discussions between parent and child more and more took place between two people, and at most among three.

Whether the discussions really went like the advice manuals said they should is not known. Simply because parents might have read a book on raising children says little about how they translated its advice into practice, even if the book gradually came to be seen as setting binding standards. At the beginning of the twentieth century, those standards were definitely moving towards what a conservative author criticized as the 'humanitarian ambitions' of her time. What she meant was the 'theory' that attributed 'children with the qualities and thus the rights of adults' and declared 'every violent act against the child's will as impermissible'. Fortunately, the author rejoiced, 'praxis in the family still ignores this theory'.[41]

Interestingly, such anti-humanitarian praxis was rarely discussed in the diaries, letters, and autobiographies of middle-class men and women. This does not mean, however, that they did not take place. Rather, they seem to have been a normal part of parenting, in bourgeois homes no less than in proletarian quarters. And since they were considered normal, they did not need to be explicitly mentioned. Helene Eyck, a Berlin merchant's wife whose diary entries from the 1880s and 1890s were almost exclusively concerned with her five sons and daughters, only touches on the fact that spankings were regularly exercised against disobedient children. In this regard, Pastor Kämpf was an exception. His family chronicle contains an entry from 20 April 1865 reporting 'the first spanking of my Agnes, ½ a dozen'. Kämpf's decision to record the event for perpetuity probably had to do with the marital argument that broke out afterwards. While his wife insisted that the 4-month-old was far too young to be beaten, the father was following the experts who counselled parents to apply corporal punishments precisely in the infant's first year of life.[42]

When reflecting on their lives, middle-class men more frequently wrote about the beatings they received from teachers or nannies than those from their parents.[43] Consciously or unconsciously, they omitted this information, either because they thought corporal punishment in the family was utterly normal or because they were ashamed of it. As a rule, the later the autobiographical text was written, the more critical the author's stance towards the way they were raised; generally, however, authors refrained from denouncing their parents. Saying that one was hit or humiliated as a child would have been to assume victimhood, something that would only become common towards the end of the twentieth century. At the same time, the chances are rather slim that there exists today a father like Kämpf who would write with a feeling of self-justification how many times he had hit his baby—even though, according to a recent study,

52 per cent of infants less than 1 year old are still smacked as reported by their parents.[44]

Personal documents and advice books reflect the shifts in conceptions of self and other, of the body and of emotions that took place in the course of the nineteenth and twentieth century. Slowly but surely, society became more sensitive about what parents and teachers did to children. Even those who promoted harsh discipline and obedience advised parents to 'unconditionally respect' children's feelings of self and not to 'demean them too much'.[45] 'Housewife, mother and doctor' Johanna Haarer, whose advice books were bestsellers in Germany in the 1930s and after, discouraged humiliation altogether. On the one hand, she vehemently distanced herself from the early twentieth-century tendency to give children more freedom and see in them an 'individual personality'. Instead, she opined, every young person should be raised 'to be a useful member of the national community', which he should serve with his individual 'talents and abilities'. On the other hand, she firmly stated: 'We never want to humiliate our children!', explaining that humiliating punishments were a thing of the 'stuffy schoolroom of past times'. Current times—meaning 1934— demanded that one raise children to 'hold their body and mind free and upright'.[46]

On this point, the National Socialist author was in agreement with the most famous paediatrician of the twentieth century, Benjamin Spock, whose books are still read today. An engaged liberal from Connecticut, Spock published *The Common Sense Book of Baby and Child Care* in 1946, selling over 50 million copies in more than forty different languages. The book clearly concluded that parents and teachers should never shame children, even if they had transgressed an important moral norm by doing something like stealing. Instead, he advised adults to consult with a child psychiatrist, a not-so-subtle nod to the pathologization of child behaviour and the medical professionalization strategies that would follow in the years to come.[47]

In West Germany, this psychotherapeutic turn took another twenty years to catch on. Previously habituated to recommend sending 'difficult' students to boarding school, by the late 1960s teachers and principals began advising parents to seek psychological treatment for their child.[48] This transformation of so-called deviant behaviour into an illness marked a new stage in the history of discipline. Up to that point, generations of children had learned what would happen to disobedient boys and girls from Heinrich Hoffmann's 1845 children's classic *Struwwelpeter*: they would be laughed at by the fish like Johnny Head-in-the-Air and would be booed at like Shockheaded Peter. Today's parents take their hyperactive, inattentive children to psychiatrists and psychotherapists, with pills and therapeutic sessions replacing public shaming. The consequences for the child are ambiguous at best. Certainly, attributing her behavioural issues to a lack of dopamine rather than to something she is herself responsible for might lessen social pressure. But such diagnoses are associated with new stigmas. Being called 'sick' might also be seen as a form of social exclusion, at least as long as the ill are a minority. With the rapid increase in ADHD diagnoses since the beginning of the century, however, that might soon change.[49]

School Discipline in Germany, East and West

Things have already changed in schools, which largely stopped using shaming during the 1970s. This shift was preceded by a long, heated debate about which disciplinary measures were legal and legitimate. Since the mid-nineteenth century, pedagogues had been advising teachers to use shaming sparingly and to refrain from shaming children in front of other pupils or in an 'undignified' manner.[50] The fact that such advice was still being dispensed in the 1920s indicates that teachers obviously continued to make use of the criticized methods on a regular basis. This ran contrary to the principles established and defended by reformist pedagogy, which became increasingly influential during Germany's Weimar Republic. State educational policies, however, refrained from issuing clear restrictions, so that shouting, railing, insulting, and hitting never disappeared from everyday school life.[51]

After 1945, the Allies, and particularly the Russians and Americans, worked to overhaul Germany's education system completely. An April 1947 decree for schools in the Soviet Occupation Zone prohibited corporal punishment altogether. Shortly thereafter, members of the SED (Socialist Unity Party) in the Berlin city council proposed that this prohibition be made law, reasoning that 'all schoolwork is aimed towards cultivating humanity and human dignity, the use of corporal punishment being not in line with these principles'.[52]

Not all schools, though, were adhering to these guidelines. Thus, in 1959, the GDR felt it necessary to renew and extend the ban, arguing that 'the use of corporal punishment or other punishments that violate the honour of the punished contradicts our schools' socialist principles of education'. East German schools instead opted to exploit the shaming power of the collective. When pupils skipped school, 'did not diligently and persistently study despite reprimands', and broke school rules, they were admonished, criticized, or censured in front of the whole class or school. In particularly difficult cases, information about the censure could be passed on to social organizations, residential councils, and leaders of factories that the child's parents belonged to. It could even be published in the local paper.[53] In this way, the collective 'organized' public opinion in order to ensure 'social contempt' and 'moral condemnation'. The pupil's 'exclusion from the collective' as a consequence of his behaviour was made 'visible for all'. After going through this 'negative judgement', 'normal relations' were supposed to be restored and the pupil allowed to return to his former place.[54] This is the precise definition of what would later be called reintegrative shaming.

West German schools refrained from such overt and aggressive forms of public shaming. But like their counterparts in the East, they could not, for a long time, bring themselves to abolish corporal punishment in all cases. Even though the federal states of Hessen and Bavaria, both of which were in the American Occupation Zone, had, in 1946, explicitly prohibited 'all demeaning punishments, particularly every form of corporal punishment and castigation' in schools, this was not sufficient to curtail teachers' habit of putting their rulers and their hands to work. In 1957, the Federal Court of Justice reminded state legislators that doing so required a formal law which had 'yet to be given'.[55]

Such a law was wanting because opinions on the subject diverged starkly, among teachers as well as among parents, jurists, and members of parliament. Many people were indeed sensitive to the humiliation that could be caused by meting out corporal punishment in front of the class. Their concern, though, was generally outweighed by the belief that the ruler was indispensable for classroom discipline, especially in elementary and non-elite schools. Teachers in industrial and rural areas, it was said, definitely needed it in order to set 'clear boundaries' for disrespectful boys.[56] Pedagogues and administrators involved in educational policy were also convinced that parents of such pupils even valued a little toughness.[57] They could refer to a 1947 Bavarian referendum in which 61 per cent of those participating supported corporal punishment in schools. Twelve years later, polls still reported an approval rate of 66 per cent.[58]

But there were also parents willing to take teachers to court. In 1953, a district court fined a teacher for eight counts of bodily harm, finding that his unusually brutal mistreatment of pupils from 7 to 12 years of age had gone far beyond what could be considered permissible. The judges referenced a 1946 ministerial decree that aimed to 'ban corporal punishment from schools' and only allowed exceptions in cases of 'extraordinary rudeness' and 'great resistance'. Neither of these criteria, the judges ruled, was applicable in this case. On appeal, the Federal Court of Justice reached the same conclusion, opining that even if one were generous enough to admit that 'modest corporal punishment by teachers is appropriate in exceptional cases', the simple 'maintenance of discipline itself could never be reason for castigating a child'. Nor did they allow it for purposes of deterrence or shaming. 'Certainly, schools should educate children to integrate themselves into society. But humiliating children before this society, as occurs when a teacher castigates a pupil, often runs contrary to this aim.'[59]

The judges' argument could not be any clearer. But not all of their colleagues shared their opinion. In 1956, another district court issued a 'not guilty' verdict in the case of a teacher who had slapped seven pupils and hit them on the hand with a cane. The district attorney appealed on the grounds that such treatment contravened Article 1 of the Federal Republic's Basic Law, because it 'violated the pupil's natural feeling of self-worth and thus her human dignity, particularly in cases where it takes place in front of the whole class'. In this instance, the Federal Court deemed the attorney's argument 'unsustainable'. Human dignity, the judges claimed, was not an absolute value, but a social convention 'determined by the progressing knowledge of moral values and the principles of human action deduced from them'. With this theory, they dismissed the district attorney's case: 'The dominant moral views in our society, which are based on the current state of knowledge, have until now declared the moderate corporal punishment of children by parents and other educators permissible and grounded in the requirements of education.' They decided that it was not the job of the court to 'assist the triumph of certain pedagogical views' that were against this dominant opinion.[60]

Another two decades would pass before pedagogical views opposing corporal punishment found the majority—and with it the courts—on their side. During this period, West German society had undergone sweeping liberalization and democratization, and the classroom was no exception. First and foremost, pupils began defending themselves against the authoritarian style of their teachers. Parents also no longer remained silent when teachers hit their sons or debased their daughters. Polls from the 1970s showed a marked change in opinion: in 1974, only 26 per cent of those polled supported corporal punishment in schools.[61] By this time, most federal state legislatures had forged the legal grounding that the Federal Court had found missing in 1957. In the words of a Berlin judge, West Germany had finally become a 'cultured state' that viewed corporal punishment as 'dishonourable and humiliating' and accordingly banned it from its schools.[62]

Fig. 13. The 'question-and-answer bee' of Pippi Longstocking's class (illustration from a 2007 French edition)

Teachers who liked to shout and curse in order to shame their students publicly were criticized too. Parents increasingly became involved and supported their children against such demeaning behaviour. Pippi Longstocking provided an exemplary course of action. Originally published between 1945 and 1948 and translated into over seventy languages, the books' eponymous heroine, a 9-year-old girl, expressly refuses to stand for shaming and intimidation. When she is chastised at school by a philanthropic lady for giving the wrong answer during an examination, she considers this 'unfair' and rebels. Instead of joining the line of shamed pupils, Pippi puts on her own 'question-and-answer bee', giving the children their self-confidence back and some candy along with it.[63]

The Power of Peer Groups

But Pippi not only fights against Miss Rosenblom's attempt at shaming her. She also defends herself against a group of boys who laugh at her because of her red hair and unconventional clothing and who take pleasure in harassing weaker pupils. Such behaviour, today known as bullying,[64] was addressed in many children's books of the second half of the twentieth century. While parents and teachers had done most of the shaming up until then, fellow pupils now took their place.

This trend is confirmed by news coverage, polls, and interviews. In 2017, a mother in Tennessee, USA, posted a video of her young son in tears over how cruelly classmates had treated him, calling him ugly and using physical violence. Within a few days, the video had been viewed 20 million times on Facebook and the child received strong support from celebrities like football and baseball players, country singers, and actors.[65] Such complaints abound. In 2009, 44 per cent of German pupils who were asked about their experiences with bullying reported they had been harassed by other pupils in one way or another, for instance by having 'mean things' said about them. One out of five said they felt treated 'as if they did not exist' and had been 'intentionally disrespected', girls more than twice as much as boys. In contrast, only a quarter of those polled said they had been humiliated by teachers in front of their classmates.[66]

In the nineteenth and early twentieth centuries, there were no such polls, making quantitative comparisons impossible. Children's books, however, offer a rich qualitative substitute.[67] An analysis of more than a hundred popular and/or prize-winning works of children's and adolescents' literature published up to the 1980s suggests that, since the mid-twentieth century, situations of shaming have been taking place far more frequently among peers than between adults and children. In almost all the books, such situations and events occupy a prominent place. Authors obviously believed them to be a familiar problem and sought to give their young readers advice on how to deal with them. When 6-year-old Tim, in Ursula Wölfel's *Tim Fireshoe* (1961), is ridiculed at school for being overweight, he gets all wound up. His father, though, tells him that he should have just laughed along with his tormentors.[68]

In Katherine Allfrey's 1963 book *Golden Island*, young Andrula is bothered by her cousin's friends, who constantly make fun of her and rejoice when she is punished at school and has to stand in the corner.

Instead of reacting to the girls' *schadenfreude* with shame, Andrula gets 'so angry' that her cousin Sassa finally 'takes a step back'.[69] Bullying is also the main topic of Judy Blume's *Blubber* (1974). Set in Pennsylvania, the novel follows a 12-year-old girl named Linda who is regularly taunted by her classmates for being overweight and wearing unfashionable clothes. Jill, one of the bullies, tells her mother about it and describes Linda as someone whose very defencelessness simply invites insult: 'There are some people who just make you want to see how far you can go.' Jill's mother thinks Linda should ignore it all or laugh it off so that she is no longer subject to mistreatment. After Jill has a change of heart and leaves the group of bullies, she herself becomes one of their targets. But instead of shrugging it off or taking it like Linda, Jill becomes a fighter, dividing her opponents and making new friends along the way. Linda, who assumes the role of the victim and lets others decide what happens to her, is definitely not the hero of the book. Rather, Jill is presented as the model that young readers are supposed to see as worthy of imitation.[70]

Already a successful children's author, Blume wrote *Blubber* after a lead bully in her 10-year-old daughter's class wielded her power to humiliate individual children publicly and force others afraid of being next to keep quiet or join her. The teacher's failure to act had allowed the conflict to get out of hand, and the children did not tell their parents out of shame for what they had gone through or witnessed. Blume wanted to break the silence. She was happy to see that her book later became required reading in teacher education. As for the critics who accused her of being too brutal, she countered them with the argument that one could only really capture school bus culture by writing in the language of the school bus: 'The kids get it. They live it.'[71]

This culture of bullying is not an entirely new phenomenon. Shaming among peers and chicanery in the classroom have been around for a long time, and things were no less rough on the playground and after school. The 1912 French children's novel *The War of the Buttons* tells the tale of a traditional rivalry between two neighbouring villages whose younger members beat each other up and curse each other. When the boys from Longeverne take a prisoner from Velrans and cut off his buttons and zippers so that he has to walk back to his friends with his trousers down and his body exposed, the Velrans boys get revenge by doing the same to the other side's leader, this time aggravated by the presence of girls.[72]

A genre prominent for shedding light on bullying practices was the boarding school novel as it developed in the 1850s and after. The plots typically took place in Britain, with its rich landscape of more or less famous boarding schools; in contrast, most German and French children attended state-funded day schools during the nineteenth and twentieth centuries. Pupils at Harrow or Eton, Westminster or Charterhouse were introduced to the school's hierarchies and rituals upon arrival. They soon got to know the hard hand of headmasters who gratuitously meted out beatings. Moreover, they were quickly initiated into the fight for status that structured relations among the students themselves. Tests of courage were normal, and those who did not pass muster were seen as sissies, giving them a rough time. Children who obeyed their parents by praying before bedtime were equally ridiculed, teased, and harassed.[73]

The fact that almost all the books include the theme of being laughed at indicates the prevalence of this experience in the everyday life of children and adolescents. Those doing the laughing were usually other children, not adults. Already at the beginning of the nineteenth century, bestselling Irish author Maria Edgeworth sought to immunize her young readers to taunting and malice. Instead, she pleaded with them to follow their own moral compass: 'When you have not done any thing wrong or foolish, never mind being laughed at.'[74] In 1834, a young American Sunday school teacher told a younger 'brother' that this 'maxim' had remained in his memory: 'No one will ever become great who is afraid of being laughed at.' Instead of falsely feeling ashamed at the 'idle laughter' of others, the adolescent should 'be firm' and act 'manly', 'despise ridicule', and refuse 'to be in servitude to other minds'.[75]

Not everyone found it easy to keep their head up in the face of 'idle laughter'. Children's books also told about children who reacted with rage and lost their temper, which, for girls, was deemed utterly inappropriate. Anne of Green Gables, in Lucy Maud Montgomery's wildly successful 1908 novel, is extremely touchy about what she perceives as insult. When Gilbert teases her about her looks, she brings her slate down on his head. In return, the teacher has her stand in front of the blackboard for the rest of the afternoon. Anne's 'sensitive spirit quivered as from a whiplash' after suffering the punishment, but she neither cries nor hangs her head. 'Anger was still too hot in her heart for that and it sustained her amid all her agony of humiliation.' Her rage is directed both at the teacher and at Gilbert. Even when the boy apologizes for having made fun of her red hair, she does not forgive him: 'Gilbert Blythe has hurt my feelings *excruciatingly*.' Though Anne is generally depicted as a bright, imaginative, joyful young person, her refusal to control her temper, regulate her anger, forgive, and say sorry is clearly depicted as a negative character trait.[76]

The most famous German girls' book of the late nineteenth century, Emmy von Rhoden's *Trotzkopf* (*Taming a Tomboy*), told a similar story. In the novel, 15-year-old Ilse is sent away to a boarding school, but angrily resists. She falls into a rage after the principal publicly embarrasses her by chastising her mediocre and careless crafts. Although her favourite teacher advises her to apologize, Ilse has no intention of doing so: 'Fräulein Raimar [the principal] was the one who deeply insulted me. I am not even going to think of asking her for forgiveness. I have never asked somebody's forgiveness and I am not going to do it now either!' Eventually, she does apologize, and feels 'lighter' than ever.[77] Even boisterous Ilse gives in and learns to look up to authority. The most important lesson she learns is that, although she initially rejected it as humiliating, asking for forgiveness can be liberating.

In Rhoden's story, the mean girls are pretty much props, while the real conflict plays out between Ilse and the school principal. With the exception of some boarding school novels that foregrounded the parallel world of pupils, this was true for most children's books of the nineteenth and early twentieth centuries.[78] William Golding's *Lord of the Flies* (1954) marked a radical shift. Originally written for adults, the novel quickly became obligatory reading for children. It tells the story of a group of British boys stranded on an island after a shipwreck, where they have to work together to survive. Two boys compete for leadership, a competition that eventually takes a violent, deadly turn. Like Joseph Conrad's *Heart of Darkness*, the story explores 'the darkness of man's heart' and the atavism of human behaviour: the relentless struggle for power, ecstatic rituals of violence, and outright cruelty. The anti-hero Jack hides his shame and inhibition behind a mask in order better to exploit the humiliation of weaker children. And even his antagonist Ralph, who stands for democratic decision making, respect, and rules, cannot manage to keep his hands clean, ridiculing his best friend Piggy because of his weight. Despite the fact that Piggy is intelligent, considerate, and responsible, the group makes him an outsider in order to ensure 'in a closed circuit of sympathy' their supposed homogeneity and unity. Thus, his contemptuous shaming and exclusion serve to integrate the other boys, and, at least for a while, the political fracture lines fade into the background.[79]

Adults only appear at the end of Golding's novel, when they put a stop to the ever-crueller conflicts between the two camps and bring the children back to the civilized world of post-war Britain. In most other children's and adolescents' books of the late twentieth century, too, adults play only minor roles. There are no mothers like the one who shames her daughter for a hole in her stocking or a tear in her dress in Elizabeth Wetherell's *Wide, Wide World* (1850). There are no grandmothers like the one in Thekla von Gumpert's *Herzblättchen* stories (1884), who shames her grandchildren for not wanting to learn how to read. And there are no Berliner aunts like the one in Clementine Helm's *Backfisch* stories (1863), who makes a 15-year-old blush for not covering her mouth when she yawns.[80] Instead, there are children who shame adults, as in Erich Kästner's 1949 novels *The Animals' Conference* and *Lottie and Lisa*, or, most prominently, children who shame other children.

What does this say about the social status of shame and shaming and the changes it has undergone over time? First, it is without question that shaming had and continues to have a central place in children's and young adults' literature. Second, it moved from something that took place between adults and children to relations among children, pupils, and members of peer groups and clubs. Third, a shift in the norms that conditioned what constituted shaming took place. Adults demanded self-control and wanted children to adhere to social norms like obedience, cleanliness, hard work, and honesty. The norms promoted by children, on the other hand, were generally geared towards producing conformity with the group by doing things like sanctioning tattling and establishing solidarity against adults. This had the unintended secondary effect of stabilizing the moral order of the adult world: just like adults, children set up hierarchies, required others to obey, and enforced rituals of shaming. Fourth, the events and behaviours seen as worthy of shame changed. Today, torn trousers might be seen as a fashion statement, but are no reason to feel ashamed, and a lack of table manners among young peers can be seen as a cool act of non-conformity. This does not mean, however, that moral pressures have somehow let up. Norms about what the body should look like have become stricter, for girls more than for boys. Overweight children are still victimized and harassed, as was Piggy in 1954, Tim in 1961, and Linda in 1974.

So, how does all this fit with modern society's liberal self-conception that wants autonomous individuals to treat each other with respect? How can it be that parents and teachers have (if slowly) learned to dispense with public shaming while many children and adolescents clearly still enjoy the practice? Social background apparently does not play a significant role here: children are bullied at elite schools just as much as they are at normal middle and high schools. Girls and boys are equally victims and bullies, if in different ways that often adhere to gender stereotypes.

One might be tempted to interpret the continued existence of bullying as a form of the old exclusion–inclusion dynamic: a group needs outsiders against whom it can consolidate itself. But if that were the case, then a single act of exclusion would be sufficient. So why is it so often the case that children are persistently made to know that they do not belong and are not respected? Why do bullies find constantly picking on the same child so attractive?

It is the feeling of having power, of being able to subjugate others against their will. Having and retaining power is not a state of being, but a process that has constantly to be given fuel. The more people participate in or approvingly witness such shows of power, the more enjoyable it is for the shamers. This is obvious in the use of physical violence and even more true for bullying.

Being a victim—at least in classic forms of face-to-face shaming—is a process as well. It develops, accelerates, or peters out in correspondence with the victim's behaviour and that of his peers. Either children act like Linda and accept their status as powerless prey of bullies who set the rules, or they fight back, defend themselves, and look for helpers. They can try to immunize themselves to shaming, reject the norms of the group that excludes them, and band up with others. Indeed, such strategies were also possible against the classic pillory, as friends of the pilloried person could change the mood of the crowd and get it on their side. Similar forms of resistance are still practised today and are often depicted in children's literature.

This is not least of all important because children and young adults generally have less power against their tormentors than do adults. They are usually less self-confident and less certain about what is wrong and what is right, which makes them more dependent on what others think of them. If they seek stability and recognition in a group, they often subject themselves to forces over which they have little control. Living outside of groups, though, is no less difficult and can again attract the attention of bullies.

The role of peer groups historically grew in correlation with a shift in family structures. Compared with the nineteenth and early twentieth centuries, children and adolescents today spend much more time among their peers. In cases where both parents work and there are few if any siblings, communication with other children gains in significance, as do peer groups. As a consequence, young people's susceptibility to being hurt by acts of shaming within their own circle and by others increases vastly.

Discipline and Humiliation in the Military

Groups often profile themselves by making joining a difficult process. New members have to be initiated and go through hazing rituals before being given the honour of membership. When the young Count Harry Kessler went to the exclusive St George's School, Ascot, in the late 1870s, the first thing he had to do was fight in a boxing match, after which the challenger and others offered to be his friends.[81]

But initiations have not always been so fair. Candidates usually found themselves in a weaker position, and members generously exploited their seniority to show the newcomer who was boss. In 1909, French anthropologist Arnold van Gennep concluded that *rites de passage* are highly volatile affairs in which initiates have to separate themselves from their old identities as a precondition to taking on a new one. The period in between is, according to Gennep, a sort of liminal phase in which the old rules no longer apply while the new ones have not yet set in. In this intermediary zone, initiates lack a solid identity and are often deliberately weakened before being accepted into the group.[82]

People subject themselves to such painful practices because they cannot live without belonging to a group. In societies in which initiation rituals are an established, mandatory, and highly esteemed part of social life, they simply have no choice. Furthermore, they hardly experience what they go through as demeaning or humiliating, but agree to it as a given. This is, presumably, different in societies that place great weight on the freedom of the individual and seek to diminish rather than bolster group bonds. If their institutions do intentionally degrade citizens, one can expect that, sooner or later, people will resist: either the general public will take offence, or those who feel demeaned will.

This can be seen in the military, which, in countries with compulsory conscription, has been one of the most inclusive institutions of modern society. Since the nineteenth century, millions of young men have marched in its ranks. They all knew that serving under the flag would be no walk in the park, even before joining. In contrast to schools, the military has historically been a 'total' institution largely separated from the rest of society. It compels its members to live in compounds and barracks and sets up its own rules, which are enforced with violence if need be. According to sociologist Erving Goffman, total institutions often use initiation rituals in order to underscore the division between inside and outside and to strip new members of their former identity.[83] In this respect, the military makes recruits swap their individual clothes for a uniform and have their hair cut extremely short. They are then subjected to harsh training and strict discipline, which aims at turning them into functioning parts of an efficient war machine.

In the 1960s, the new West German army was rocked by its first big scandal. Several drill sergeants were accused of 'constantly demeaning treatment of subordinates' and taken to court. The main culprit, though, did not think he had done anything wrong. 'I trained', he said defiantly, 'as I myself was trained.' Most recruits had silently endured the abuse, in part out of fear of being subjected to worse, in part out of a false conception of camaraderie. Some were blinded by the elite, masculine attitude of their superior and confused brutality with toughness. In the end, only a few had the courage to speak out.[84]

Magnified by the media, the public's outrage signalled a change in how the military was generally perceived. In a liberal, democratic society, so the argument went, the military should not have any special privileges and was to respect the human dignity of its members. Thus, degrading recruits was no longer seen as acceptable. With every new scandal, ideas of what constituted degradation and humiliation were broadened. Soldiers were forced to eat raw pigs' livers, consume alcohol until they vomited, and commit obscene sexual transgressions: the list of demeaning practices used by training officers as tests of toughness grew longer and longer. Recruits and parents reacted, the press reported, and state attorneys intervened.[85]

The mistreatment of soldiers had already been a topic of discussion in the late nineteenth century, when Germany's Social Democratic Party took every opportunity to criticize the military as a repressive instrument of the imperial state. But among the population at large, the military maintained a good reputation as the preeminent 'school of masculinity'. When things got a little rough every once in a while, this was generally accepted as part of the schooling experience. As late as 1956, 63 per cent of West German women and 55 per cent of men agreed that 'today's youth' needed the military because it taught them 'order and decency'.[86]

This view of the military as an educational institution had been around since the early nineteenth century, when, following the French model, the Prussian state implemented compulsory military service for young men. At the same time, it outlawed physical punishments such as hitting and running the gauntlet on the grounds that these practices violated the honour of the new citizen-soldiers. Still, it took a long time to make the 'freedom of the soldier's back', as officer August Neidhardt von Gneisenau called it, a reality.[87] Even after the 1808 statutes had been passed, recruits were not treated with care. When representatives at the 1848 Frankfurt Parliament expressly stated that corporal punishment was 'wholly unworthy' of the 'dignity of free men' and the 'dignity of a people who have achieved sovereignty', they were thinking first and foremost of the military.[88]

In Britain, with its professional army and navy, military authorities were even less concerned with issues of dignity and respect. Flogging was outlawed as late as 1881 in the army (and only suspended in the navy). Although the House of Commons and the press did take notice of what an 1860 article called 'Britannia's Shame', the public outcry fell short of affecting the policies of military leaders.[89] Even during the First World War, the War Office kept its ears shut when it came to abolishing demeaning practices. Interestingly, such demands were voiced with explicit regard to the large number of volunteers joining the war effort for patriotic reasons. In an angry opinion piece published in the *Illustrated Sunday Herald*, the former soldier Robert Blatchford heavily criticized the British army for administering what he called 'a contemptible form of torture' and a 'disgrace to the Flag'.[90]

What he was referring to was officially named 'Field Punishment No. 1'. According to the *Manual of Military Law*, it was a castigating measure 'for any offence committed on active service' and consisted in the culprit being temporarily 'attached . . . to a fixed object' by irons,

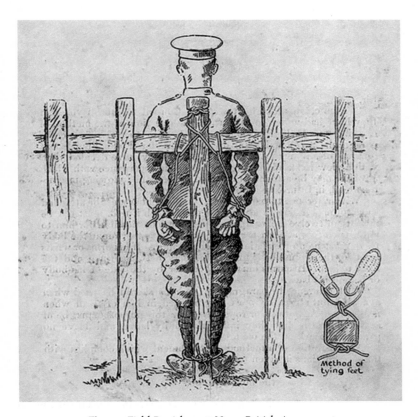

Fig. 14. Field Punishment No. 1, British Army, 1917

straps, or ropes.[91] During military campaigns, such punishment had proven effective and efficient, and so it continued to be applied after the war broke out in 1914. This time, however, it not only targeted professional soldiers, whose social reputation was rather low anyway. It also affected volunteers who had, in Blatchford's words, 'left good posts or good work to fight for their country'. When they found themselves punished for small disciplinary transgressions by being 'tied by the neck, waist, hands and feet to cart wheels', this was felt to be a gross 'indignity'. After witnessing an artilleryman 'stretched out, cruciform-fashion, his arms and legs wide apart, secured to the wheel', a private confided in his diary: 'I don't think I have ever seen anything which so disgusted me in my life and I know the feelings amongst our boys was (sic) very close to mutiny at such inhuman treatment.'[92]

When Blatchford made the soldiers' 'hatred of a degrading punishment' public, he clearly hit a nerve. Since the army's composition had changed dramatically since 1914, with millions of civilians volunteering, the public showed genuine interest in those 'patriots' being decently and respectfully treated. The government was soon flooded with protest telegrams and letters. Trade union chapters passed resolutions against the 'humiliating form of punishment', and the House of Commons discussed it as well. Even some army commanders distanced themselves from the practice, likening it to 'the stocks or pillory'. But Douglas Haig, as Commander-in-Chief of the British Armies in France, insisted on maintaining the method. He did pay lip service to public opinion, though, by slightly changing the physical position of the offender so as to avoid the 'unfortunate' impression of 'crucifixion'. Instead of men being tied up 'with their arms extended', they were now to keep their arms to their sides or behind their back. The War Office happily accepted Haig's recommendation and had illustrations of the new position sent out to the battalions.[93] Whether this compromise managed to appease people's indignation about what they considered 'savage', 'barbarous', and 'boche-like' is unclear. In any case, Field Punishment No. 1 continued to be generously meted out by courts martial abroad and was only finally abolished in 1923.

In the country of Boches and Huns, as Germany was called by Blatchford and many of his compatriots, the punishment of 'tying' was equally attacked—and formally banned six years earlier. As in Britain, it had a longer tradition. When it was practised during the Franco-German War of 1870–1, soldiers and even some officers were acutely aware of its 'ignominy', since it obviously disgraced the 'individuality of the patriot'. Still, such 'cruel' disciplinary measures were found necessary in order to maintain order among the troops.[94]

While those measures did not yet cause a major stir in the early 1870s, they did during the First World War. More and more soldiers—volunteers as well as conscripts—complained and felt dishonoured and debased. Their feelings were multiplied and popularized by the national press. After frequently coming under parliamentary fire from Social Democrats and liberals, 'tying' was finally banned in May 1917 by the minister of war. As in Britain, army commanders were not amused. In August 1918, General Paul von Hindenburg tried to persuade the minister to allow soldiers to be tied up in cases of 'cowardice and other serious transgressions, which unfortunately have become regular occurrences'. The response was unambiguous: 'The punishment of tying is degrading. In some cases, those subject to the punishment have taken their own lives immediately after.'[95]

Letters and diaries proved the minister's point. Consider the case of 34-year-old conscript Martin Hobohm, a historian by profession who wrote in April 1917: 'It is not discipline that makes army life hard, but the unnecessarily injurious fashion in which it is meted out . . . There is no greater test of nerves than to constantly be insulted, challenged, threatened while carrying out difficult duties. It is nonsense to say that one should not let it bother him: the feeling of honour is a natural force in man, it cannot be shut off.'[96] A soldier on the Eastern Front made a similar argument in June 1917. He wrote that he would

be glad to take a few weeks leave, if only to get away from this unbelievable, unnecessary aggravation for a while and no longer to see the gratuitous injustices that are done to us and that we must silently accept, because all institutions and laws are turned against us and we of course do not want to make ourselves unhappy for our entire lives. Into what sort of slavery have we been thrown, we, who used to feel ourselves free people and who did not believe that we would be capable of suffering the smallest insult or other injustice without it being punished?[97]

Ten years later, Hobohm had to evaluate professionally the 'social issues in the army as a partial cause of the German defeat'. His assessment was that, 'in our generation', punishments like tying up soldiers were perceived as 'unspeakably despicable, a remnant of traditional brutality' and an attack on 'human dignity'. In 1912, Hobohm's university teacher Hans Delbrück had still placed the postulate of the 'army organism' above the dignity of the individual soldier. But the 'World War generation' saw things differently, which, according to Hobohm, was a symptom of 'the gradual expansion of civic dignity'.[98]

Of course, human and civic dignity were not identical. While the former was shared by everyone independent of their social position or political belonging, the latter only befitted the members of a given society bound by constitutionally defined rights and duties. Yet the dignity of the citizen included human dignity. When soldiers felt insulted and demeaned, they made a claim to both types of dignity. They also emphasized how nobody would accept such treatment in civilian life, and considered it shameful and unworthy of 'free people'. Ordinary conscripts thus demonstrated a sensitivity that would have been hard to detect in former times. By the early twentieth century, concepts of dignity had obviously pushed their way into the feeling and reasoning of men who were no longer willing to take violations and insults without making a noise. As citizen-soldiers, they felt entitled to demand that their human and civic dignity be equally recognized in the army.

Such instances of resistance and resentment notwithstanding, it still took another fifty years before these views were to become commonplace enough to be able to mobilize public action. Only in the 1960s did large swathes of West German society begin to reject the notion that the military should be permitted to discipline soldiers with degrading practices, no matter what the transgression to be punished. What was no longer acceptable in the school playground was now destined to disappear from the barracks as well.

Initiation Practices: Self-effacement and Empowerment

Interestingly, the humiliating acts committed by those of the same rank and age were less criticized than violence carried out by officers, even though some soldiers did complain about being abused by comrades. The latter often acted at the behest of non-commissioned officers and passed on the treatment that they had experienced themselves. Men who were not as physically or mentally fit as the others were particularly taunted. Moreover, there were traditional pecking orders among the soldiers, with young recruits being forced to polish older soldiers' boots and serve them in other ways. If they refused to obey, the 'old ghost' of the barracks would make them suffer for it during the night.[99]

Since young soldiers stood up against such maltreatment considerably less than against the brutality and unfairness of their superiors, they might have accepted it as the downside of the cherished camaraderie that the military was famous for. Furthermore, they had long since been used to the experience that seniors had more power than juniors and might, from time to time, play nasty tricks on them. This is what happened in the 'wild' gangs of adolescent boys and girls as much as in schools and in college. British boarding schools were known as hotbeds of a form of subordination called 'fagging' that lasted well into the late twentieth century. When Eton's headmaster, in 1977, suggested that 'fagging' be abolished as an 'anachronistic' tradition, many students protested vehemently.[100] They found much to be gained from a system that granted older boys the power to exploit and bully younger ones until the latter moved on to become fag masters in their own right. Laying the older boy's breakfast, building his fire, and being sent on errands were normal chores; being ridiculed, harassed, and caned seem to have been no less normal.[101]

Fig. 15. University freshman flees paddle-wielding senior after being dunked in the 'Fountain of Knowledge', New York University, 1946

At university, the system continued, and does so to this very day. Whenever a student aims to join a fraternity or sorority in the United States or Great Britain, they have to undergo a pledge period of one or two months in order to prove their loyalty and devotion. They are forced to follow orders diligently, serve the older brothers and sisters, and put up with the latter's often demeaning and cruel behaviour. For some, this feels like 'slavery'; others adore it as a method of community building. Things become worse on the day of initiation. Now that the pledge period is over, the student is fully accepted into the organization. But as a final proof of allegiance, she is subjected to a number of tests that might involve sexually abusive and humiliating acts. While fraternities are infamous for their physical hazing rites, sororities also employ a number of bodily practices that expose and harass women for their weight or the size of their breasts. 'It was disgusting', a student admitted later. 'But it was like a ceremonial ritual. Everyone before you did it, so you have to do it too.'[102]

Hazing is defined in a major study from 1999 as 'any activity expected of someone joining a group that humiliates, degrades, abuses or endangers, regardless of the person's willingness to participate'.[103] Why young people might be inclined to join that group and let themselves be humiliated, degraded, and abused, can be learnt from the film *Goat*. Premiered at the Sundance Film Festival in 2016, the film takes place in the present at a typical American college campus with manicured lawns and stately buildings. Young people of both genders walk around in flip-flops and shorts, study in seminars and libraries, and go through their *éducation sentimentale* in dorms and sorority and fraternity houses. The film studies the experience of one freshman, Brad, at a fraternity where his older brother is already a member. The older brother teaches the younger how great it is to be among the frat boys: he will enjoy a sense of community, respect from others, easy sex, and always enough booze. Along with the other pledges, Brad then runs the gamut of classic hazing transgressions in order to see if the other frat brothers will let him in. The point is less to prove one's courage or serve the members than simply to allow the others to abuse the hazee in any way possible. Nothing is off limits: Brad has to drink urine, dip his head in the toilet, bleat like a goat, squirm around in the mud, chug warm beer until he vomits, bow before the pledge master and be spat on by him, stand on a wall and act like he is having sex. The threat of being forced to penetrate a goat is always there, and all forms of humiliation take place in the presence of the initiated.

The film is based on a novel that draws on the personal experiences of its author and narrator, Brad Land.[104] The stories told in *Goat* correspond with what is known, through personal interviews or anonymous articles, about the 'secret life' of fraternities and sororities.[105] But hazing also plays out in youth sports and athletic teams, and has done so for quite some time.[106] Around 1900, things got so out of hand at the University of Illinois that the administration had to intervene and ended up expelling some students. As a form of ritualized rivalry between classes, hazing began disappearing in the early twentieth century, but it is still a prominent feature of college life at many American schools.[107] Some colleges have established hazing websites that inform students about their rights and encourage them to resist such practices. Even in the codes of fraternities and sororities, hazing as part of the pledge process has been officially banned. In truth, however, it has just gone 'underground' and is still an ingrained part of student subculture. Protected through vows of silence, humiliating rites of passage are thus kept from ever seeing the light of day.

For those in on the game, debasing rituals are both meaningful and exciting. They enable members of the group to gain power and reconfirm their sense of belonging, in good things and in bad. If students have a tendency to sadism, they might even enjoy running others through the mud. The fact that the mud is usually made of excrement says a lot, as does the constant simulation and discussion of sexual practices and the use of paddling.

But why do young men and women subject themselves to this kind of treatment? Why do they freely submit to such degradation? Researchers view hazing as a variation on classic rites of initiation and passage, in which the initiated person shows himself or herself worthy of the group. Some tend to see hazing as a form of play that has no further consequences.[108] But can that really be? Neither Brad Land nor the students interviewed by anthropologist Peggy Reeves Sanday in the 1980s say anything about hazing having a playful character.[109] A continuous source of scandal since the 1990s, the fact that hazing rituals frequently lead to death also speaks against this reading.

What the accounts of young men and women do attest to is the sense of insecurity they feel about their status during the transition from family to college. They react by looking for a group that gives them some social stability and emotional strength. Belonging to a fraternity or sorority bolsters their self-confidence and helps them to find their place in an unfamiliar environment. After paying the price of entry, they are promised lifelong brother- and sisterhood, which makes doubts about oneself seem small in comparison. Some even think the degrading rituals have a deeper meaning, allowing the young men and women to erase themselves so that they can begin anew with an identity that is up to the challenges of life. 'We all dissolved under the abuse. We all felt worthless, *but now we're all together and we feel good.*' Others consider such abuse as providing life skills badly needed to survive in American society. A few members lucidly analyse the maltreatment as a play of power and dependency: 'They tear you down, so they can build you back up again.'[110]

Things were not all that different in German student associations. In contrast to American fraternities, however, they had their heyday in the nineteenth and early twentieth centuries; as of today, they find themselves at the margins of university culture. They too had attributed considerable significance to initiation rituals, and thus sought to destroy the old identity of the initiate in order to forge a new one. In the early modern period, it had been custom at German universities for new arrivals to be publicly beaten, insulted, and mocked by older students. In 1536, Martin Luther explained with slight irony the sense of the ritual to Wittenberg students: 'it teaches us to recognize ourselves, who we are and how we are, and to humiliate ourselves before both God and men'.[111] After the universities officially replaced the hazing ritual with entry exams in the eighteenth century, many student associations kept the tradition alive, but only for their own members. Thus, students no longer had to go through general and compulsory initiation rituals. If they wished to join a fraternity, though, they deliberately consented to a host of denigrating practices.

Unlike American fraternities and secret societies, which tend to take vows of silence, German 'Burschenschaften' or 'Corps' were historically rather open about their hazing and fagging practices. In numerous papers and recollections, they proudly wrote about what it meant to be a 'Bursche' and how one gained admittance to the association. Students apparently longed to undergo the 'rites of violence' and took an active part in them. The initiation ritual consisted of a sword fight with strict rules. The two students stood as equals, had the same weapons and could try to compensate for possible physical weakness with technique and agility. There was nothing demeaning about it; indeed, many were like novelist Thomas Mann's youngest brother Viktor, who spoke of his excitement at having the chance to prove his masculinity. An initiate only had to be ashamed if he bowed out in fear. Those who stood their ground and received the famous cut beneath their eye could leave the fight with their heads high.[112]

There were other student rituals and conventions, however, that did not give the prospective members a chance to assert their masculine prowess. In the 'fox classes', for instance, novices learned about internal and external hierarchies, and the 'fox baptism' was all about degrading subjugation. The 'beer session' demonstrated how silly they looked when they were completely drunk and at the same time forced them to keep a stiff upper lip in their abject state. The strict regimentation of the hours of the day constantly reminded the young men of their 'freely accepted unfreedom' (Viktor Mann) and made pursuing other interests and friendships rather impossible. But even those who felt burdened by being chained to all the duties and rules stuck with it and retained their positive attitude. Most members would later claim that in their fraternity years, they learned to 'stand strong' and grew to be 'useful members' of a larger group. They kept in contact with their fellow students and profited from their relations with the 'old boys' just as they helped new generations to progress. Thus, the initial humiliation paid off, often in cash.[113]

Women's Dignity: Rape and Sexism

Concerning 'the other sex', German student associations differed considerably from American fraternities. Up until the 1960s, young women who were invited to the associations' dances (though tellingly not to their drinking parties and duels) were called 'Couleur-Damen' and were treated with utmost respect and politeness. In the nineteenth century, they were often the daughters of professors; after 1908, when German universities started accepting female students, they could be classmates. Old ladies today still talk about how much they enjoyed the chivalric and gentlemanly conduct and how comfortable they felt among the young men. They would shake their heads in bewilderment if they were told about gang rapes on American campuses in which frat brothers happily participate. They would be similarly stunned to hear about entire sorority pledge classes forced to have sex with frat brothers.[114]

German university life in 1900 or 1960 cannot be compared with what is happening today on the other side of the Atlantic Ocean. Conceptions of gender have been thoroughly transformed and sexual relationships among students have become more common. This has causes beyond the fact that most American institutions of higher education have been made co-ed since the 1960s. In no other area did social norms in the latter half of the twentieth century change more than in regard to sexuality, and universities were no exception to this shift.

As early as the 1970s, intimate connections on campus were seen as normal, even if American universities sought to project the image that they were prohibited in their dormitories in order to appease parents. While there is no doubt that sexual assaults did take place, talking about rape was taboo. When someone was indeed accused of rape, it usually remained within the university's disciplinary system, where it was suppressed by administrators more concerned with preserving their institution's reputation. Moreover, victims also had a difficult time telling others what had happened to them because of the shock and shame associated with being the object of sexual violence. Those who did go to the police were often told that they were at least partially responsible for what had been done to them. Only when feminists began discussing the issue in the 1970s did attitudes begin to change. In 1971, the New York Radical Feminists organized a public 'Rape Speak Out', which was followed up with a conference, and, four years later, journalist Susan Brownmiller's aptly titled manifesto *Against Our Will*. The book was an international success, and in 1995 the New York Public Library included it in its list of the 100 most important books of the twentieth century.[115]

Making rape into a topic of political discussion was difficult, not least because it was mostly committed in a space without witnesses by a person whom the victim knew: marital partners, friends, classmates. In contrast, gang rapes on college campuses had an audience and were definitely marked as acts of humiliation. In the 1980s, American professor of anthropology Peggy Reeves Sanday conducted interviews with the perpetrators and victims of such gang rapes. Frat members who took part in them were clearly aware of the humiliating nature of the crime. At the same time, they strongly believed that their victim was complicit, reasoning that they themselves had had to go through a similar victimization during their hazing rites. Since they had willingly consented to being demeaned, they assumed that the girls had tacitly agreed as well. They chose to ignore the fact that their often heavily inebriated victims were never asked for consent.[116]

Certainly, the frat boys' self-justifications cannot be applied without qualification to other cases of gang rape reported ever more frequently by the press, non-government organizations, and other institutions.[117] Not many rapists—and particularly not those who act in groups—think or speak about why they violate women. But alongside the demonstration of power, what psychologists call 'bonding' almost always plays a role: the collective act serves to forge a bond between those who observe, cheer, and even film each other in the act. The videos often end up on the internet, which turns the humiliation of the victim into a spectacle for all to see.

Gang rapes are undoubtedly one of the most extreme forms of public degradation that women around the world (and, though less prominently, men) are subjected to. Contrary to appearances, they usually take place not in civilian life, but during political and armed conflicts.[118] In 1949, the Geneva Convention forbade warring parties from committing 'outrages upon personal dignity, in particular humiliating and degrading treatment' against non-participants and prisoners of war.[119] Between 1992 and 1995, however, the Bosnian War made the horrors of mass rape painfully and publicly real. In Europe, this was the first time such acts had been witnessed since the excesses of the Second World War, which still live on in the collective memory.[120] The new war witnessed large-scale and systematic acts of violence orchestrated not only to degrade the (mostly Muslim) women, but also as part of a campaign of ethnic cleansing through forced impregnation. Public outrage was so great that in the year 2000, the International Criminal Tribunal for the former Yugoslavia in The Hague tried three Bosnian Serbs for rape, torture, slavery, and assaults against personal dignity in fifty documented instances. A year later, they were convicted and received long sentences; the court rejected an appeal in 2002.[121]

The complaint filed by the German feminist Alice Schwarzer at the Hamburg Regional Court in 1978 was of an entirely different sort. Along with other famous and non-famous women, Schwarzer accused the then most popular magazine in Germany, *stern*, of reducing women to sex objects and violating their dignity by regularly depicting scantily dressed or nude females on their front covers. The suit against such weekly sexism was meant to make an example of *stern*, as many other print media used the same tactics to attract (male) readers. The idea was old: sex sells, a naked female bottom or breast would increase sales. The Women's Council supported Schwarzer and her co-plaintiffs, but the court threw out the case, finding that, because they made up a majority of the population, 'women' could not constitute a group capable of being maligned as such.[122] The Press Council, responsible for enforcing journalistic ethics, also considered

Schwarzer's complaint illegitimate and refrained from punishing the magazine. Nevertheless, the very fact that 'human dignity' and its significance for women were debated in public led feminists to view West Germany's 'first sexism trial' as a success.[123]

One form of public humiliation that has never made it to court is the 'walk of shame' known from the intimate world of American dorm life. The website *Urban Dictionary* describes it as 'the walk across campus in the same clothes as yesterday after you slept with someone and spent the night in their dorm room'.[124] Although the wording appears gender-neutral, it is usually applied to women for the simple but superficial reason that their party clothing, messed-up hair, and smeared make-up stand out more than do men's rumpled pants and shirts. In effect, this makes their sexual activities more visible. But above all and more profoundly, the use of the term 'shame' reveals a double standard against women whose sex lives are just as free and self-determined as those of men. It goes back to the traditional pre-scriptions that a woman should show sexual 'purity' and restraint, morals that apparently continued to play a role in the liberal world of the late twentieth century. *Quod licet Jovi non licet bovi*, what men are allowed to do, women are not.

Whether or not the shaming really occurs is not entirely certain. When the retailer Urban Aid markets a 'Shame on You Kit' with wash products ('If you have to do the "walk of shame" at least you will be clean'), the slogan suggests a sense of irony. Shame here only comes in quotation marks and is, it seems, no longer a real-life issue.[125] This might be seen as affirming the 1970s feminist motto: the shame is over.[126] Women might also have Madonna's 1983 song 'Burning Up' on their minds, in which the pop icon sings: 'I am not the same, I have no shame, I am on fire.' Indeed, the Sexual Revolution of the 1960s and 1970s radically challenged the notion that women should be ashamed of their bodies and sexuality.[127] Yet not everyone went as far as the legal assistant turned stripper who assured her mother and the readers of *stern* in 1969 that, while she had been terribly ashamed when she started her new career in Hamburg's red light district, she now felt 'just as good' as before, 'only a bit freer, more open, less ashamed and happier'. She therefore recommended that every woman with 'reservations' do a striptease once in her life.[128]

Without shame did not mean without dignity, though. As it was the young woman's own free decision, taking off her clothes in front of a mostly male audience did no damage to her personal dignity. If she had been forced to it, it would have. But where should one draw the line between free will and forced consent? What about the naked cover girls who provoked Alice Schwarzer to sue *stern* for sexism a decade later? On the one hand, they could equally claim that 'the shame is over' and happily pose for high-paying photographers. On the other hand, and this is how many feminists argued, there are asymmetric power relations at work, since men—photographers, journalists, editors, and readers—are in a position to exploit women and turn them into sexualized objects.

Such asymmetry was also addressed in 2017 when the #MeToo campaign went viral on social media. Sparked by public allegations against film producer Harvey Weinstein that he had sexually harassed, assaulted, and raped dozens of women, the campaign shed light on the ongoing transgressions of powerful men against dependent or less powerful women. Furthermore, it spoke of the deep shame that those women had endured through being treated like sex objects. Shame, with regard to women's bodies, was obviously not yet over and had prevented those assaulted from striking back immediately. Once they did, often many years or even decades later, they frequently referred to the shameful experience of humiliation and to the sense of dignity that had been violated by their abuser's actions.

Trial by Media and the Pillory of Public Opinion

When the *New York Times* and *The New Yorker* broke the news of the accusations against Harvey Weinstein, they did what a critical press was supposed to do: inform the public of issues and problems that the public should know about. At times, this function has been likened to that of the pillory, which had exposed wrongdoers to the broader public. During National Socialism, the media exerted its pillorying power with particular passion and zeal. Some newspapers even introduced a section explicitly titled 'On the pillory' and published the names of 'Aryan' men and women who entertained social or sexual relations with Jews.[129] In the early 1920s, local papers in occupied territories had similarly subjected German women to the disdain of the public for engaging in 'horizontal collaboration' with the occupying forces.[130]

Be it explicitly or implicitly, newspapers had indeed increasingly taken on the role of 'social pillory'. Germans were not the only ones talking about the 'Zeitungspranger' or 'trial by media' as early as 1800.[131] In England, where the press enjoyed far greater freedom, newspapers had been printing defamatory articles since the eighteenth century. Whether on political, moral, or religious grounds, the articles served the purpose of damaging—or even destroying—their targets' reputation. In 1728, a judge complained that 'this offence has now grown so common, that if a man goes into a coffee house, it is uncertain whether he lays his hand upon a newspaper, or a libel'. Magazines like *London Spy* and *The Night-Walker* castigated vice and immorality, but did not give names—unlike in the real pillory, they did not want to subject anyone to the abuse of 'the rabble'. Instead, they called on the conscience of those who knew they were being talked about and hoped they would change their ways. As one publisher stated, 'our design is to reform, not to expose'.[132]

All over Europe, print media have been known as an excellent venue for shaming and embarrassing people since the early modern period. Vituperative publications, whose authors generally remained anonymous, enjoyed great, if local circulation. They were posted on the doors of churches and town halls or on the gallows, took up political, social, and moral issues, and generously named names.[133] These 'pasquils' were first-rate irritations for city and state officials, who intervened with corresponding gravity. In 1794, the Prussian General Law Code dictated that 'the pasquil, if it be desired by the insulted person, be burned in public by the executioner'. In the 1830s, jurists and politicians heatedly debated whether this was still in line with 'contemporary ways of thinking'. Many argued that the authors of such publications, who 'in their own words want to put the honour of their fellow citizens on the pillory of public opinion', should themselves be tied up on the public square.[134]

By penalizing written diatribes, the state disallowed its citizens a practice that it wanted to retain for itself, but only on the condition that the transgressor was found legally guilty. It was indeed the privilege of the state to post convicts' names on the gallows, put them in the pillory or, after the second half of the nineteenth century, publish their sentence in an official paper. The rule of law was put first, and this is what distinguished state actions from private pasquils or social shaming administered by villagers and townspeople on their own volition. Nevertheless, drastic punishments were not enough to keep people from arrogating the state's privilege for themselves and 'placing others on the pillory out of revenge, party interest and other dishonourable motives'. Defamatory writings had in fact become 'more frequent' in the 1830s and 'the style of thinking that tends towards such acts has been more strengthened than weakened'.[135]

Such a tendency can be identified on many levels. Even if early modern practices like riding the skimmington or the stang became less and less frequent after the beginning of the nineteenth century, other forms of collective shaming persisted.[136] Tin-canning went on in Northamptonshire right into the 1930s. As an eye-witness recalled: 'This was done when a couple were caught in a compromising situation. The young bloods of the village used to make an effigy and parade round the village banging tin trays, cans and buckets and stop outside the culprit's house and give a concert.' These charivari parades targeted not only sexual transgressors, but also economic frauds. Muffled men banging tin cans 'would stop outside the fishmongers for example and shout insults— "How much rotten fish have you sold today?" and so on at different places round the village'. Although the local authorities had the men summoned and fined, the latter did not care: 'They held a dance and that raised enough money to pay all the fines.'[137]

In Canada, charivaris or 'shivarees' took place throughout the nineteenth and early twentieth centuries. They were mostly instigated by 'idle young fellows in the neighbourhood' who noisily expressed disapproval against contentious marriages and made 'the night hideous'. In the USA, tarring and feathering was used to publicly shame those who had committed crimes of immorality. After enjoying a politically motivated popularity in the 1760s, the practice was later directed against 'Negro criminals', antislavery advocates, labour organizers, and pacifists. The Irish Republican Army continued to tar and feather its enemies and opponents until the 1970s. In 1971, during 'the Troubles', Catholic women in Northern Ireland used the same measure to humiliate and punish 'soldier dolls'—women who went out with British soldiers.[138]

Labour disputes provided another welcome opportunity to publicly shame those who did not play along. In 1923, miners who went on strike against the occupation of the Ruhr region by French and Belgian troops erected pillories with the names of those who had broken the strike.[139] Italian workers, in the 1960s and 1970s, insulted and mocked strike-breakers while forcing them to walk through a human corridor. When such *cortei interni* involved foremen and executives, workers banged on tins and struck cowbells, thus reviving the tradition of rough music or charivari. As one Fiat employee put it, these actions 'deprived the boss of his power. In the march, so many bosses were humiliated.' In turn, workers felt empowered by shaming the powerful.[140]

Rough music, which had a long tradition throughout Europe, was also deployed against Italian parish priests who, after 1870, showed open contempt for the new liberal state and made their distaste known to people who fully embraced it. Formerly reserved, above all, to punish immorality or sexual transgressions, practices of popular justice took on a decidedly political character during the nineteenth century. As the lawyer defending several French *charivariseurs* in 1832 explained, 'it is not about resuscitating the charivari of the old regime against marriages that were badly manufactured—the century is too advanced for that'. Instead, charivaris now targeted politicians and administrators who were considered corrupt, unjust, and deceitful, or who simply held political opinions disdained by their opponents. The prefect of Pas-de-Calais, for instance, was sanctioned by a charivari because, among other things, he had attended a party organized by a right-winger. He shared the fate of being publicly mocked, cursed, and shamed with Bayonne judges who had, in 1832, sentenced a *charivariseur* to two years in prison.[141]

The state indeed came down hard on those who, as the French minister of the interior declared in 1833, attacked the 'freedom of opinion, the respect of individuals, and public peace'. For their part, defendants praised the charivari as emphasizing the 'honest people's' voice against 'parliamentary bavardage'.[142] Such statements clearly signalled a new sense of political entitlement and implied a harsh critique of political personnel and procedure as they had developed after the revolutionary upheavals of the late eighteenth century. Engaging old-style humiliation and carnivalesque inversion to make themselves heard and listened to, people—*l'honnête homme du peuple*—merged modern and traditional forms of protest. Alongside the evolution of democracy and parliamentary representation there continued to exist popular shaming practices that challenged authority and power hierarchies.[143]

Print media helped both to enlarge and to intensify the scope of public shaming. Satirical journals and the emerging socialist press served as a forum of critique that generously employed the language and imagery of denigration, ridicule, and debasement. Following in the footsteps of traditional pasquils, they epitomized the defamatory 'style of thinking' that contemporaries found amplified during the 1830s. Still, periodicals fulfilled other functions as well. Individual readers used them to advertise goods and services, announce marriages, and publish obituaries. People even apologized to others and retracted insults in newspapers, a practice documented as early as the eighteenth century in England.[144] But they also did the opposite, paying cash for the chance to insult and shame others publicly. In 1903, a husband who had recently moved out of the house published a notice in seven Alsatian newspapers: 'Warning: I hereby declare that I will under no circumstances pay for the debts of my wife, Maria, born S.' Being called a spendthrift embarrassed and even offended Maria. It made her feel that 'her credit had been damaged', so she sued and demanded her husband publicly retract his statement.[145]

The press thus offered people a new arena for their personal and professional conflicts and for subjecting their opponents to the gaze of public opinion. Yet journalists also defined and pursued their own agenda. No longer satisfied with playing the role of mere chroniclers, they took pride in waging social or political campaigns and putting pressure on those they accused of wrongdoing. A famous case was that of Maximilian Harden, editor of the weekly *Die Zukunft* (*The Future*). In 1906, he started a campaign against Kaiser Wilhelm II's entourage by labelling them as homosexuals; other papers soon joined. Harden's articles bore many traits of public shaming and were received as such. The journalist was consequently sued for libel by one of the men he had accused of being in a gay relationship.[146]

The Freedom of the Press versus the Right to Personal Honour

German law placed strict limits on what journalists could say and write, and the suits against them were legion. In the 1880s, prosecutors began putting their repressive powers to work primarily against the social-democratic press, and some editors spent more time behind bars than at work. While any criticism of the monarchy or the Emperor and his family could be tried as *lèse-majesté*,[147] politicians usually filed libel suits, as did Bismarck and many others. Among the very few members of parliament who deliberately refrained from suing were the socialist leader August Bebel and the left-liberal representative Eugen Richter. Both believed libel suits to be an instrument of political censorship that they chose to dispense with.[148]

According to Article 193 of Germany's penal code, newspapers could not be prosecuted so long as they pursued 'legitimate interests' in their reporting and showed restraint in the 'form of expression'. Interests were considered legitimate when they aimed at 'combatting immorality among the people, furthering scientific and political knowledge, or advancing the welfare of the people'. Under no circumstances was the press permitted to give in to what was called the 'satisfaction of curiosity' and the 'repulsive craving to excite oneself about serious crimes'.[149] The courts made their decisions in line with these principles: when editors could successfully demonstrate that they had acted to 'teach' and not 'entertain' their readership, libel suits against them were generally dropped.[150]

Thus, when the press sought to shine a light on social and political problems and those responsible for them, they had to consider carefully whether their reporting would be seen as serving legitimate interests. What that meant was, of course, interpreted in different ways. The Imperial Court tended towards a rather restrictive reading, which garnered sharp criticism from social democrats and liberals.[151] In the Weimar Republic, when political opinions were moving towards the extremes, politically motivated insults became ever more frequent. Communist and National Socialist papers were in virtual competition for who could transgress norms of respect the most. While laws adopted in 1922 and 1930 did make it illegal to insult, slander, or demean members of government, courts generally used these laws against the leftist press and looked the other way when it came to National Socialist and other far-right periodicals.[152]

Friedrich Ebert, the first president of the Weimar Republic and a Social Democrat, was the target of a veritable onslaught of defamation. Between 1919 and 1925, he received tons of letters littered with insults like 'trash rascal', 'filthy saddler', 'ox', and 'old drunken pig'. He was told that he would soon be 'chopped up' and 'shot on the heap' and that his corpse would be 'smeared with shit'.[153] The invectives unleashed against the president by left- and right-wing papers were extraordinarily nasty and circulated freely even though Ebert never tired of filing suits. A communist periodical in 1921 called him 'trash' and described him as a 'representative of the profiteer's republic, bloated lieutenant of the Hohenzollerns, devotee of smoking and wine bottles'. Another article accused him of gluttony, because 'otherwise he would not have such a shameless pot-belly'.[154]

Ebert's belly was, indeed, widely known, since it had been shown to all in a 1919 issue of the republic's most popular newspaper, the *Berliner Illustrirte Zeitung (BIZ)*. On the day Ebert was sworn into office, the paper's front page featured a photograph of him and minister Gustav Noske in their bathing suits at the Baltic Sea. The picture caused a furore and was reprinted countless times, mostly by far-right and conservative papers that wanted to malign the republic they so despised.

The editor of the *BIZ* and the head of the liberal Ullstein publishing house that owned the paper apologized to Ebert for their 'regrettable error'. Claiming that they had in no way intended to disgrace the republic or insult the president, they stated that, quite the contrary, they had wanted to popularize Ebert as a normal person like you and me.[155] In fact, the paper had been printing pictures of politicians in everyday scenes since the times of the Empire. In 1902, they showed Chancellor Bernhard von Bülow on the beach in his vacationing place at Norderney. In contrast to the Ebert photograph, however, the chancellor was fully dressed and his wife wore 'bright beach clothing, shadowed by a large hat'. The 26 April 1903 issue followed Bülow on holiday in Capri; again, he was wearing a hat, suit, and boots. On 30 June 1906, the *BIZ* even depicted the Kaiser with suit and summer hat visiting the Bülows in Norderney. On 1 April 1910, after Bülow had transferred his office to Theobald von Bethmann Hollweg, the paper's front page featured both chancellors 'on Easter holiday in Rome'. The picture was clearly a fake: for one, it had both men taking a dip in the river Tiber far too early in the year. In addition, it adorned the gaunt Bethmann Hollweg in a striped bathing suit and showed the chubby

Fig. 16. Friedrich Ebert and Gustav Noske at sea, August 1919

Bülow shirtless, which made both of them look utterly ridiculous. As one would expect, many readers felt provoked by the unstatesmanlike take, forcing the *BIZ* to explain that it was all just an April Fool's joke: 'Bülow and the Chancellor did not bathe in the Tiber', either with or without bathing suits.[156]

Against this background, the publication of Ebert's photograph could only be seen as an affront, which is precisely how it was used by a prominent conservative periodical. They were the first to print it and later sold it as a postcard. When Ebert sued them, the judge declared the dissemination of the picture unlawful, but let the editor off without punishment. The freedom of the right-wing press held more weight in the courts than did the dignity of the president.

In 1933, the freedom of the press to criticize the government and its representatives was brought to an abrupt end. Insulting the 'Führer' and his ministers was not the only thing to be made illegal. 'Groups or communities who, according to the people's healthy sentiment, are bearers of their own honour' could now sue for libel too, among them the military and the Nazi party.[157] At the same time, new publishing laws expanded the concept of what constituted legitimate interest. Under its guise, the press was permitted to call out and humiliate certain individuals and social or ethnic groups, but only if doing so was 'approved of by the people's healthy sentiment'.[158] This was assumed—and generously given—whenever the press castigated 'race traitor' women or citizens who defied the boycott against Jewish merchants.[159]

After 1945, legal scholars, practitioners, and politicians returned to pre-Nazi laws and precedents, reaffirming the right of the press 'to act openly in the name of legitimate public interests without having to fear being punished for libel'.[160] However, West Germany's constitution, ratified in 1949, did place some limits on the freedom of the press by guaranteeing the 'right to personal honour'. According to Theodor Heuss, who, as a member of the Parliamentary Council, was co-responsible for drafting the Basic Law, such limitations were important 'because defamation and false reporting about an individual's private and public life ought not to be permitted. We dispensed with particular protection against defamation for men of public life in order to avoid anything that looks like the Law for the Defence of the Republic and because all people enjoy the same right to have their personal honour protected.'[161]

Once in office, the Federal Republic's first government did make some concessions on this front. In 1951, parliament agreed to introduce mild punishments for disparaging the state, its symbols, and constitutionally ordained institutions. Beyond that, penal law shielded individuals active in 'political life' from libel and insult. In the 1960s, though, opinions on what kind of limits could be placed on free speech began to change. One reason was that the political instrumentalization of the judiciary was increasingly coming under fire. When it convened in Berlin in 1979, the Russell Tribunal studied the human rights situation in West Germany, placing particular focus on the 1972 law prohibiting 'enemies of the constitution' from holding public office as well as on the anti-terrorism laws passed in 1976 and 1977. At the same time, the convention of defence lawyers passed a resolution demanding the abolition of the passages on libel in the criminal code.[162]

Another reason could be found in the notable and profound liberalization of West German society. Curtailing journalists' right to inform the public by prioritizing issues of personal honour was seen as contradicting the liberal principles of democracy and transparency. The Federal Court of Justice felt the winds of change, too, and in a 1966 decision let an 'inappropriately harsh expression of opinion' pass.[163] Likewise, the Federal Constitutional Court came to side with press freedoms over the right to personal honour.[164]

While West Germany's legal culture was by now moving closer towards the American system with its emphasis on free speech, there were strong counter-currents. In the 1980s, legal scholars and practitioners began criticizing the 'barbarization of political communication' and saw 'witch-hunts, pillories, and mental torture' on the rise. They mourned the 'lost honour of the citizen' and pressed for improvements in the means of forming and expressing public opinion.[165] The critics were not swayed by the fact that the European Court of Human Rights affirmed 'the primacy of free political debate over their participants' interests in their own reputations'.[166] Indeed, the press itself often proved their point. In 1974, Nobel Prize for Literature laureate Heinrich Böll found himself at the centre of a smear campaign orchestrated by the *Bild* tabloid for his alleged support of Red Army Faction terrorists. In response, he wrote the novel *The Lost Honour of Katharina Blum*. Serialized in *Der Spiegel*, the novel attacked sensational journalism and called out its tendency to wreck the lives of its targets without providing any evidence of the charges.[167]

Whereas Böll's was a clear case of politically motivated character assassination, other subjects lent themselves to exposure too, and trials were a good place to start.[168] Many defence lawyers deplored the 'unrestrained admission of photographers and radio broadcasters into the courtroom', a practice that thrust defendants 'before a techno- logical pillory that is worse than the pillory of the Middle Ages'. Unsurprisingly, one wrote, defendants 'often fear the *public pillory* of the press more than any possible sentence'.[169] This held particularly true for 'juicy stories' that attracted journalists' attention because of 'the person of the defendant or the action or both'.[170] Such stories were promised and delivered by the 1985 trial against the famous boxer Gustav Scholz, who had while drunk murdered his wife, or by the trial of a couple who had held a young girl captive for months, raping and torturing her. Having turned 19 by the time the trial began, the girl contributed to her own 'public embarrassment' by signing an exclusive contract with the *Bild* tabloid and contributing details. Other papers, however, distanced themselves from what they called the 'modern media pillory'. The inevitable exposure not only of perpet- rators, but also of crime victims led many serious journalists to doubt the principle of public trials.[171]

Despite the criticism, tabloids happily continued to exploit and expose people for commercial interests. Betting on scandals, naming and shaming proved an easy way to increase sales. Starting in the 1980s, private TV channels cashed in as well. A watershed was reached in the early morning of 14 February 2008, when TV cameras were on hand as the private home of a major CEO was searched on suspicion of tax evasion. Many found the affair deeply unsettling. It was one thing for the press not to want to pass up a chance to report on the inglorious fall of a prominent person. But it was another that they had received information from institutional insiders who obviously wished the CEO to be publicly paraded. As far as the *Frankfurter Allgemeine Zeitung* (FAZ) was concerned, the CEO had been deliberately put on a 'social pillory'. The blunt staging of his arrest had brought him 'dishonour', 'ignominy', and 'ostracization': 'The lattice of the front garden became so well known that even tourist buses drove by to check it out.'[172]

Using words like dishonour, ignominy, and pillory, the FAZ critically referred to shaming practices from former times when human dignity was not yet universally respected. A statistical analysis shows that since the 1990s, such words have appeared with increasing frequency in the paper. One might trace this back to an actual rise in public shamings, from which would follow more regular media reporting. But it might also be that journalists have come to reject these practices more categorically than they did in the past.[173] To refrain from naming and shaming did not mean handling an accused CEO with kid gloves. Mob justice, however, was to be avoided at all costs, and so was *schadenfreude*.

What the 2008 case made crystal clear was that close cooperation between criminal justice, law enforcement, and the media, while an everyday affair in the USA, is considered unacceptable in Europe. Since the nineteenth century, European journalists have had the right to report on public trials, and have had no reservations about making use of this right. Unwritten rules of journalistic ethics, though, kept them from being there before charges had even been filed, which is why the CEO's public arrest was so sharply criticized. That things work differently in the USA was brought to everyone's attention in

2011. In New York, French politician and presidential hopeful Dominique Strauss-Kahn was accused of sexual assault and attempted rape. The image of 'DSK' in handcuffs being escorted to the courthouse by police officers was printed around the world and caused a great deal of indignation among Europeans. The so-called 'perp walk' or 'walk of shame' is common practice in the USA and is deliberately intended to humiliate. Some police departments even provide skilful choreographies for the press, which is eager to print the photographs.[174] This all appeared strange in Europe's legal culture, where the honour and dignity of the individual person enjoys greater protections, a fact emphasized by French, Dutch, and German commentators alike.[175]

Consensual Degradation on TV

Sensitivity towards anything that smells of public humiliation has reached a historic high, a fact evidenced by people's tendency not only to defend themselves against such acts, but also to refuse to play the role of onlookers. The fine-tuning of people's sense for distinguishing between dignified and undignified behaviour began with nineteenth-century liberals finding fault with demeaning forms of legal punishment. As of the late twentieth century, the degrading depiction of people in print and digital media has become a primary target of criticism.

But what can be said about situations in which people freely consent to their own public degradation and even act to further it? Since the advent of the new millennium, consensual degradation has become an everyday phenomenon that can be witnessed at any time on the television screen. One of the pioneers of this trend was the TV series Big Brother, first aired in the Netherlands in 1999. The format has since spread throughout Europe and much of the rest of the world. The show depicts the 'real lives' of people constantly under surveillance as they live together, compete with each other, and complete tasks together. Tasteless acts with a high embarrassment quotient are normal and the limits of what is considered disgusting are regularly put to the test. If the housemates want to stay and win cash prizes at the end, they have to withstand all the trials. From the history of the show, it seems the incentives are sufficient to make some people assent to just about anything.

Reality television also appeals to those who turn to it as a last resort for help that they otherwise cannot afford. They seek advice from doctors, nutritionists, or dating experts, and they pay the price of being humiliated by the host and ridiculed on social media. For fourteen years, *The Jeremy Kyle Show*, copying *The Jerry Springer Show* in the USA, exposed the most vulnerable members of British society to public sneering and spatting. Humiliation was its very 'backbone', and it successfully invited millions of viewers to laugh at others' expense. Only when a contestant took his life after filming an episode was the programme permanently cancelled in May 2019.[176]

Other shows, too, deliberately make use of shaming strategies. In the British-made *Pop Idol* franchise, a jury judges young talents in a tournament-style elimination process, evaluating the singers' voice, clothing, and performance. One of the judges, Simon Cowell, became particularly renowned for his insulting comments, which were clearly intended to increase the show's entertainment value. The German version of the series followed a similar pattern. However, in Germany, faced with complaints in 2007, the Commission for the Protection of Minors in the Media conducted an investigation into the 'social-ethical disorientation' caused by the show and hit it with a fine. In 2010, it again lambasted the 'degrading behaviour of the jury', which 'intentionally humiliates the young candidates in front of millions'.[177] But those millions—mostly adolescents—did and do not seem to care, apparently thoroughly enjoying the public shaming.

Based on *America's Next Top Model*, the casting show *Germany's NTM* has also been the subject of critique. Aired weekly since 2006, the show revolves around aspiring young women seeking to gain a foot in the door of the modelling industry. Enticed with contracts, publicity, and cash prizes, contestants have to pass a number of tests and let themselves be photographed in questionable poses: being covered in salad dressing, lounging around half-naked in a bar made of ice, and pole dancing are just a few examples. Some find this demeaning.[178] But the audience likes the entertainment and remains loyal to the show. Fascination is supplemented by *schadenfreude* over the wannabe models' bloopers, whether it be tripping over themselves or struggling to speak.

The desire to see others flop seems to guarantee the show's high viewership. But why do thousands of young women subject themselves to the casting machine, only in order to be humiliated in front of millions? Maybe they simply lack judgement or just have their 'eyes on the prize', or their desire for quick fame and riches is great enough to keep them on the show. The potential for success, it appears, is so attractive and seductive that contestants are willing to put a price tag on their dignity.

Some see the casting-show madness as an expression of our neo-liberal world, which forces people to present themselves on the market as flawless, efficient, success-oriented machines. But beauty pageants, which have been around since the beginning of the twentieth century and saw a boom in the 1950s, have long since featured similar values: young women line up to be judged on their looks in order to get some fame and money.[179] What is new about the twenty-first century's casting shows is the way they stage and exploit failure for the delight of an audience. Before a winner can be declared, all other participants must be eliminated, and every minute misstep is scrutinized at great length. Some of this parallels the initiation rituals of fraternities and sororities in the sense that self-degradation is made into a condition of belonging.

A key difference, though, is that frat hazings are generally conducted in front of an audience limited to group members whereas the TV shows are seen the world over. While the viewers are anonymous, they prove to be highly present and active, judging the behaviour and ratings of contestants in countless forums, both online and offline. With shows like *Big Brother* and *American Idol*, viewers themselves turn into judges and often serve to validate the shaming strategies of moderators and jurors. Although they could just as well undermine these strategies, they rarely do so—which points to the limits of a culture of dignity that has yet to make itself part of all spheres of society.

Online Shaming

The use of digital media to publicize the humiliation of others is another indicator of these limits. The extent of the problem has become a nightmare for many, because the internet puts no constraints on how widely a humiliating video, image, or text can be proliferated. Moreover, the internet has changed the function and character of the act of shaming itself. In video recordings of gang rapes, the perpetrators place the helplessness of their victims on display, and the same goes for the fad of attacking random people on the street for the purpose of recording it, cynically termed 'happy slapping'.[180] Among many young people, being defenceless is considered a flaw and the word 'victim' an insult. Those who engage in these new forms of humiliation seek not to punish someone for transgressing a norm, but simply to revel in their own power and the powerlessness of others.

The internet has provided these asymmetrical—and often tragic— displays of power with a forum that almost seems tailored for the purpose. On the one hand, it has removed shaming from its classical social contexts and functions. Rather than serving to chastise transgressions, solidify a sense of community against an outsider, or initiate a new member, acts of humiliation on the internet make humiliation into an end in itself. One might see this as a sign of social disintegration and anomie, in that the economy of individual enjoyment and self-assertion has replaced socially valid norms and conventions. On the other hand, the enjoyment factor still needs social validation, just like the classic forms of shaming and humiliation, and the internet delivers here like no other. Simply put, content on the internet is visible to anyone with a connection, enabling perpetrators to demonstrate their power to degrade others in pure form for an infinite community that watches and posts comments.

Such phenomena fly in the face of a society that purports to place paramount value on non-violent communication, mutual respect, and esteem for human dignity. Aside from sociopathic extremes like 'happy slapping', the alarming frequency of hateful language and shaming insults on social media is an affront to these values. Even on sites where users can no longer hide behind the mask of anonymity, both the immediacy and physical disconnect of online communication invite people to insult and attack others in a way that defies description. Not least of all, this affects adolescents and even children, who are confronted with forms of cyber-bullying of utmost cruelty. In one instance that took place in 2013 in Italy, a 'friend' spread rumours on Facebook under a false name that a 14-year-old girl would sleep with anyone, which ultimately led to the girl being gang raped.[181]

Adults, too, cannot escape being shamed on the internet, particularly when they have achieved some degree of celebrity.[182] Politicians and journalists, above all, have had to accustom themselves to receiving hate mail, and social media abound with public humiliations of the worst sort. Defamatory letters have certainly been around for a long time, and the ones targeting kings, queens, presidents, and ministers can still be read in state archives. What is new, however, is, first, their frequency and the breadth of circulation enabled by digital technologies. Second, their language has become ever more brutal, particularly when they are directed against women. Male rape and torture fantasies seem to know no bounds, as is testified by prominent female journalists and politicians who are flooded with such postings. Third, humiliation is increasingly moving beyond media celebrities and people holding public office. In theory and in practice, everyone might wake up to find themselves on a list of shame, insulted for being fat, promiscuous, too far to the right or left, homosexual, a sexual harasser, a tax evader, a water-waster, or a bad driver. In short, anyone can attack anyone at any time on the internet, where their speech acts can proliferate without limit or expiration date.[183] In contrast to the classic news media, the internet has a long memory—once something is there, it is very difficult to get rid of it.[184]

This also distinguishes online shaming from the face-to-face acts of shaming common in the pre-digital world. For one, it is now far easier to demean someone who is not present, especially in cases where the perpetrator might be secretly ashamed of what he is doing. And it has become considerably more difficult for victims of online attacks to defend themselves. How would Pippi Longstocking deal with bullies if they made fun of her hair and clothes on the internet instead of in real life? Would she shame them with her cleverness? Laugh it off? Move to another school? These things are hardly possible any longer, or would make little sense, because the internet follows everyone everywhere, stopping time and levelling space.

Thus, with digital media, social shaming has taken on a new dimension. It is geared far more towards stigmatization than towards punishment and reintegration. It progressively adopts elements of humiliation that aim to degrade, debase, and exclude. People demeaned in such fashion can hardly return to their social group unscathed. As with Martin Kippenberger, they often remain standing in the corner long after class is over.

3

HONOUR AND THE LANGUAGE OF HUMILIATION IN INTERNATIONAL POLITICS

A cts of public humiliation are not only directed at individuals or social groups. They are also a reality in international relations. Sometimes they are contained within the world of language, and sometimes they spill over into military conflicts. Historically, this has been nothing uncommon, as the Swiss diplomat Emer de Vattel confirmed in 1758: 'Every nation, every sovereign, ought to maintain their dignity by causing due respect to be paid to them; and, especially, they ought not to suffer that dignity to be impaired.' In the case that the prince's dignity was injured, he 'has a right to demand, even by force of arms, the reparation of an insult'.[1] This also applied to the prince's diplomats. According to Julius Bernhard von Rohr's 1733 book on 'ceremonial science', the prince who does not receive 'satisfaction' might start a war.[2]

Today, political leaders have become more cautious in making declarations of war. Humiliation, however, is just as much an instrument of international politics as it was in times past, and violating the conventions of diplomatic ceremony can still cause serious issues. When US president Barack Obama took a trip to China in 2016, he had to disembark Air Force One on an improvised set and walk onto the tarmac without red carpet. American media—above all, social media—saw in this an intentional mistreatment of the guest of state, not just a technical mistake.[3]

But diplomatic ceremony is not the only sphere that lends itself as a stage for the politics of humiliation. When Iranian students tried to force the extradition of the shah by taking American diplomats hostage after the 1979 Islamic Revolution, they were clearly violating international law, which guarantees the immunity of foreign emissaries. International conventions would thus demand that the Iranian government apologize for the incident (which to date has yet to occur). The United States took the event as a flagrant act of shaming that damaged its prestige. For President Jimmy Carter and National Security Advisor Zbigniew Brzezinski, nothing less than 'national honor' was at stake. Carter thus ordered a military rescue mission to put an end to the 'international humiliation', and even though it turned out to be a spectacular failure, Brzezinski maintained that it would have been 'shameful and unworthy of America' not to have tried.[4]

In short, honour and attempts to violate it have long played a role in international politics, where honour means power and the inability to defend it means weakness. Questions of power have thus frequently been negotiated in the language of honour, and the argument that a state's honour had been disrespected has often been used as leverage in claims to power. Such strategies saw a marked upturn as international relations began attracting increased publicity and taking on new resonance. All over Europe and the USA, the late nineteenth century gave rise to a national public that paid close attention to how its own government acted and reacted on the international stage. Since then, 'the people' and the media have tended to inflate the significance of supposed acts of disrespect, transforming them into do-or-die questions of national existence.

Lord Macartney and the Emperor of China

At the end of the eighteenth century, international politics generally were not yet much exposed to the public eye. So, when Lord George Macartney set sail for China on the HMS *Lion* on 26 September 1792, hardly anyone took notice. Macartney had been tasked by King

Fig. 17. *The Reception,* caricature by James Gillray, 1792

George III with negotiating better trade conditions with China for the East India Company and with installing a permanent embassy. Accompanied by a delegation of about a hundred people, he brought with him precious gifts and manufactures for the Qianlong Emperor who, so the British hoped, would thus be charmed into fulfilling their wishes.

Not long after their arrival, Macartney and his men realized that their mission was not going to run quite as they had planned. Although they were treated politely and given everything they needed, the preparations for meeting with the emperor were complicated and time consuming. The whole affair was a test of patience for both sides. The Chinese viewed Macartney as a negotiator whose experience stood in inverse relation to the intensity with which he made his demands. He was also not the first international emissary to visit Beijing. Since the mid-seventeenth century, sixteen diplomatic missions had made their way from Europe to China for the purpose of negotiating trade relations. Jesuit missionaries had been living in China since the sixteenth century and were prized as scholars and precision mechanics.[5] Besides, the Chinese regularly received vassal rulers who had to pay tribute.

However, with the exception of Russia, the emperor did not maintain relations with any Western countries, which were viewed as barbaric. The exception was strategic: China gave the tsar extensive religious, economic, and cultural privileges in order to keep him out of China's conflicts with Mongolian lords. When the Kangxi Emperor sent his emissary to St Petersburg in 1712, he advised him to conform to Russian rituals and rules. This stood in marked contrast to the norm for tribute-paying heads of state, who were forced to follow Chinese customs when they received visitors from Beijing.[6]

Peter I exploited the concession when he sent Count Lev Ismailov to the Chinese capital in 1719–20 to negotiate better trade conditions for Russian merchants. He told his ambassador to hand his letters of credence to the emperor personally and in no way to perform the kowtow. In doing so, the tsar knew perfectly well that Ismailov would be violating one of the central elements of Chinese court ceremony, which demanded that every visitor fall to his knees three times and touch his head to the ground nine times altogether. After being respectfully received, Ismailov did as he was ordered and insisted on directly presenting the letter without kowtowing.

The emperor was not amused. He considered Ismailov's request 'presumptuous' and out of tune with Chinese ceremonial customs. Above all, he urged him 'to give up his unreasonable pretensions of delivering the letter with his own hands, as he was no more than a representative of his master'. As a mere envoy, he could not expect to 'receive the same honours as those that would be paid to the Czar, if personally present in Peking'. When Ismailov did not comply, the emperor sent several officials and translators to convince him. They told the Russian that when Chinese envoys were dispatched to

Moscow, they would gladly follow Russian customs, and went so far as to say that they would appear before the tsar without head covering, even though in China only convicted criminals walked around bareheaded. In order to prove he was serious, the highest-ranking official took off his hat in front of the Russian diplomat, thus committing an unheard-of act of self-degradation. Impressed, the count changed his mind. On the day of the audience, he 'immediately prostrated himself before the table, holding up the tsar's letter with both hands'. Irritated at the long back and forth, the emperor let him remain in this posture for a while before finally taking the letter—without the intervention of a courtier—directly from the diplomat's hands.[7]

The whole scene was witnessed and recorded by Italian priest Matteo Ripa. It is a particularly potent example of the kinds of power games played on the chessboard of international relations in the eighteenth century. The ceremony was the place where questions of honour were negotiated, and who was received by whom according to what rules served as a measure of power and submission. To break the rules was impolite. In the middle of the eighteenth century, British politician Lord Chesterfield explained to his son Philip that every courtly custom was just as meaningful as it was meaningless, and that if one did not want to make a fool of oneself, one had best just follow the local conventions.[8] In their relations between one another, European states generally sought to stick to this principle. But when it came to China, they often tested the limits.

Macartney certainly did, and this despite the fact that the higher-ups at the East India Company told him to adhere to Chinese customs and not to think too much about the peculiarities of courtly ceremony, so long as he could do so without violating his own honour and that of his king. According to Macartney's diary, the British did endeavour 'always to put the best face upon everything, and to preserve a perfect serenity of countenance upon all occasions. I therefore shut my eyes upon the flags of our yachts, which were inscribed "The English Ambassador bringing tribute to the Emperor of

China", and have made no complaint of it.'[9] He did refuse, however, to 'kneel down upon both knees, and make nine prostrations or inclinations of the head to the ground'.[10] Nevertheless, the British ambassador could not help but be impressed at the artful considerations that his Chinese hosts made when discussing court ceremony:

> They began by turning the conversation upon the different modes of dress that prevailed among different nations, and, after pretending to examine ours particularly, seemed to prefer their own, on account of its being loose and free from ligatures, and of its not impeding or obstructing the genuflexions and prostrations which were, they said, customary to be made by all persons whenever the Emperor appeared in public. They therefore apprehended much inconvenience to us from our knee-buckles and garters, and hinted to us that it would be better to disencumber ourselves of them before we should go to Court.[11]

But Macartney remained steadfast in declining to accept the advice and instead insisted that they follow 'the etiquette of the English Court', which is to say, kneeling on one knee and kissing the monarch's hand. His first duty, he explained to the Chinese officials, was to please his own king, and prostrating clearly ran contrary to his notions of what that meant.[12]

A few days of calm passed before the officials brought up the topic again. Macartney wrote: 'It seems to be a very serious matter with them, and a point which they have set their hearts upon. They pressed me most earnestly to comply with it, said it was a mere trifle; kneeled down on the floor and practised it of their own accord to show me the manner of it, and begged me to try whether I could not perform it.'[13] When he realized that they would not let up, Macartney wrote a letter explaining that he would prefer to adhere to English customs. But he also offered a compromise: he would follow local conventions if a Chinese courtier of the same rank performed three prostrations before a portrait of the British king. The Chinese dismissed the offer as 'unwarranted haughtiness' and scolded the English as 'ignorant barbarians' who did not deserve to be treated 'with too much courtesy'. While Macartney still 'dwelt upon the propriety of something to distinguish between the homage of tributary Princes and the ceremony used on the part of a great and independent sovereign', the officials eventually gave up. He was permitted to meet the emperor as he would meet his king: he would kneel upon one knee, but without kissing the emperor's hand, 'as it was not the custom in China'.[14]

For the British envoy, refusing to go along with the Chinese ceremony was a matter of national honour and official dignity. He insisted that both rulers were of equal standing (though he himself was obviously convinced of Britain's superiority) and believed that the prostration ritual put this in question. The fact that the Chinese finally let him have his way was viewed by Macartney as a superb achievement. His secretary George Staunton likewise celebrated it as a victory for 'reason, accompanied by temper and perseverance', and thought it indicated a significant alteration in the Chinese government's attitude towards Western states.[15] For the Chinese, however, there was no shift in mindset; there was just annoyance about British 'ignorance' and contempt for the 'barbarians' from a faraway land who had little to say or give that would be of interest.[16]

At least, that is what the Qianlong Emperor, then at the height of his power, wrote to the British king when he sent the latter's ambassador home empty-handed. He praised George III for his 'sincere humility and obedience' and thanked him for the 'tribute articles' that 'have been sent from afar across the sea'. But he was dismissive of the king's efforts to place a permanent trade ambassador in China, since 'this does not conform to the Celestial Empire's ceremonial system, and definitely cannot be done'. Furthermore, he wrote, his empire had 'never valued ingenious articles, nor do we have the slightest need of your Country's manufactures'.[17]

The Imperial Edict, composed in verse, left no room for doubt that the Qianlong Emperor viewed George III as an obsequious supplicant who humbly offered his gifts 'with reverence and affection', as did other vassal rulers. The notion that another country might be on a level with China was inconceivable for the emperor, as was the concomitant notion that he treat another ruler as his equal. The kind of reciprocity based on mutual recognition that his predecessor had arranged with Russia was not something the powerful Qianlong Emperor was willing to consider. In contrast to Russia, China did not depend on Britain's economic or military good will.

The emperor was ready to tell all of this to the king long before Macartney—like Ismailov before him—began his long-drawn-out negotiations for the right kind of court ceremony. The Imperial Edict had been drafted by the Grand Council in early August 1793, a whole two weeks before the bilateral talks on prostration and bows were started. The emperor made it official on 23 September, nine days after receiving Macartney in audience. Thus, even though the Chinese were 'extremely displeased' with the British envoy's stubborn resistance, it played no role in the emperor's decision, which had already been made in advance.[18]

Macartney had not anticipated this. He was caught off guard, and all the more so as he had viewed the officials' acquiescence to his wishes on the matter of ceremony as a good sign. But he and his men had clearly drawn the wrong conclusions from their hosts' accommodating behaviour. Indeed, their willingness to allow him to bow rather than insisting that he touch his head to the ground nine times was more a matter of lack of interest than of courtesy.

The British delegation's perception that they were being treated condescendingly was another misunderstanding. Johann Christian Hüttner, who had come along on the voyage as the private tutor of Staunton's son and as a translator, called the Chinese courtly customs 'demeaning' and wrote that they could not be reconciled with 'the dignity of a British envoy'.[19] This was all strange for the Chinese, for whom showing respect by prostrating before the person of praise was completely normal. Children did this with their parents, the living with the dead, subjects with their emperor, and the emperor with his predecessors and God. Everybody owed somebody respect, and prostrating was an adequate gesture for showing it. He who knew his place in the world was well aware of what was demanded of him without being humiliated or ashamed by it. Quite the contrary, by kowtowing, one was able to partake of the power of the venerated person.[20]

The Chinese believed that Europeans were putting their 'barbaric' ignorance on display by not understanding and accepting this. In cases when they did conform, they were considered 'agreeable and polished' and were gladly seen at court. When the Dutch East India Company sent a delegation to China in 1794, they readily complied with local etiquette and prostrated along the road the emperor passed on his way to his summer residence. He saw this as a sign of their 'desire to be civilized by Chinese culture' and treated their 'dutiful submission' with grace and generosity.[21]

Sovereign Equality and Diplomatic Ceremony

In contrast, the British insisted on the concept of equality and their rights of sovereignty. A 1771 entry to the *Encyclopaedia Britannica* defines 'sovereign' as a concept that, 'in matters of government, is applied to the supreme magistrate, or magistrates, of an independent government or state: by reason their authority is only bounded by the laws of God, of nature, and the fundamental laws of the state: such are kings, princes, etc.'[22] The venture of independent sovereignty did not blend with being looked at like a vassal, which is why the British delegation were so irritated when their gifts for the Qianlong Emperor were labelled articles of tribute.

The principle of sovereign equality was established in Europe in the seventeenth century. It pronounced that sovereign states stood in a relation of parity to one another, and even though some had more territory and power than others, they still negotiated as equals. The precept was first officially inscribed into international law after the Napoleonic Wars—in 1815 at the Congress of Vienna and in 1818 at the Congress of Aix-la-Chapelle. But by the signing of the Peace of Westphalia that ended the Thirty Years' War in 1648, it had already been acknowledged as a key element of international relations.[23]

At the same time, installing ambassadors in other European nations to carry out a state's diplomatic affairs with other states became the norm. Up into the nineteenth century, personal meetings between monarchs remained rare events, as kings and queens preferred to travel in their own countries rather than go abroad.[24] Therefore, ambassadors took on the role of representing their sovereigns' interests in interstate communication. Treatises on international law and manners books taught them what kind of behaviour was expected of them, and they also received advice from the field of ceremony studies, which began flourishing around 1700.[25]

The French court long set the trends in diplomatic ceremony and attached special honours to the ambassadorial office. As the direct representatives of their lords, ambassadors were not treated much differently than kings would have been: they were called 'your excellence' and they got to walk, sit and stand to the right of the foreign monarch.[26] But who carried the title and the honours that came with it was decided by the sovereign receiving the ambassador, not the king or prince he represented. This could give rise to controversy. French kings in the eighteenth century would not receive German diplomats, thus refusing to acknowledge their princes as sovereign equals. There were also gradations in ceremonial signs of respect. Western European customs held that ambassadors could keep their hats on when attending an audience. In the French court, however, Swiss ambassadors were forced to remove theirs, which the Swiss viewed as disparaging treatment that undermined the dignity of their sovereign.[27]

Practices like not taking one's hat off in front of a king were, according to Lord Chesterfield and Emer de Vattel, 'in their own nature indifferent'. But as long as 'the usages and manners of the age' accepted them 'as proper expressions of the respect due to the representative of a sovereign', they gained 'real value and a settled signification'. In Vattel's own words, the 'law of nations' therefore 'requires that we should pay deference to such institution'. Failing to do so could lead to problems for both parties. If an ambassador did not behave properly in the presence of a foreign sovereign, the latter might feel that his honour was being challenged. On the other side, the respect or lack thereof shown to a diplomat was equally shown to his lord. Even ordinary citizens could cause issues. If they insulted an ambassador, their government owed, as Vattel stated, 'full satisfaction to the sovereign who has been offended in the person of his minister'.[28]

This is precisely what happened in 1708 at the end of Russian ambassador Andrei Matveev's mission in London.[29] After being given his farewell audience, Matveev asked his creditors to present their bills. His inability to pay the high sum immediately made one creditor suspicious enough to have him arrested and held in a sponging-house for a few hours. The ambassador firmly protested against such undignified treatment to Queen Anne and considered it an 'affront offer'd His Czarish Majesty himself in person of his ambassador...the greatest violation of the law of nations'.[30] The event was extremely embarrassing for the queen, and Secretary of State Henry Boyle assured the Russians that she would do everything to offer the tsar all possible 'satisfaction'. In February 1710, Charles Whitworth handed Peter I a royal letter that expressed the queen's 'appropriately great dissatisfaction and repugnance concerning such a senseless act inflicted upon a publick minister' and begged for forgiveness.[31] The tsar accepted Anne's apology as 'a mark of her goodwill and favour'. He also found no issue with the royal letter's claim that the British government had taken 'endeavours to use all practicable methods towards due satisfaction', even if he would have liked to have seen the perpetrators punished more harshly. If 'due satisfaction' had been denied, however, the tsar could have secured it 'through war', and international law would have been on his side.[32]

This case, which was widely discussed at European courts of the time, illustrates well the complexity and fragility of international relations. On the one hand, it demonstrates how susceptible to conflict the early modern system of diplomacy really was. Rather than make relations between sovereigns easier, it could often do just the opposite: the more rules there were, the more chances for transgressions, which could, if needed, be quickly blown out of proportion. It was no matter of coincidence that in 1652, the Viennese court tasked a secretary with keeping track of all of its ceremonial customs and practices, and thus with ensuring that no faux pas were committed.[33] In Britain, the Matveev affair led Parliament to pass a detailed law that gave ambassadors legal immunity.[34]

On the other hand, the affair shines light on the great significance of ceremonial forms and their wider resonance. When the British envoy met with the tsar in 1710, he was not alone. 'All the noblest lords of the Empire were present, as were all foreign ministers at His Majesty the Czar's court'. Whitworth and Peter I held their discussion in the presence of powerful, influential men, and the topic was clearly of general interest.[35]

Another effect of the public reception was to make the British queen's apology known. The apology affirmed both the principle of sovereign equality and the notion that the ambassador was the direct representative of the person and dignity of his sovereign. The conclusion to be drawn was that the humiliation of an ambassador was equal to the humiliation of his lord and that the offended prince had the right to demand satisfaction from the monarch whose subject had carried out the humiliating act. In other words, an apology from the creditor or the constable who arrested Matveev would have been insufficient. Queen Anne herself had to step up and ask the tsar to forgive the 'grave insult which had been inflicted on the person and character of the ambassador' in order to prevent things from getting out of hand.[36]

During the Moscow meeting, great pains were taken to maintain form and suppress any doubt about the principle of equality among European sovereigns. The British envoy was received by the tsar with all appropriate ceremony, and he was allowed to take off his head covering before approaching the tsar, who was also bareheaded. He bowed three times before the Russian emperor and repeated the gesture when he left. He personally handed Peter the royal dispatch and explained its contents in English. There was no trace of ceremonial shaming during the entire reception. Instead, the tsar and

Charles Whitworth met in the style of aristocratic men of honour, as equals taking part in an *affaire d'honneur*.[37]

Finally, the affair demonstrates how flexible and diverse ceremonial symbols were in the eighteenth century. Vattel viewed it as a privilege of European ambassadors that they did not have to remove their hats. But in Russia, things were different: here, the honour consisted in being permitted to see the tsar un-hatted. In the end, the most important thing was the recognition of equality expressed in the reciprocity of the gestures.

In European politics, sovereign equality and reciprocity were jealously guarded. France's tendency to distinguish between important and unimportant states in ceremonial honours caused just as much resentment as did the gestures of superiority made by the Viennese chancery. In his 1799 report on the journey to China described above, George Staunton wrote that the 'arrogated superiority' of the Chinese court reminded him of the tone and attitude that was once assumed by the Holy Roman Empire towards other European powers.[38] Such attitudes, however, were quickly falling out of style.

The Polyvalence of Ceremonial Gestures: The Kiss on the Hand

At least in Europe and among Europeans, the airs of 'arrogated superiority' experienced one last revival during Napoleon Bonaparte's expansionist reign. His defeat paved the way for a new European order, which, despite acknowledging Britain and Russia as hegemons, was still serious about recognizing the sovereignty of all states. Even the peace negotiations with France were conducted according to the principle of mutual respect. Napoleon's former foreign minister Charles-Maurice de Talleyrand attended the Congress of Vienna as an equal and was viewed by the other foreign ministers as such.[39] While the countries that had been invaded by French troops had suffered both materially and symbolically during the occupation, the feelings of humiliation found no voice in the diplomatic setting.[40] The fact that Napoleon had been forced to abdicate the throne and the Bourbons were back in power certainly contributed to the dignified atmosphere, but the conventions of post-revolutionary diplomacy did their part too, ensuring that a politics of revenge would not emerge victorious.

The more universal these conventions became within Europe, the more indignation Europeans expressed at the signs of inequality they discovered outside of Europe. Instances included the Qianlong Emperor's refusal to treat European envoys as representatives of sovereigns and not just payers of tribute, as well as the hierarchical treatment common in Maghrebi courts, where consuls and envoys from Christian nations stood at the bottom of the ceremonial ladder. Viewed as infidels, they had to wait until the last Muslim subject had kissed the ruler's hand before being allowed to perform the ritual. The very act of kissing a ruler's hand as an expression of gratitude for privileges like freedom of religion also gradually began to be met with resistance. In 1794, the French commissioner to Tunis, Jean-Baptiste Lallement, repudiated the ceremony as profoundly displeasing; two years later, consul Bonaventure Beaussier wrote that it was a 'humiliating piece of etiquette for republicans'. Nevertheless, he accepted the gesture as 'a custom consecrated by time' rather than fighting it as an act of submission.[41]

Indeed, Paris had directed its diplomats to 'respect the political, civil and religious laws' of the host country instead of tossing out in revolutionary fervour the 'old diplomacy' with its 'ridiculously ostentatious ceremonies'. As foreign minister Charles François Lebrun explained in 1793, the French people viewed all other peoples as equals. But so long as traditional privileges and pretensions remained the norm elsewhere, France should not unilaterally abandon her traditional rights.[42] When it came to altering ceremonial customs, French diplomacy left the initiative to its English-speaking counterparts. Beginning in 1816, American and British consuls attending audiences in Tunis simply left it at a short bow. The Americans made an argument similar to that made by Lord Macartney in Beijing: an American would never kiss the hand of the president, so why should they have to kiss the hand of the Bey? In 1836, the French consul finally followed suit, telling Mustafa Bey that the hand-kiss was 'uncommon in the Christian courts and even in Constantinople', and that it ran contrary to 'the dignity of the representative of the French nation'. Six years previously, a French–Tunisian treaty had already abolished the payment of gifts, *alias* tributes.[43]

Thus, the Europeans and Americans rewrote the rules of international relations according to their own tastes. Rather than adhere to local customs, they insisted on what they held to be dignified. At the same time, when non-European ambassadors came to visit, they were expected to conform to European customs, which, for their part, were often not so different from what was practised outside of Europe. In London, kissing the monarch's hand was normal and remained so. In 1793, Macartney even offered to kiss the Qianlong Emperor's hand. When British consuls refused to kiss the Tunisian Bey's hand, they thus dispensed with the principle of reciprocity, implicitly denying the other's equality and taking the high ground.

Europeans usually justified their unwillingness to comply with foreign conventions by denouncing them as demeaning and humiliating. But why then was a hand-kiss demeaning in Tunis while it clearly was not in London? They could not have had an issue with the gesture itself, which was rather unambiguous. The very fact that one had to bow one's head in order to kiss a monarch's hand showed him or her honour. But honour was never a zero-sum game, as honouring someone did not necessarily imply a loss of honour on the part of the one doing it. Like the Chinese interpretation of the kowtow, he who honoured the king took part in the latter's honour. Thus, being allowed to kiss the hand of the monarch might even have been seen as a privilege. This was obviously the case in Württemberg, where until 1781 only the aristocratic students of the military academy were permitted to kiss the duke's hand. Non-noble students had to make do with the hem of his robe.[44]

From this perspective, the European ambassadors' refusal to kiss the hand of the Tunisian ruler indicated that they attached little importance to the privilege of having a part in his honour, and, in fact, considered the latter to be of little value. The Bey's honour capital was no longer seen as being equal with that of European rulers, and the principle of sovereign equality obviously did not apply. In turn, Europeans placed a higher premium on their own honour, demanding that they be treated with corresponding deference. Making such demands reality necessitated power, which more and more states managed to accumulate, demonstrate, and perform during the long nineteenth century.

From Genuflecting Reverences to Bowing

At the same time, European societies underwent radical social and political changes. Relations between rulers and their subjects were recalibrated, and new modes of communication came into being. It was in this very context that Austrian Emperor Joseph II decreed, in 1787, to abolish the custom that men and women kiss the hand of 'the highest lord and of all members of the royal house'. This decision did not, to be sure, concern foreign diplomats, who were still expected to kiss the hands of royalty at the Viennese court. Rather, it concerned the emperor's subjects, who up until then had been expected to kiss the emperor's hand when presenting him with a petition. Joseph II also forbade them from performing all 'the genuflecting reverences and kneeling'.[45] As early as 1734, Duke of Württemberg Carl Alexander had stated that kneeling was a form of reverence 'owed to God alone' and that bowing before people was a 'vexatious abuse'. In 1783, the king of Prussia voiced his agreement and stated that this should be told to all citizens.[46]

On the one hand, these alterations were made to draw a starker line between secular and religious forms of veneration, and thus emphasized the separation between church and state. On the other, they gave expression to the shift in the relation between the monarch and his people. The new body language articulated the transformation of cap-in-hand subjects into self-confident citizens who could no longer be expected to kneel in reverence. Standing upright before their ruler was more in line with their reformed status.

Contemporaries viewed these moves as a sign of progress, and the fact that they compared them with the state of things outside Europe was no coincidence. In 1787, German encyclopaedist Johann Georg Krünitz expressed satisfaction that Joseph II's decree had abolished the 'Asiatic, degrading fashion' of 'bowing before one's despots', reasoning that nothing was 'more demeaning to man's dignity than the slavish habit of bowing before governing men'. He saw the custom's origins in 'the Orient, where the people suffering under the iron yoke of arbitrary power view their rulers not as fathers of the fatherland, but as half-gods'. The Protestant author did not miss the occasion to remind readers that in Europe, such lack of culture was only custom-ary at papal audiences, where even foreigners were expected to 'get on their knees' before the pope, while he spoke to them 'without giving them the most minute sign that they may stand'.[47]

Krünitz's outrage at the pope's 'demeaning' behaviour was triggered by the fact that the pope performed it in his capacity as a head of state. As the head of the Catholic Church, he would have been justified to expect the gesture from fellow Catholics, since kneeling was by then accepted as a centuries-old convention of Christian ritual. Originally, however, early Christians, like Jews, had venerated their God while standing in order to distinguish this form of veneration from that shown to kings, which took place in a kneeling position. Only when Christians came under imperial rule in the fourth century did they adopt the courtly customs of the Byzantine Empire. But even then, kneeling remained reserved for certain times of the year. On Sundays and between Easter and Pentecost, the Resurrection was celebrated standing.[48]

Still, many people had, over time, spoken out in favour of kneeling in prayer. Drawing on the belief that there was a close connection between the body and mind, gesture and feeling, St Augustine wrote in the early fifth century: 'And I know not how it is, that, while these motions of the body cannot be made but by a motion of the mind preceding, yet by the same being outwardly in visible sort made, that inward invisible one which made them is increased: and thereby the heart's affection which preceded that they might be made, groweth because they are made.'[49] By giving expression to their devotion and humility through bodily movements, believers did more than just render their feelings visible—they further strengthened and intensified them. Nearly 900 years later, Thomas Aquinas made a similar claim when he said that signs of humility like kneeling not only give expression to a believer's devotion, but also 'incite our affections to submit to God'.[50] In 1659, French philosopher Blaise Pascal touched on this point again, writing that internal and external thoughts and feelings had to coincide if one wanted to be close to God. For him, hoping for God's help by making external gestures without true belief was an act of superstition, while inner devotion without external expression was a sign of arrogance. Such arrogance, as he saw it, was predominantly shown by members of the aristocracy, who were too proud to kneel.[51]

Genuflection as a form of *deditio* was consecrated in medieval and early modern ritual and was not limited to the religious sphere. When Charles V defeated the alliance of Protestant princes in 1547, the first demand made in the capitulation treaty was that the defeated apologize on their knees. And so, the princes kneeled for half an hour before the emperor, begging him for forgiveness. This act was particularly problematic for Protestants, as the turn away from the Catholic Church and the pope had compelled Protestant rulers to seek to separate religious and secular power. The genuflection, however, obscured the lines. Followers of Calvin rejected it without compromise so long as it was not performed before God alone, while Lutherans proved more flexible. But they, too, refused to kneel before the pope.[52]

In Protestant churches, genuflection as a form of religious reverence eventually was discarded. Protestants began kneeling only on special occasions, and even then, it was out of 'habit', not because of an official imperative.[53] In the 1830s and 1840s, things came to a head in Bavaria. Until 1803, soldiers there had to kneel before the altar when they went to church; afterwards, they could get away with clutching their hat and bowing their head. In 1838, the king commanded his men to kneel during the Eucharist, which provoked an outcry from the Protestant high consistory, who objected that soldiers of his confession would do no such thing. Protestant representatives in the Bavarian parliament complained too. Finally, in 1845, Ludwig I, who wanted to establish parity between the confessions in his kingdom, reinstituted the earlier custom, so that neither Catholic nor Protestant soldiers were required to kneel.[54]

Genuflection also fell out of favour as a demonstration of respect before persons of high rank or age. The custom of actually touching one's knee to the ground was supplanted by the custom of simply bending the knee. In the course of the nineteenth century, even this custom came to be—at least for men—substituted by a modest bow.[55] A German etiquette manual published in 1800 stated: 'The greater and nobler the person to whom you are supposed to show reverence, the lower you should bow your head and back; but not so low that your backside should form a parallel line with your head.' Later etiquette guides would admonish their readers never to bow 'too deeply or slavishly', and 'also, one should not remain in the bowed position for too long'. In the 1870s, bowing itself became taboo, with one guide stating that 'the body must remain straight' and the bow consist 'only in a deep nodding of the head'. Only when showing veneration to 'high-positioned persons' should one slightly bow one's torso, another guide declared, quickly following up with the reminder that one must 'immediately reassume a straight posture with head held up'. The dominant opinion at the turn of the twentieth century was that a bowed back and bent knees were undignified for a true man and that the gesture cut a 'ridiculous figure'.[56]

In contrast, women had to continue performing the old genuflection and bowed their entire torso forward. As early as 1775, Justus Möser, a German jurist and administrator, mocked this 'ridiculous imitation of the French bow'. Instead, he praised the noble 'pride of a woman who stands up straight and greets her guest with a friendly glance'.[57] Nevertheless, the custom of bowing ultimately became the dominant one. Practised by women throughout their lives, it was by no means restricted to the upper classes. Women and girls curtsied everywhere they met someone of standing, whether noble or bourgeois, and maids in urban households curtsied before guests and their employers.[58]

These different bodily postures reflected the cultural differences between men and women. In the nineteenth century in particular, great weight was placed on putting such differences on display and internalizing them in all spheres of life, all the way down to gestures. An upright posture was seen as distinguishing men from women, slaves, and animals, and was supposed to denote freedom, autonomy, and independence. It was also seen as marking the difference between Europeans and non-Europeans. In 1868, the Swiss-born law professor Johann Caspar Bluntschli exhorted that 'free men' from 'civilized states' do not bend their knees, because their 'dignity' was irreconcilable with the 'unreasonable demands' they encountered in 'despotic, especially Oriental courts'. Bluntschli would probably have considered the British custom of genuflecting until one's knee touched the ground an 'undignified demand'. In continental courts, ambassadors only had to bow three times, which seemed to be, in the academic's opinion, more befitting of the dignity of free men and the 'dignity of the represented states'.[59]

The British in India: Colonial Humiliation and 'Native' Etiquette

In 1615, Sir Thomas Roe bowed three times in the court of the Mughal emperor Jahangir in Agra. Roe had travelled to India on the orders of James I to lobby for the East India Company. Although it was custom for supplicants to get on their knees when approaching the emperor, Roe requested that he be allowed to follow British conventions, which was 'freely granted'. Thus, as he later wrote in his journal, he bowed once after entering the outermost circle, again after entering the inner circle, and a last time directly before the emperor, giving him a letter from the British king and gifts that were 'well-received'.[60] In 1795, Colonel Michael Symes did something similar when the British governor-general of Bengal sent him from Calcutta to Burma. Even though kowtowing was customary in the court of the Burmese king, Symes was allowed to skip it after asking.[61]

In contrast, the majority of residents who represented the interests of the East India Company in the courts of Indian princes more or less conformed to local and regional customs. Some adopted local clothing and lifestyles, while a few even converted. For its part, the company hired experts on India to advise its members on matters of protocol and diplomacy.

Beginning in the 1820s, however, the tone shifted. Indian princes, and the Mughal emperor himself, sent more and more complaints to the governor-general about disrespectful behaviour. In one incident, a resident had delivered the obligatory gifts (*nazr*) with only one hand. When asked about it, the resident claimed that he found the ceremony 'humiliating' and had thus paid it little mind. Governor-General William Bentinck reprimanded him for his insubordination in 1830, admonishing him that he best adhere to the 'established etiquette to which all natives of Rank attach so much importance'.[62]

Yet Bentinck's predecessor William Amherst had had problems with the *nazr* too. Viewing it as a form of tribute, he refused to give the customary gifts to the emperor on a visit in 1827, which did not go down well. The emperor protested that Amherst had robbed him 'even of the cheap gratification of the usual ceremonials of address, so as to humble me, as far as possible, in the eyes of all ranks of people'.[63] For his part, Amherst wanted to avoid any appearance of being subordinate to the Indian ruler. The payments that the East India Company was contractually obligated to give the emperor were thus reinterpreted as a salary or pension and from then on dispensed without formal ceremony.[64]

While the British saw this as a way to assert their power and independence, the Indian monarch viewed it as a flagrant act of humiliation. According to Major-General John Malcolm, who worked for the company and advised Governor-General Francis Rawdon-Hastings, such issues were a double-edged sword. Speaking to his assistants and officers in 1821, Malcolm stated that, on the one hand, it was important for them to remain Europeans and not submit to local customs, because otherwise 'every impression of our superiority' would disappear. On the other, they should avoid all possibly demeaning actions, as it was 'sufficiently galling' for the Indians to 'have foreign masters'. If those masters went pronouncing their 'superiority' too openly, it would be seen as an intentional act of humiliation. Therefore, he concluded that the British should treat Indians with 'kindness' and pay respect to 'their customs and usages'. The more powerful Europeans (Malcolm used 'British' and 'European' as synonyms) became, the 'more relaxed' they could be about ceremonial matters. If the Indian princes sought to cover up their real loss of power by placing more weight on 'the forms of station', it would be politically irresponsible to 'deny it gratification'.[65]

Malcolm's advice was, however, not entirely heeded. Either the British colonials stuck to their own etiquette and forced Indian rulers to comply, or they let the Indians practise their 'native' reverences without returning them in kind. Again and again, the British administration had to command officials to treat the 'sensitive' Indians with respect and politeness.[66] After 1858, when the British Crown formally annexed India into the British Empire, the imperial attitude of superiority became omnipresent. Indeed, the British adopted the Indian Durbar, where rulers traditionally held audiences. Lord Charles Canning, the first viceroy of India, used such occasions to honour princes and others who had remained loyal during the 1857 rebellion, thus tightening their ties to the new state. Still, the Indian participants of the 1877 Imperial Durbar were mere background actors at an event that celebrated the empire itself. The ceremony was centred on the queen's proclamation as the empress of India, with Victoria not even present.[67]

This changed in 1911, when King George V and Queen Mary attended the Delhi Durbar. In contrast to 1877, Indian princes now played a more active role. Nevertheless, Viceroy Charles Hardinge was the first to be allowed to show the king reverence by bowing three times and then kneeling to kiss his hand. After him came a group of Indian rulers led by the Nizam of Hyderabad, who, following Muslim custom, bowed and placed his right hand over his heart. Others greeted with a 'salaam' or gave a military salute. The maharaja of Baroda was the only one who fell out of line. Wearing simple and 'inappropriate' clothing, he bowed once when he approached George V, did not look at the queen, and then turned his back to the couple as he walked away swinging his cane (usually carried by the white sahibs and used to thrash their Indian subjects). While official reports took no notice of the incident, rumours abounded. When the viceroy heard that Baroda was a 'hot-bed' of resistance against British rule, he demanded that the maharaja send a written apology, which came quickly and did not spare on professions of loyalty. Hardinge had the letter published in The Times, with the paper adding that the maharaja should let this 'humiliation' serve 'as an effective warning'.[68]

Europeans in China: Fighting against the Kowtow

Demanding an apology had ultimately become one of the key instruments of imperialist politics of humiliation as they played out during the second half of the nineteenth century. The formalities of greetings and paying respect were also easily exploited to this end, a fact that the British were well aware of when expanding their informal and formal power in India. At the Delhi Durbar of 1911, they demonstrated that they were willing to accept Indian conventions, so long as this acceptance could be interpreted as a recognition of British superiority. They never forced local persons of power to adopt English practices of reverence.[69] But they did succeed early on in being exempted from having to participate in 'native' ceremonies.

They tried this in China, too, though with less success. In the eighteenth century, the East India Company began expanding to the Far East, using diplomatic means to further their interests. The Chinese, however, were less ready to cooperate and compromise than were the various Indian princes and the Moghul emperor, whose power was slipping away by the day. Both Macartney and his successor Amherst had ultimately failed in their missions to establish permanent trade relations with China, missions during which the issue of kowtowing had played an important role.[70] After the 1830s, the company began preferring military options in pursuing its commercial interests, and the two Opium Wars weakened China to the point where its status was degraded to that of an informal colony of Western powers.

In the Treaties of Tianjin, signed in 1858, Great Britain, France, Russia, and the United States forced China to allow them to open permanent embassies in Beijing, and two years later, after further fighting and massive destruction, China formally acknowledged their right to do so. The British representative, Lord Elgin, who would become Indian viceroy in 1862, placed particular weight on symbolic gestures. Article 3 of the Sino-British treaty dictated that all diplomatic ceremonies seen as 'derogatory' for British ambassadors be dispensed with. In return, it promised that the British would show the same ceremonial respect towards the Chinese emperor as they did towards the sovereigns of independent European nations.[71]

While the treaties with France, Russia, and the United States merely stated that both sides' diplomats 'shall at all times have the right to correspond on terms of perfect equality', the treaty with Great Britain finally brought the long struggles over the kowtow to an end. Elgin succeeded in getting rid of an obligation that had irritated Macartney and Amherst and clearly offended British sensibilities. The British now turned the tables and, under the auspices of equality, forced Chinese dignitaries to adhere to the European ceremonial regime, both in China and in Europe.

The Chinese court was highly sensitive to this imperial gesture of the 'barbarians', who, according to the treaties, were no longer to be called such. Even though the Beijing government had to open its ports and allow missionaries to enter, it continued to resist the symbolic defeats. Beginning in 1861, European countries could theoretically set up embassies in the capital, but the emperor found all kinds of reasons not to receive and acknowledge the ambassadors.

At the same time, doubts were growing as to whether this policy of passive resistance actually benefited China. Gradually, the new Zongli Yamen, the Ministry of Foreign Affairs that had been established in 1861, started developing an interest in questions of international law. In 1863, American minister Anson Burlingame had his interpreter William Martin translate Henry Wheaton's *Elements of International Law* into Chinese, which was authorized by the imperial court a year later.[72] In 1865, Robert Hart, a high-ranking British officer in the Chinese Maritime Customs authority, urged the government to play a more active role in international diplomacy by receiving and dis- patching ambassadors, learning foreign languages, and becoming versed in international law. The Zongli Yamen then asked the opinion of leading provincial officials, and a majority voted for modifying court ceremonies and finding a compromise acceptable for all sides. They concluded that it was neither feasible nor desirable to treat the Europeans in the same way as envoys from tributary states like Annam (later Vietnam) and Burma. The Zongli Yamen accepted the vote and passed it on to the emperor.[73]

Receiving Western ambassadors and changing ceremonial conven- tions seemed all the more pressing because the Treaty of Tianjin was about to be revised. The hope was that diplomatic concessions would help China secure better conditions for itself. Intellectuals also pleaded for opening the country to outside knowledge, skills, and technology. In 1863, the Confucian reformer Feng Guifen suggested establishing a school for Western languages and science in Shanghai, arguing that learning about and from the foreign conquerors was imperative. He claimed that only then would China be able to recapture its original power, renew and strengthen itself, and leave behind 'former humiliations' that had been done to it by the 'barbarians'.[74]

For European ambassadors who had been waiting to be received by the emperor since 1861, the breakthrough came in 1873. On 29 June, the representatives of Great Britain, Russia, France, the Netherlands, and the United States were given an imperial audience; Thomas Wade took detailed notes on the event for the British foreign secretary. Standing before the emperor, the five men briefly bowed three times and placed their letters of credence on a long table. Then they stepped back in the customary fashion, 'à reculons', bowing three times again. Wade used emphatic words when describing this rather prosaic scene, claiming that never before had the Chinese Empire so 'broken with the tradition' (which was not true). The significance of such change should by no means be 'undervalued', because 'an important beginning has been made': 'We appeared face to face with the Emperor, standing, because we represented Governments the equal of his own.' Finally, he said, China had given up its claims to being 'greater and better' than all other states.[75]

Still, the Europeans had much to complain about, since, as Wade mentioned, the reception was not exactly in line with Western standards and usages. After long negotiations, they came to an agreement with the Zongli Yamen about the ceremonial rules to be observed during audiences. The American minister Charles Denby praised the agreement as 'the recognition of the international equality of each and every nation with China, which is the chief moral element of an audience'. For Denby's German colleague Max von Brandt, the significance lay in the fact that what 'was offered by the Chinese as an act of grace and courtesy came to be seen and ultimately established in the run of the negotiations as a right of the foreign representatives'. In front of the 'hundreds of witnesses' who were present at the 1891 imperial audience, this right had been demonstrated, and there could be no further doubt 'that the position taken by the foreign dignitaries vis-à-vis the emperor was wholly different from the position that he demanded and received from the Chinese and other Asians'.[76]

Von Brandt was talking about the ambassadors' gestures—bowing three times twice remained the norm—and the spatial arrangements. In 1873, European ambassadors had been received in a hall of the outer palace. Two decades later, they were allowed to enter the inner palace, which, as the German sinologist and translator Otto Franke knew, had hitherto been 'anxiously guarded' and closed to foreigners. Franke noted 'with satisfaction' that the Chinese court had thus finally arrived at solving the longstanding ceremonial issues by giving the Western-ers what they had been fighting for during the last hundred years.[77]

By speaking of satisfaction, Franke was using a concept from the vocabulary of honour: he who maligned another man's honour must give him satisfaction. Franke, who was sympathetic to China, believed that this was precisely what the Europeans had achieved after a full century of having their honour besmirched. The symbol par excel-lence of the degradation they believed to have suffered was the kowtow. After 1873, when it was formally struck from Chinese–European diplomatic protocol, Europeans and Americans stood upright before the emperor's throne, in contrast to the Chinese and envoys from tributary countries.

There was one Asian country that also joined the anti-kowtow alliance to Beijing's profound irritation: Japan. For centuries, China had exerted considerable political and cultural influence on the island nation, and the shogunate had adopted Chinese conceptions of a hierarchical world order and the respective court etiquette. In 1691, at an audience in Edo (later Tokyo), the representative of the Dutch East India Company had to approach the throne 'on his hands and knees'. Having reached the shogun, he 'bow'd his forehead quite down to the ground, and so he crawl'd backwards like a crab, without uttering a single word'.[78]

The Meiji Restoration of the 1860s and 1870s transformed many aspects of Japanese politics, including diplomatic customs. The open-ing of the country to foreign diplomats and trade led the Japanese to embrace international law and receive ambassadors according to European conventions. When foreign secretary Taneomi Soejima visited Beijing in 1873, he therefore insisted on being treated like a Western diplomat and refused to kowtow. His Chinese hosts were astonished, reminding him of the two nations' shared cultural heritage and asking why the Japanese were not resisting Western customs. Soejima admitted that some older court officials had committed suicide and that others had attacked European diplomats on their way to the palace. While the Chinese might consider these men 'true patriots', he saw things differently: although courage and loyalty were good, it would have been better for them and their country if they had shown intelligence and good judgement too. Simply avoiding the changes, he believed, demonstrated the men's lack of insight into what was strategically necessary and sustainable for relations with other countries. And so, he concluded, this was why he was insisting on being received by the Chinese emperor according to international protocol: namely, by bowing three times.[79]

But Japan did more than put itself above Chinese court customs. It also challenged Chinese dominance in Korea, a country that had traditionally paid tributes to China. By defeating the powerful Chinese fleet in 1895, Japan was able to bring Korea into its sphere of influence. Capping off a half-century of gradual losses of power, China had now given up its status as the premier regional power to Japan. This was particularly disturbing for Chinese elites. Being humiliated by a country that had for centuries stood in the shadow of their own and was now successfully buddying up with the imperial Western powers was found much worse than the humiliations brought on by those powers themselves.[80]

Another newcomer to the scene was the German Empire, which had been making its presence known in China since the 1870s.[81] When Edmund von Heyking assumed the ambassadorship in 1896, the tone in Sino-German relations shifted dramatically. Heyking's confident, eloquent wife Elisabeth made liberal use of insulting expressions about the 'filthy barbarians who do not need European ambassadors, but rather European masters—the sooner the better!' In her letters, she proclaimed that it was high time Germans take their place 'at the grand Chinese trough, where the best seats have already been occupied by the Russians and the French'.[82] Her wish was fulfilled in 1898, when the German Empire forced the Chinese to concede Kiautschou (Jiaozhou) Bay.

Satisfaction and Regrets

The Kiautschou Bay concession was preceded by a series of Chinese riots that gave Germany a welcome excuse for taking military action after first fomenting conflict by diplomatic means. When officers of the German battleship *Cormoran* were assaulted 'with stones and filth by the screaming mob' in October 1897, ambassador Heyking reported the event to the local governor and made intentions to 'demand satisfaction'. Shortly after, he received news that a German Catholic mission in Shandong had been attacked and two priests had been murdered. He decided to resolve the matter with the battleship quickly, urging the Chinese authorities to send a 'letter of apology', perform a twenty-one-gun salute to the German flag, and punish the perpetrators. He got what he wanted, and so Germany had obtained 'satisfaction'.[83]

Heyking then turned his energies to the attack on the mission, making similar, but much more severe claims. He wanted all ministers of the Zongli Yamen to come to the German embassy and personally apologize for the attack. Wilhelm II, however, instructed his ambassador to put off these 'demands for expiation' for a while. Instead, the Kaiser performed a 'manly act' and gave orders to occupy Kiautschou Bay. Chinese officials protested and called on Germany to leave the area immediately. Prince Qing told the German ambassador that the situation was highly 'humiliating' and that Germany had 'raped China in a way that it would not dare against any other country'.[84]

Under international law, the military intervention was wholly unjustifiable. Seeking reparations and 'satisfaction' after attacks on diplomatic posts and persons, in contrast, was not, and there were many precedents. In 1870, rioters in Tianjin destroyed the French consulate, a cathedral, and a Catholic orphanage, killing multiple Europeans and Chinese who had converted to Christianity. In response, Western representatives wrote a collective note to the Zongli Yamen demanding that it punish the perpetrators and take effective steps to ensure the security of foreigners. Of the various offences, the French legation considered the pulling down and destruction of the French flag as the most serious. This insulted them more than the assault of French diplomats and the murder of French citizens. In order to avoid military retaliation, the Chinese were called upon to dispatch a high-ranking dignitary to Paris with a formal letter of apology.

As in 1708, when Queen Anne had her special envoy in Moscow personally apologize for the attack on the Russian ambassador to London, the Chinese emperor sent Wanyan Chonghou to Paris. At first, he was not received because the French minister in Beijing was still waiting in vain for an audience at the Chinese court. When he was finally able to hand the emperor's letter to the French president Adolphe Thiers, the latter could not but realize that it contained neither an apology nor an expression of regret. The emperor merely assured the French head of state that his government was not responsible for the events in Tianjin and that he was still interested in maintaining peaceful, friendly relations with France. Nevertheless, Thiers expressed his 'satisfaction' and his hope that the Chinese would treat French consuls and foreign missionaries more respectfully in the future.[85]

In 1875, British interpreter Augustus Raymond Margary was murdered in the border region between China and Burma. Ambassador Wade used the so-called Margary Affair to settle scores with the Chinese government, attributing the violent act to the 'hostility of the official or the lettered class, who have not learned, or will not understand, that the government of the foreigner is the equal of his own'. He wanted a clear signal from Beijing that international officials were to be treated not as enemy aliens, but as guests of the emperor. Moreover, he demanded that an emissary be sent to London to express the government's regret. The ministers of the Zongli Yamen approved dispatching a diplomat, but they initially resisted sending a letter of apology along with him.[86]

But when Guo Songtao left to become the first Chinese ambassador to London in 1877, he had the letter in his bag. Addressing the queen, the emperor stated that the Chinese 'profoundly regret and lament' the event. He explained that he had appointed Guo 'to proceed to your Majesty's country to give utterance, on our behalf, to the sentiments we have at heart'.[87] It is doubtful that the sentiments were genuine, however. In 1878, the empress dowager told Guo's successor Tseng Chi-Tse about her concern that the constant riots against foreign churches and buildings in China might stoke trouble. Tseng agreed, and explicitly referred to the Margary incident that had caused the court 'work and worry day and night'. Although he found it perfectly natural that the Chinese people and its ministers 'hated' foreigners, he argued that 'we must plan gradually to make ourselves strong before anything can be done. The destruction of one church or the killing of one foreigner by no means avenges our grievances or wipes out our humiliation. At present many Chinese do not understand this principle.'[88]

Recorded by Tseng in his diary, this conversation with the empress dowager reflects the severity of the feelings of humiliation experienced by the Chinese, as does their reaction to the occupation of Kiautschou twenty years later. These feelings were present in the internal communications of high-ranking government officials just as much as they were in the writings of many intellectuals and reform groups. Changing the situation, in their view, required systematic self-strengthening instead of individual acts of violence.

When Chinese dignitaries complained about such humiliation to foreign representatives, their arguments fell on deaf ears. Instead, they were referred to the rules of international law, which dictated that states pay reparations for material damages and grant satisfaction for moral and political insults. This was indeed the case. Still, states were free to decide what they were willing to accept as satisfaction. They could choose between harsher and more lenient measures, spanning from a military salute of the flag and oral or written apologies all the way to extravagant acts of atonement in which ambassadors had to hand-deliver official regrets and laments to the head of the maligned state.[89] The fact that China was often forced to perform the most severe—and on the international stage most seldom seen—acts is indicative of the intentional politics of humiliation pursued by Europe in the Middle Kingdom.

During the nineteenth century, those states that made demands for satisfaction generally had more military, economic, and political power than their other. In 1856, the British took advantage of an incident that they considered humiliating to request a written apology from the local authorities in Canton. When the Chinese refused, a British squadron assailed the city and set off the Second Opium War. At home, this was sold as a 'vindication of the national honour' and, despite parliamentary criticism, met with the approval of the electorate.[90] In 1863, Edward Neale, Britain's deputy chargé d'affaires in Japan, demanded that the shogunate apologize for the murder of a British businessman by a samurai. Neale rejected the government's mere expression of regret as insufficient and insisted that the Japanese take full and unilateral responsibility. Eventually, they consented in order to prevent things from escalating, apologizing and paying out a huge sum of money. But Neale was not finished yet. He also wanted the province in which the murder took place to apologize and offer material reparations, in addition to punishing the perpetrator. The daimyō refused, arguing that the businessman had behaved disrespectfully and had deserved to die. In response, Neale had the Royal Navy attack the city of Kagoshima.[91]

Twenty years later and strengthened by the Meiji Restoration, Japan forced Korea to send an envoy to Tokyo to apologize for an attack on the Japanese embassy and the murder of a military adviser.[92] In 1886, Japan demanded an apology from China after Chinese sailors stationed in Nagasaki ran wild through the streets, harassing women and killing policemen who intervened. But since China still felt militarily superior, it refused.[93]

In short, apologies were not a matter of course in international relations. They had to be squeezed out of governments and were often offered only after threats of serious sanctions. For those who finally gave them, they were humiliating, a clear sign of powerlessness.[94] It was precisely for this reason that the choice of words turned out to be a very sensitive issue, a point well illustrated by Ambassador Wade's insistence in 1876 that the Chinese envoy sent to London was on a 'mission of apology' in order to give the British government 'satisfaction'.[95]

In this sense, international relations were repeating, albeit on a larger scale, a practice not uncommon in social relations. In 1811, the Prussian king had abolished the legal instrument of 'private satisfaction', which dictated public apologies for doing injury to another's honour. Officially asking for forgiveness, so the king and his councillors argued, was seen as 'insulting' and 'humiliating'.[96] In Great Britain, too, men had a tough time apologizing, even when they knew they had done something wrong, as the example of Robert Louis Stevenson discussed in Chapter 2 illustrates. In Germany, France, Italy, and Russia, men of honour preferred to duel with sword or pistol rather than apologize for insults.

Thus, European diplomats knew exactly what they were doing when they forced 'missions of apology' upon the Chinese. In their own eyes, they were only taking revenge for humiliation they themselves had suffered, and the British and Germans were particularly thin-skinned in this respect. When Guo Sungtao arrived in London in 1877, *The Times* published a curt editorial stating that the Zongli Yamen had hopefully learned its lesson and would in the future stop treating European representatives like 'humble petitioners of contemptible foreign States'.[97] Ambassador Heyking, too, never missed an opportunity to complain about alleged humiliations. When the diplomatic corps was received by the Chinese emperor in February 1897, the

German envoy made the mistake of trying to leave the audience hall through the central entrance, upon which a minister grabbed him by the arm and pointed the way to the side-door. Heyking found this insulting and demanded an apology. The Zongli Yamen, however, told him that he had gone the wrong way, and his American colleague Denby, who was tasked with mediating, agreed. Elisabeth von Heyking was seething: 'Old Denby is unfortunately half Sinicized and belongs to a school for which we moderns have no sympathy. He comes from a time when the ambassadors here had to laboriously work just to be received and proudly rested on these laurels.' In contrast, the 'moderns' she was speaking of came from a 'time more focussed on reality, and they do not allow themselves to be impressed upon by the Chinese. It was very curious how old Denby constantly came back to old protocols and actually served as the advocate of the Chinese.'[98]

Three years earlier, Otto Franke had described the current protocol as 'entirely sensible' and, discussing the multiple doors leading to the reception room, wrote: 'So long as the ambassador was the bearer of a letter from his sovereign, he was allowed to pass through the most distinguished entrance, that is, the middle stairway with carpet and the middle door, which was otherwise only used by the emperor; in contrast, he exited through the left side-door.'[99] Heyking, however, refused to admit the faux pas and insisted that the Chinese apologize. In the end, he got his way: the minister who had grabbed him by the arm came to the embassy and formally asked for forgiveness. Although the Chinese went to considerable lengths in accommodating foreign demands and sensibilities, European observers continuously took offence at how rudely their representatives were treated at the Beijing court.[100]

The Berlin Kowtow Affair of 1901: Who Humiliates Whom?

The year 1901 put an end to all of that. After the Boxer Rebellion had broken out, the eight allied powers reacted with uncompromising military and political might. The Chinese government had to meet a series of draconian conditions: alongside harsh punishment for the attackers and their supporters, the allies demanded immense financial reparations—and the explicit abolition of the kowtow for diplomats. In reality, this had been a non-issue since 1873. But the Europeans, Americans, and Japanese used the situation to emphasize once again the principle of 'perfect equality' between sovereign states, 'without any loss of prestige on one side or the other'.[101]

They were also unanimous about the first item on the list of conditions. It obligated the Chinese to apologize for the murders of the German ambassador Clemens von Ketteler and the chancellor of the Japanese delegation, Akira Sugiyama, who had both been killed during the rebellion.[102] Speaking for the Germans, Secretary of State for Foreign Affairs Bernhard von Bülow had immediately made it clear that such an act of 'expiation' was a 'question of satisfaction' and 'a matter of national honour'.[103]

Not long thereafter, Kaiser Wilhelm II received a telegram from the Chinese emperor, who 'most deeply lamented and regretted' Ketteler's murder and stated that a drink offering would be made in his name. The emperor also sent the Japanese Tenno his regrets, arranged for religious ceremonies to be held for Sugiyama, and appealed to the long tradition of good relations and mutual respect between the two neighbouring countries. While the Tenno accepted the regrets 'with satisfaction' and advised the emperor to appoint a new government, Wilhelm II was more guarded. He replied that he could not view the drink offering as 'expiation' for the 'misdeed' and made further demands.[104]

Having to 'expiate' was new and strange language for diplomats, as up to then, satisfaction and apology had been the dominant notions prescribed by international law. These practices had originated in the social discourse of aristocratic honour, while 'expiation' belonged to the domain of theology. Its Lutheran interpretation spoke of a 'redress for guilt caused by transgression of a law'. This demanded that the 'sinner' feel regret and 'suffer punishment that fits the transgression'. The concept gradually drifted from its religious home into the world

Fig. 18. Caricature of Wilhelm II demanding expiation in *Punch*, 10 October 1900

of law. In civil trials, and divorce and libel trials in particular, 'expiation' was often made a condition of the amicable resolution of legal disputes.[105]

'Expiation' had considerably greater moral overtones than 'apology', and the frequency of the word's use in diplomatic documents since the late nineteenth century attested to its special emotional potency. The Chinese emissary who was sent to Berlin in 1901 to deliver the emperor's formal apology was quickly fashioned as the 'expiation-prince'; six years later, a popular German encyclopaedia memorialized him as such. In 1902, another encyclopaedia listed 'kowtow' in its table of contents for the first time, a notion that until then was unfamiliar to most Germans.[106]

But how and why did the kowtow find its way into a German lexicon? Kaiser Wilhelm II was to blame. In the summer of 1901, he started a chain of events that riled diplomats, journalists, and ordinary citizens and that made the kowtow, defined as a 'ceremony of the deepest subjugation', into a popular conversational topic. After Wilhelm's tight-lipped response to the Chinese emperor's early telegram, the diplomatic corps in Beijing had urged the Chinese government to dispatch an 'extraordinary mission' to Berlin, led by an imperial prince and expressing the emperor's sincere regrets about Ketteler's murder. So in July 1901, Prince Chun boarded a German ship to do just that. Even before his arrival Wilhelm II tried everything in his power to make sure that the prince's visit would be as uncomfortable as possible. He knew that he was acting in line with public opinion, which, according to the twice-daily *Berliner Lokal-Anzeiger*, was waiting for the 'essential satisfaction'.[107]

Exactly who gave the Kaiser the precise idea of what such satisfaction should consist of is unknown.[108] As a matter of fact, Senior Master of Ceremonies and Lord Marshal August zu Eulenburg told the Foreign Office on 8 July that the prince and his delegation were to be received at the Berlin Palace on 27 August. Foreign Secretary Oswald von Richthofen then asked Professor of Sinology Carl Arendt about 'questions of etiquette' and how one might communicate to the Chinese government that the prince was being received 'not as a guest of high honour, but as a supplicant'. Arendt, who had worked for twenty years as an interpreter at the Prussian-German Embassy in Beijing, replied that, because 'there is no true Chinese ceremony for cases like this', the Germans should just stick to European customs, with which the Chinese were, by then, quite familiar. At the same time, he recommended slight variations in protocol that would convey the message and avoid everything 'that might look like a celebratory reception of the prince'.[109]

Just to be certain, Richthofen also asked the current ambassador to Beijing for his opinion. Mumm von Schwarzenstein basically confirmed Arendt's advice and explicitly warned against adopting 'Oriental ceremonies'.[110] Richthofen passed this along to Eulenburg and suggested that he plan every minute detail, such as 'the number of steps that the envoy must make when approaching His Majesty, and the distance from His Majesty that he must maintain, the type and number of bows, the issue of headcoverings, etc.' On 6 August, Eulenburg broke the news to the Foreign Office: 'His Majesty the Kaiser and King insists that the entire delegation of the prince only approach the throne on their knees during the audience, as is custom towards their own emperor; the entrance of the prince himself need only be accompanied by the customary three bows in intervals, beyond which further determinations may be made.'[111]

When Eulenburg informed the Chinese ambassador Liu Hai-kwan about the ceremony, the latter immediately contacted his superiors back in Beijing. He returned to the German Foreign Office multiple times pleading that the kowtow be dispensed with, asking that, if nothing else, at least the prince's interpreter, Lieutenant General Yin Chang, be left out of it. After all, he argued, Wilhelm II had made Yin Chang a member of a high order of merit in 1898, and he was, moreover, the designated future Chinese ambassador to Berlin. Forcing him to get on his knees would profoundly embarrass him in front of the other members of the diplomatic corps. Meanwhile, in Beijing, Prince Qing and Li Hongzhang considered the Kaiser's demand 'in every sense a gesture of humiliation. This is a matter of national dignity.' They asked Mumm to contact his government, 'because this ceremony has never been customary when Chinese ambassadors are received in Europe, does not fit with European culture and civilized manners, and in China itself, where reforms are currently being undertaken, they are thinking of getting rid of the kowtow as something no longer in step with the times'. But Wilhelm II would hear none of it. He repeatedly gave orders that the whole delegation had to kneel: 'There is no reason to make an exception for future ambassador Yin Chang. On the contrary, it will be very useful if it is made clear to him from the beginning that one cannot insult the German Kaiser without being punished.'[112]

In the meantime, Liu Hai-kwan had travelled to Genoa to meet Prince Chun after his long journey and to brief him about the diplomatic calamity.[113] The prince also viewed it as an attack on the 'honour of the nation' because, as he noted in his diary, *guikou*, or 'kneeling and kowtowing', was not customary in international relations.[114] The ministers of the Zongli Yamen instructed him by telegram not to perform the kowtow and not to continue on to Germany before the conditions of the audience had been cleared up. On 25 August, a telegram from Basel arrived at the Foreign Office: 'Prince Chun ill, travel delayed indefinitely.' On the same day, Chinese chargé d'affaires Kinginthai visited Richthofen in Berlin and confided that 'he was convinced that the sudden illness would be cured if we allow the prince's delegation not to perform the kowtow and satisfy ourselves with Tschingan, that is, kneeling on one knee, the right'.[115]

Richthofen passed this on to Wilhelm II, who immediately made it known that he 'would not budge a finger from what He has decreed. It is a mission of expiation and this must under all circumstances be maintained.' Although many, including the chancellor, tried to persuade him otherwise, he remained adamant: 'I don't care what happens, I'll send fighter squadrons to China again.' Since, as he confidentially admitted, 'the King of England and Lascelles (the British ambassador in Berlin) knew that he had demanded the kowtow, he could not disavow himself in front of them.'[116]

That was the crux of the matter: the Kaiser did not want to lose face in front of Great Britain by retracting his demands. But the Foreign Office feared that it was precisely the Kaiser's intransigence that would embarrass Germany in front of the whole world. On 23 August, *éminence grise* Friedrich von Holstein wrote with great foresight in a letter to the chancellor about how he thought things would play out: neither the Chinese government nor Prince Chun would be

> lacking in good advice. One can surmise that they will be told that Germany has placed itself in the wrong with its exaggerated demand and will thus, in the case that China refuses it, not be able to do anything, because all other powers that have asked China to undertake a mission of expiation have disapproved of Germany's behaviour.

Holstein concluded that it was 'indeed' the case that there was not much the Germans could do: 'The land and sea forces still there are insufficient to intimidate the Chinese, and one can certainly assume that our good friends have felt it their duty to inform the Chinese government of this and of our isolation concerning the kowtow question.'[117]

But the Kaiser did not care and stuck to his guns. Meanwhile, the Beijing diplomatic corps wondered why the audience in Berlin kept being delayed. US ambassador William Rockhill was well informed on the matter, and Mumm asked him about the kowtow and the Macartney mission (Rockhill had published an article on it in 1897).[118] The topic was discussed at every diplomatic dinner, and every bit of information heightened the suspense. It was known that Li Hongzhang—who since the 1870s had been the most powerful man in Chinese foreign policy—had urged Prince Chun not to give in. Finally, on 4 September, the news came that the Kaiser had folded: 'The Chinese are jubilant.'[119]

Indeed, the Kaiser had backed down. What finally convinced him was not Richthofen's (correct) argument that foreign powers 'like Russia, maybe also Japan, view the kowtow as too demeaning for China and thus our insistence upon it is politically disadvantageous'. Nor was it his own people, who were tired of China and would hardly be willing to accept the refusal to kowtow as a good reason for another military intervention. The argument that Wilhelm II was finally able to yield to was, to everyone's surprise, religion.[120]

During a conversation with the German consul in Basel, Prince Chun's interpreter Yin Chang mentioned that the kowtow had a 'religious tinge'. When Richthofen heard this, alarm bells went off in his head. He commissioned a report and explained to the Kaiser that a ceremony with a decidedly 'religious character' could not be demanded by foreign leaders. From a Christian perspective, it would be sheer 'blasphemy' if the Chinese were to kneel before the German Kaiser, and it would also gravely violate 'religious feelings in Germany'. The argument had no basis in fact, but it did the trick, and Wilhelm changed his mind. After talking to the chancellor, who had interrupted his vacation to rush back to Berlin, Wilhelm II 'graciously' declared on 1 September that the issue had been resolved. He stated that the usual three bows would be sufficient and that only the prince and Yin Chang would have to attend the audience while the rest of the delegation waited in the anteroom. On 2 September, the Foreign Office informed the German consul in Basel and the Chinese chargé d'affaires in Berlin, and Prince Chun's illness abruptly ended. Two days later, the audience took place at the New Palace in Potsdam with a slight change of protocol: the Kaiser only gave the prince the 'planned honours of escorting and guards' after he had received him and the 'expiation' had been completed.[121]

And thus was drawn to a close the conflict that had held international diplomats on the edge of their seats for a whole month. A situation that Wilhelm II had created intentionally to humiliate the Chinese had turned into a drama in which Germany's international reputation was at stake. The Kaiser was willing to take considerable military risks and put aside political prudence in order to avoid losing face. The chancellor and Foreign Office were only able to bring him from this (self-)destructive course of action with great effort; whether or not he actually believed the religion argument is another matter. At any rate, it gave him the chance to retract his demands in an honourable manner, which, as Richthofen assured, would be crowned by 'a complete, impressive success for Germany, both domestically and internationally'.[122]

The foreign secretary, however, was wrong. The affair was perceived as honourable neither in Germany nor abroad, where all major newspapers had constantly reported on it.[123] With the exception of the socialist press, the initial conviction that China had deserved to be 'humiliated' was widely shared. The London *Times* thought it wholly correct that the Chinese government 'taste the humiliation they have brought upon themselves'.[124] The conservative Catholic *Bayerische Curier* viewed the 'humiliation' of the 'expiation-prince' as 'satisfaction for insulted German national sentiment'.

Berlin's *Lokal-Anzeiger* applauded the 'moral humiliation' of the Chinese, while the *Münchener Neueste Nachrichten* considered the 'external forms' of the audience as only satisfying for those 'who did not place exaggerated demands of humiliation on the expiatory mission'.[125] But it was precisely such exaggerated demands that came to irritate people. *The Times* found it 'hardly conceivable' that the government of an enlightened nation 'borrowed from the servile etiquette of the Far East', writing that this would neither be approved of by 'the enormous majority of educated Germans', nor 'increase foreign reputation' in China.[126]

Indeed, as the *Times* correspondent in Beijing reported, the Chinese were 'chuckling over the result', while the Russian legation, which had advised the Qing court 'to keep firm', was 'ingeniously seeking to take credit to themselves'. The *Washington Post* agreed that the resolution of the conflict was a victory for Chinese diplomacy and that the expiatory mission did not attest to German imperial superiority. Satirical magazines were 'full of caricatures just now showing the Chinese Dragon triumphant and gloating over the retreating allies, who are represented as withdrawing in a sadly disgruntled condition after having failed to reduce the Oriental monster to submission'.[127] The Viennese weekly *Floh* mocked the Germans, who had capitulated in the face of Chinese resilience and 'made fools of themselves'. In *Simplicissimus*, Theodor Heine drew a cartoon depicting the short 'expiation-prince' thumbing his nose at a tall cuirassier while explaining to his interpreter that in China the gesture meant: 'I beg your forgiveness.' On Berlin's Friedrichstrasse, merchants got in on the action with a figurine that sold in droves: one side depicted 'John Chinaman' with a drooping moustache, ironically described by the *Berliner Damen-Zeitung* as a 'real image of melancholy'. But if one pulled on a paper band, 'the melancholic moustache pops up and takes on a jolly, even proud character'. Printed on the figure were the words: 'Prince Chun—before and after the kowtow!' The humorous object reflected well 'the mood of Berlin residents', who had closely followed how the 'underdog' had come out on top.[128]

Fig. 19. *Der Sühneprinz* (The expiation-prince), cover of a humoristic composition by Otto Reutter, *c.*1901

Over the course of a few weeks, German politics had thus attracted the laughter of the European and Asian world.[129] The centuries-old debate over the kowtow as a major element of Chinese ceremony ended with this laughter. Initially conceived of as a way to humiliate

China, the Kaiser's plan backfired and ended up humiliating Germany, a fact that was immediately suppressed in the country's official memory.[130] In China, too, the diplomatic victory did little to smooth over the fact that three days after Chun's audience in Potsdam, on 7 September 1901, the country signed the Boxer Protocol, another in a line of Unequal Treaties that documented China's long descent in the face of the West and Japan. The Protocol included arrangements for the erection of a commemorative monument to Ketteler, which was unveiled in 1903; many Chinese saw this as a sign of dishonour. In 1924, the by then republican government declared 7 September a 'day of national shame'. By the early 1940s, there were more than 100 such days on the Chinese calendar. The memory of shame and humiliation had become a central feature of Chinese nationalism. Even today, the 'century of humiliation' is a term still used in China to denote the period from the First Opium War in 1839 to the Communist Revolution in 1949.[131]

Honour and Shame, War and Peace in Europe

China was not alone in adopting humiliation as a central term in its political lexicon. Europeans used it as well. Even though the old fights for pre-eminence in ceremonial matters had been settled in the early nineteenth century and the equality of European states established, Europe's leaders still had a tendency to feel insulted and humiliated for just about anything. In international relations, honour continued to play a central role, and the more it was transferred from individual monarchs to the state and the nation, the more conflicts between states were characterized as struggles for national honour.

The 'nationalist nonsense' of the late nineteenth century, as Friedrich Nietzsche criticized it in 1885,[132] gave the language of honour an exceptional acerbity and made it widespread in a way that it had not been in earlier times, when politics was still an arcane activity of elites. Now, fired up by the press and nationalist associations, every citizen could personally identify with the honour of their country and interpret anything that might be seen as an attack on the nation's honour as an attack on their own. Combined with the internationally acknowledged right of states to demand satisfaction for moral and political insults, this would ultimately have grave consequences. As the liberal Carl Welcker wrote in 1847, states often viewed 'illegal violations of their honour as justified grounds for war', and now they could do so with the full support of their own populations.[133] Propaganda helped train public opinion to support political power plays unquestioningly. During the 1901 Kowtow Affair, the German government placed considerable weight on the notion that the Chinese people get the 'right impression of the expiatory mission', thereby completely failing to comprehend political relations in China, which did not allow 'the people' to participate in politics.[134] At the same time, politicians in Berlin anxiously kept an eye on the reactions of the national 'press and public', who they believed had to be 'spoon-fed' political decisions.[135]

In 1870, too, German citizens had been spoon-fed the decision to go to war with France. This proved to be an easy task, since Napoleon III had declared war first. The French emperor had promised his nation a *satisfaction éclatante* for the insults from Prussia that France had allegedly been suffering since 1866. In the intervening period, political communication was filled with references to 'humiliation', 'degradation', and insulted national honour. Both sides feared a loss of prestige in Europe and among their own people, particularly Napoleon, whose authoritarian reign was supported by plebiscite. This was not the least in a list of reasons why the French government wanted war with Prussia and did everything it could to bring it about. In its efforts, Paris found a congenial partner in Berlin's chancellor Otto von Bismarck. His carefully crafted Ems Dispatch, which exposed French ambassador Vincent Benedetti's taboo behaviour towards King Wilhelm I, was viewed as an affront against France's national honour. For his part, Wilhelm I was aggravated that Benedetti had demanded a 'letter of apology' from him, because this offended 'my personal [honour] and the honour of the nation'.[136]

All of these insults and explanations were carried out in public. National citizens were bombarded with information and took an active part in the whole drama. Governments gave their messages directly to the national press, while journalists did their own research and stoked up aggression independently. Even socialist papers printed fired-up articles, talked about the supposed attacks on national honour, and urged politicians to act forcefully. 'National feeling and national honour' had become, in Bismarck's words, 'powers' of 'great moral force', and public opinion had developed into an important element of power. Accordingly, no politician wanted to 'compromise' himself in its eye.[137]

All sides portrayed themselves as victims, and everyone felt that they had been humiliated and insulted without themselves having humiliated or insulted anyone. It was always the other who was looking for trouble, whereas the accusers were just acting in self-defence. In extreme cases, countries stylized themselves as taking revenge for past humiliations. Wilhelm Camphausen's double watercolour

Fig. 20. Wilhelm Camphausen, *Vergeltung* (Vengeance). Tilsit 1807. Sedan 1870. Watercolour, before 1885

'Vengeance' could be interpreted in this way. In the painting, Camphausen, who had been hired to follow the Prussian Army to France, contrasted the mythic image of Queen Luise vainly asking Napoleon Bonaparte for a lenient peace in 1807 with an image of France's surrender in 1870. After his defeat in Sedan, Napoleon III, nephew of Napoleon I, appeared before Luise's son Wilhelm to give up his sword. Both were moments of great humiliation, and the painting made clear that the latter was vengeance for the former, thus restoring Prussia's and Germany's honour.[138]

The multiple versions of Anton von Werner's famous painting 'Proclamation of the German Empire' had a similar function. They drew attention to the paintings in the Hall of Mirrors at the Palace of Versailles that celebrated the victories and triumphs of Louis XIV, including the annexation of Alsace as a French province—now to be 'returned' to Germany. Likewise, the military chaplain explained in his sermon at the event that the proclamation had 'repented the shame that was once heaved upon our German people from this place and from this royal throne'.[139]

Almost a half-century later, the humiliation that France had suffered was revenged at the exact same place. In June 1919, delegates representing the victors of the First World War met in Versailles to sign a peace treaty with Germany. It was no coincidence that the French prime minister Georges Clemenceau, who had fought against the Germans in 1871, chose the Hall of Mirrors for the signing ceremony. The two Germans—Social Democrat Hermann Müller and Johannes Bell of the Catholic Centre Party—were not allowed to sit at the large table. They were brought in, allowed to sign, and escorted away. In the hotel, Müller, who had until then tried to contain himself, collapsed in a cold sweat. On the same evening, after the 'worst hour of my life', he travelled back to Berlin.[140]

There were others who were also not so happy about the ceremony. Edward House, adviser to the American president Woodrow Wilson, found it reminiscent of a Roman triumphal procession, where 'the conqueror dragged the conquered at his chariot wheels'. He deplored the fact that the signing lacked any 'element of chivalry' and that it 'was elaborately staged and made as humiliating to the enemy as it well could be'. British diplomat Harold Nicolson empathized with the German ministers, who, as members of the new post-revolutionary government, had had no part in the war politics of the German Empire.[141]

In Germany, the Treaty of Versailles was seen as a humiliating peace, and politicians of all parties strove to distance themselves from it. The War Guilt Clause, which forced Germany to accept complete responsibility, and the harsh reparations that the country was forced to pay made Germans feel dishonoured. The far-right relentlessly mobilized against the treaty and defamed Müller and Bell, who had reluctantly signed it, as dishonourable traitors. Other 'fulfilment politicians' were murdered on the street.

The military occupation of the Rhineland, another term of the treaty, was seen as particularly humiliating, above all the stationing of French units that included soldiers from Africa. In 1920, the entire Weimar National Assembly with the exception of the Independent Social Democrats voted for a resolution declaring this an 'indelible dishonour' for Germany and a 'horrifying danger' for German women and children. Even Social Democratic president Friedrich Ebert, in a 'call on the world', strongly spoke out against the 'provocative offence against the laws of civilization' that 'coloured troops of the lowest culture are stationed to watch over a people of such high spiritual and economic significance as the Rhinelanders'.[142] In the same vein, a leaflet condemned the 'unheard of humiliation and rape of a highly cultivated white race by a half-barbaric coloured one'.[143]

They did not mean 'rape' in an exclusively figurative sense, but were playing on the sometimes forced, sometimes consensual relationships between soldiers from French colonies and German women. The children of these relationships were derogatorily referred to as 'Rhineland bastards' by broad swathes of the population. In an article for the *Sunday Times*, a Conservative MP who had served as a British officer in the war and toured the occupied territories in 1921 called them

Fig. 21. Cover of the satirical magazine *Kladderadatsch*, 30 May 1920

'grotesque creatures', 'pathetic little witnesses to the horrors of this Blotch on the Rhine'. He wrote that he had nothing against humiliating Germany, but that he was fiercely against allowing blacks to rule over whites. This, he argued, was 'searing the soul of Germany and building up in her heart a desire some day to punish indignity with greater indignity'. His prognosis was that this would automatically lead to another war.[144]

Right-wingers and National Socialists hurried to fulfil this prophecy. After 1933, Hitler sought revisions to the Treaty of Versailles and ordered the 'grotesque creatures' to be sterilized so that the 'black horror' would not procreate, thus 'destroying' the 'white race' from within and taking it 'from its cultural and political height'.[145] He constantly used 'honour' and 'shame' in his rhetoric, and grasped at every opportunity to publicly humiliate his political opponents, both domestic and foreign. When German troops marched into Paris on 14 June 1940, the 'Führer' had the train car in which the French, British, and Germans had signed the armistice on 11 November 1918 in Compiègne removed from the museum and taken back to its historical site. On 22 June, the second armistice was signed here. According to minister of propaganda Joseph Goebbels, the ceremony was 'not a demonstrative humiliation' and neither 'hate' nor 'revenge' played a role in it. 'But', he wrote, 'the ignominy of 1918 is now over. One feels born again.' The car in which the Allies had once 'humiliated' Germany was brought to Berlin and exhibited in the city centre.[146]

Steps Small and Large in Post-war Diplomacy

Whether the cycle of humiliation and revenge could be broken after 1945 was no minor question. Symbolic gestures were attributed great significance and were given close attention. Before the Federal Republic's first chancellor Konrad Adenauer received the Occupation Statute from the Allied High Commission in September 1949, lengthy negotiations had been undertaken to ensure that the act did not have 'a humiliating character'. The French and Americans in particular had been accommodating. 'Contrary to protocol', Adenauer reported, André François-Poncet had approached him and shaken his hand upon arrival. Thus, from the very beginning there was 'a friendly atmosphere' that clearly facilitated the difficult situation.[147]

For his part, Adenauer used the polite gesture to make a small, but important move. According to the Allies' protocol, only the commissioners were to stand on the carpet; the chancellor was supposed to step on it after the head commissioner's address. But Adenauer did not stick to the official choreography. When François-Poncet advanced to greet him, Adenauer came up to him, 'and thus stood on the carpet as well', just like the representatives of the Western occupying forces. None of them, the chancellor happily noted, objected.[148]

John McCloy later recalled that he welcomed Adenauer by saying: 'I can well imagine what you're thinking. Surely you're thinking of Canossa.'[149] With 'Canossa', he was referring to Holy Roman Emperor Henry IV's walk to Pope Gregory VII in 1077 to repent and have his excommunication taken back. Since the nineteenth century, it had been used as a metaphor for a humiliating act of political submission. Bismarck's statement in 1872 that 'we are not going to Canossa, neither in body nor in mind' had continued to reverberate.[150] Everyone present at Hotel Petersberg, the seat of the Allied High Commission, was familiar with the language of humiliation. But after the bitter experiences of the first half of the century, nobody wanted to make use of it any longer. Just as international treaties sought to commit signatories to the protection of human dignity and mutual recognition, so the post-war conception of international relations was based on the 'principle of sovereign equality', as the 1945 United Nations (UN) Charter put it.

This implied both the rejection of physical and military violence and dispensing with acts of humiliation. In 1948, the UN gave an example of the new diplomatic style when it chastised Israel for the murder of UN mediator Folke Bernadotte. Officials were not sparing in their criticism of the Israeli government for doing little to catch the murderers, and UN secretary-general Trygve Lie demanded an official apology. After much hesitation, Israel issued a lukewarm statement saying that the government regretted and disapproved of the incident. Still, Lie declared himself satisfied and did not pursue any further measures.[151]

Such a conciliatory tone stood in stark contrast to the treatment suffered by Greece at the hands of Italy in 1923, when Italian general Enrico Tellini, working on behalf of the League of Nations to help mediate border disputes between Greece and Albania, was murdered along with three members of his delegation. Italy's duce Benito Mussolini held the Greek government responsible and, in the style of Wilhelm II, occupied the island of Corfu. He demanded high-sum reparations, the execution of the murderers, and an apology for the 'grave offence' that had 'profoundly offended and exasperated' public opinion in Italy. The Greek government and press were outraged at what they perceived as an attack on the 'honour' and 'sovereignty of the State'. The London *Times* seconded and condemned Italy's intent 'to inflict the bitterest humiliation upon Greece'. Yugoslav politicians compared the demands with the 1914 Austrian ultimatum to Serbia.[152]

After 1945, these kinds of asymmetrical gestures of humiliation gradually lost their legitimacy and force. The 1919 Covenant of the League of Nations had already required its members to maintain 'open, just and honourable relations', without, however, condoning the kind of violence-based honour later touted by Italian Fascism and German National Socialism. The fact that these regimes and their political ideas had lost the Second World War paved the way for an international order that held up principles of sovereign equality, territorial integrity, and political independence over questions of honour.[153] Although such principles did not remain uncontested during the Cold War, the language of honour and humiliation was largely absent in post-war political communication. In communist countries, honour was hardly ever mentioned in the context of foreign policy, and the West avoided it, too.[154]

Even the newly independent states of Africa and Asia that had successfully cast off the yoke of colonial rule did not, in the 1950s and 1960s, play the card of national humiliation. Although political and intellectual leaders by no means hid their feelings of being hurt and insulted by colonial and imperialist powers, they chose instead to focus on future relations of equality and collaboration. In 1960, Patrice Lumumba, prime minister of the Republic of the Congo, gave a fervent speech at the proclamation of independence in which he addressed the 'noble and just struggle' against 'the humiliating slavery that had been forced upon us'. A day earlier he had signed a treaty of friendship with Belgium that he considered 'a sister nation, to whom we say: "We need you, just as you need us. We hope that the friendship between our two peoples, who are now equals, will take the concrete form of fruitful economic, scientific, and cultural cooperation."'[155] In a similar vein, Frantz Fanon, in his seminal 1961 book *Les Damnés de la Terre (The Wretched of the Earth)*, put far more emphasis on the new states' demand for material reparations and restitutions than on the moral dimension of the anti-colonial struggle.[156] It took until the 1990s for moral politics to re-enter international relations, where it found, in the form of official apologies, global acceptance. According to a 2001 UN resolution, though, such apologies, or expressions of regret, should not themselves 'take a form humiliating to the responsible State'.[157]

The Politics of Apology and Willy Brandt's Warsaw Genuflection

But there were hurdles on the way to reaching this consensus, and what different parties understood by humiliation varied considerably. The notion that apologizing was a sign not of weakness, but of moral and political strength, only slowly gained footing, and even then, it was not accepted by all. In 1958, during a visit to the former Gestapo prison in Warsaw, Social Democratic politician Carlo Schmid signed the visitors' book 'with deep shame at this site of German disgrace'. Back home, he was accused of dragging Germany's 'national dignity' through the mud.[158] In 1965, Polish bishops were confronted with similar criticism for their 'Pastoral Letter' to their 'German Brothers'. Within a 'culture of hate', they intended to build bridges between the two countries and made a bold move: they granted forgiveness for the crimes committed by Germans against Poles during the war, and they asked for forgiveness for crimes committed by Poles against Germans during forced expulsion after the war. In keeping with Christian tradition, they conditioned their offer on their addressees' willingness to repent: 'Where there is no recognition of guilt, there is no forgiveness.' The German bishops, however, could not bring themselves to admit their own culpability, all the while interpreting the Polish plea for forgiveness as an admission of guilt. Only the Protestant churches were willing clearly to acknowledge 'mutual guilt' and to support serious steps towards reconciliation—above all, that West Germany recognize the Oder–Neisse Line as the Polish border.[159]

In Poland, the communist government reacted harshly to the bishops' move, and most priests and believers distanced themselves from it. Looking back at the event, parliamentary representative and later prime minister Tadeusz Mazowiecki stated that Polish society was not yet ready for such a step.[160] The Protestant memorandum, too, was highly controversial in the Federal Republic, and its authors received threats and were called traitors. Those Germans who had been forced to leave their homes in the former eastern parts of Germany after the war were outraged. Nevertheless, two-thirds of those who spoke out during the debate supported the memorandum.[161]

This was the context in which the first state visit of a West German chancellor to Warsaw took place in 1970. The agenda was to sign treaties 'normalizing' German–Polish relations, which included the recognition of all borders. Most of those present at the signing ceremony described the event as 'sober' and 'not particularly moving'.[162] Thus, nobody could have predicted that the visit would go down in history as a moral and political milestone. The 7th of December started in the usual mode. Before the signing, Willy Brandt laid a wreath on the Tomb of the Unknown Soldier. He then drove to

Nathan Rapoport's 1948 memorial to the Warsaw Ghetto Uprising. The sculpture was not a normal stop for foreign dignitaries, but Brandt had already made known his intention to see it. After he laid down a wreath and straightened out its edges, he took a few steps back and—to the astonishment of all—kneeled. He remained in the position long enough for photographers to imprint the moment into celluloid for eternity.

As the Germans arrived at the president's office shortly thereafter, the Polish politicians had already been informed about what had happened. But nobody spoke about the event and what it meant, as translator Mieczysław Tomala later recalled.[163] The gesture was too surprising and too confounding. Statesmen kneeling was anything other than an everyday affair; in fact, it was outright unheard of.

Interpreting Brandt's genuflection as a gesture of humility seemed plausible in Catholic Poland. But Brandt was neither Catholic nor, for that matter, religious. Moreover, he bore no personal responsibility for what the Germans had done to Poland during the war. As a socialist, he had left Germany in 1933, only to return after the war. Why, then, did he kneel?

Members of Brandt's delegation asked themselves this question as well. Late at night, over one or more glasses of whisky, Egon Bahr, close friend and secretary to the Chancellor's Office, remarked 'with great shyness and bashful excitement': 'That was crazy.' Brandt replied that 'he had the feeling that laying a wreath was not enough'. He said the same to a journalist: 'This morning I knew it: that it would not be so simple as other wreath ceremonies, just bowing one's head. This is a whole different dimension.' Twenty years later, he wrote in his memoirs: 'I had not planned anything, but I had left Wilanów Castle, where I was staying, with a feeling that I must express the exceptional significance of the ghetto memorial. From the bottom of the abyss of German history, under the burden of millions of victims of murder, I did what human beings do when speech fails them.'[164]

In retrospect, he did the right thing. The Warsaw Genuflection found great resonance in the Western media and quickly became an iconic symbol of the new 'Ostpolitik', for which Brandt received the Nobel Peace Prize in 1971. But the genuflection was more than a sign of political change in West Germany. It was also an important event in the history of modern diplomacy, an emotional act that clearly distinguished itself from standard practices and ceremonies. Brandt, who was usually more reserved, could not express his feelings in any other way than in a gesture of humility. Without knowing it, he was drawing on a longstanding cultural practice. When a newspaper tried to make the corny joke that the chancellor, who came from a Protestant background, had kneeled before the Jewish monument like a good Polish Catholic, he responded in irritation that they were 'missing the point'.[165]

The point was certainly not to perform an act of self-humiliating devotion following the Catholic model. Nevertheless, Christian rituals of repentance—also common in Protestantism—probably inspired the gesture, which was immediately interpreted as an admission of guilt and a plea for forgiveness. In that sense, Brandt was writing history. Even in the face of political apologies that came after, his genuflection was the most remarkable and memorable of them all, singular and unrepeatable.[166] Brandt's evocative body language gave it its emotional force. While the text of the Warsaw Treaty used succinct, dry words in stating Germany's role in the war and Poland's status as victim, Brandt's genuflection communicated not only mourning, but also regret and humility. At the same time, his straightened back was the posture of a man who himself was not complicit and who nevertheless assumed responsibility for the crimes of his nation.

It was shocking for many. Novelist Günter Grass, who had followed the chancellor to Warsaw, wrote in his diary that the 'immediate benefit of this trip' was the 'regained capacity to feel moved'. He recalled that on the morning of 7 December, even the Polish hosts showed signs of 'astonishment, shock, and shame': 'They thought they knew German behaviour; this was new for them.' Not least of all, Prime Minister Józef Cyrankiewicz, a survivor of Auschwitz and Mauthausen, was touched, stating: 'Only he could have done that',

Fig. 22. Cover of *Der Spiegel* 51/1970

and that the Poles had understood him. Brandt recalled that on the
way to the airport, Cyrankiewicz took him by the arm and said that
the gesture had moved many and that his wife had telephoned with a
friend in Vienna and both had cried.[167]

Reactions in West Germany were quite different. An instant survey conducted by *Der Spiegel* showed that 48 per cent held Brandt's gesture for 'overdone', while 41 per cent found it 'appropriate'; 54 per cent of those between 30 and 60 years of age disapproved.[168] Press reports also spanned a wide spectrum. Long before the trip, conservative papers had branded the recognition of Poland's western border as a 'treaty of shame' that no decent German would sign. Not surprisingly, they considered Brandt's genuflection 'undignified' and wrote that it smacked of treason, capitulation, and subordination. One letter to the editor saw only one parallel in world history: Henry IV's Walk to Canossa.[169] Grass had feared this would be the response: 'How will they report on it back home? Will the tendency to defamation exploit it to distort the genuflection into a kowtow?'[170]

There it was again, the kowtow. Having taken the stage in 1901 as a deliberate act of political humiliation, it had survived in cultural memory and could be used to twist Brandt's gesture of humility into a gesture of humiliation. What was novel, however, was the explicit emphasis on the gesture's emotional dimension. To be sure, that dimension had not been altogether lacking in the 1901 events. But in 1970, emotions clearly captured the spotlight and were made into a political bone of contention. While some praised Brandt's gesture as an authentic expression of shame, mourning, and deeply felt pain, others criticized 'the big cudgel of emotion'. According to a conservative politician, 'emotions' and 'concepts like reconciliation, friendship, trust, and peaceableness' do not speak to 'political reason, but for the heart and temper'. He thus read the act as a questionable, inappropriate show of 'demonstrative morality'.[171]

French president Georges Pompidou had a similar take, while East German media preferred just not to report on the genuflection at all. In the Polish press, the photo was touched up so that it looked like Brandt was standing before the monument rather than kneeling. In contrast, many Western papers printed the picture of the kneeling chancellor on the front page and praised the gesture as courageous and powerful.[172]

Moral Politics

Two or three decades later, Brandt's gesture was remembered positively as a 'sign of change', both in Germany and abroad. In some countries, it was even seen as an exemplary act of political apology and reconciliation deserving of imitation. In 1997, a Croatian scientist demanded that the Serbian government perform a similar symbolic gesture, and in the same year, China let Japan know that it believed it was commendable.[173] In 2014, China's official press agency Xinhua drew a contrast between Brandt's Warsaw Genuflection and the Japanese prime minister's recent visit to the Yasukuni Shrine, where military officials guilty of grave war crimes are memorialized. Xinhua wrote that 'the moment Brandt knelt down, his nation stood up', and that while Brandt's 'silent apology' had renewed international trust and reverence for his country, Shinzo Abe had refused to grapple honestly with the history of violence that his country had unleashed in Asia in general and China in particular.[174]

Demands that nations—and not only Japan—self-critically come to terms with their past have become louder and more frequent since the 1990s. This marks nothing less than a political sea change. Morality and agreement about what constitutes good and evil have become a central political issue in many places, challenging the classic understanding of politics as a game of power. The end of the Cold War seemed to offer a chance to overcome ideology-driven friend–enemy relations and us-versus-them mentalities. Politicians became less exclusively attached to asserting their own national interests and showed openness and care for others' concerns. This shift in perspective was pushed forward by human rights discourse, which has been growing in prominence since the 1970s. But it also reflects a move towards relational subjectivization, which seeks to place the suffering of the subject front and centre, and promises healing in the form of empathy and recognition. Vulnerability, mindfulness, attention to others' needs: these concepts have paved the way for a culture centred on the victim. Both in the media and in politics, this culture has gained widespread acceptance.[175]

As a consequence, a great number of apologies have been made on the international stage over the last three decades, chiming in an 'age of apology'.[176] In 1990, Soviet president Mikhail Gorbachev expressed deep regret over the massacre of Polish prisoners of war in Katyn in 1940 after decades of Soviet denial, denouncing it as one of the greatest crimes of Stalinism. In March 1995, Lithuanian president Algirdas Brazauskas visited the Knesset and asked forgiveness for his fellow Lithuanians who had murdered and plundered Jews during the Second World War.[177] In the same year, French president Valéry Giscard d'Estaing departed from the claim that Vichy was not France, which had been the official position since Charles de Gaulle, and apologized for the fact that the French people and the French state had actively participated in the deportation of Jews to the camps.[178] And in 1997, when Queen Elizabeth II took her third trip to India, she brought with her a speech in which she decried the 1919 Amritsar massacre as a 'distressing' example of the sad and painful episodes of British–Indian history. During her visits in 1961 and 1983, she had made no mention of it.

But even in 1997, words were still being chosen carefully. The new Labour government wanted a powerful apology for British soldiers' massacre of hundreds of unarmed Indian civilians. Officials, however, advised it that doing so might encourage former colonies to make similar demands. Thus, the queen opted for general words of regret, placed a wreath at a memorial to the event, and briefly bowed her head. Many Indians were disappointed, pointing to Germany and Japan as countries that had more decisively admitted their guilt.[179] Indeed, Japan had found words of apology, particularly towards Korea. While in 1984, Emperor Hirohito cautiously stated that there had been an 'unfortunate past' in the two countries' relations, eight years later, Prime Minister Morihiro Hosokawa expressed 'profound remorse and regret' that 'past Japanese actions...caused unbearable suffering and sorrow for so many people'.[180]

In contrast to the demands for satisfaction of the nineteenth and early twentieth centuries, these apologies were not for transgressions of individual citizens or groups for whom the government bore abstract responsibility. Instead, these apologies were attempts of the current governments to distance themselves entirely from actions officially committed or tolerated by their predecessors. When addressed to citizens and representatives of foreign states, such admissions of culpability have often been particularly difficult. Things have generally been less complicated when it comes to domestic conflicts. In 1993, South African president Frederik Willem de Klerk apologized for apartheid, and shortly thereafter, ANC president Nelson Mandela apologized for acts of violence committed by the African National Congress. In 1997, American president Bill Clinton apologized for the 'shameful' and 'racist' Tuskegee experiments that involved infecting African-American men with syphilis for 'scientific' purposes between 1932 and 1972. In 2008, Kevin Rudd, prime minister of Australia, apologized to Australian Aborigines, and in the same year, Canadian prime minister Stephen Harper apologized to indigenous peoples in Canada for forcing their children into state-run boarding schools.[181]

Balancing accounts with former colonies was a more intricate affair. Colonial powers like Great Britain and France have placed considerable weight not only on being charged for their crimes, but also on being praised for their civilizational accomplishments. Accordingly, in 1997, the queen discussed, alongside the 'moments of sadness', those of 'gladness'. In 2007, French president Nicolas Sarkozy apologized for the undeniable crimes of the colonial system. But he also reminded his listeners in Senegal and Algeria of all the good things the French had done, like constructing ports, roads, hospitals, and schools. In a speech to students in Dakar dripping with pathos, he refused to express regret on the grounds that sons could not be held responsible for the crimes of their fathers. Moreover, as he had stated during the elections, he considered regret a form of self-hatred that had to be overcome so that the French could win back their national honour and pride. In Algiers, he left the evaluation of French–Algerian history to the judgement of future historians, resting satisfied with honouring 'all victims'. This did not placate the Algerian minister of the interior, who drily remarked that an apology would have been 'useful'.[182] In 2013, sixteen years after the queen's visit, British prime minister David Cameron came back to Amritsar. But he too refused to apologize and only called the massacre a 'deeply shameful event in British history'. Whether or not he himself felt shame is not known.[183] But even if he did, it would have remained an inward, private feeling as long as he failed to recognize it as a call to active 'counteraction', as West German president Theodor Heuss had done in 1955.[184] Such counteraction would have automatically been accomplished with an admission of guilt, which, in contrast to shame, is an act directed towards the outside, to the victims. For them, it would have been 'useful', both as a performative expression of recognition and as symbolic reparation.[185] But the expectations of victims often contradict the historical narratives of perpetrators. In such cases, political apologies—even without genuflection—carry an aftertaste of self-humiliation.

This is why the conservative Tea Party Movement organized the 'Restoring Honor Rally' in Washington, DC in 2010. Some protesters believed that US president Barack Obama had done disservice to the honour of the nation by 'apologizing for everything we ever did'. Such apologies, they thought, had robbed them, the citizens of the United States, of their personal and political self-respect. During the 2016 presidential race, Republican Sarah Palin accused Obama of 'kowtowing' to America's enemies.[186] Similar tones have been struck in recent debates over history classes and cultural politics in France, Hungary, and Poland. The more conservative the speakers are, the more critical they are of the readiness to apologize. According to Gérard Larcher, president of the French Senate, those who support a 'culture of repentance' undermine national pride. In 2016, Polish minister of culture Piotr Gliński echoed the same sentiment. The leader of Poland's Law and Justice party Jarosław Kaczyński has repeatedly criticized the 'pedagogics of shame', stating that Polish children and adolescents should learn to feel a sense of honour and pride in their homeland.[187]

Honour and pride have not only stood in the way of researching the dark chapters of national histories and apologizing to those who suffered during them. Honour and pride are also at stake in the performative gestures that are part of international relations. In 1994, when US president Bill Clinton bowed before the emperor of Japan on his visit to the White House, even the liberal *New York Times* criticized the 'obsequent' gesture, which it said ran contrary to America's republican traditions. Fifteen years later, President Obama was harshly reprimanded for bowing before Saudi King Abdullah. The conservative *Washington Times* called it a 'servile gesture' and a 'full-out genuflection' that demeaned the 'power and independence' of the United States.[188]

All of this demonstrates important things about the contemporary status of the politics of humiliation. First, it draws attention to the enormous power wielded by the modern press. Thanks to the comment sections on websites, its reach in the twenty-first century has grown well beyond traditional print and photo journalism. The public and the press speak in a loud, polyphonic voice. Political opponents are quick to shout out when they think they have discovered something that diminishes national reputation and self-esteem. In such contexts, the word 'kowtow'—the absolute symbol of political subjugation and self-humiliation—finds liberal use.[189]

Second, the cases mentioned show that the moralization of politics is a multi-faceted, complex development. The trend that Willy Brandt started with his 1970 genuflection provided occasion for heated domestic controversies. What have been praised by some as forward-looking gestures of reconciliation, others have sought to admonish as humiliating, backward-looking rituals of repentance.

Third, the mixture of politics and morality in foreign relations has become a pointed weapon in the competition for state power and influence. The fact that China rarely misses an opportunity to remind Japan of Brandt's model and to demand a similarly powerful apology is less a matter of morality and more a matter of politics. The conflict over how to interpret the past is part of a game of power in which both countries play hardball. By depicting itself as the victim of earlier aggression and degradation, China is seeking to bolster and legitimate its contemporary interests, both towards its own citizens and towards the rest of the world. Similar calculations are behind the 'culture of humiliation' prominent in some Arabic countries and the 'humiliation syndrome' plaguing Russian politics under President Vladimir Putin.[190]

Thus, the politics of humiliation remains an eminently important force in international relations. Beyond diplomatic ceremonies and gestures, history and its interpretation offer explosive material that can be used to buttress allegedly legitimate claims to power and 'respect' in the face of allegedly derogatory acts of interference and domination. Past injustices are taken to justify the policies of the present. Even the new world order established after the Second World War and then again after 1989 has not completely done away with such dynamics. Piggy-backing on the rebirth of morality and the emotional language of respect and recognition, stakeholders in serious conflicts—both domestic and international—eagerly play on the themes of damaged national honour, dignity, and pride, threatening revenge and demanding satisfaction.

For some time, it had seemed as if such sentiments and behaviours were manifestly on the decline, at least in large parts of Europe. Without a doubt, this was due to the fact that supranational institutions had been created to dampen conflicts and provide a forum for sober-minded, pragmatic debate. Likewise, Europeans have learned that pride and humility, honour and shame are not irreconcilable opposites, but can all be a source of moral and political strength. The French, for instance, can be proud of the 1789 Revolution and be ashamed of the use of torture during the Algerian War of Independence. Germans can be proud of their democratic rebirth after 1945 and the *Wirtschaftswunder* without denying their guilt, shame, and responsibility for Nazi crimes. Britain can have, to quote Queen Elizabeth II once again, moments of sadness and gladness when it comes to colonial and post-colonial relations. These emotional concurrences did not pop up overnight, but are the result of long, often painful interactions in schools and universities, media, and politics. They are never finished and never set in stone. Every consensus can be dissolved, as demonstrated by recent events. When it is, regret might again be interpreted as a sign of weakness and trumpeting one's honour as a sign of strength.

Close Connections

At this point, readers might wonder what actually connects the politics of humiliation operating on the international stage with the demeaning practices performed within modern societies and among social actors. What joins the early modern pillory and today's media shaming with Queen Anne's apologies and the last German Kaiser's urge to humiliate high-ranking Chinese diplomats?

Particularly remarkable is the fact that the same vocabularies have been used in both domestic and international situations: honour and dignity, shame and disgrace, shaming and humiliation. The bodily postures associated with these feelings and practices have been similar too: dignity is expressed in an upright posture, bestowing honour and paying homage with bowing reverence. Kneeling was long customary for those asking for forgiveness, receiving orders, or suffering corporal punishment.

The meanings attached to these gestures, however, have not always been the same. Bowing before a high dignitary demonstrates a different form of honour than bowing in the name of human dignity. While honour of the first sort derives from an office or social status, the latter is seen as inborn and inalienable.[191] In the nineteenth and twentieth centuries, both were signified with the word 'honour', and people spoke of both 'universal human honour' and the 'honour' of the state and nation.[192]

National honour is still around, and it is so jealously guarded precisely because it is so easily insulted. It is touted with the same unconditionality that inheres in what used to be called human honour and is today called human dignity. For many, the fact that states and nations have honour and insist on having it recognized seems to be just as much a matter of course as the claim that all human beings have honour or dignity that must be respected. The link between individual and collective notions of honour can be found in the concept of the princely ruler as the initial and prime bearer of honour. Since the early modern period, this personal, dynastic form of honour has been gradually transferred to the state and later to the nation as the imagined community of individual citizens.

Be it on the interstate or inter-personal level, honour and shame are structurally and systematically tied to relations of power. As a rule, only those who have power and want to prove it can shame and humiliate. This holds for states as well as for teachers, bosses, and bullies. Power is not something static, but has to be constantly tested out and reconfirmed through the demonstration of others' lack of it. Peer groups use similar politics of shaming and humiliation, as do states, particularly in the era of imperialism and colonialism. What they have in common is, among other things, the importance of the public as active participant and observer. Without an audience, the humiliating 'processions' forced upon 'race traitors' and political enemies by the Nazis and the 'expiatory missions' of the Chinese would have been pointless. In cases where large numbers of people have refused to take part, the spectacles have failed.

Such failed instances of intentional acts of humiliation have, throughout history, been rarer in international relations than they have been when attempted by social actors, whose use of humiliation has come under increased criticism. The case of China in 1901, in which the humiliated state managed to turn things around and humiliate the humiliator, was only possible with massive support from third parties and has remained the exception to the rule.

CONCLUSION

No End in Sight

This book began with stories and episodes and it ends with history: with the history of European modernity, an epoch that has elevated individual freedom and human dignity to its highest values and defended them against all kinds of attacks. However, this modernity is not and has never been a shrine of respectful, empathic, violence-free human interaction. New forms of unfreedom and degradation were born in the shadows of the Enlightenment, whether it be in colonies, in total institutions like the military, or in boarding schools and religious homes. Targeted shaming and even humiliation have played a central role in the history of modernity, and were only dampened very late and against much resistance.

At the same time, the arenas and agents of power underwent changes, as did the perpetrators and victims. While the state generally stopped using shaming as a way to enforce norms, society began identifying new groups to be singled out for discrimination and humiliation. In their role as communicators, initiators, and fanners of the flames, the media took on an important moral-political function. They worked and continue to work as symbolic pillories where disliked citizens are put on exhibition and foreign policy is analysed for signs of intent to humiliate. Today, nobody seems safe from the media pillory.

History in Fast Motion: Public Shaming and Its Critics

In 1773, Johann Georg Schlosser, a lawyer from Frankfurt, moved with his wife Cornelia née Goethe to Emmendingen, a town of about 2,000, to fill the position of senior bailiff. As a devoted reformer, Schlosser ordered the night watchman to knock on the window shutters of indebted citizens at four o'clock every morning and cry out: 'Wake up and get to work so that you can pay off your debts!'[1] The point was not just to wake the slumbering debtors, but to make enough noise to be heard by neighbours, thus publicly shaming those who failed to fulfil their duty of paying off lenders in a timely manner.

We do not know what effects this measure had. Did the rudely awakened debtors really feel ashamed? Did they change their work ethic? Did neighbours find the new bailiff's measure appropriate? Did the shouting of the night watchman bother them, or did they lie back with self-satisfied *schadenfreude*? There are no records of protest or criticism, and we might surmise that the intervention was accepted as being rather moderate. Compared to earlier forms of public shaming, it really was—after all, at least the indebted citizens did not end up on the pillory. Schlosser was certainly a lot more liberal than the Bielefeld mayor who, in 1817, came up with the idea of setting up a pillory for beggars at the town hall where they could be put on display for a few hours.[2] But still, the repeated public admonition early in the morning shamed and embarrassed debtors, no doubt intentionally.

More than two centuries later, similar practices of shaming are still used, albeit not by official authorities. In Spain, private debt collectors have found it convenient to publicly shame people into settling their bills. They turn up in eye-catching costumes and conspicuously labelled cars in order to grab everybody's full attention. A *cobrador del frac* or 'black shadow' standing outside an office, house, or restaurant clearly marks the owner as someone who has not paid his debts. The business is predicated on shame, and it yields high success rates.

Fig. 23. A *cobrador del frac* (debt collector in tailcoat), Madrid, 2006

Apparently invented in Ecuador, it has spread to many other countries even though legislatures usually try to prohibit such aggressive practices. Under British law, the harassment of debtors can be legally punished on the grounds that it subjects a person to 'alarm, distress or humiliation'.[3]

That the state—both legislators and executives—actively protects citizens from being humiliated is a relatively new development. In the late eighteenth century, public officials found it perfectly all right to name and shame people into norm-abiding behaviour. A hundred years later, such practices were still around, but stood under increasing criticism. In Saxony, for instance, municipal administrations denounced citizens who did not pay their local taxes by publishing their names and addresses in official circulars or newspapers. In addition, pub and restaurant owners were told to post the names in their establishments and refuse service to them. In the 1880s, social democrats frequently raised the issue in parliament. Their spokesperson August Bebel did not have anything against keeping 'malicious' tax evaders out of the pubs and dance halls until they had paid their debts. But he strongly opposed the 'very severe public branding and injury to honour'. Reading out the names of debtors at public gatherings and publishing them in newspapers and restaurants was, he argued, the same as 'putting them on the pillory'. It was 'ugly and degrading' and 'conflicts with the principles of modern legislation'. He was joined by liberal members of the legislature and, in the end, by the Saxon government as well.[4]

When Bebel referred to the principles of modern legislation, he was talking about the removal of public and corporal punishment from the penal codes and the law's tendency to defend the honour of the individual. Beginning in the late eighteenth century, hanging someone out to dry for everyone to see was increasingly viewed as problematic. Respect for citizens' sense of honour and human dignity led legislators gradually to move away from disciplining crimes with shaming, and by the mid-nineteenth century, these corrective techniques had all but disappeared from the penal codes. Even publishing the debts of the indebted like Schlosser did in Emmendingen might now be seen as an insult that itself could be grounds for criminal prosecution or a civil lawsuit.

This development reflected shifting views on civil rights and the limits of the state. Born out of the French Revolution, the new *citoyen* demanded that their honour be protected not only against attacks by other citizens, but also from encroachments by the state. It was a matter of broad consensus that the types of public corporal punishment practised with regularity until the 1840s injured the sense of honour of those who suffered them and did lasting damage to both their sense of self-esteem and their respectability in the eyes of others. Using beatings to shame stood in conflict with the purposes of modern penal policy—namely, improvement and resocialization— and the principle of acknowledging the dignity of all, including those who had violated the law.

Once the protection of human dignity was legally codified, citizens could go even further and insist on repealing sanctions that, in their view, negatively affected their dignity. In 1956, the district court of Hamburg sentenced a student to prison for homosexual activities and grave insult. The university then started disciplinary proceedings against the student, which ended with his expulsion two years later. The judgement, along with the penal court's decision, was posted in the university's main building for a month. The student, however, protested, arguing 'that the punishment of public shaming violates the [Federal Republic of Germany's] Basic Law'. It was not the judgement itself or the expulsion that gave occasion to his suit (although prosecuting homosexuality as a crime was coming increasingly to be called into doubt). Rather, the student claimed that the shame caused by the publication of the convictions contravened the law of the land: it was neither in sync with the protection of honour guaranteed to all citizens, nor could it be reconciled with the principle of the sacrosanctity of human dignity spelled out in the constitution's first article. Yet it still took the university until 1965 finally to adopt a disciplinary code that dispensed with such methods of public chastisement.[5]

Situations like those in Hamburg and Dresden illustrate two things: on the one hand, the types of public punishment that had been largely abolished by the mid-nineteenth century continued to have resonance among jurists and public administration through the twentieth century, even if in comparatively mild forms. On the other, official shame sanctions clearly faced resistance. Disapproval grew over time and found expression in the protests of Saxon social democrats and liberals and the grievances of the Hamburg student. The aversion to public humiliation was motivated by the concept of individual freedom, which granted everyone the right to be treated decently, independent of what they have done. This principle made compounding a punishment by publicly embarrassing the convicted no longer tolerable. By demeaning people and willingly exposing them to the contempt and *schadenfreude* of others, these practices stood in direct conflict with the moral economy of the new civil society and its values of respect, tact, and politeness.

Popular Justice and the Powers of Society

That such values would come to determine the language of public discourse could not have been anticipated around 1800. Nevertheless, liberals had already begun criticizing what they viewed as a politics of humiliation, which they saw being carried out not only by the state's penal institutions and courts, but also in traditional reprimands and practices meant to embarrass and shame members of a local or professional community. While these practices were widespread in early modern Europe, nineteenth-century states tried to stamp them out in order to consolidate their monopoly on the legitimate use of physical force.[6]

But this was easier said than done. In 1826, shipbuilders in Bristol stigmatized a fellow worker for blacklegging by tying him to a mast and dragging him around town. Skipping ahead 100 years, miners in the Saar region put up shaming posts to publish the names of strike breakers. As late as the 1970s, Italian workers used rough music and *cortei interni* to humiliate bosses and supervisors. In Russian villages, it remained standard practice to publicly shame thieves and fraudsters well into the twentieth century—whether the shaming was accompanied by physical violence depended on the severity of the crime.[7] Such sanctions were always extrajudicial. Either the violation was not legally punishable, as in Bristol, the Saar, and the Italian factories, or courts were too far away and not trustworthy, as in Russia. But beyond these sorts of pragmatic concerns, the power of popular justice for building community should not be underestimated. Through exposing transgressors to public disdain, the community asserted its power and readiness to condemn and exclude. At the same time, it reinforced the validity of its own rules and conventions and strengthened members' feeling of belonging. This is, at the very least, how those who participated in the act of shaming felt about it.

Under National Socialism, a similar connection between exclusion and inclusion was brought to bear in practices of public humiliation like parading 'race traitors' through the streets or putting 'enemies of the people' on display. Things were not all that different in 1960s China. During the Cultural Revolution, young men and women sought to depose the formerly sacrosanct authorities of state, society, and family.[8] The deeper their victims sank, the greater the collective feeling of empowerment experienced by the perpetrators. They were utterly convinced that they were doing the right thing by defending the revolution against alleged counterrevolutionaries. The German stormtroopers too thought they were protecting the *Volksgemeinschaft* when they humiliated men and women accused of violating the new norms of the regime.

Thus, in the twentieth century, the power of smaller groups and communities was transferred to large units such as 'the people' or 'the nation'. It was in the name of the people that semi-state actors went out to sanction, punish, shame, and humiliate without inhibition. Generally speaking, societies that place primacy on the social embeddedness of the individual and their obligation to act in accordance with the common good tend to give secondary status to the rights of the person and their entitlement to respect. In this vein, the National Socialists' motto 'You are nothing, your people is everything' meant that the rights of citizens were to be placed behind the interests of the community.[9] In the former socialist states, too, the collective was ranked over and above the needs of the citizen, and public shamings were a part of everyday life. In East German schools and factories, it was nothing uncommon for those who had fallen short of ideological demands to find their names published in newspapers or displayed on banners. In the China of the 1950s and 1960s, giving somebody a white flag marked them as a straggler and made them a target of public opprobrium.[10]

The official justification was always that the shamed had to be taught a lesson so that they could successfully be reintegrated into society. Proponents of shame sanctions in the USA use a similar argument, and so does Australian criminologist John Braithwaite. Since the 1980s, he has been an ardent defender of reintegrative shaming, which he believes is wholly distinct from stigmatizing forms. Differing in content but not in form are recent proposals to use shaming as a weapon of the powerless against the powerful by publishing the names of white-collar criminals or polluters on the internet. But in reality, the clear line between 'good', reintegrative shaming and 'bad', demeaning humiliation is impossible to sustain.[11] No form of shaming is without stigmatization and exclusion, even if its primary aim is to reintegrate and improve the 'delinquent'.

Equally problematic is the usurpation of morality by social and political movements that claim to act in the name of the common good and that view shaming as a legitimate means to achieve this end. In 2012, left-wing politicians suggested that Germany's Ministry of Finance should publish the names of wealthy tax evaders on the internet. This was met with stark resistance. Returning to traditional forms of public shaming stands, as critics maintain, in conflict with the rule of law and opens the door to arbitrariness: applied to the tax evader today, it might be expanded to people who drive too fast or those with certain sexual preferences tomorrow.[12]

Such arguments reflect liberal convictions that place high value on individual freedoms and, consequently, deeply mistrust collective shaming and the 'common sense' feelings of popular justice that inform it. As totalitarian regimes have demonstrated again and again, such 'common sense' can easily be influenced by propaganda and mobilized against the 'enemies' and outsiders of the day. Even when shaming is used against those in power, it has always taken a mean, ugly shape. As the Talmud says: 'He who insults a person in public is morally as guilty as if he had shed blood.'[13]

Victims of Shaming: Shameless Women and Cowardly Men

There has never been a lack of reasons for why people are publicly shamed. Early modern societies punished thieves, fraudsters, counterfeiters, and those accused of insult and libel with the pillory, beatings, and branding. Less severe violations were generally taken care of within guilds or local communities. Last but not least, acting contrary to sexual mores could subject one to forms of public ridicule that were often accompanied with violence.

Modern societies did indeed bid adieu to public shaming as a punishment carried out by the state. But they generally retained practices of shaming, particularly against women and female sexuality. In the nineteenth century, middle-class families raised their daughters to be 'coy', feel shame for little tears in their dresses, and blush in the presence of young men. Women who became pregnant out of wedlock could no longer allow themselves to be seen in 'good' society, unless, of course, their family succeeded in quickly marrying them off, even if that meant with a man from a lower social class.

Yet female sexuality was not just a family affair. State and society too made it into their own concern. During National Socialism, 'Aryan' women who slept with Jewish men or forced labourers from another country were demeaned in public. After the Second World War in countries liberated from German occupation, tens of thousands of women rumoured to have had relations with the occupying forces had their heads shaved in public and were prodded through the streets. They were accused of desecrating their own honour and, even worse, the honour of the nation. In the 1970s, Catholic women in Northern Ireland who dated British soldiers faced the same treatment. After having their hair cut off, they were tarred and feathered and bound to street lamps. Here too, shaming was not carried out by the state, but by social groups.[14]

While women have apparently had to be constantly shamed in order to stay on the politically and socially prescribed path of sexual virtue, men have never been subjected to the same standards and strategies. There are no records that French or Dutch men who did forced labour in Germany during the early 1940s were ever publicly shamed back home for their romances with German women. In contrast to female honour, male honour has traditionally been viewed as a matter not of sexuality, but of prowess and courage. A boy who is afraid and shows it has problems. His friends, peers, parents, and

Fig. 24. The white feather campaign, Great Britain during the First World War

siblings call him a wuss or a sissy. Whoever wants to escape such embarrassment has to submit to all kinds of tests without blinking an eye, tests that made English boarding schools of the late nineteenth and early twentieth centuries notorious. These tests live on in fraternity and military hazing rituals.[15]

Things are particularly dramatic when a man is called a coward in front of a group of women. Precisely this happened in Great Britain immediately after the outbreak of the First World War, when some young women displayed their patriotism by giving white feathers to men on the street who were not wearing a uniform. The white feather was a symbol of cowardice and was immediately understood as such by the gifts' recipients.[16] This seriously bothered many men, and quite a few signed up for the army after the embarrassing experience. The idea was spurred on by Vice Admiral Charles Cooper Penrose-Fitzgerald, but the act itself lay in the hands of women, which made it all the more shameful for the unfortunate men. In 1938, Virginia Woolf looked back on the campaign, writing that, in the end, 'a man still feels it a peculiar insult to be taunted with cowardice by a woman in much the same way that a woman feels it a peculiar insult to be taunted with unchastity by a man'.[17]

Campaigning and Resisting

Even if the number of feathers actually handed out was limited, the shaming campaign left, according to Woolf, an 'immense psychological impression'. In contrast to recruitment posters that also used shaming tactics, the white-feather campaign affected men in a very personal way.[18] The difference between the two strategies is not at all trivial. While men could simply look past the posters, there was no way to escape the immediacy of the feathers.

The distinction between the shaming of a collective and the shaming of an individual person explains why political and commercial shaming campaigns have almost always failed. In 1951, bakers from West Berlin walked through the city with a cage that held 'Mr. Dishonour and Ms. Shame' captive: the message was that the couple was buying bread in East Berlin, thus doing economic damage to the more expensive bakers in the West. Likewise, the city council mounted an energetic public relations campaign against buying in East Berlin, publishing posters, short films, and slides, all, however, without any marked success.[19] It did not shame because it did not reach people on a personal level. General moral appeals and warnings do not work, a fact demonstrated by campaigns against fare dodgers in public transportation. But the feeling of shame evoked by being escorted off the train by a conductor in front of other passengers might cause those without a ticket to think twice next time.[20]

Therefore, shaming campaigns that make a direct impact on individuals are far more effective. A poster that hung in the window of a Moscow shoe store in March 1959 provides a good example. It displayed caricatures of men and women from the neighbourhood who had shoplifted or engaged in double-dealing, each depicted with their name, year of birth, and address. This measure probably did a lot more than trying to convince people that not stealing was in the interest of the common good and the socialist economy.[21]

Yet embarrassing individuals is frowned upon in liberal societies because it does injury to human dignity by exposing people to the condemnation of others. Thus, train conductors are not really out to shame fare dodgers personally. In public institutions, officials generally seek to avoid any form of degrading or humiliating behaviour. Those working in unemployment and welfare offices are directed to treat their clients with manners and respect. Part of this treatment has been the new architecture of unemployment offices—at least in Germany—that turned them from 'ignoble' dens in the 'back alleys of society' into modern, transparent service centres in malls or on main streets.[22]

Nevertheless, some welfare recipients still report the feeling that they are being shamed. Their sensitivity towards shame is closely linked to the loss of social status. But it also testifies to the internalization of social norms about performance standards. In modern societies which are based on individual work and achievement, not earning one's own money and being dependent on others is considered a social stigma. Many find it 'demeaning to the nth degree' when it becomes visible and they have to pay for their groceries with food stamps rather than cash. For the same reason, many also avoid taking advantage of food banks, where their precarious circumstances are put on display for all to see.[23]

The 'shamefaced poor' of the nineteenth century behaved in a similar way, doing all they could to keep their neediness out of sight. To respect their concerns, the charities and women's associations that helped them made sure that their names remained confidential.[24] Expectations and conventions changed with the shift from church and local poor relief to state-run welfare systems. Afterwards, those eligible no longer had to feel ashamed when applying for financial support; instead, they could be confident about their right to be supported.[25] As a general rule, applicants were not held at fault for experiencing tough times. In periods of high unemployment or inflation, this was bolstered by the fact that it was the fate of many to have to seek assistance.

People can also become resistant to shame when they reject the validity of social norms. A person who condemns the principles of wage labour and maximum achievement might not feel shame when using food stamps, even in times of full employment. Likewise, a person who goes to the opera in jeans and a t-shirt and ignores the judgemental glances and comments of high society is hard to shame. A precondition of being shamed is that one accepts the norms that one has transgressed.

Since the second half of the twentieth century, acceptance of majority norms can no longer be taken for granted. First, lifestyles have become more pluralistic: some social groups have values and customs that are not shared by others outside their group, but which are nevertheless tolerated and respected. Second, a process of de-formalization has softened or invalidated behavioural conventions that used to be rigid and obligatory. Many issues that might have been an occasion for shame and shaming fifty years ago are now seen as unproblematic. Finally, social emancipation movements have criticized and fought against traditional notions of shame and practices of humiliation. American and European feminists declared shame an outmoded tool of repression used by patriarchal societies. Since inventing the slogan 'Gay Pride' in 1969, gay and lesbian activists have expressed their denunciation of shame at all kinds of public demonstrations. The feminist motto 'the shame is over' held validity for them too.[26]

But this does not mean that people in modern societies have no honour and are thus more resistant or indifferent to shame than their forefathers and foremothers.[27] What have changed are notions of what honour is and who is able to grant it or take it away. Traditionally, inherited membership in social groups and estates vested one with honour and determined how it could be asserted or withheld. By and large, honour was measured by the position that one held in the social pecking order and by whether one acted as one's position prescribed. Today things are different. Individuals rather than social groups make claims to honour, or, as we now say, respect and recognition.[28] In the modern era, social groups have far less power and control over the lives of their members. Indeed, the material conditions of highly differentiated societies render impossible the politics of collective shaming common in early modern communities and guilds. In principle, people can freely move, change their occupation, or quit a club or association in order to avoid being shamed. Moreover, belonging to social groups is no longer the primary source of self-worth and self-esteem.

As an overall tendency, shaming has thus lost ground in modern societies. Nevertheless, it is still around. Every group uses shaming techniques to confirm its own codes of behaviour and bring transgressors into line. Such techniques are particularly prominent among adolescents. But adults, too, do not live on desert islands. Everyone has family, colleagues, neighbours, classmates, friends, and acquaintances whose recognition they value.[29] If recognition is withheld or replaced by open contempt and disrespect, even the mobile, urban, autonomous citizen of high modernity feels vulnerable and injured.

Liberalization

In a somewhat paradoxical way, she feels even more vulnerable than her traditionally minded ancestors. The more societies are beholden to the protection of human dignity, the more they tend to increase their members' sensitivity to social degradation and defamation. In this sense, there has been a considerable increase in sensitivity towards shaming over the last few decades. Petitioning against school sports competitions and their allegedly humiliating effects would have been unthinkable in the 1950s. People socialized in cultures of respect and recognition will have different ideas of what constitutes 'dignified' treatment from those who have grown accustomed to experiencing disrespect and subjugation from a young age. The liberalization of social institutions since the 1960s has contributed decisively to elevating individual expectations of personal decency and individual capacities to detect and reject degrading treatment.

But these changes did not happen on their own. Although some nineteenth-century educators had warned against intentionally humiliating children and shaming them in front of their peers, these ideas only became broadly accepted decades later. In West Germany, the first widescale debates on bad practices of child rearing took place in the 1960s and 1970s. In 1952, the Federal Court of Justice overturned a lower court's ruling against two parents for child abuse. The parents had tied up their 'rotten' 16-year-old daughter and cut her hair so short that she 'could not let herself be seen in public'. In the Federal Court's opinion, such measures were adequate for 'making the girl ashamed not only of the punishment she received, but also of the reprehensible nature of her behaviour'.[30] Against this sentence, the Federal Constitutional Court's 1968 decision that a child's human dignity is guaranteed by the Basic Law and must be respected and protected by state and society was a bombshell.[31] Up to that very day, generations of pedagogues and advice authors had defended the position either that children have no sense of personal dignity or that it is not developed enough for a few beatings to do it much damage.

It took a decade after the Constitutional Court's ruling for legislators to pass laws that forbade 'demeaning and undignified childrearing methods'. But what exactly is dignity, and what constitutes demeaning treatment? Courts have been called upon to answer this question again and again, and their answers have been neither unified nor conclusive. As the Federal Court of Justice stated in 1957, human dignity is neither absolute nor unchangeable; thus, it is subject to historical change. Insofar as new 'moral values' and 'views' come into being and gain social validity, views of what constitutes their violation change too.[32]

In 1986, a lower court found that hitting an 8-year-old child with an object was demeaning. In their decision, the judges wrote that children 'also perceive such treatment as demeaning, because it is too similar to the treatment of animals, who are normally beaten not by hand, but with objects'. Significantly, the judges did not question the parents' right to hit their children. They were just repulsed by the use of a water hose to do it, which in their eyes lowered the child to the level of an animal. In the end, the Federal Court of Justice overturned the decision on the grounds that it was 'too narrow', which opened the social and political debate anew. A law passed in the year 2000 granting children the right to a violence-free upbringing seems to have put a tentative end to the discussion: 'Corporal punishment, mental injuries, and other demeaning measures are prohibited.'[33] The 2004 British Children Act was not quite as radical. To be sure, it did abolish the 'moderate and reasonable' defence that had helped to justify corporal punishments under certain conditions. But it still allowed parents to resort to 'light smacks' if necessary.[34]

Britain (as well as many US states) also took far longer to get rid of the humiliating practice of administering beatings at school. Despite continuous criticism, head teachers, local courts, and legislators held on to such practices well after continental European countries had stopped them. In 1978, the European Court of Human Rights intervened in the case of 15-year-old Anthony Tyrer, sentenced by a juvenile court on the Isle of Man to three strokes with a birch for attacking a classmate. Although British courts had finally been forbidden from sentencing people to beatings in 1948, this did not apply to the juvenile courts on the Isle of Man. Tyrer was flogged in the presence of his father, a doctor, and three police officers. He then appealed to the National Council for Civil Liberties for help, which brought his case to the European Commission of Human Rights. The court ultimately found that Tyrer's punishment had treated him as an 'object in the power of the authorities' and violated his right to 'dignity and physical integrity' as guaranteed by the European Convention on Human Rights. The island's residents saw things differently. However, the decision gave support to parents who campaigned against the use of corporal punishment, whether it be from police officers, teachers, or headmasters. In 1986, the UK Parliament reacted by passing a law forbidding hitting in state schools, and about a decade later, these protections were extended to pupils of the UK's private schools.[35]

A letter sent to pupils at a school in Lisburn, Northern Ireland in 2016 shows how much pedagogical practices have changed since then. According to its mission statement, the public primary school on Harmony Hill—*nomen est omen*—aims 'to encourage and develop a sense of self-esteem' as well as 'respect for self and others'. Such values were reflected in the letter to the 11-year-olds. It reminded them that they should not be too disappointed if their grades were not as high as they had hoped. 'We know that each one of you has worked very hard and with a great attitude. No score can ever take that away from you. In fact, we believe that your attitude and who you are as a person is much more important than any mark on a test.'[36]

The letter quickly went viral on the internet, garnering the school much praise. It demonstrates well the cultural shifts that have thoroughly transformed the relationship between teachers and students in many, if not all places. While teachers formerly used to embarrass students with lower grades in front of the entire class, shaming is now seen as old-fashioned.

Bullies

Harmony Hill Primary School also adheres to a strict anti-bullying policy. Its purpose is to protect pupils not from disciplinarian teachers, but from the everyday forms of harassment that weaker pupils often face at the hands of the stronger. Here, too, the school is following the latest trends. As recent studies show, aggressive shaming generally takes place among schoolchildren and within peer groups. While most parents and teachers now avoid shaming for both moral and educational reasons, many children and adolescents try to assert their power and increase their status by humiliating others. Children's books started problematizing bullying in the second half of the twentieth century and many states in the USA have passed laws against bullying in schools.[37] This too demonstrates the growing sensitivity towards practices that violate a person's feelings of self-respect and dignity.

The function of bullying, however, has undergone considerable changes over time. Children have always hit each other—the boarding school novels of the nineteenth century are chock full of examples. They fought for position in the pecking order with physical and emotional violence. But repeated harassment over longer periods was the exception, and alliances between classmates were rarely stable. Students who were shamed could regain respect and find their place in the group again. Nowadays, though, bullies have a different intention. Adolescents who constantly harass and degrade others want to stigmatize, not shame in a way that would enable and allow reintegration. The ones who film their acts seek an even more radical form of exclusion, or at least accept it without much thought. All that matters for them is securing their dominance by putting it on public display—the nastier, the more impressive.

And, one might add, the more enduring. Posting shows of power on the internet ensures they will be seen by a large number of people. Things that would have only reached a small circle before the times of Facebook and Instagram now stick to victims (and perpetrators) like feathers on tar. They thus tend to have a long-lasting effect on the lives of those impacted. Debasing practices like tarring and feathering have been abolished in the name of human dignity, and the same goes for the classic pillory. But while being exposed to the public gaze on the old pillory only took a couple of hours or days, images on the internet stay in circulation far longer and reach a potentially worldwide audience.

At the same time, the internet is democratic and participatory. Users choose what information to consume, what to share, and what not to.

They can refuse to give attention to bullies and they can oppose them rather than publicly or privately gawking at the suffering of victims. Resistance is possible on the internet, even more so since perpetrators are not persons of authority and do not act in the name of the state. Therefore, all citizens have the power to decide whether they will allow people to be publicly shamed and demeaned. To beat the bullies, they do not need new laws or police measures. Alongside attentive teachers, colleagues, and fellow citizens, they simply have to have a functioning moral compass, a capacity to make judgements about social situations, and a talent for mobilizing others. In the end, if bullies fail to garner any attention or only get negative responses, their strategy for fun will quickly go up in smoke.

Humiliating and shaming are always connected with claims to power and the desire to exert it with the approval of others. Without public assent, power is worthless. Of course, there are acts of subjugation that go on between two people without the presence of another. But they belong to the world of psychotherapists and novelists. What interests the historian is the politics of humiliation, which depends on public staging and involves an audience that watches and claps at what it sees. In the absence of spectators, those who shame fall into irrelevance.

This is true of contemporary shaming platforms on the internet that turn everybody into a potential perpetrator or victim. The same goes for some television shows that expose people to millions of viewers and make them look ridiculous or contemptible. If the objects of derision allow it to go on without resisting, it means that they prefer negative attention to none at all, that their desire for recognition is so great that they are prepared to be humiliated for it. In contrast to Kant's dictum, human dignity does indeed have a price here: the notorious fifteen minutes of fame, which is more often than not fifteen minutes of shame.

Liberal societies can do nothing to stop citizens from staging themselves as objects of shaming or from watching others do the same. But their institutions can and should make sure that they do not play a part in it. At the very least, they must intervene when shaming takes on brutal forms and shame is exacerbated with violence.

Gestures of Humility or Signs of Respect?

Such a case occurred in 1935 near Stargard, Pomerania. A worker complained about a superior who had called him the laziest man in the factory. The boss was taken from his home by a group of people who proceeded to walk him through town to the worker's house. After arriving, they forced him to kneel down and apologize in a clear act of self-humiliation.[38] In present-day China, some employers still make employees who fail to meet sales targets get on their knees and publicly beg for forgiveness.[39]

Forcing someone to kneel has always meant subjugating that person. As in the cases of the Pomeranian superior or Chinese executives, this can take the form of an arbitrary ritual of atonement or apology and be coupled with unmistakable signs of power and degradation. But people also kneel of their own free will. Kneeling before God is an expression of individual humility that is highly valued in many religious cultures. Well into the nineteenth century, kneeling was seen in many parts of the world as a sign of obeisance towards those of higher rank. In China, children kneeled before their parents and courtiers before the emperor; in Europe, servants kneeled before their masters and subjects got down on their knees when petitioning the prince.

But kneeling gradually fell out of favour, especially among European men. During the process of bourgeois emancipation, they came to view it as a gesture of the enslaved and the unfree. Showing respect now needed little more than a nod of the head. But while men stood upright and restricted gestures of humility to the church and very special occasions, women had to follow a different set of rules. They were expected to do 'more than simply bow' and instead 'drop their entire body by bending their knees in a singular fashion'. This gesture had to be 'arduously practised', preferably in front of a mirror.[40]

Gestures are nothing natural, and they never were. In the best-case scenario, they could be made into second nature with considerable practice. But they are also not entirely artificial or arbitrary. 'In many cases', wrote Johann Georg Sulzer in 1773, they are 'a precise reflection of a person's inner state'. Around the turn of the nineteenth century, some viewed bodily gestures as 'translators of your sentiments', and in 1872, Darwin called them the 'language of the emotions'. He claimed that they made emotions more intense, and psychologists like Wilhelm Wundt joined him in this observation. Gestures also helped forge relationships with other people and, Sulzer theorized, had an immediate effect on their 'mood and attitude'.[41] When girls, up until the 1960s, curtseyed, they made the recipient of the symbolic gesture feel elevated and revered. At the same time, the girls were supposed to experience feelings of deference, respect, and possibly even subordination.

The British court, which continued to expect men to kneel long after the practice had been abolished on the European continent, has also kept the convention of curtseying alive. Even German chancellor Angela Merkel curtseyed a little before the queen during a 2014 visit. Only Chancellor Helmut Schmidt's wife Loki refused to curtsey on the grounds that it would have been contrary to her 'personal convictions' as a proud citizen of a republic (meaning Hamburg).[42] The queen's reaction to Ms Schmidt is not known. But such gestures are closely watched by audiences both at home and abroad. Politicians who bow their heads too deeply might be harshly criticized, as President Barack Obama learned in 2009 after meeting the emperor of Japan. His bowing gave Republicans an occasion to admonish him for what they called a 'degrading kowtow'.[43]

Kowtowing has had a negative connotation among Western diplomats since the late eighteenth century. It was primarily associated with China and its courtly ceremonies, in which domestic officials and foreign emissaries alike had to kneel before the emperor and touch their heads to the ground multiple times. European ambassadors viewed this practice as demeaning. They were unable to reconcile it with the ideas of state sovereignty and equality that had been developing in Europe since the early modern period and that had become standard principles of diplomacy after 1818. Moreover, it stood contrary to feelings of national honour, which had gained considerably in significance in the age of nationalism and democratization. Public opinion often reacted sharply to what were perceived as signs of disrespect in interstate relations and urged heads of state to demand satisfaction as codified in international law.

This was no easy task for the state that had to give it. Similar to private atonement, diplomatic apologies in the nineteenth century were felt to have something humiliating about them. When the imperialist powers of Europe made an art of forcing them out of foreign—and particularly Chinese—diplomats, it was to precisely this effect. While around 1800 China could still afford to compel British emissaries into kowtowing and then send them home empty handed, the situation changed dramatically after the country lost two wars against Great Britain and France. The changes not only affected courtly ceremonies. China also had to send emissaries regularly to Paris, London, and Berlin to atone for infringing on the national interests and sensibilities of European ministers and subjects. This was the politics of humiliation on full display and was understood by everyone involved as such.

Apologizing has remained a touchy subject in international diplomacy until this very day. This stands in contrast to the customs of social interactions, where apologizing is known as a sign of respect and good manners and usually does no damage to the self-esteem of the person making the apology.[44] In the distrustful eyes of the public, ceremonial acts in international relations are like power seismographs that pick up every little vibration made by shifts in mutual recognition and obeisance. Commentators pay painfully close attention to who bows how deep in front of whom. In 1970, for instance, the majority of West Germans disapproved when Chancellor Willy Brandt kneeled before the Monument to the Ghetto Heroes in Warsaw because they thought it weakened their government's position in its negotiations with Poland.

Many Americans have also been unable to reconcile presidential apologies with their sense of national pride and honour. When a Chinese fighter pilot died in a crash with an American surveillance plane in 2001, President George W. Bush's expression of regret for the event was criticized by conservative intellectuals as a sign of 'profound national humiliation'. They claimed that China had 'brought the United States to one knee'. Others insisted that Bush had not apologized, but had simply expressed 'sincere regret'. The speaker for China's Ministry of Foreign Affairs, however, rejected this interpretation, claiming that the letter from Washington had expressed *shenbiao qianyi*, which can be translated as a 'deep expression of apology or regret'.[45]

These spats over what words were used and what means what recall the semantic juggling act performed by China and Germany a century earlier, when the German emperor's attempt to humiliate China symbolically backfired, giving the weakened Middle Kingdom a rare victory. Contemporary China views the 'century of humiliation' not only as a past era, but also as a reminder that the country should never again let itself become a plaything of outside interests. This idea continues to inform the country's foreign policy and its insistence on being treated as an equal.

Yet this has little to do with what observers of Chinese culture call the nation's peculiar obsession with 'saving face'. They claim that losing face in China is seen as a sign of weakness and inferiority.[46] But is this really a Chinese—or Asian—peculiarity? Does it not also hold true of Europeans and Americans? Wilhelm II justified his resistance to taking back his demands that the Chinese emissaries kowtow by claiming that it would compromise his stance in the eyes of Edward VII. He too wanted to save face and assert his honour. Linguists have shown that many, if not all cultures have developed and express 'face wants', or the desire to be recognized and affirmed and not shamed and humiliated.[47]

Power and Dignity

We cannot adequately understand the 'dialectics of recognition' in international and social relations without grasping the dimension of power that permeates them. In this regard, philosopher Hans-Georg Gadamer's argument that every act of non-recognition leaves behind a 'feeling of humiliation' seems overly simplistic.[48] After all, my emotional reaction to somebody's refusal or failure to return my greeting depends on how important this person is for me. If I am of a lower status, the lack of response makes me aware of my subordinate position and causes me shame. If I am in the superior position, it might irritate me, but it certainly will not humiliate me. My feeling of self-esteem will not be affected, even if it happens in front of a group of people.

In short, public humiliation only works in the context of asymmetrical power relations. For sure, power plays a role in almost all social interactions, but only under certain circumstances does it mutate into an offensive politics of humiliation. This requires well-defined power differences, and at least one party has to want to put these differences on display for a third party. Moreover, the politics of humiliation has to be staged in a public place where it can find resonance and support. This happened in the age of imperialism, became accepted diplomatic practice in Europe after 1918, and has reached new peaks in international history since Donald Trump was sworn in as the forty-fifth president of the United States in 2017.

Under Trump's government, the outright humiliation and derision of foreign leaders—like 'Rocket Man' Kim Jong Un from North Korea—has entered everyday politics. At the same time, the president has put an end to apologies that he considered demeaning and out of place. In May 2018, he told US Naval Academy graduates: 'We are not going to apologize for America. We are going to stand up for America. No more apologies.'[49] As Trump and his followers saw it, apologies were a sign of weakness and self-humiliation, particularly in the highly competitive world of international relations.

Within this world and backed by international law, states assume similar rights and responsibilities to those held by individual persons in liberal societies. They both lay legitimate claim to dignity and honour. Yet, there are major differences in how their claims are asserted and what they are based upon. While the dignity of the state needs strength, the dignity of humans needs protection. Donald Trump, in his 2018 speech, closely linked the 'respect' that America commanded to its 'fighting force' and military efficiency. Individuals, in contrast, are highly vulnerable. The violent excesses of the 1930s and 1940s give evidence of how quickly and radically human dignity can be disposed of. In many European countries, the strong state and its willing helpers crushed the dignity of those they hated all while loudly touting the state's quasi-sacred 'honour'.[50]

The concept of human dignity has been around in European societies since the late eighteenth century. It was developed when liberal and 'enlightened' minds began to contest the forms of public corporal punishment that, in their view, degraded man to the status of an animal and dishonoured him in front of his fellow citizens. The idea was not to save people from suffering pain and cruelty at the hands of rulers, but to treat them as feeling, thinking beings rather than allegedly senseless animals.[51] After 1945, it became obvious that this idea had failed over large swathes of the globe.

Since then much has changed. In the Federal Republic of Germany, human dignity has been elevated to an inalienable right. When the Constitutional Convention proposed a first draft of the Basic Law, Article 1 clearly defined the relation between state and individual: 'The state exists for the people, not the people for the state. Human dignity shall be inviolable. To respect and protect it shall be the duty of all state authority.'[52] But what should be considered a violation of human dignity was an object of debate, and even the courts were not in agreement. What some viewed as degrading and humiliating was viewed by others as a legitimate way to teach someone a lesson.

Over the last few decades, erstwhile divergent positions have come closer. As a general trend, the definition of what constitutes an attack on human dignity has been expanded. Equally, debates on dignity and degradation have become broader, more intense, and more constant. This has less to do with a factual increase in acts of humiliation and more to do with a heightened sensitivity towards them, both in private and in public. Shaming is now criticized, with moral and juridical force, as an act of physical or mental violence. It is no longer a matter of whether someone feels shamed or humiliated. Rather, the definition of what humiliation is follows out of a society's or social group's symbolic codes and cultural conventions.

Thus, not every refusal to return a greeting can be seen as an attack on human dignity. The severity depends on the significance attributed to it. For its part, this significance is not an individual decision; rather, it is socially constructed. In our age of decreasing social formality and increasing pluralization, a missed greeting is overall less important than it might be in societies or milieus that place considerable weight on formal signs of recognition and deference. It is up to individuals to decide whether they want to let it irritate them or not. People who have adopted the kind of Stoic placidness propagated by the philosopher Martha Nussbaum will simply look away while others will react with shame or rage (psychologists call the latter a defence against shame or a reversal of affect).[53] Such defence strategies have grown more common with the rise of narcissistic patterns of feeling during the late twentieth century. People who make their self into the centre of attention and desire social recognition more than anything else will be more sensitive when it is denied them. Lowered self-esteem can then be experienced as a personal crisis and become a national obsession. In this vein, California created a 'Task Force to Promote Self-Esteem' in 1987 with members from churches, schools, and the business community.[54]

The rapid rise in significance undergone by the concept of humiliation over recent years and decades thus turns out to be an element of a new moral economy. This economy has primarily gained credence in liberal and democratic nations, whose citizens demand respect and recognition not only from the state, but also from one another. It is precisely because expectations are so high that sensitivity increases to things perceived as personally humiliating, which in turn helps explain why phenomena like bullying meet with great resistance. In contrast, societies whose behavioural norms are primarily centred on group belonging place less weight on the individual's feelings. They seldom appeal to the notion of human dignity, if at all, and when they do, it is often with a different understanding of what it means.

It is unknown whether Mohamed Bouazizi self-immolated in 2010 because he saw his human dignity degraded by the repression of the Tunisian police or because he felt his sense of self-respect offended by being slapped by a female officer. As someone who was not at home among polyglot intellectuals and professionals oriented towards European values, such notions and the feelings associated with them might have been completely foreign to him. His notion of 'self' was certainly different from that of a 26-year-old Californian Google employee or a university student in Berlin. And his understanding of honour and dignity was probably not the same as that of men of the same age and social status in Europe or North America.

Thus, when Tunisian journalists interpreted Bouazizi's public suicide as a protest against 'degradation and humiliation', they looked beyond these differences. And it was precisely this way of framing the act that sparked a political firestorm. Indeed, the desperate act of the young street vendor might not have much in common with demands for individual respect or acknowledgment of victimhood made by those engaged with Western identity politics. However, the message that he would no longer let himself be pushed around by the authorities found immediate resonance. 'Dignity' was given a political meaning that recalled the early years of the European anti-humiliation project and its engagement for the right of citizens not to suffer degradation at the hands of the state.

The European project ultimately unfolded as a long negotiation between state and citizens. Drawing on the concepts of human dignity and civil liberties, citizens were able successfully to delegitimize the state's use of humiliation and shaming in public institutions. But this should by no means be seen as a story of linear progress and unmitigated success. Rather, history has repeatedly confronted us with new social sites of shaming. And it has not just been the lower-class 'mob' that has had its fun humiliating and deriding others. Apart from staging their own spectacles of humiliation, middle- and upper-class observers have taken open or secret pleasure in watching such acts and in doing so have made them possible.

The increasing respect for others' desire to be recognized thus stands contrary to the widely felt need to use humiliation in order to gain power and attention and thereby improve one's social, political, or cultural position. Whether such strategies are successful depends upon how the public reacts. Does it go along with them and approve—or does it fight back and defend liberal values of human dignity and personal honour? The question remains open, and history is not at its end.

NOTES

Introduction

I wish to thank Kerstin Singer for her excellent help in researching and editing and Uli Schreiterer for his constructive criticism and helpful suggestions. He read the entire manuscript, some sections more than once. I am also grateful to Juliane Brauer, Timon de Groot, Uffa Jensen, Anja Laukötter, Margrit Pernau, Anne Schmidt, and Max Stille for commenting on individual chapters. Collaborating with Adam Bresnahan, who translated the book from the original German, was wonderful. For the English edition, the text has been thoroughly revised and rewritten.

1. Badie, *Humiliation*, 135–6; Gero von Randow, 'Jetzt kommt das Volk', *Die Zeit*, 20 January 2011 (with quotes from Tunisian journalist Sihem Bensedrine and other witnesses); Aleya-Sghaier, 'Tunisian Revolution'. All translations from German and French sources are those of the author unless otherwise noted.
2. Ahmet Davotoglu, 'We in Turkey and the Middle East Have Replaced Humiliation with Dignity', *The Guardian*, 15 March 2011, https://www.theguardian.com/commentisfree/2011/mar/15/middle-east-dignity-common-destiny, accessed 31 June 2018; Thomas Friedman, 'The Politics of Dignity', *The New York Times*, 31 January 2012; Klein, 'Humiliation Dynamic' and Lindner, *Enemies*, which contains many examples; Zink, *Humiliation*, 7–20.
3. 'Supporter Bearing "Idiot" Sign Stands with Defiant Driver', *Cleveland 19 News*, 18 July 2009, http://www.cleveland19.com/story/20091870/supporter-bearing-idiot-sign-stands-with-defiant-driver, accessed 11 April 2017.
4. Amanda Hess, 'The Shaming of Izzy Laxamana', *Slate*, 12 June 2015, http://www.slate.com/articles/technology/users/2015/06/izabel_laxamana_a_tragic_case_in_the_growing_genre_of_parents_publicly_shaming.html?wpsrc=kwfacebookdt&kwp_0=35576, accessed 11 April 2017.
5. Weber, *Economy and Society*, 53.
6. Williams, *Shame and Necessity*, ch. 4; Miller, *Humiliation*, 117 ff.
7. Tangney, 'Self-conscious Emotions', 543, 545; Taylor, *Pride*, 53, 59, 67; Scheff and Retzinger, *Emotions*; Deonna et al., *In Defense*.

8. Kästner, *Classroom*, 42, 60, 92, 104–7, 112–13, quote 60.

9. United Nations Office of the High Commissioner of Human Rights, *Universal Declaration of Human Rights*, http://www.ohchr.org/EN/UDHR/Pages/Language.aspx?LangID=eng, accessed 11 April 2017.

10. Czeguhn, 'Verhältnis'. Three-quarters of all constitutions explicitly mention human dignity and the dignity of the person (Baets, 'Utopia'). See Pfordten, *Menschenwürde*; Weber-Guskar, *Würde*; Basic Law of the Federal Republic of Germany (Grundgesetz, GG), https://www.bundesregierung.de/Content/EN/StatischeSeiten/breg/basic-law-content-list.html, accessed 5 December 2017.

11. Whitman, *Harsh Justice*, 100–1. The wealth of literature on the development of human rights has mostly focused on the twentieth century and has paid little attention to the history of the concept of 'human dignity'. See Eckel, *Ambivalenz*; Eckel and Moyn, *Moral*; Hoffmann, *Human Rights*. For a contrast, see McCrudden, 'Dignity'.

12. Foucault, *Discipline*, 77–8, 91.

13. Margalit, *Decent Society*, 1, 41; see the similar argument in Bieri, *Art*, 35 ('Dignity is the right to not be humiliated'), 172. In contrast to Margalit's and Bieri's philosophical reasoning, legal theorist and historian James Whitman argues that one should distinguish between (legal) cultures with 'laws of civility' (like France and Germany) and those, like the USA, with laws of 'decency'. See Whitman, 'Enforcing Civility', esp. 1287–95.

14. Braithwaite, *Crime*; Rossner, 'Reintegrative Ritual'; Münster, 'Wiederentdeckung'.

15. Cesarani, *Final Solution*, 250–1.

16. Court ruling, 17 March 2016 (Urteil des OLG München v. 17.3.2016–29 U 368/16—Internetpranger).

17. *Chinese School*.

18. Aaron J. Klein, 'Israel and Turkey: Anatomy of a Dissing War', *Time*, 14 January 2010, http://content.time.com/time/world/article/0,8599,1953746,00.html, accessed 11 April 2017.

19. Philip Oltermann, 'Merkel Lets Comedian Face Prosecution for Erdoğan Poem', *The Guardian*, 15 April 2016, https://www.theguardian.com/world/2016/apr/15/angela-merkel-agrees-prosecution-comedian-erdogan-poem, accessed 11 April 2017.

20. Court ruling, 15 March 1989 (BGH-Urteil v. 15.3.1989–2 StR 662/88, margin number 15). See Schönke et al., *Strafgesetzbuch*, 28th edn (2010), 1742 ff.

21. Bourdieu, 'Dialektik'. In Remarque's novel two strangers meet and curse each other out. Each tries to be original and, ultimately, they end up having respect for one another: Remarque, *Three Comrades*, 46–7. For a psychoanalytic perspective on defences against shame, see Wurmser, *Mask*, 194–203.

22. A study of the 1950s and 1960s showed that German state attorneys categorized only 5 per cent of charges of insult as being in the public interest: Christiansen, *Beleidigung*, 87–8.

23. Offenberger, *Jews*, 31–67.

24. See Klein, 'Humiliation Dynamic', 117–18 on the difficulties of clearly separating humiliation from shame. The New York psychiatrist differentiates by claiming that people view shaming as deserved and humiliation as undeserved. See also Miller, *Humiliation*, 117–24, 164.

25. Hörnle, 'Würdekonzept', 102. See also Landweer, 'Sich-gedemütigt-fühlen'.

26. The (London) *Times Digital Archive* shows 10,155 hits for 'humiliation' between 1785 and 1985 and only 313 for 'shaming'. In articles saved in the archives of the German newspaper the *Frankfurter Allgemeine Zeitung* between 1949 and 2016, the word 'Demütigung' (humiliation) appears ten times more frequently than 'Beschämung' (shaming), though after the 1970s the discrepancy is less extreme. Source: http://faz-archiv-approved.faz.net/intranet/biblionet/r_suche/FAZ.ein, accessed 7 September 2016. See also Miller, *Humiliation*, p. x.

27. See, for example, Noellner, *Verhältniss*, 4–5; Köstlin, *Abhandlungen*, 3, 5; Binding, *Lehrbuch*, 137. Whitman's argument that the post-1945 European (continental) emphasis on human dignity grew directly out of the older concern for honour is not altogether convincing, since it pays too little attention to the fact that, from the late eighteenth century, more emphasis was placed on the difference between 'intrinsic' and 'extrinsic' honour, thereby devaluing social honour. This development is also neglected by Margalit when he connects the concept of human dignity historically to the notion of social honour (*Decent Society*, 43).

28. Court ruling, 18 November 1957 (BGH-Urteil v. 18.11.1957–GSSt 2/57, quote at margin number 17); Geppert, 'Straftaten'; Hilgendorf, 'Beleidigung'.

29. Elena Toledo, 'Mexican Teachers Union Punishes "Traitors" with Walk of Atonement', *PanamPost*, 2 June 2016, https://panampost.com/elena-toledo/2016/06/02/mexican-teachers-union-walk-atonement/, accessed 11 April 2017; 'Outrage in Mexico over Public "Teacher Shaming"', *The Telegraph*, 2 June 2016, https://www.telegraph.co.uk/news/2016/06/02/outrage-over-mexican-teacher-shaming/, accessed 11 April 2017.

30. Piyush Srivastava, 'Shaved & Made to Ride Donkey—Two Sides of the Intolerance Coin in Heartland', *The Telegraph (Calcutta)*, 31 January 2016, http://www.telegraphindia.com/1160131/jsp/nation/story_66748.jsp#.V4d3 UXptBXt, accessed 11 April 2017.

31. In the entry on 'humility' in his *Dictionary of the English Language* from 1785, Samuel Johnson quoted the influential theologian Richard Hooker: 'When we make profession of our faith we stand; when we acknowledge our sins, or seek unto God for favour, we fall down; because the gesture of constancy becometh us best in the one, in the other the behaviour of *humility*.' (Ibid., i. 983).

32. Preuß, 'Demut'; Zink, *Humiliation*, 23 ff.; Nietzsche, *Beyond Good and Evil*, 153 ff.; Paulsen, *Regierung der Morgenländer*, 129, 134.

33. Elias, *Civilizing Process*, 414–21.

34. Simmel, 'Psychologie der Scham'.

35. Lewis, 'Shame'; Wurmser, *Mask*, 16–17, 308; Nathanson, 'Timetable', 5; Williams, *Shame and Necessity*, 222.

36. Marx, 'Eighteenth Brumaire', 103.

Chapter 1

1. Behrens, *Scham*, 205; Rexroth, *Deviance*, 110–22. See also D'Artagnan, 'Rituel Punitif'.

2. ALR stands for Allgemeines Landrecht für die Preußischen Staaten (Prussian General Law Code). For its origins and its approach to penal policy, see Evans, *Rituals*, 133–40. Patent from 13 January 1787, §33, Justizgesetzsammlung 611/1787, in *Joseph des Zweyten*, 15; Bitter, *Strafrecht*, 118.

3. Lidman, *Spektakel*, 187, 189; Lidman, 'Schande', 208–9.

4. Dülmen, *Der ehrlose Mensch*, 81; Smith, 'Civilized People', esp. 33.

5. Burke, *Speeches*, 156–9. See also Bartlett, 'Sodomites'.

6. Evans, *Rituals*; Spierenburg, *Spectacle*; Friedland, *Seeing Justice Done*.

7. Schreiner, 'Verletzte Ehre', 279.

8. Lidman, *Spektakel*, 165, 370; Wettlaufer, 'Schand- und Ehrenstrafen'.

9. Koziol, *Begging Pardon*, 181–2; Schreiner, 'Verletzte Ehre', 281–5; Neumann, 'Beschämung'; Ingram, 'Shame Punishments', esp. 300.

10. Ibid., 306; Nash and Kilday, *Cultures of Shame*, 37; Thompson, 'Rough Music'.

11. Davis, *Society*, 100, 105–6, 110–11, 116–17.

12. Nash and Kilday, *Cultures of Shame*, 33–4.

13. Neumann, 'Beschämung', 281.

14. Garrioch, 'Verbal Insult', 108.

15. At least this is suggested in a moral tale published in Johann Evangelist Fürst's *Bauernzeitung aus Frauendorf* (viii, no. 5, 28 January 1826, 33–5). The publisher was a Bavarian court official who stood up against the pillory.
16. Beattie, *Crime*, quote 464.
17. Boswell, *Johnson*, iii. 31.
18. Ammerer, '"Durch Strafen"', 317.
19. Schwerhoff, 'Verordnete Schande', 171; Ingram, 'Shame Punishments', 298, 300; Sharpe, 'Decline', 80; Shoemaker, 'Streets of Shame', 240; Frank, *Gesellschaft*, 194; Beattie, *Crime*, 465.
20. Frank, *Gesellschaft*, 198.
21. Schwerhoff, 'Verordnete Schande', 174, quote 181; Ingram, 'Shame Punishments', 298, 300; Ammerer, '"Durch Strafen"', 320.
22. Bergk, *Beccaria's Abhandlung*, 197, xxii.
23. Morley, *Defoe*, 219–56; Moore, *Defoe*, ch. 1; Nash and Kilday, *Cultures of Shame*, 81–5.
24. Leibetseder, *Hostie*, 143–4.
25. Foucault, *Discipline*, 115–20, 232–5.
26. Shoemaker, 'Streets of Shame', 245; Davis, 'I Can Bear Punishment', quotes 101.
27. Cordingly, *Cochrane*, 247–52; Shoemaker, 'Streets of Shame', 245; Smith, 'Civilized People', 37.
28. *Edinburgh Annual Register for 1815*, 29–31; Sharpe, 'Decline', 81; Shoemaker, 'Streets of Shame', 240.
29. Rush, *Enquiry*, quotes 5, 10, 14, 18.
30. Dufriche de Valazé, *Loix Pénales*, 343–4; Muyart de Vouglans, *Loix Criminelles*, 63–4; Hentig, *Strafe*, i. 423–6.
31. Globig and Huster, *Abhandlung*, 83.
32. Whitman, *Harsh Justice*, 113–16; Smirra, *Entwicklung*, 83–9; Foucault, *Discipline*, 112.
33. *Novum Corpus Constitutionum Prussico-Brandenburgensium* (hereafter NCC), ii (1756), no. 64, 115 (rescript from 10 July 1756). Svarez used the same formulation in 1792 in his lessons for the prince (*Vorträge*, 28).
34. Sonnenfels, *Grundsätze*, 442.
35. *Gesetzrevision*, i. 69.
36. Gräff et al., *Ergänzungen*, 336–7 (rescript from 10 October 1794). The 'Spanish mantle' was a wooden, barrel-formed coat placed on the convicted. Also out of wood, the 'shrew's fiddle' was primarily used against women, as its name suggests.

37. Evans, *Tales*, 100–1, offers examples into the 1830s.
38. Article 22 of the 1810 *Code Pénal* prescribed that every person sentenced to 'perpetual hard labour; to hard labour for time; or to solitary imprisonment; shall, before he undergo his punishment, be set in the pillory in the market-place, and shall remain there exposed to the view of the people for one hour; above his head shall be placed a label, containing, in large and legible characters, his name, profession, dwelling-place (*domicile*), his punishment, and the cause of his condemnation' (*The Penal Code of France*, 6).
39. *Collection complète des lois*, 121–54, here 131. According to Mittermaier, *Strafgesetzgebung*, i. 277, after this change the balance of dishonouring and corrective punishments was reversed: Between 1825 and 1831, 60 out of every 100 sentences were dishonouring, whereas after 1832 it was only 40. Many German states still had penal codes that contained honour punishments and the pillory.
40. Smirra, *Entwicklung*, quote 143.
41. Landsberg, *Gutachten*, 47.
42. Grolman, *Grundsätze*, 77.
43. Helfer, 'Denkmäler', 65; Lottner, *Sammlung*, i (1834), quotes 110, 231.
44. Geheimes Staatsarchiv Preußischer Kulturbesitz (hereafter GStA) Berlin, I. HA Rep. 84 a, Nr. 49545: Letters of the Prussian Minister of Justice von Kamptz to King Friedrich Wilhelm III, 5 March 1837, 9 June 1837 and letter to Kamptz, 2 August 1837.
45. Leitner, *Sammlung*, v (1838), 118: Royal decree of 18 April 1835. The ALR supplemented the death penalty and life sentences with being whipped by the executioner.
46. Svarez, *Vorträge*, 27. On beatings as a form of exerting domination see Koselleck, *Preußen*, 641–59.
47. *Gesetzrevision*, i. 110–11 (Motivating Reasons to the First Draft of the Revisor from 1827). On Klein see Kleensang, *Konzept*, 195–213.
48. In 1798, a report by the Prussian college of medicine in Bayreuth concluded that a mild chastisement should be achieved for both sexes by hitting them with a paddle, while a 'hard punishment for both sexes' should be achieved by cutting a 'half-inch thick, three feet long half-fresh switch of hazel bush' and hitting them, 'according to the constitution of the subject', 40, 50, and up to 80 times over the span of one or two days, 'all ad posteriora, the least dangerous place to do it' (Wahrhold and Antistiani, 'Diebstahl', quote 150).
49. 'Zwey merkwürdige Verordnungen', quotes 37–8. The ALR only required that the 'bodily constitution of the punished' be taken into consideration (Part 2, Title 20, Section 10, §50).

NOTES TO PAGES 34−9

50. Kant, *Groundwork*, 46.
51. Kant, *Metaphysics*, 225; see also Bayefsky, 'Dignity'; Darwall, 'Kant'.
52. Beattie, *Crime*, quotes 462, 461.
53. Ingram, 'Shame Punishments', 295–6; Dabhoiwala, 'Sex and Societies', quote 297.
54. Smith, 'Civilized People', 38. See Beattie, *Crime*, 463–4, for more (and similar) examples.
55. *Gesetzrevision*, iv.i/i. 43.
56. Emsley, *Crime and Society*, 262; Shoemaker, 'Streets of Shame', 237–8; Smith, 'Civilized People', 39; Sharpe, 'Decline', 83.
57. Cox, *Crime*, 95.
58. Grolman, *Grundsätze*, 85; Hudtwalcker, 'Züchtigungen', 175. Even in the heated debates on corporal punishment that took place during the revision of the Prussian penal code in the 1830s and 1840s, it was a matter of consensus that 'public chastisement is not to be permitted, because it deeply humiliates the criminal, can lead to greater furore during commotions, and is irreconcilable with the decision to abolish public punishments, even for severe crimes' (*Gesetzrevision*, iv/i. 40, from the minutes of the state commission's meeting on 21 April 1838).
59. Mittermaier, 'Züchtigung', esp. 657. Gießen's Court Counsellor of Justice Noellner similarly argued in 1843 that the 'reprehensibility' of corporal punishments was primarily due not to their being public, but to their being 'demeaning' (Noellner, 'Bemerkungen', quote 202).
60. *Gesetzrevision*, v. 306–7.
61. Landsberg, *Gutachten*, 29, 47.
62. *Gesetzrevision*, i. 112; v. 293, 297; vi. 599.
63. Ibid., v. 299–300.
64. Wick, *Ehrenstrafen*, 7; Welcker, 'Infamie', 393, cited 'the insult to human dignity' as a strong 'argument against corporal punishment'. Similar were Noellner, 'Bemerkungen', 192; Arnold, 'Erfahrungen', esp. 274–8.
65. Jagemann, 'Strafe', 241.
66. Ibid., 230; Hudtwalcker, 'Züchtigungen', esp. 164, 179.
67. *Gesetzrevision*, iii. 273.
68. Ibid., v. 304; Royal Decree, 6 May 1848, in: *Gesetz-Sammlung* (1848), 123.
69. Mittermaier, 'Züchtigung', 661–2.
70. Mommsen, *Grundrechte*, 27–8. The author was commenting on the Frankfurt Constitution, which did away with 'the pillory, branding, and corporal punishment' (Sellert and Rüping, *Studien- und Quellenbuch*, ii. 52). See also Kesper-Biermann, 'Gleichheit'.

71. Zedler, *Universal-Lexikon*, i (1732), 467.
72. *Allgemeines Landrecht für die Preußischen Staaten*, 697 (Part 2, Title 20, Section 10, §§607−9).
73. Globig and Huster, *Abhandlung*, 81. At the same time, the authors did not believe it was right to punish an aristocrat who had 'scathed the honour of a lower person' as harshly as if the opposite were the case, because he would then, with the loss of his good name, give up 'much more . . . than he had injured'.
74. Beattie, *Crime*, 463.
75. Klein, 'Darstellung', 118.
76. Crosby, 'Fighting for Honor', sees few differences between cities and the countryside for the period between 1650 and 1730.
77. Garrioch, 'Verbal Insult', 106, 115; Dinges, *Maurermeister*; Walton, *Policing*, 43.
78. Frank, 'Ehre und Gewalt', 322.
79. Andrews, 'Press'.
80. Jensen, 'Chicaneur', 167. Cf. Gleixner, *'Das Mensch'*. On the Prussian law on servants, see Pape, *Wiedereinführung*, 4.
81. NCC, ix (1792), no. 3, 657−66.
82. Klein, 'Darstellung', 118.
83. *Jahrbücher für die preußische Gesetzgebung, Rechtswissenschaft und Rechtsverwaltung* i (1813), 6−7 (Decree from 23 May 1812), quote 7.
84. *Gesetzrevision*, iv/i. 37; see also ibid., vi. 850.
85. Frevert, *Emotions in History*, ch. 2.
86. Behrens, *Scham*, 185.
87. Weber, *Injurien*, esp. 92−5, quotes 94, 120 (includes a reference to the University of Leipzig's faculty of law sentencing a student in 1634 to an apology and declaration of respect for kissing a woman without her consent); Fuchs, *Um die Ehre*, 48, 252.
88. Garrioch, 'Verbal Insult', 107; Walz, 'Schimpfende Weiber', esp. 186; Gowing, *Domestic Dangers*; Crosby, 'Fighting for Honor', 296.
89. James, 'Frauenstrafen', 314. On head shaving, see the contemporaneous account in Krünitz, *Oekonomische Encyklopädie*, xx (1780), 496−8; Schwerhoff, 'Verordnete Schande', 167; Hentig, *Strafe*, i. 411−12.
90. Helfer, 'Denkmäler', 73, on a Rhenish case. On the increasing conflation of honour and virginity after the sixteenth century, see Burghartz, 'Geschlecht'.
91. *Gesetzrevision*, iii. 5, 136, 271.
92. Gräff, *Ergänzungen*, 329; Evans, *Tales*, 117.
93. Meister, 'Schamhaftigkeit', 131.
94. *Gesetzrevision*, iv/i. 43 (from the minutes of 21 April 1838).

95. Royal Edict, 18 December 1848, in *Gesetz-Sammlung* (1848), 423. Still, penal law continued to privilege the kind of honour reserved for bourgeois and aristocratic men that found its expression in duelling (Frevert, *Men of Honour*).

96. Buddeus, 'Ehrenstrafen', 455; Köstlin, *Abhandlungen*, 3, 5; Fahne, *Ehrenkränkungen*, 11.

97. Distinctions elaborated in Grolman, *Grundsätze*, 88.

98. Pape, *Wiedereinführung*, 20, 57. See also Evans, *Tales*, 105–14. On similar developments in Austria, see Malfèr, 'Abschaffung'.

99. Mittelstädt, *Freiheitsstrafen*, pp. iii, 11, 18, 24–5, 57, 81–2. See also Rosenblum, *Beyond*, 36.

100. Rittner, *Mittelstädt's Broschüre*, 34; Schwarze, *Freiheitsstrafe*, pp. viii, 42–3, 45; Streng, *Studien*, 192.

101. Mittelstädt, *Freiheitsstrafen*, 85–6.

102. Frank, *Strafgesetzbuch*, 41.

103. Goltdammer, *Materialien*, i. 107–8, 224; ii. 345 (§30, §163 StGB).

104. Landsberg, *Gutachten*, 47, 290; Feuerbach, *Betrachtungen*, i. 188; Weber, 'Hauptforderungen', quote 617; *Oeffentlichkeit, Mündlichkeit*, 418, 466.

105. Welcker, 'Infamie', 395, 400. Similar is Wahlberg, *Ehrenfolgen*, 59.

106. Ortmann, *Verhandlungen*.

107. Müller, *Suche*; Siemens, *Metropole*. Many newspapers regularly ran courtroom reporting, e.g. the *Berliner Abendpost* in its supplement 'The courtroom'.

108. Schwarze, *Freiheitsstrafe*, 14.

109. *Schleswiger Nachrichten*, 26 August 1902; Habermas, *Thieves*, 244–80.

110. Wahlberg, *Ehrenfolgen*, 36.

111. Whitman, 'Enforcing Civility' (with a comparison of Germany, France, and the USA). See also Goldberg, *Honor*. On French law (with far fewer libel suits), see Pin, 'Honneur'; on the USA, see Nelson, 'Honor'.

112. Köstlin, *Abhandlungen*, 7, 12.

113. Ibid., 48, 79. Similar is Binding, *Lehrbuch*, 134, 144. On criminal statistics from 1903, see *Brockhaus' Kleines Konversations-Lexikon*, i. 1024.

114. This was prescribed by §200 of the Empire's penal code. On civil suits and measures of atonement, see Liepmann, *Beleidigung*, 126; Hahn, *Materialien*, 277.

115. Frank, *Strafgesetzbuch*, 259; Binding, *Lehrbuch*, 163; Köstlin, *Abhandlungen*, 80.

116. *Gesetz-Sammlung* (1811), 149 (the royal decree permitted plaintiffs who had been insulted in pasquils to make the punishment public); *Gesetzrevision*, i. 667–8 (quotes from the report by Kircheisen and Hardenberg from

30 January 1811). See also Bors, 'Abbitte'; Moosheimer, *Actio*, 23–30; Schulte, *Strafe*, 52–74; Goldberg, *Honor*, 21.

117. Liszt, *Lehrbuch*, 247. See also Schwarze, *Commentar*, 524. Cf. Fuchs, 'Erörterung'.

118. *Entscheidungen des Reichsgerichts in Strafsachen*, vi. 180–4, Rep. 3153/81 (Court ruling from 17 April 1882). Friedrich Wilhelm III had, in 1811, given the same reasons for abolishing the legal instrument of 'private satisfaction' as reparation for insults.

119. Wahlberg, *Ehrenfolgen*, 50.

120. *Entscheidungen des Reichsgerichts in Strafsachen*, xvi. 73–7, Rep. 1077/87 (Court ruling from 17 May 1887), quote 75.

121. See also Fuchs, 'Erörterung', 425–6; Quanter, *Schand- und Ehrenstrafen*, 200. As early as 1869, experts working on a penal code for the North German Confederation voted against including court reprimands as a form of punishment because they were 'unusable due to their shaming and humiliating character' (*Motive zu dem Entwurfe*, 18).

122. *Gustav Radbruchs Entwurf* (1922), 5–6, 8, 35, 53–4. On the Weimar Republic see Rutz, *Genugtuung*; on respective laws in other countries see Hüttel, *Bekanntmachung*; on Switzerland see Kuhn, *Bekanntmachung*.

123. See pp. 54–65.

124. Schomburg, 'Bekanntmachung'.

125. *Gesetzblatt der Deutschen Demokratischen Republik*, i (1957), 643–7. On the GDR justice system, see also Sperlich, *Social Courts*.

126. From the court ruling (Rechtsprechung: Strafrecht, in: *Neue Justiz* 14 (1960), 731–4).

127. From the court ruling (Rechtsprechung: Strafrecht, in: *Neue Justiz* 16 (1962), 548–9); directive no. 12 from 22 April 1961, in: *Gesetzblatt der Deutschen Demokratischen Republik*, iii (1961), 223–8.

128. Ibid. The East German penal code that went into effect in 1968 confirmed the revisions made after 1957 and permitted the publication of sentences in order to spur on the 'mobilization' of the population against 'certain forms of criminality' (*Gesetzblatt der Deutschen Demokratischen Republik*, i (1968), 1–48, here 18, §50); Neuhof and Schmidt, 'Anwendung'.

129. Directive no. 12, 22 April 1961 (see note 127).

130. Decree of the State Council of the German Democratic Republic on the basic task and method of the organs of the administration of justice, 4 April 1963, in: *Gesetzblatt der Deutschen Demokratischen Republik*, i (1963), 33–5 (the second section is on the conflict committees); Betts, 'Property',

esp. 219, 239–40; Sperlich, *Social Courts*, 55–64; Görner, 'Erfahrungen'; Lohmann, 'Gerichte'.

131. Görner, 'Erfahrungen', 715–16.

132. The highest court praised the 'conscious discipline' of the workers in 1961 and believed the 'education of delinquent, undisciplined citizens' to be necessary (directive no. 12, 22 April 1961, see note 127).

133. Schulz, 'Elemente', 44–5, 48. In 1959, the influential jurist and later attorney general of the GDR, Josef Streit, commended the workers' courts in Czechoslovakia: 'The convicted see it as a greater disgrace when they are made to speak before the disciplinary committees instead of in court . . . The courtroom does not have such an atmosphere of intolerance' (Streit, 'Gedanken', 39). Benjamin, *Konfliktkommissionen*, 118, places similar emphasis on 'the strong rational and emotional effect that conflict committees had on transgressors. Characteristic are the often heard remarks of the accused that they would prefer a court hearing over the social organ of justice.' For similar claims regarding the Soviet Union, see Schejnin, 'Kriminalität', esp. 226. See Haerendel, *Gerichtsbarkeit*, esp. 231.

134. Reiland, *Gerichte*, 20–55; Hamann, *Ehrengerichtsbarkeit*; Schönfeldt, *Schiedsmann*, esp. 3–5 and ch. 3. On Soviet comrades' courts, see Gorlizki, 'Delegalization', esp. 422. On similar practices of social shaming in Soviet youth organizations (Komsomol) in the 1950s and 1960s, see Tsipursky, 'Coercion', esp. 61–3. On the comrades' courts set up in Chinese factories and mines after 1953, see Cohen, *Criminal Process*, 52, 103–4, 170–9.

135. http://www.documentarchiv.de/ns/nat-arbeit.html (§§35–55), accessed 21 May 2018; Gusko, 'Sinn und Ziel', esp. 263, 266; Frese, *Betriebspolitik*, 244–50; Bootz, *Hamburger Rechtsprechung*, 136–52, on the praxis of honour courts in Hamburg.

136. Freisler, 'Ehrenwahrung', 10; Schaffstein, 'Bedeutung', quotes 271.

137. Dahm, 'Erneuerung', 824 (Dahm, a member of the party and SA since 1933, was, together with Schaffstein, the main representative of the toe-the-line Kiel School); Dahm, 'Ehrenschutz', 2497–8; Schaffstein, 'Bedeutung', 271; Rietzsch, 'Strafen', 137. See Brezina, *Ehre*; Waldow, *Ehrenschutz*.

138. *Denkschrift des Zentralausschusses*, 114 (Freisler led the committee and composed the chapter on the 'Penal system'); Schaffstein, 'Bedeutung', 271; Dahm, 'Erneuerung', 832; Rietzsch, 'Strafen', 141–2. Freisler's drastic 'thought-provoking impulses' caused considerable furore. See, among others, Hentig, 'Pranger'; Bader-Weiß and Bader, *Pranger*, 151. Freisler also wrote the foreword to the booklet by Kluetz, *Volksschädlinge am Pranger* (the author was the head of the press office of the district court of Berlin).

139. Doerner, 'Gerichtsberichterstattung', 146; *Deutsche Justiz* 99 (1937), 709 (quote from the district court judge K. Schäfer, who was also a member of the committee on penal law).

140. Wildt, *Hitler's Volksgemeinschaft*, ch. 6.

141. *The New York Times*, 19 August and 4 September 1933.

142. Dodd, *My Years in Germany*, 28–30.

143. Przyrembel, *'Rassenschande'*, 73; Przyrembel, 'Ambivalente Gefühle'; Wildt, *Hitler's Volksgemeinschaft*, 174. In 1933 in Essen, a number of citizens wrote anonymous letters to the *National-Zeitung* complaining that Centre Party politician Hirtsiefer had been paraded through the streets; they viewed this as a 'cultural disgrace' and a relapse to medieval times ('Schwielenheinrich und die Spießbürger', *National-Zeitung*, 20 September 1933).

144. On medieval and early modern traditions, see Wettlaufer and Nishimura, 'History', 200, 215; Ingram, 'Shame Punishments', 292–3; Buddeus, 'Ehren-strafen', 457. On shame processions, see Schwerhoff, 'Verordnete Schande', 161.

145. Pollack, *Topographie*; Botz, *Nationalsozialismus*, 94–5; Gedye, *Bastionen*, 294–8; Offenberger, *Jews*, 31–67.

146. See Kuhlman, *Reconstructing Patriarchy*, 39–69, on the international and transnational 'Rhineland Horror' campaign.

147. Maß, 'The "Volkskörper" in Fear'.

148. Krüger, 'Selbstjustiz'; Wigger, *'Schwarze Schmach'*, 131; Martin and Alonzo, *Charleston*, 159; Lebzelter, '"Schwarze Schmach"'. Public humiliations increased after the departure of the occupying forces. Some newspapers published a 'strumpet's pillory' with a black mourning border; in 1925 in Essen-Bredeney, a 'pillory was set up in various places' listing the names of so-called Frenchmen's darlings (Krüger, 'Selbstjustiz', 122, 125).

149. Wildt, *Hitler's Volksgemeinschaft*, 186.

150. As early as 1930, National Socialists had proposed a national bill to 'protect the German nation' from racial treason; it wanted to punish mixed mar-riages with Jews by the loss of civil privileges and civic honour. The law was finally passed in 1935 after all opponents had been silenced. See Wildt, *Hitler's Volksgemeinschaft*, 167–8, 188–92.

151. *National-Zeitung*, 12 and 20 September 1933; Bücker et al., *Nikolaus Groß*, 140–2. On the 'processions' of non-Jewish persons, see Wildt, *Hitler's Volksgemeinschaft*, 181–9.

152. Kerbs et al., *Gleichschaltung*, 122–6; *Washington Times*, 23 March 1933, 1; *Daily Herald* (London), 24 April 1933, 8; Bömer, *Das Dritte Reich*, 78–9. The London *Times* printed a report about the scene in Nuremberg witnessed

by Martha Dodd and another on the Brandenburg town of Neuruppin, where a girl had been paraded around by SA officers with a sign hanging around her neck that made her 'transgression' known to all: she had failed to stand when the 'Horst Wessel Song', used as the anthem of the NSDAP, was being sung. The time of the 'spectacle' was published in the local newspaper to ensure a large crowd (Times, 23 August 1933, 10).

153. Denkschrift des Zentralausschusses, 113–14.

154. Wildt, Hitler's Volksgemeinschaft, 189–90 (quote Schacht), 190.

155. Ramm, 20. Juli, quotes 495; see also Schlabrendorff, Secret War, 303–16. Schlabrendorff was arrested on the Eastern Front on 17 August 1944 after the attempt to assassinate Hitler; he was acquitted on 16 March 1945 by the People's Court, but instead of being released, he was moved around to multiple concentration camps before being freed by American troops.

156. Langhoff, Rubber Truncheon, 179.

157. Łuczak, Położenie, 36–7, quote 37 (letter from Himmler to Hitler's deputy Rudolf Hess, 8 March 1940).

158. Tholander, Fremdarbeiter, 59–63; Storr, Zwangsarbeit, 51–5; Förtsch, '"Empörung"'; König, '"Deutsche Frau"', esp. 112–17; Heusler, '"Straftatbestand"'; Herbert, Fremdarbeiter, 79–82, 125–7.

159. Tholander, Fremdarbeiter, 64; König, '"Deutsche Frau"', 115–16; Kundrus, '"Umgang"'. When Martha Vollrath (who had had relations with a 'filthy Pole') was publicly shaven bald in Altenburg, Thuringia in February 1941, the punishment was announced by loudspeaker in a somewhat defiant tone: 'While to some this judgement might seem harsh, it is completely in line with the sentiments of the German people' (Altenburger Landeszeitung, 7 February 1941). I would like to thank Ms Grit Baum of the Landesarchiv Thüringen/Staatsarchiv Altenburg for her friendly support in researching this incident.

160. Heiber, Rückseite, 234–5 (circular by Martin Bormann, 13 October 1941), quote 234.

161. Gribbohm, 'Nahrung'. Even party members and Nazi sympathizers often found Freisler's conduct in trials to be 'harsh, unjust and unfriendly' (Koch, In the Name of the Volk, 172). For an overview, see also Rachlin, 'Freisler and the Volksgerichtshof'.

162. At the time, only press photos from the courtroom were published, not the film material: the Deutsche Wochenschau did not release a newsreel nor did the longer cuts in Verräter vor dem Volksgericht go to the cinema. After Goebbels showed it to him on 29 August 1944, Martin Bormann, head of the Party Chancellery and one of Hitler's closest confidantes, spoke out

against distributing it among the regional leaders, because 'an undesirable discussion over the conduct of the trial could easily follow'. It was only in the 1970s that parts of the recordings were shown in West Germany (Tuchel, 'Volksgerichtshof').

163. Schlabrendorff, *Secret War*, quote 318; Ramm, 20. *Juli*, 161–7, 202–6; Mühlen, *Angeklagten*, 199–200, 297–8, 308. See also the report written immediately after he was freed in 1945: Schultze-Pfaelzer, *Kampf*, above all 21–39.

164. Report by Thierack to Bormann, 8 September 1944, in: Hofer, *Nationalsozialismus*, 356; Goebbels, *Tagebücher*, part ii, xiii. 225 (entry from 4 August 1944), 211–15 (3 August 1944); Goebbels, *Reden*, ii. 342–59; Kershaw, *Hitler 1936–1945*, 689. The *Völkische Beobachter* described the accused as 'self-serving, pitiful little traitors' who projected an 'appearance of human abjection' and 'squalidness'; it quoted Freisler, who ranted about the 'moral self-emasculation of this coward' (article from 10 August 1944, 1–3).

165. Vyshinsky quoted in Boiter, *Trotsky*, 21 ('Liars and clowns, insignificant pigmies, little dogs snarling at an elephant, this is what this gang represents'). Vaksberg, *Prosecutor*, 80–3, 107–9. Vaksberg states that such insults were published by the press on commands from 'above', but that renowned authors also adopted the language of the prosecutor for themselves. On the Stalinist ritual of 'criticism and self-criticism', see Riegel, 'Rituals'; Unfried, 'Foreign Communists', esp. 185–8. On China, see Cohen, *Criminal Process*, chs 8, 9.

166. Warring, 'Relations'; Frommer, 'Denouncers'; Vervenioti, 'Women'.

167. Guillaume de Morant, 'La véritable histoire de la tondue de Chartres', *Paris Match*, 22 August 2014, http://www.parismatch.com/Actu/Societe/La-veritable-histoire-de-la-tondue-de-Chartres-583028, accessed 4 August 2016.

168. Röger, *Kriegsbeziehungen*, 128–43. In contrast to France, such campaigns generally took place during the occupation. After the liberation of Poland there were other scapegoats to be found, above all ethnic Germans.

169. Laurens, '"Femme"', 157; Kelly, 'Reconstruction'; Virgili, *Shorn Women*, esp. 96–7; Kitchen, *Legacy*, ch. 2; Gugglberger, 'Täterinnen'; Roberts, *Soldiers*.

170. John, '"Haarabschneiderkommando"', quotes 337, 344. The last quote comes from an interview conducted in 1996. On the 'Amiliebchen' (Americans' darlings), see Biddiscombe, 'Dangerous Liaisons'; Zur Nieden, 'Fraternisierung'; Reif, '"Recht"', esp. 368; Domentat, 'Hallo Fräulein'.

171. Weckel, 'Shamed by Nazi Crime'; Weckel, 'Disappointed Hopes'.

172. Kämper, *Schulddiskurs*, 296; Peitsch, '"Antifaschismus"', 3. In an 1843 letter, Marx had written of the 'national shame' he as a German felt towards the

retrograde political situation in his country and attributed to it a revolutionary force: 'Shame is a kind of anger which is turned inward. And if a whole nation really experienced a sense of shame, it would be like a lion, crouching ready to spring' (Marx, *Letters*, 133).

173. On 'collective shame', see Kansteiner, *German Memory*, 205–8 (first quote 207–8); Eitz and Stötzel, *Wörterbuch*, i. 383 ('Kollektivschuld'); Hurrelbrink, *8. Mai 1945*, 93.

174. On the prevalence of the culture of shame, see Assmann and Frevert, *Geschichtsvergessenheit—Geschichtsversessenheit*, 94. Such post-war debates on shame (in contrast to guilt) tell a different story than that analysed by Ruth Leys in her book *From Guilt*. Leys identifies a recent shift from guilt to shame as the dominant emotional paradigm of trauma theory. As she sees it, feeling guilty implies accepting responsibility and agency, whereas feeling shame does not. As shown above, in post-war Germany, shame was closely connected to personal agency and responsibility. Morat, *Tat*, 369–70, 377 (quotes by Jaspers 369); Olick, *House*, 208–312; Lethen, *Cool Conduct*, 170–86, on Carl Schmitt's concept of 'shame cultures'.

175. Strittmatter, *Nachrichten*, 333.

176. Ian Johnson, 'China's Brave Underground Journal-II', *The New York Review of Books*, 18 December 2014, http://www.nybooks.com/articles/2014/12/18/chinas-brave-underground-journal-ii/, accessed 17 August 2016, with a picture of the party member's humiliated son; Zhensheng, *Red-Color News Soldier*; Dikötter, *Cultural Revolution*, 112–25, 159–63, 178–80, 211–16. Even before the Cultural Revolution, the government had used 'informal' administrative sanctions, which publicly demeaned transgressors in a fashion similar to traditional local forms of castigation (Cohen, *Criminal Process*, 17, 20, 26–7, 51, 164–5; Dikötter, *Tragedy*, 67, 167–71; Dikötter, *Mao's Great Famine*, 36–7, 304–5).

177. Ian Johnson, 'China's Brave Underground Journal-II', *The New York Review of Books*, 18 December 2014, http://www.nybooks.com/articles/2014/12/18/chinas-brave-underground-journal-ii/, accessed 17 August 2016.

178. Nussbaum, *Hiding*, esp. 232; similar Whitman, 'What is Wrong', esp. 1088; Whitman, *Harsh Justice*, 24–5; for proponents' arguments, see Etzioni, 'Back to the Pillory?'; Kahan, 'Alternative Sanctions'.

179. Nomos 4000/1958 (https://en.wikipedia.org/wiki/Law_4000/1958, accessed 17 August 2016). See Kornetis, *Children of the Dictatorship*.

180. Zhensheng, *Red-Color News Soldier*, esp. 102–13. See the image at https://www.scmp.com/photos/china/2170061/cultural-revolution-through-lens-chinese-photographer?page=3, accessed 7 October 2019.

181. The cases of men being shorn in Greece have a different meaning than when the measure was used against 'shameless' women. At the time, long hair was seen as effeminate; the crewcut was thus more a way of forcing re-masculinization than an emasculation in the mode of Samson.

182. Bailey, *Strengthen the Country*, 48; Frodsham, *Embassy*, p. lv.

183. This difference is overlooked by Foucault, *Discipline*, and Whitman, 'What is Wrong'.

184. This does not mean that cruel treatment of animals was permitted. It is no coincidence that animal protection groups began popping up all over Europe in the nineteenth century. However, they argued their goals based not on the dignity of the animals, but on the grounds of avoiding pain. See Eitler, 'Übertragungsgefahr'.

Chapter 2

1. Kooistra, *Erziehung*, 78.

2. According to Hartmann, *Kippenberger*, 17, the artist created the sculptures in 1989 in reaction to a series of particularly negative criticisms. He was familiar with corporal punishment and disciplinary measures ('prison') from his years spent in boarding schools (Kippenberger, *Kippenberger*, 70–95, 362–3).

3. *Taschenbuch für teutsche Schulmeister 1789*, 594; Englmann, *Volksschulwesen*, 291: As late as 1870, kneeling was commonly used as a school punishment; *Gesetze und Vorschriften für die Studirenden*, 13–14.

4. Gibson, *English Vice*, 69, 100–6.

5. 'Über Dorfschulen', 25; *Taschenbuch für teutsche Schulmeister 1789*, 594; *Zeit- und Handbüchlein*, 14.

6. Scheidler, 'Dürfen in der Schule', esp. 139; *Pädagogisches Real-Lexicon*, 12. In 1909, such punishments were deemed a common 'ignominy' 'in a time of pedagogical barbarity' that 'today nobody is speaking out against' (*Encyklopädisches Handbuch der Pädagogik*, ix (1909), 9).

7. Quotes from the 1910 school regulations issued by the London County Council (Newell, *Last Resort*, 21).

8. Ibid., 22; Rowbotham, 'When to spare', 116, states for the Birmingham School Board in 1877: 'For decency's sake, girls were generally either caned on the backs of their legs, or on their hands. Boys were usually caned or flogged on shoulders, back or buttocks.' As to the children's viewpoint, see Middleton, 'Experience'. For a personal account of an Eton College student in the 1950s, see Benthall, 'Invisible Wounds'.

9. Gibson, *English Vice*, 65–79, 99–112; Ellis, 'Corporal Punishment'.

10. Thom, '"Beating Children"', 263. See, for Germany, Schumann, 'Legislation'.

11. Monroe, *Cyclopedia*, v. 91. Around 1900, demeaning practices of teachers in US schools included, alongside beatings, cursing and public admonition, 'notes of complaint to parents, a roll of dishonor displayed publicly, low grade in deportment' as well as 'ridicule', which was considered 'one of the most potent, as well as most dangerous forms of disgrace' (ibid., 90). According to Gershoff et al., *Corporal Punishment*, 1, thirty-one US states have, as of 2015, banned the practice, nineteen states have not. It is particularly common in rural areas (Han, *Corporal Punishment*).

12. Baier et al., *Kinder und Jugendliche*, 57. A total of 44,610 pupils of all genders and school levels were surveyed. See also Singer, *Würde*.

13. Bernd Kramer, 'Mutter startet Petition #bundesjugendspieleweg', *Der Spiegel*, 25 June 2015, http://www.spiegel.de/schulspiegel/leben/bundesjugendspiele-mutter-startet-petition-bundesjugendspieleweg-a-1040475.html, accessed 23 December 2015.

14. Anne-Kathrin Gerstlauer et al., 'Ehrenurkunde, wem Ehrenurkunde gebührt', *Die Zeit*, 25 June 2015, http://www.zeit.de/sport/2015-06/bundesjugendspiele-petition-anekdoten-erinnerungen, accessed 23 August 2016.

15. *NCC*, x (1798), no. 46, cols 1663–8, regulation from 23 June 1798, quote 1668.

16. Koselleck, *Preußen*, 643–52; Pape, *Wiedereinführung*, 4. One 'moderate corporal punishment' was considered to be 'five beatings with a leather whip on a clothed body part'. Prussian laws on the relation between servants and masters remained in force until 1918.

17. *Encyklopädie der Pädagogik*, i (1860), 59.

18. Rousseau, *Emile*, 217; Matthias, *Benjamin*, 200, spoke of an 'acquired sense of shame'.

19. Schröder, *Prügelstrafe*, 30–4, quote 31 (from 1905). But corporal punishment against Africans also came to be discredited. After harsh criticism in the German parliament, the Imperial Colonial Office began efforts in 1907 to curtail its use in German colonies (ibid., 87–118). On corporal punishment by British colonists in India, see Sen, *Disciplining Punishment*; Singha, '"Rare Infliction"'.

20. Klencke, *Mutter*, 486–8 (emphases here and in the following quotes in original).

21. On the increasing influence of advice literature on practices of childrearing, see Berg, '"Rat geben"'; Keller, *Ratgeber*.

22. Klencke, *Mutter*, 486–7, 555.

23. Ibid., 551–2, 575–6, 509, 495–6.

24. Humphrey, 'Duties', 42. Humphrey used the words 'to bring under' and 'to break' when describing his view that children should be raised to see obedience as their highest duty. Similar is Klencke, *Mutter*, 575.

25. Sulzer, *Versuch*, 185, 165–7. Born in 1720, Sulzer became a tutor in 1743 and, in 1747, a professor at the Joachimsthal Gymnasium in Berlin.

26. Ibid., 166–7.

27. Matthias, *Benjamin*, 97. See also Heusinger, *Familie Werthheim*, 242–3, who posited the rule: 'A child who lies must never be publicly scolded or punished for this, and barring utmost need for it, should not even be publicly reminded of it' (243).

28. Lhotzky, *Soul*, 61.

29. Kabisch, *Geschlecht*, 168, 172, 174.

30. Lindner, *Handbuch*, 110.

31. Klencke, *Mutter*, 551–2, 575–6, 509, 495–6.

32. Twain, *Huckleberry Finn*, 121.

33. Foerster, *Lebenskunde*, 40–1.

34. Foerster, *Lebensführung*, 307; Stevenson, *Letters*, 160–1 (letter from June 1874).

35. Nöstlinger, *Cucumber King*, 125–6. The book received the 1973 German Youth Literature Award for the category children's books.

36. Lüngen, 'Charaktererziehung', quotes 194–5; see also Foerster, *Jugendlehre*, 421.

37. Matthias, *Benjamin*, 103, see Kay, 'How Should We Raise Our Son Benjamin'. Similar is Wilhelm, *Züchtigung*, 61–6. Dr Edmund Abb, author of a manual on childrearing first published in 1915 and reprinted into the 1950s, believed that young children's 'feeling of honour is not highly developed', which is why beatings would have no 'damaging effects' (*Lehrbuch*, 168; see also Abb, *Erziehungskunde*, 122–5).

38. Bar, 'Lehre', esp. 183.

39. Schnell, *Ich und meine Jungens*, 137–8. The author was a teacher at a grammar school.

40. Schulz, *Mutter*, 63. First published in 1907, the book saw its eighth edition in 1923.

41. Wilhelm, *Züchtigung*, 65–6.

42. Helene Eyck, *Tagebuch 1876–1898*, 5, 12 (private collection of Frank and Rosemarie Eyck, Calgary, Canada); Budde, *Weg*, 152. Dr Heim of Berlin wrote in his diary in 1797 that he hit his young daughter Ida 'on the bottom with my hand, because she was being stubborn and screamed, which brought all my other children to cry profusely' (*Tagebücher*, 104).

43. Budde, *Weg*, 363. If authors did write about beatings, they mostly mentioned fathers and, interestingly, nannies as perpetrators (Gibson, *English Vice*, 52–3).

44. Nobes and Smith, 'Punishment', 276. The study was based on self-reports of ninety-nine families living in urban areas in and around London.
45. Hetzer, *Seelische Hygiene*, 53.
46. Haarer, *Deutsche Mutter*, 261; Haarer, *Unsere kleinen Kinder*, 236–40, quotes 239–40. Her advice book *Unsere Schulkinder* (Munich 1950) made no mention of humiliating children and instead emphasized: 'Our punishments may not ever embarrass the child' (p. 123). On Haarer and other childrearing manuals, see Gebhardt, 'Eltern', and Gebhardt, *Angst*.
47. Spock, *Common Sense Book*, 323–5.
48. Gass-Bolm, 'Ende', 455; Tändler, 'Erziehung', esp. 100–1.
49. Denise Foley, 'Growing up with ADHD', *Time*, http://time.com/growing-up-with-adhd/, accessed 28 August 2016. According to a 2006 study conducted by the *New York Times*, between one-quarter and one-half of all US children who normally spend their summer vacations at camp take medication daily. Allergy and asthma medicines were at the top, but pills against behavioural abnormalities and psychic problems were so common that one no longer had to dispense them disguised as vitamin pills to avoid stigmatization (Jane Gross, 'Checklist for Camp: Bug Spray. Sunscreen. Pills', *The New York Times*, 16 July 2006, http://www.nytimes.com/2006/07/16/us/16camps.html?_r=1, accessed 30 August 2016).
50. *Real-Encyclopädie des Erziehungs- und Unterrichtswesens*, i (1863), 225–6; *Lexikon der Pädagogik*, i (1913), cols 450–2. Even in 'institutional pedagogy', which dealt with 'problematic' children, humiliations were supposed to be used 'with great caution', a 1912 commentary on an article advised. The article's author, the Catholic teacher Bernhard Schelle, had recommended that his colleagues take hard measures against defiance: 'Such a pupil must be humiliated so long that he comes and begs for forgiveness ... Otherwise, your reputation is undermined and the little brat triumphs.' *Blätter für Anstalts-Pädagogik* 2 (1912), 36 (Schelle), 80 (Schieffer's comment). As to flogging in British reformatory and industrial schools, see Gibson, *English Vice*, 76–82.
51. In 1918, 1922, and 1923, respectively, Mecklenburg-Schwerin, Saxony, and Thuringia prohibited corporal punishment in state schools ('Kein Züchtigungsrecht für Heimerzieher und Lehrer', *Zentralblatt für Jugendrecht und Jugendwohlfahrt* 64 (1977), 2172, esp. 218). Hessen's state school law of 1921 allowed the disciplinary methods permitted in 1904 to remain, which included censure by the teacher or principal, detention, and corporal punishment. 'Dishonouring and demeaning punishments', however, were to cease (Bach et al., *Volksschulwesen*, 50, 282–3). In a Prussian decree from

1928, the Minister for Science, Art, and Education stated that 'just as in pedagogical theory, so too in pedagogical practice has corporal punishment come into disrepute. I wish that the punishment would accordingly continue to taper off and disappear altogether' (Kluger, *Volksschule*, 171).

52. Uhlig, *Dokumente*, i. 240; *Berliner Zeitung*, 24 October 1947.

53. Baske and Engelbert, *Zwei Jahrzehnte*, ii. 54 (regulation from 12 November 1959, §34). On school praxis, see Geißler, *Geschichte des Schulwesens*, 294.

54. Berg, *Theorie der Strafe*, 31, 63−4, 67.

55. Court ruling, 23 October 1957 (BGH-Urteil v. 23.10.1957–2 StR 458/56, margin numbers 35–6); refers to Hessen's ministerial decree of 13 May 1946.

56. Heber, 'Sinnhaftigkeit', 116. Girls were hardly ever the topic of discussion; they were viewed as less defiant and were not allowed to be hit out of concern for their shame and decency. See pp. 80–1, 85 and the decree of the Prussian Education Ministry from 29 March 1928 (Kluger, *Volksschule*, 171). Lower Saxony's decree of 27 October 1946 referred to it when forbidding corporal punishment for girls and only allowing it for boys in exceptional cases.

57. 'Über die Frage, ob dem Lehrer ein Züchtigungsrecht zusteht', *Juristen Zeitung* 9 (1954), cols 752–6, here 754–5 (BGH-Urteil v. 14.7.1954–5 StR 688/53); Court ruling, 23 October 1957 (BGH-Urteil v. 23.10.1957, margin number 45: 'Most parents do not have a problem with teachers meting out corporal punishment on justified occasions for the purpose of education . . . The contested judgement notes that at a parents' conference convened by the defendant in the school year 1953/54, after a long discussion, 80% of the parents in attendance declared their assent that their children receive corporal punishment.')

58. Gass-Bolm, 'Ende', 444, 457; Gass-Bolm, *Gymnasium*, 112 ff., 215 ff.; Schumann, 'Schläge', 39–40.

59. 'Über die Frage, ob dem Lehrer ein Züchtigungsrecht zusteht', 753 (see note 57). On the case of the teacher Kurt Weckwerth in Hanover, see 'Machen Sie was', *Der Spiegel*, 30 September 1953, 12–14.

60. Court ruling, 23 October 1957 (BGH-Urteil v. 23.10.1957, margin numbers 1, 10, 28–9, 50).

61. Gass-Bolm, 'Ende', 457; on stronger, more critical engagement of parents in schools, see Schumann, 'Asserting'. As to similar developments in Britain with parents' and pupils' groups campaigning against corporal punishment in the late 1960s, see Newell, *Last Resort*, 35–7. But Newell also quotes opinion polls from the mid-1960s when parents overwhelmingly favoured caning 'when other methods have failed' (ibid., 30).

62. Kopp, 'Zu dem Urteil'. As early as 1955, the judge had criticized corporal punishment as unconstitutional and unacceptable in a 'cultured state'.

63. Lindgren, *Pippi in the South Seas*, 40–52. By 2015, 30 million copies of *Pippi Longstocking* had been sold in Germany alone; worldwide the number is 66 million (*Badische Zeitung*, 10 September 2015).

64. Cf. the definition given by the American government on 'What is Bullying', https://www.stopbullying.gov/what-is-bullying/index.html, accessed 6 August 2018.

65. Maggie Astor, 'A Nation Answers a Sobbing Boy's Plea: "Why Do They Bully?"', *The New York Times*, 11 December 2017, https://www.nytimes.com/2017/12/11/us/bullying-video-keaton-jones.html, accessed 19 July 2018.

66. Baier et al., *Kinder und Jugendliche*, 57.

67. On the historical significance of children's literature for the development of readers' emotions, see Frevert et al., *Learning how to Feel*.

68. Wölfel, *Tim Fireshoe*, 5. The book was originally published in German and received the German Youth Literature Prize in 1962. The English version is from 1963.

69. Allfrey, *Golden Island*, 13–14, 20, 148, 150, was awarded the German Youth Literature Prize in 1964 and was translated into English in 1966, as well as into several other languages.

70. Blume, *Blubber*, 62, 89, 148.

71. 'Judy Blume on the Web', http://www.judyblume.com/books/middle/blubber.php; https://www.amazon.com/Blubber-Judy-Blume/dp/148141013X#reader_148141013X, accessed 29 August 2016.

72. Pergaud, *War of the Buttons*, 4, 17–18, 28–9, 50, 52. The book was made into a film twice, in 1962 and 2011.

73. The most famous boarding school novels were *Tom Brown's Schooldays* by Thomas Hughes, published in 1857, and Frederic Farrar's *Eric: or Little by Little* of 1858. In Rudyard Kipling's *Stalky & Co* (1899), the cadets read Farrar's book and laugh at its overt morality (ibid., 49, 64–5, 105–6, 137, 239).

74. Edgeworth, *Early Lessons*, 77. Edgeworth's texts were also reproduced in European and US school books and newspapers.

75. 'Letters to a younger Brother No. XII: False shame', 88.

76. Montgomery, *Anne of Green Gables*, 156–9. The book has sold 50 million copies as of today, has been translated into twenty languages, and has been adapted for musicals, plays, and films.

77. Rhoden, *Trotzkopf*, quotes 78, 83–4, 96, 98. The book was translated into English in 1898, but with some alterations to this passage, cf. Rhoden, *Taming a Tomboy*, 100–21.

78. As to such exceptions, see Rudyard Kipling's *Stalky & Co*, which is mostly about friendships and bullies among students and less about teacher–pupil relationships.

79. Golding, *Lord of the Flies*, quotes 248, 29. The book has been translated into thirty-nine languages and had, in Germany alone, fifty editions between 1956 and 2008. In the USA, it remains required reading for ninth-grade students. The author received the 1983 Nobel Prize for Literature and the book has been filmed twice.

80. Wetherell, *The Wide, Wide World*, 28; Gumpert, *Herzblättchens Zeitvertreib*, 93; Helm, *Backfischchen's Leiden*, 8.

81. Kessler, *Gesichter und Zeiten*, 102–3. See also his biography: Easton, *Red Count*, 24, 26.

82. Van Gennep, *Rites of Passage*; Turner, *Ritual*.

83. Kühne, 'Soldat', 349–50; according to Erving Goffman, 'total institutions' included boarding schools, correctional institutions, and psychiatric clinics (Goffman, *Asylums*).

84. 'Tauglich II', *Der Spiegel*, 21 August 1963, 20–2; 'Tiefste Gangart', *Der Spiegel*, 13 November 1963, 52–9; 'Solche Bengels', *Der Spiegel*, 18 December 1963, 25.

85. On the most recent case, which dealt with demeaning initiation rituals and training techniques, see Matthias Gebauer, 'Bundeswehrausbilder zwangen Soldatin zum Stangentanz', *Der Spiegel*, 14 December 2017, http://www.spiegel.de/politik/deutschland/bundeswehr-skandal-in-pfullendorf-sadistische-praktiken-in-der-ausbildung-a-1134529.html, accessed 5 April 2017.

86. Wiedner, 'Soldatenmißhandlungen'; Frevert, *Nation in Barracks*, 10–11, 21, 60–1, 111, 170–99.

87. In a publication from 9 July 1808, Gneisenau made general conscription contingent upon the 'freedom of the soldier's back' on the grounds that 'a beating is considered an outrageous insult by all estates'. Friedrich Wilhelm III followed the plea on 3 August 1808 and decreed the abolition of corporal punishment, which was only retained for second-class members of the military, i.e. for those who had committed grave offences and been found guilty by criminal courts (Pertz, *Gneisenau*, i (1864), 385–7). See also Voigt, *Gesetzgebungsgeschichte*.

88. *Verhandlungen der deutschen verfassunggebenden Reichsversammlung*, i. 288.

89. Gibson, *English Vice*, 168–77. The possibility of reintroducing naval flogging was only taken from the table in 1949.

90. Robert Blatchford, 'Why "Crucify" Tommy?', *Illustrated Sunday Herald*, 29 October 1916, 5.

91. *Manual of Military Law*, 721.
92. Sheffield, *Leadership*, 64–5; see also Graves, *Goodbye*, 147; Coppard, *With a Machine Gun*, 76.
93. *In their Own Words*, 164–7; Messenger, *Call-To-Arms*, 370–3.
94. Delbrück, 'Rezension', 517.
95. *Quellen zur Geschichte des Parlamentarismus*, 1303, 1317, 1320, 1324–5, 1333–5; *Die Ursachen des Deutschen Zusammenbruches*, 394–5.
96. *Die Ursachen des Deutschen Zusammenbruches*, 82–3 (emphasis in original).
97. Ziemann, *Front*, 116.
98. *Die Ursachen des Deutschen Zusammenbruches*, 87.
99. Wiedner, 'Soldatenmißhandlungen', 173, 184–6; Frevert, *Nation in Barracks*; Kühne, *Kameradschaft*, 80–1; Lehmann, *Infanterie*, 18–26.
100. 'Eton Students Want to Carry on Fagging Tradition', *The Telegraph*, 3 March 1977.
101. Gibson, *English Vice*, 116–19. British boarding schools also knew the custom of the headmaster delegating his right to flog to senior pupils (ibid., 69).
102. Robbins, *Pledged*, 258.
103. Quoted in Gervais, 'In the Name of Obedience', 206.
104. Land, *Goat*. The book was quickly reviewed in all major American newspapers (*The New York Times*, 29 February 2004; *The Boston Globe*, 29 February 2004).
105. Ford, 'Fraternal Order'; Dundes and Dundes, 'Elephant Walk'; Nuwer, *Hazing Reader*; Moisey, *Fraternity*; Robbins, *Pledged*; Govan, 'Old School Values'; Whaley, *Disciplining Women*, 87–115. Psychologists view hazing as a form of 'prosocial humiliation' with grave psychological effects (Klein, 'Humiliation Dynamic', 103–4).
106. According to a 1999 study, 80 per cent of college athletes reported being subjected to denigrating initiation rites, quoted in Alberts, *Coaching Issues*, 159; see also Johnson and Holman, *Making the Team*.
107. Solberg, 'Pranks'; Horowitz, *Campus Life*.
108. Mechling, 'Paddling', esp. 63; Mechling, 'Hazing'. See also Mechling's ethnographic study of the Boy Scouts, *On My Honor*.
109. Sanday, *Fraternity Gang Rape*.
110. Ibid., quote 149 (emphasis in original); Whaley, *Disciplining Women*, 107; Robbins, *Pledged*, quote 256–7. That hazing bolsters the individual's social dependency on the group is demonstrated by empirical data from Keating et al., 'Going to College'.
111. Füssel, 'Riten', 645.
112. Mann, *Wir waren fünf*, 327; Frevert, *Men of Honour*, 85–115.

113. Blattmann, '"Laßt uns den Eid"'; Möller, *Wissenschaft*, 123 ff. For a mostly positive account of his time as a 'Bursche', see Mann, *Wir waren fünf*, 326–31; mixed, but at the end positive is the account of the famous Berlin Egyptologist Erman, *Werden*, 101–10. Explicitly negative is the account of writer Kurt Martens, who even described his time spent at boarding school as an endless series of humiliating experiences and as 'the worst year of my life': he had to serve older pupils as their 'slave' and they harassed him with 'bullying, ridiculous tasks, physical abuse' (*Lebenschronik*, 47; on his time as a 'Bursche', see ibid., 98–100).

114. Sanday, *Fraternity Gang Rape*; Robbins, *Pledged*, 61.

115. Brownmiller, *Against Our Will*; https://www.nypl.org/voices/print-publications/books-of-the-century, accessed 1 September 2016.

116. Sanday, *Fraternity Gang Rape*, 150. See also Neumann, 'Gang Rape'.

117. International numbers can be found at https://en.wikipedia.org/wiki/Gang_rape, accessed 1 September 2016.

118. Known as a leftist, in 1973 the Italian actress Franca Rame was kidnapped by a group of neo-fascists in Milan, who then tortured and raped her (with the cooperation of the police, as it was later discovered). She was so traumatized by the experience that she was only capable of telling her husband Dario Fo about it two years later. It took until 1978 before she spoke about it in public (Andrew Gumbel, 'Dario Fo Looks Back in Anger on Era When Italy's Rulers Had His Wife Beaten and Raped', *Independent*, 7 March 1998, https://www.independent.co.uk/news/dario-fo-looks-back-in-anger-on-era-when-italys-rulers-had-his-wife-beaten-and-raped-1148763.html, accessed 2 August 2018).

119. 'Convention (III) relative to the Treatment of Prisoners of War. Geneva, 12 August 1949', https://ihl-databases.icrc.org/ihl/WebART/375-590006, accessed 1 August 2018.

120. On sexual violence during the Armenian Genocide during the First World War, see Bjørnlund, '"Fate"'; on gang rapes during the Second World War see Mühlhäuser, *Eroberungen*, 73–155; Sander and Johr, *BeFreier*; Gebhardt, *Crimes Unspoken*.

121. Iacobelli, '"Sum"'; Jerome Socolovsky, 'Jetzt bekommst Du ein bosnisches Baby', *Der Spiegel*, 20 March 2000, http://www.spiegel.de/politik/ausland/vergewaltigungen-in-bosnien-jetzt-bekommst-du-ein-serbisches-baby-a-69669.html, accessed 2 August 2018; Askin, 'Prosecuting', esp. 333–41.

122. *Neue Juristische Wochenschrift* 33 (1980), 56–8 (Decisions in civil law: BGB §823; StGB §185: 'Die Frauen keine kollektiv beleidigungsfähige Personengruppe').

123. Schwarzer, *PorNo*, 203–45; Rudolf Augstein, 'Die Frauen schlagen zurück', *Der Spiegel*, 3 July 1978, 76.
124. http://www.urbandictionary.com/define.php?term=walk%20of%20shame, accessed 1 September 2016.
125. Lunceford, 'Walk of Shame'.
126. Millett, 'Shame is Over'; Meulenbelt, *Shame is Over*.
127. Steinbacher, *Sex*, 295–324; Herzog, *Sex after Fascism*, chs 4–6.
128. 'Schämt sich eine Strip-tease-Tänzerin', *Stern*, 28 January–3 February 1969, 155. The nightclub dancer's desires for the future were, nevertheless, predictably conventional and not feminist: she wanted to marry a man 'who can give me everything, including money' and to 'be true to him'. Continuing to work as a legal assistant or stripper was out of the question.
129. Przyrembel, *'Rassenschande'*, 185–200.
130. Krüger, 'Selbstjustiz', 120–3.
131. [Haken], *Ausstellungen*, 77.
132. Shoemaker, 'Decline', 122–4. On local newspapers and their work as 'shaming machines' in (late) Victorian England, see Croll, 'Street Disorder', esp. 259 ff.
133. Rublack, 'Anschläge'. Weber, *Injurien*, 33, referred to the long tradition of so-called 'shame portraits'; they were exhibited in public and had the function of sanctioning 'breaches of contract and trust'. Contracts often contained a passage in which both parties freely consented to submitting themselves to this punishment. The practice was banned as an intolerable form of private revenge in 1577.
134. *Allgemeines Landrecht für die Preußischen Staaten*, 697 (Part 2, Title 20, Section 10, §621); *Gesetzrevision*, iii. 341–2; as to the French politics of printed libels and calumnies before and during the revolution, see Walton, *Policing*, 41 ff., 116 ff.
135. *Gesetzrevision*, iii. 311, 341–2.
136. Hazlitt, *Faiths and Folklore*, 551–2, 563.
137. Grimes, *Like Dew*, 6–8.
138. Greenhill, *Make the Night Hideous*, quote 21; Irvin, 'Tar, Feathers', esp. 227–8; 'Ulster Women Tar 2 Girls for Dating British Soldiers', *The New York Times*, 11 November 1971.
139. Mallmann and Steffens, *Lohn*, 158, 168. In 2016, Mexican school teachers who refused to join the strike against the government had to wear placards that denounced them as traitors and their hair was publicly cut: 'No fueron maestros los que nos raparon', *El Universal*, 1 June 2016,

http://www.eluniversal.com.mx/articulo/estados/2016/06/1/no-fueron-maestros-los-que-nos-raparon-dice-profesor#imagen-1, accessed 26 July 2018.

140. Favretto, 'Rough Music', quote 241.

141. Ibid., 230; Fureix, 'Charivari', quote 67.

142. Ibid.

143. As to the co-presence of modern and traditional forms of protest, see the articles in Favretto and Itçaina, *Protest*. They contest Charles Tilly's sharp chronological distinction between 'old' and 'modern' repertoires of protest (old = parochial, bifurcated, particular, patronage-based; modern = cosmopolitan, autonomous, modular): Tilly, *Contentious French*, 46, 391–2.

144. Shoemaker, 'Streets of Shame', 251.

145. *Entscheidungen des Reichsgerichts in Zivilsachen*, lx. 12–20, Rep. VI. 104/04 (decision from 9 January 1905). See also the Berlin creditor's trial of 1902 (see note 109 in Chapter 1).

146. Goldberg, *Honor*, 136–8.

147. Hall, 'Kaiser'; Hartmann, *Majestätsbeleidigung*. In 1907, the Reichstag decided, on the initiative of the Kaiser, to punish *lèse-majesté* more mildly.

148. Goldberg, *Honor*, 74, 84–5.

149. Binding, *Lehrbuch*, 154.

150. Frank, *Strafgesetzbuch*, 253.

151. Liepmann, *Beleidigung*, 38–9; Bar, 'Lehre', 162; according to Quanter, *Schand- und Ehrenstrafen*, 204, the publication of court proceedings was 'a modern form of shaming . . . which should only occur when it is really deserved'; in the face of numerous 'abuses', he found plausible 'a certain animosity of administrative institutions towards the press'.

152. This is according to the analysis by Berchem, *Oberlandesgericht Köln*, 290.

153. Bundesarchiv Berlin, R 601/17: anonymous letter, received on 14 September 1921. The file contains countless threats and personal attacks, most signed by the aggressor.

154. Bundesarchiv Berlin R 601/18: Letter from the Office of the President to Reichstag Representative Richard Meier, 4 July 1921; similar is the Letter to the Prussian Minister of Justice from 6 July 1921.

155. Mühlhausen, 'Weimarer Republik'; Mühlhausen, *Ebert*, 790, 912 ff.

156. *Berliner Illustrirte Zeitung*, 17 August 1902, 26 April 1903, 30 June 1906, 1 and 10 April 1910.

157. Schönke, *Strafgesetzbuch* (1942), 404. The so-called Treachery Act of 1934 punished with prison sentences statements that allegedly damaged the government or the NSDAP. A 1935 revision to penal law applied the

same protections against defamation enjoyed by state and government to the manifold organizations within the National Socialist movement (Waldow, *Ehrenschutz*, 23–4).

158. Schönke, *Strafgesetzbuch* (1942), 419–20.
159. See above pp. 56–9; Schaffstein, 'Bedeutung', 271.
160. Schönke, *Strafgesetzbuch* (1947), 426–7.
161. Tettinger, *Ehre*, quote 12. Nolte, *Beleidigungsschutz*, 13, rightly points out that Heuss confused the Law for the Defence of the Republic with the emergency decree of the president from 1931, which in turn served as the model for §187a, adopted in 1951.
162. Krutzki, '"Verunglimpfung"'.
163. Court ruling, 21 June 1966 (BGH-Urteil v. 21.6.1966–VI ZR 261/64, in *Entscheidungen des Bundesgerichtshofs in Zivilsachen* xlv. 296–311). In 1951, the court still demanded the use of 'the most careful means' and placed 'particularly strict' limits on attacks in the press (BGH-Urteil v. 26.10.1951–I ZR 8/51, in ibid., iii. 270–85).
164. In 2015, the district court in Munich followed a similar line of argumentation when it refused to hear the complaint of a woman who felt that her personal rights had been violated because she and her hateful Facebook posts had been put on the 'pillory of shame' by the *Bild* tabloid. The German Press Council also acknowledged in the story a 'public interest that transcends personal rights' (http://www.presserat.de/presserat/news/pressemitteilungen/datum/2015/; 1 December 2015, accessed 6 September 2016). But in 2016, the Munich appeals court found in her favour: *Bild* was permitted to print her posts, but not her photo identified by name (OLG München, Urteil v. 17.3.2016–29 U 368/16).
165. Tettinger, *Ehre*, 27, 42; see also Mackeprang, *Ehrenschutz*, 13, 15–6; Stürner, 'Ehre'. According to Nolte, *Beleidigungsschutz*, 6, the critics had, by 1992, become, 'if not the majority, at least a strong, well-heard minority'.
166. Kübler, 'Ehrenschutz'.
167. Böll, *Lost Honour*.
168. Bösch, 'Skandale'; Bösch, *Geheimnisse*.
169. Bitzer, Eberhard, 'Wider die Diktatur der Jupiterlampen', *Frankfurter Allgemeine Zeitung*, 16 May 1959, 2; Dahs (sen.), *Handbuch*, 110. Dahs was known as the 'star lawyer' of the German government.
170. Dahs (jun.), 'Referat', p. K 10: 'the reporting seeks to stir up or satisfy emotions like distrust, jealousy, self-righteousness, condescension, hate, schadenfreude, etc'. On the long tradition of court reporting, see Müller, *Suche*; Siemens, *Metropole*; for an example from the 1920s, see Goldstein, 'Künden' (Goldstein was the court reporter of the *Vossische Zeitung*).

171. Gerhard Mauz, 'Ich habe nichts als meine Pflicht getan', *Der Spiegel*, 11 March 1985, 103–12, quote 106; Helmut Kerscher, 'Wenn Opfer am Pranger stehen', *Süddeutsche Zeitung*, 31 January 1985, 4.

172. Joachim Jahn, 'Milde gegen Reumütigkeit?', *Frankfurter Allgemeine Zeitung*, 16 January 2009, 3; Fröhling, *Pranger*, 279 ff.

173. Kerscher, 'Wenn Opfer am Pranger stehen' (see note 171), 4. A full-text search of the digital archive of the *FAZ* from 1949 to today showed that the number of articles in which the words 'Pranger' (pillory) and 'Demütigung' (humiliation) appeared increased considerably more than the number of articles in which words like 'Wetter' (weather) and 'Politik' (politics) appeared. The increase was particularly marked in the 1990s. The search used the databases 'F.A.Z. 49–92' and 'F.A. Z. BiblioNet (1993 ff.)' of the licensed 'F.A.Z.-Bibliotheksportals' at http://faz-archiv-approved.faz.net/intranet/biblionet/r_suche/FAZ.ein, accessed 7 September 2016.

174. According to Hagglund, 'Protections', 1765, the phrase 'perp walk' has been in use among New York photographers and police officers since the 1940s; it entered common use in the 1980s. The *New York Daily News* ran the headline 'Walk of Shame' on its 16 May 2011 edition. New York mayor Michael Bloomberg agreed with French critics that the perp walk was 'humiliating', but he did not think this was a problem (http://www.slate.com/articles/news_and_politics/crime/2011/05/walk_the_walk.html, accessed 6 February 2017).

175. 'Perp Walk', *The Economist*, 18 May 2011, http://www.economist.com/blogs/democracyinamerica/2011/05/arrest_dominique_strauss-kahn, accessed 23 March 2017.

176. Amelia Tait, 'British Reality TV Is a Theater of Cruelty', *The New York Times International Edition*, 20 May 2019, https://www.nytimes.com/2019/05/18/opinion/jeremy-kyle-show-love-island.html, accessed 29 May 2019.

177. 'DSDS vs. Jugendschutz', *Digital Fernsehen* 3 (2010), 8.

178. Walter, *Living Dolls*, with numerous examples.

179. Cohen et al., *Beauty Queens*.

180. Hilgers, *Gewalt*.

181. Nick Squires, 'Teenage Girl in Italy Gang-raped after Friend Posted She Was "available" on Facebook', *The Telegraph*, 26 November 2013, http://www.telegraph.co.uk/news/worldnews/europe/italy/10475408/Teenage-girl-in-Italy-gang-raped-after-friend-posted-she-was-available-on-Facebook.html, accessed 4 September 2016.

182. Ronson, *Publicly Shamed*.

183. Köhler, 'Online-Pranger'; Matthias Heine, '"Shaming" ist der Shitstorm gegen Wehrlose', *Welt*, 28 May 2015, https://www.welt.de/kultur/article141592209/ Shaming-ist-der-Shitstorm-gegen-Wehrlose.html; http://www.liebl-net.de/ pranger/pranger.php, accessed 14 September 2016.

184. Despite their divergent modes of proliferation, analogue and digital media work together harmoniously, which immensely bolsters their potential to shame. Since the 1990s, newspapers and television have adopted digital technology, while at the same time using blogs and social media as sources of information. See Pörksen and Detel, *Skandal*; Petley, *Media*.

Chapter 3

1. Vattel, *Law of Nations*, 153–4.
2. Rohr, *Einleitung*, 413.
3. Mark Landler and Jane Perlez, 'Obama Plays Down Confrontation with China over His Plane's Stairs', *The New York Times*, 5 September 2016, http://www.nytimes.com/2016/09/05/world/asia/china-obama-group-of-20-summit-airport-arrival.html?_r=0, accessed 17 April 2018.
4. Brzezinski, *Power*, 492–3, 500. See also Houghton, *US Foreign Policy*, 73, 177, 218; Klein, 'Humiliation Dynamic', 95, 115.
5. Xiaomin and Chunfeng, 'Late Qing', esp. 413; Spence, *Memory Palace*.
6. Hsü, *Rise*, 114–17.
7. Massie, *Peter*, 819; *Memoirs of Father Ripa*, 115–26; Rockhill, *Audiences*, 25–6.
8. Chesterfield, *Works*, 159, 479, letters to his son, 21 August 1747 and 22 September 1752. Napoleon endorsed this principle after British emissary Lord Amherst visited him in his exile on St Helena in 1817 and told him about his mission to China, which had failed in part because of the kowtow ceremony. Napoleon said there was no question that one had to adhere to the ceremonial conventions of the host, and that trying to hold to one's own customs in foreign courts also found no justification in international law (O'Meara, *Napoleon*, ii. 177–9).
9. Cranmer-Byng, *Embassy to China*, 88.
10. Ibid., 85.
11. Ibid., 84.
12. Ibid., 85.
13. Ibid., 90; cf. Cranmer-Byng, 'Embassy to Peking', 157–9.
14. Cranmer-Byng, 'Embassy to Peking', 157–8; Cranmer-Byng, *Embassy to China*, 119.
15. Cranmer-Byng, *Embassy to China*, 153–4; Staunton, *Account*, 71.
16. Cranmer-Byng, 'Embassy to Peking', 157–8.

17. Ibid., 134, 137; see also Xiaomin and Chunfeng, 'Late Qing', 414–15; Harrison, 'Qianlong Emperor's Letter'.
18. Cranmer-Byng, 'Embassy to Peking', 133, 158.
19. Hüttner, *Nachricht*, 121.
20. Williams, *Middle Kingdom*, 800–1; Jochim, 'Audience Ceremonies'; Rawski, *Last Emperors*, 205; Hevia, *Cherishing Men*, 224; Hevia, 'Sovereignty', esp. 184, 187.
21. Rockhill, *Audiences*, 29; Van Braam, *Account*, 285; Duyvendak, 'Dutch Embassy', esp. 65, 88; Pritchard, 'Kotow', esp. 197–9; Blussé, 'Peeking'.
22. *Encyclopaedia Britannica*, iii (1771), 618; Grimm, *Souveränität*.
23. Fassbender, 'Westphalia, Peace of (1648)', 18–22; Duchhardt, 'Das "Westfälische System"', esp. 399.
24. See Paulmann, *Pomp*, above all chapters 1 and 2 on interstate relations in the eighteenth and early nineteenth centuries. In the second half of the nineteenth century, international meetings between monarchs became an important element of European politics. See also Paulmann, 'Searching'.
25. Jones, *Encounters*, 52–6; Vec, *Zeremonialwissenschaft*.
26. Stollberg-Rilinger, 'Honores Regii', esp. 9–12.
27. Vattel, *Law of Nations*, 463–4.
28. Ibid., 462–4.
29. For a detailed account, see Hartley, *Whitworth*, 69–77; Hennings, *Russia*, 220–37.
30. 'Royal letter from G.I. Golovkin to Charles Whitworth', 16 September 1708, in: Dixon, *Britain and Russia*, 72–4, here 73.
31. 'Account by Charles Whitworth', February 1710, in: Dixon, *Britain and Russia*, 91–3, here 92.
32. Ibid.; Hennings, *Russia*, 228; Rothstein, *Peter*, 93; Kemmerich, *Grund-Sätze*, 7, 40, 42, 49; see also Lamberty, *Mémoires*, 168–76, 230–40; Hartley, 'Clash'.
33. Wentker, 'Besuch', 136.
34. 'Act for Preserving the Privileges of Ambassadors' (1709) in: Lamberty, *Mémoires*, 240–1.
35. Kemmerich, *Grund-Sätze*, 49; Hennings, *Russia*, 229.
36. 'Royal letter from Queen Anne to Peter I apologizing for the assault in London on A. A. Matveev', 19 September 1708, in: Dixon, *Britain and Russia*, 74–5, here 75.
37. Hennings, *Russia*, 234–5.
38. Staunton, *Account*, 80.
39. Schroeder, *Transformation*, 508–9, 517–38.
40. For an example of feelings of national humiliation, see Heim, *Tagebücher*, 140 ff.

41. Windler, 'Diplomatic History', 96–7.
42. Frey and Frey, 'Reign', 723.
43. Windler, 'Diplomatic History', 97–8; Windler, *Diplomatie*, esp. chs 3.2 and 4. Up until the 1890s, the USA did not dispatch ambassadors, but only consuls, because the notion of ambassadorship conflicted with the Americans' understanding of republicanism. Instead, they tried, as Samuel Adams had done in 1778, to use ceremonial forms 'that are adapted to the true republican principles' and thus to dispense with expressions of honour wherever possible (Köhler, 'No Punctilios', 438).
44. Uhland, *Karlsschule*, 98, 176.
45. *Wiener Zeitung*, 10 January 1787 (decree from 4 January 1787); Beales, *Joseph II*, 437–8. In his memoirs, English prison reformer John Howard describes how the emperor shook his hand after a private conversation in December 1786. Howard's biographer repeats the 'generally received opinion' that the philanthropist had at first declined to meet with the emperor due to his 'aversion to the rule of court etiquette, which required persons presented to the sovereign to kneel before him; an act of adoration which he would never pay but to the Supreme.' But at their meeting, the emperor dispensed with it and shortly thereafter abolished the ceremony altogether (Brown, *Memoirs*, 466, 469–71). Krünitz, *Oekonomische Encyklopädie*, xli (1787), 419; Frötschel, 'Mit Handkuss'; Schürmann, *Tisch- und Grußsitten*, 169–80; Stollberg-Rilinger, *Emperor's Old Clothes*, 257.
46. Krünitz, *Oekonomische Encyklopädie*, xli (1787), 418–19; Hausen, *Portefeuille*, 480.
47. Krünitz, *Oekonomische Encyklopädie*, xli (1787), 417, 419; Paulsen, *Regierung*, 107–49.
48. Koziol, *Begging Pardon*, 9–10, 181; Schmitt, *Raison des gestes*, 289–90.
49. See also Saint Augustine, 'Miscellany', 229: 'For when someone seeks to pray, he arranges his limbs just as it occurs to him at the time that his body is best disposed to arouse his mind.'
50. *The Summa Theologica of St Thomas Aquinas*, ii, 2nd part, 84, 2, 71.
51. Pascal, 'Pensées', 1219 ('il faut que l'extérieur soit joint à l'intérieur pour obtenir de Dieu'). Similar is Ratzinger, *Spirit*, 190–1: 'When kneeling becomes merely external, a merely physical act, it becomes meaningless. On the other hand, when someone tries to take worship back into the purely spiritual realm and refuses to give it embodied form, the act of worship evaporates, for what is purely spiritual is inappropriate to the nature of man. Worship is one of those fundamental acts that affect the whole man. That is why bending the knee before the presence of the living God is something we cannot abandon.'

52. Stollberg-Rilinger, 'Kneeling', 154–5, 164–9; Stollberg-Rilinger, *Emperor's Old Clothes*, 250–8, on kneeling during throne investitures; Althoff, *Macht*, 200 ff.; Althoff, 'Grundvokabular', 149–64; Althoff, 'Compositio', 72.

53. *Pierer's Universal-Lexikon*, viii (1860), 602–3. On contemporary Catholicism, see Ratzinger, *Spirit*, 184–94.

54. Dorn, 'Kniebeugungsfrage'.

55. Wildeblood and Brinson, *Polite World*, 132–5, 164–98, 225–7, 248–51.

56. Claudius, *Anweisung*, 117; Alberti, *Complimentirbuch*, 86–7; Ebhardt, *Ton*, 3rd edn, 324; Ebhardt, 13th edn, 285; Franz, *Ton*, 73. Cf. the succinct definition given by a British manual from 1884: 'Bowing is merely a graceful inclination of the head and body from the waist' (*Cassell's Household Guide*, ii. 14). In 1898, British sociologist Herbert Spencer claimed that bowing was the last remainder of prostration, which he viewed as the posture of a defeated, subjugated man. He attributed it to bellicose, militaristic societies and found it more widely spread on the European continent than in Britain, where it was primarily practised among aristocrats and in the navy (Spencer, *Principles*, ii. 118–19, 122, 141–2).

57. Möser, *Phantasien*, 130.

58. Moreover, many typically female tasks were done kneeling, such as scrubbing the floor. Cf. Davidoff, 'Class and Gender'.

59. Bluntschli, *Völkerrecht*, 135. According to Adelung, *Freiherr von Meyerberg*, 37, 73, in the seventeenth century bending one's knee was also in line with 'German custom' and was practised in 1661 by the ambassadors of Holy Roman Emperor Leopold I at the court in Moscow. In contrast, it was 'old Russian custom' to touch one's head to the ground. In 1679, during an audience at the Brandenburg prince-elector's court in Berlin, ambassadors from Moscow 'at various moments touched their whole face to the ground' (*Ceremonial-Buch*, 65). The custom of bowing three times came from Louis XIV's court at Versailles (Sabatier, 'Itinéraires').

60. Foster, *Embassy*, i. 108. See also Flüchter, 'Ceremonial'; van Meersbergen, 'Repertoires'.

61. Arnold, 'Salutation'.

62. Fisher, 'Resident', esp. 431–5, 451–2. See also Dalrymple, *White Mughals*.

63. Arnold, 'Salutation', 196. On the differing 'cultural codes' of the British and Indians and the misunderstandings to which they gave rise, see Cohn, *Anthropologist*, 635–82.

64. Ibid., 463–99, 632–82.

65. Malcolm, *History*, ii. cclxiii–cccii. On the fetishization of such 'honours' in the colonial context, see Dirks, *Hollow Crown*, 355 ff., 385 ff.

66. *Manual of Indian Etiquette*, 6 (the manual also included Malcolm's instructions from 1821, 7–17); El Edroos, *Etiquette*, 14.

67. Cohn, *Anthropologist*, 654 ff.; Nuckolls, 'Durbar Incident', 530; *The Historical Record*, 205.

68. Nuckolls, 'Durbar Incident', 537–8, 555–6; Cohn, *Colonialism*, 128–9. Interestingly, official accounts did not mention the incident (e.g. Fortescue, *Narrative*, 153; *The Historical Record*, 227–8), but the scene was captured on camera—https://www.youtube.com/watch?v=4RH9Zj4TKok, accessed 27 March 2017—and later shown in British music halls (Nuckolls, 'Durbar Incident', 544).

69. Lord Hardinge not only practised these customs in 1911 at the Delhi Durbar. In 1910, after King Edward's funeral, he attended a meeting 'of all the Members of the Privy Council . . . at St. James's Place in the presence of King George [V], when the announcement of his accession to the Throne was read and each Privy Councillor in turn on bended knee swore allegiance to the Sovereign' (Hardinge, *Old Diplomacy*, 189).

70. On Amherst's 1816 mission, which included the experienced Staunton, see Hsü, *Rise*, 164–5; Gao, 'Kowtow Controversy'. Like Macartney, Amherst also refused to perform the kowtow.

71. Wang, 'Audience Question', 618. To compare the texts of the treaties, see http://www.chinaforeignrelations.net/node/144 (Great Britain), 162 (France), 206 (USA), 233 (Russia), accessed 7 April 2017. Eben von Racknitz, *Plünderung*, analyses the height of the Second Opium War, when the British and French intentionally destroyed the Yuanming Yuan (Old Summer Palace) as both a punishment and a way to teach the Chinese a lesson (231–8). The event came to be imprinted upon Chinese cultural memory as a 'symbol of national humiliation' (306–7).

72. Wheaton, *International Law* (on ambassadors: 217, 273–84). Martin also translated other texts of international law into Chinese, including Bluntschli's book on the topic. See Teng and Fairbank, *China's Response*, 98; Svarverud, *International Law*, 88–98; Xiaomin and Chunfeng, 'Late Qing', 431.

73. Wang, 'Audience Question', 619–21; Hsü, *Rise*, 302–3.

74. *Sources of Chinese Tradition*, 235–7. In 1878, a similar argument was made by the young Ma Jianzhong, who studied at Sciences Po in Paris and worked as an interpreter for the new ambassador Guo Songtao (Bailey, *Strengthen the Country*, 49–52). See also Desnoyers, 'Self–Strengthening'.

75. *House of Commons Parliamentary Papers*, China, no. 1, 1874, 3–4. (Mr Wade to Earl Granville, 7 July 1873).

76. Mr Denby to Mr Blaine, 28 January 1891, in: *Papers Relating to the Foreign Relations of the United States*, doc. 348, 363–5, quote 364; Brandt, *Dreiunddreißig Jahre*, iii. 277–8.

77. [Otto Franke,] 'Die Audienz der fremden Gesandten in Peking zur Feier des sechzigsten Geburtstages der Kaiserin Ex-Regentin', *Der Ostasiatische Lloyd*, 23 November 1894, 133–4, quote 134.

78. Kaempfer, *History*, ii. 531.

79. McWilliams, 'East', esp. 257; Tsiang, 'Sino-Japanese Relations', esp. 15–16.

80. Paine, *War*, 253 ff.

81. Hu, 'Preußenbild'; Steen, 'Resistance'.

82. Heyking, *Tagebücher*, 205.

83. Ibid., 232–4; Herold, *Reichsgewalt*, 270–1; Gottschall, *By Order*, 155 ff.

84. Herold, *Reichsgewalt*, 272–3; Heyking, *Tagebücher*, 234, 238.

85. Biggerstaff, 'Ch'ung Hou Mission'.

86. Wang, *Margary Affair*, 70, 79, 97, 99, 111.

87. *House of Commons Parliamentary Papers*, China, no. 3, 1877, 91 (Letter of Apology from the Emperor of China, October 1876); Frodsham, *Embassy*, xxv–xxvi, 118–19, 121, 187.

88. Teng and Fairbank, *China's Response*, 105. Of course, Tseng Chi-Tse performed the kowtow at the beginning of the conversation and remained kneeling the entire time.

89. Bissonnette, *Satisfaction*, 85–110; Przetacznik, *Protection*, 217–20.

90. Lord Palmerston's Address to the Electors of Tiverton, in: *The Times* (London), 24 March 1857, 9; *Hansard's Parliamentary Debates*, vol. 144, 1857, 1155 ff. (debates on 24, 26, 27 February, 2 and 3 March 1857, with strong references to 'national honour'); Wong, *Deadly Dreams*, 193 ff.

91. Hashimoto, 'Collision'; Denney, *Respect*, chs 9–22; Satow, *Diplomat*, 77–94. The businessman had indeed severely violated Japanese rules of politeness and respect (*Japanische Etikette* (1887), 156–7).

92. Keene, *Emperor of Japan*, 377; Deuchler, *Gentlemen*, 135.

93. Kamachi, 'Chinese'. The Nagasaki affair was brought to an amicable ending through the mediation of the German ambassador to Tokyo, Theodor von Holleben.

94. Frodsham, 'Record', esp. 411; Frodsham, *Embassy*, xxv–xxvi.

95. *House of Commons Parliamentary Papers*, China, no. 3, 1877, 80 (Sir T. Wade to the Prince of Kung, 26 October 1876).

96. *Gesetzrevision*, i. 667.

97. *The Times* (London), 9 February 1877, 10.

98. Heyking, *Tagebücher*, 207. (Heyking coins the highly pejorative verb 'verchinest' here.)

99. [Franke], 'Audienz', 134 (see note 77).

100. Heyking, *Tagebücher*, 209, 257; Wolf, *Wanderungen*, 48–68.

101. MacMurray, *Treaties*, i. 278–320, quote 308; Hevia, 'Making China', esp. 387–91.

102. MacMurray, *Treaties*, i. 278–94.

103. *Die Grosse Politik*, xvi. 55 (quote Bülow), 155.

104. *House of Commons Parliamentary Papers*, China, no. 5, 1901, 16 (The German Emperor to the Emperor of China, 30 September 1900), 117–8 (Letters of the Emperors of China and Japan); Kürschner, *China*, part 2, cols 381–3.

105. *Kirchliches Handlexikon*, vi (1900) 480; *Meyers Großes Konversations-Lexikon*, xix. (1909), 192.

106. Ibid., xi (1907), 539; *Kirchliches Handlexikon*, vi (1900), 480. The 1902 entry on 'kowtow' stems from the newly revised 14th edition of *Brockhaus' Konversations-Lexikon* (x. 655). The revised anniversary edition from 1898 had not yet included an entry on the word.

107. *Berliner Lokal-Anzeiger*, 5 January 1901, evening edition, 1. See also Fitzpatrick, 'Kowtowing'.

108. The diplomats in China speculated over the person's identity. (Ruxton, *Diaries Satow*, i. 135, 1 September 1901).

109. Politisches Archiv des Auswärtigen Amtes (hereafter PA AA), R 131819, memorandum by C. Arendt, 15 July 1901; cover letter, 15 July 1901.

110. Ibid., telegram no. 443, received 17 July 1901.

111. Ibid., Richthofen to Eulenburg, 31 July 1901; Eulenburg to Foreign Office, 6 August 1901.

112. PA AA, R 18506, Deputy Secretary of State Richard von Mühlberg to Heinrich von Tschirschky, 20 August 1901; Tschirschky to Mühlberg, 23 August 1901; telegram no. 506 from Mumm, received 23 August 1901. For the Chinese perspective, see Chang, *Relations*, 161 (who draws on the memoirs of the Chinese ambassador: Liu Hai-kwan, *Gēngzi hǎiwài jìshì*). I would like to thank Sonia Li Qingyang for paraphrasing and translating these memoirs with respect to the kowtow affair. They also contain telegrams from and to the Qing government, here Prince Qing and Li Hongzhang to Liu Kunyi, 23 August 1901, ii. 124–5.

113. According to Franke, *Erinnerungen*, 111, the Chinese delegation had already been informed at Port Said about the planned ceremony: 'The Chinese were very upset about the news, but they hardly showed it. South Chinese members of the mission stated they would rather be beheaded than accept

this dishonour. During the trip to Genoa they resolved not to cross the German border until the issue of the ceremony was decided in agreement with Beijing.' Franke, who coincidentally was on the same ship, had 'indeed been informed of everything, but fortunately (I) was not asked my opinion; I would honestly have not been able to give the Chinese any other advice.'

114. 'Chun qinvang shi De riji', 151. I would like to thank Prof. Dr Angelika Messner, Dr Zihui Wu, and Prof. Dr Dagmar Schäfer for their translations and expertise. A German version of the diary entries that, however, only begins on 2 September 1901 can be found in Leutner, 'Musterkolonie', 503–7. On the various forms of non-verbal greetings in China, see Wilkinson, *Chinese History*, 105–8.

115. PA AA, R 18506, telegrams from Consul General Irmer of Genoa, 23 and 24 August 1901; Foreign Office to Chancellor Bülow, 24 August 1901; telegram from Eiswaldt from Basel, 25 August 1901; Richthofen to Tschirschky, 25 August 1901.

116. Ibid., two telegrams from Tschirschky, 26 August 1901; the second telegram was addressed to Richthofen as 'private' and confidential.

117. Ibid., Holstein to Bülow, 23 August 1901. By 'good friends' he probably meant the Russians.

118. Ruxton, *Diaries Satow*, i. 134, 31 August 1901; Rockhill, 'Diplomatic Missions'. In 1905, Rockhill wrote that the Kotow Affair of 1901 was 'perhaps not the most interesting, but certainly the most amusing, incident in the whole history of the kotow question' (*Diplomatic Audiences*, 52).

119. Ruxton, *Diaries Satow*, i. 135, 2 and 4 September 1901.

120. PA AA, R 18506, pro memoria by Richthofen, 28 August 1901; Richthofen to Mumm, 29 August 1901. According to Liu Hai-kwan, *Gēngzi hǎiwài jìshì*, i. 7–8, it was the former German consul in Tianjin Albert Edwin von Seckendorff ('Si Gende') who likely changed the Kaiser's decision. Seckendorff advised the Kaiser: 'Kowtow ("*guibai*") is a ritual dedicated only to the God ("the Sky") and Jesus, it is therefore very dehumanizing and humiliating to force someone to do such a thing. Chinese officials take a very firm stance regarding their dignity [...] There are also the opinions of other countries to be taken into account. It is unworthy to lose so much for so little.' The Kaiser then slowly 'came to his senses'.

121. Ibid.; PA AA, R 18507, telegram from Richthofen to Consul Eiswaldt; telegram from Richthofen to Emperor Wilhelm, 2 September 1901; telegram from Hülsen, 3 September 1901. Richthofen himself judged the religion argument to be 'more or less correct'; most German experts had rightly rejected it as incorrect or only partially correct (PA AA, R 18506,

Richthofen to Mumm, 29 August 1901; report by Carl Arendt, 30 August 1901; letter by Consul Oskar von Seckendorff, 31 August 1901). See also Reinders, *Responses*, esp. 106–7.

122. PA AA, R 18506, pro memoria by Richthofen, 28 August 1901.

123. These reports did not always line up with the facts. For instance, Japanese newspapers and the British Reuters news agency reported that Wilhelm had demanded a kowtow from the prince himself and not just from his entourage (PA AA, R 18507, telegrams from Mumm, 31 August and 2 September 1901). The word itself also led to misunderstandings, as kneeling was not identical with kowtowing. The statements of the Kaiser and the head of court administration only mentioned that the Chinese should 'lower themselves to their knees' or 'fall to their knees'. 'Kneeling' was also the topic of discussions with the Chinese ambassador on 20 August 1901. In contrast, Prince Chun wrote in his travel diary that German diplomatic protocol demanded from his entourage *guikou*, which meant 'kneeling and kowtowing'. Prince Qing also spoke of 'kowtow' in his talks with the German ambassador in Beijing. After that point, 'kowtow' made its way into the Germans' communications. On 1 September, the German Foreign Office corrected that the reception ceremony would not involve 'kowtow, but rather simply the entourage kneeling' (PA AA, R 18507, telegram from Mumm). See Klein, 'Sühne-geschenke'. Fitzpatrick, 'Kowtowing', is not aware of such—partly intentional—misunderstandings and has a few other misinterpretations as well (Yin Chang was not the 'ex-ambassador to Germany', but the designated new ambassador, which would have made the kowtowing even more awkward for him).

124. *The Times*, 2 September 1901, 7.

125. PA AA, R 18507, Prussian legation in Bavaria, 6 September 1901 (press review); *Berliner Lokal-Anzeiger*, 5 September 1901, evening edition; Hetze, 'Feindbild'.

126. *The Times*, 2 September 1901, 7, and 5 September 1901, 3.

127. Ibid., 5 September 1901, 7; *The Washington Post*, 4 September 1901, and 8 September 1901, quote 8.

128. *Der Floh*, no. 35, 1 September 1901; *Simplicissimus*, no. 27, 1901; *Berliner Damen-Zeitung*, 29 September 1901. But some publications insulted the Chinese prince as a 'girly creature' (*Berliner Damen-Zeitung*, 8 September 1901), so scared he peed his pants (*Kladderadatsch*, 1 September 1901). The *Berliner Tageblatt*, 27 August 1901, evening edition, quoted the *Allgemeine Schweizerische Zeitung* as saying that the prince was a 'a total weakling', his

interpreter a 'little pigtailed wuss in his little skirts and woman's jacket and fine little Chinese booties'. Berlin humorist Otto Reutter composed a couplet about the kowtow affair, cf. www.otto-reutter.de. Thanks to Robert Ostermeyer for providing the image (fig. 19).

129. *Berliner Tageblatt*, 28 August 1901, morning edition; 30 August 1901, morning edition; 3 September 1901, evening edition; Franke, *Erinnerungen*, 111.

130. Müller, *Wirren*, ii, does not say anything about the kowtow question. Kürschner, *China*, part 2, col. 411, only references 'some formalities'. A similar tendency can be found in Schönburg-Waldenburg, *Erinnerungen*, 182–3 (the author was Wilhelm II's aide-de-camp in 1901). In 1920, the former interpreter and director of the Chinese salt administration in Shandong, Friedrich Wilhelm Mohr (*Gedanken*, 212), criticized the 'overtly embarrassing mission of expiation'.

131. MacMurray, *Treaties*, i. 278–94; Callahan, *China*, 31–125; Wang, *Never Forget Luo*, 'Humiliation'; Callahan, 'Insecurities', which discusses this narrative in school books, museums, national holidays, films, novels, and songs.

132. Nietzsche, *Beyond Good and Evil*, 148.

133. Welcker, 'Injurie', 409.

134. PA AA, R 18506, telegram, Richthofen to Mumm, 25 August 1901. See the similar commentary of the *Berliner Tageblatt*, 6 September 1901, morning edition.

135. PA AA, R 18507, telegram from Mumm, 31 August 1901; PA AA, R 18506, pro memoria by Richthofen, 28 August 1901.

136. Aschmann, 'Ehre', all quotes 157, 159, 166, 169–70, 172; Aschmann, *Preußens Ruhm*, 367–465, quote 454.

137. Aschmann, *Preußens Ruhm*, Bismarck's quotes 357, 359, 397.

138. The painting belonged to Wilhelm I's private collection. On the surrender of the sword in 1870, see Steller, *Diplomatie*, 34–7. On French sentiments of revenge after 1871, see Schivelbusch, *Culture*, ch. 3.

139. Toeche-Mittler, 'Kaiserproklamation', 21.

140. MacMillan, *Paris*, 27, 474 ff.

141. House, *Papers*, iv. 502; Nicolson, *Peacemaking*, 366–71; see also MacMillan, *Paris*, 476–7.

142. Ebert, *Schriften*, ii. 290; Wildt, *Hitler's Volksgemeinschaft*, 166; see also Wigger, 'Against the Laws', here 116; Maß, 'The "Volkskörper" in Fear', 235–9.

143. Wigger, 'Schwarze Schmach', 96. On the 'black horror', see also Collar, *Propaganda War*, 94–129; Wigger, 'Against the Laws'.

144. Edward A. Bagley, 'The Black Watch on the Rhine', *The Sunday Times*, 23 October 1921.

145. Hitler, *Mein Kampf*, 449; Pommerin, 'Sterilisierung'.
146. Goebbels, *Tagebücher*, part I, viii. 185–6, 22 June 1940.
147. *Der Auswärtige Ausschuß*, 4 November 1949, 16.
148. Adenauer, Memoirs, i. 184.
149. McCloy, 'Adenauer', 422. McCloy used the Canossa metaphor again in his speech at the opening of the America House in Stuttgart in 1950, saying that in the USA, nobody demanded that the Germans 'walk to Canossa', but that Americans did demand that they take a critical approach to their mistakes, reminding them that 'humility leads to strength and not to weakness'; http://usa.usembassy.de/etexts/ga4d-500206.htm, accessed 16 December 2016.
150. *Verhandlungen des Deutschen Reichstags*, 4 May 1872, 356.
151. Ilan, *Bernadotte*, 224–41; Marton, *Death*, 241–70; Sohn, *Cases*, 267–8.
152. Barros, *Corfu Incident*, 56, 58, 60, 66–7.
153. *The Paris Covenant*, 3.
154. Saurette, 'You Dissin Me?'. American president John F. Kennedy did not let himself get drawn in when Soviet leader Nikita Khrushchev, at the 1961 Vienna summit, accused the USA of wanting to 'humiliate the USSR and this cannot be accepted' (Patterson et al., *Foreign Relations*, v. 229). Like in East Germany, honour in the Soviet Union was a means of domestic politics aiming at integration and social duty; national honour hardly played an official role any more (http://dic.academic.ru/dic.nsf/ogegova/266338, accessed 28 December 2016, with thanks to Pavel Vasilyev). For the GDR, see *Meyers neues Lexikon*, ii. 806; Speitkamp, *Ohrfeige*, 220–1, 240–3.
155. *Lumumba Speaks*, 219, 221.
156. Fanon, *The Wretched*, 79–81. Fanon had joined the Algerian Liberation Front in 1955. As to colonial 'pathways of humiliation', see Badie, *Humiliation*, 67–86.
157. http://www.refworld.org/docid/3ddb8f804.html, accessed 20 December 2016. The articles 'On Responsibility of States for Internationally Wrongful Acts' were worked out by the International Law Commission of the General Assembly.
158. Weber, *Schmid*, 599. In his lecture at the University of Warsaw, whose rector had invited him, Schmid added: 'If there can be no collective guilt in the sense of the word used in penal law, still, every honest German knows that his conscience is burdened by the crimes committed against the Poles.'
159. Żurek, 'Kominek'; Żurek, 'Briefwechsel', quote 72; Greschat, 'Memorandum', quote 37; Feindt, 'Semantiken'. On the origins of the Protestant

memorandum, see Rudolph, *Kirche*, 86–149. On the 'culture of hate' in Poland, see Krzemiński, 'Kniefall', 1081–2.

160. Kerski et al., *'Wir vergeben'*, 98.

161. Greschat, 'Memorandum', 37–8.

162. Behrens, *'Durfte Brandt knien?'*, all quotes 85.

163. 'Eine Geste ohne Worte', *Tagesspiegel*, 7 December 2010, http://www. tagesspiegel.de/politik/willy-brandts-kniefall-1970-eine-geste-ohne-worte/ 3591058.html, accessed 20 December 2016.

164. 'Plötzlich wurde es ganz still', *Süddeutsche Zeitung*, 5 December 2010, http:// www.sueddeutsche.de/politik/der-kniefall-willy-brandts-ploetzlich-wurde- es-ganz-still-1.1031988, accessed 16 December 2016; Bahr, *Zu meiner Zeit*, 341; Hermann Schreiber, 'Ein Stück Heimkehr', *Der Spiegel*, 14 December 1970, 29–30; Brandt, *My Life*, 200.

165. Schreiber, 'Ein Stück Heimkehr', 29–30 (see note 164). On the media reception, see also Rauer, 'Symbols in Action'.

166. Gibney and Roxstrom, 'Status', 928; Teitel, 'Apology'.

167. Grass, 'Tagebuch' (entry from December 1970); Schreiber, 'Ein Stück Heimkehr', 30 (see note 164); Brandt, *My Life*, 200.

168. 'Kniefall angemessen oder übertrieben?', *Der Spiegel*, 14 December 1970, 27.

169. Comments from the press can be read in Behrens, *'Durfte Brandt knien?'*, 51–124; 'Letter to the Editor', *Der Spiegel*, 14 December 1970, 7; Kießling, 'Täter', esp. 217–8; Schneider, 'Brandts Kniefall'; Wilkens, 'Kniefall'.

170. Grass, 'Tagebuch', 81.

171. Kießling, 'Täter', quotes 217. See also Schneider, 'Warschauer Kniefall'.

172. Krzeminski, 'Kniefall', 1086; Wolffsohn and Brechenmacher, *Denkmalsturz?*, esp. 47, 53–8.

173. Rauer, 'Geste', esp. 145, 148.

174. 'Abe Disgraces Japan Where Brandt Honored Germany', *China Daily*, 2 January 2014, http://www.chinadaily.com.cn/kindle/2014-01/02/content_17210924. htm, accessed 17 December 2016.

175. Hoffmann, *Human Rights*; Moyn, *Last Utopia*; Barkan, *Guilt*; Ahmed, *Cultural Politics*, ch. 5; Conradi and Vosman, *Praxis*. For a critical perspective, see Giglioli, *Critica*.

176. Marrus, 'Apologies'; O'Neill, *Honor*, 177–192; Bruckner, *Tyranny*.

177. Nobles, *Politics*, 156 ff., with numerous other (often incorrect) references.

178. Marlise Simons, 'Chirac Affirms France's Guilt in Fate of Jews', *The New York Times*, 17 July 1995, http://www.nytimes.com/1995/07/17/world/chirac- affirms-france-s-guilt-in-fate-of-jews.html, accessed 10 April 2017.

179. John F. Burns, 'In India, Queen Bows Her Head Over a Massacre in 1919', *The New York Times*, 15 October 1997, http://www.nytimes.com/1997/10/15/world/in-india-queen-bows-her-head-over-a-massacre-in-1919.html, accessed 10 April 2017.

180. Nobles, *Politics*, 156–7; Nobles erroneously states 1985 rather than 1984. 'Policy Speech by Prime Minister Hosokawa Morihiro', 23 August 1993, http://japan.kantei.go.jp/127.html, accessed 10 April 2017.

181. Edwards, 'Apologizing'; Nobles, *Politics*, 71–138; 'Presidential Apology', 16 May 1997, https://www.cdc.gov/tuskegee/clintonp.htm, accessed 10 April 2017.

182. Speech by Nicolas Sarkozy, 10 July 2007, http://discours.vie-publique.fr/notices/077002208.html; 'Le discours de Dakar de Nicolas Sarkozy', http://www.lemonde.fr/afrique/article/2007/11/09/le-discours-de-dakar_976786_3212.html; 'Le discours de Nicolas Sarkozy, 6 mai 2007', http://www.liberation.fr/france/2007/05/06/le-discours-de-nicolas-sarkozy_9889; 'Discours de Nicolas Sarkozy à Alger, 4 décembre 2007', http://www.afrik.com/article13062.html; 'Le discours de M. Sarkozy sur la colonisation jugé insuffisant par le ministre de l'intérieur algérien', http://www.lemonde.fr/afrique/article/2007/12/03/le-discours-de-m-sarkozy-sur-la-colonisation-juge-insuffisant-par-le-ministre-de-l-interieur-algerien_985462_3212.html, all accessed 11 April 2017.

183. Cameron stated that an apology was no longer necessary because 'the British government had "rightly condemned" the massacre at the time'. 'David Cameron Marks British 1919 Amritsar Massacre', http://www.bbc.com/news/uk-politics-21515360, accessed 10 April 2017. This was, in the best case, only half true, see Sayer, 'British Reaction'.

184. See above, p. 69.

185. Carranza et al., *More than Words*, https://www.ictj.org/sites/default/files/ICTJ-Report-Apologies-2015.pdf, accessed 11 April 2017.

186. Barbaro, Michael, 'The Most Mystifying Lines of Sarah Palin's Endorsement Speech', *The New York Times*, 20 January 2016, https://www.nytimes.com/2016/01/21/us/politics/sarah-palin-endorsement-speech-donald-trump.html; Amy Gardner et al., 'Beck, Palin Tell Thousands to "Restore America"', *The Washington Post*, 29 August 2010, http://www.washingtonpost.com/wp-dyn/content/article/2010/08/28/AR2010082801106_2.html?sid=ST2010091201877, all accessed 12 February 2017.

187. 'Poland's Leading Daily Feels Full Force of Jarosław Kaczyński's Anger', *The Guardian*, 23 February 2016, https://www.theguardian.com/world/2016/feb/23/poland-jarosaw-kaczynski-gazeta-wyborcza-law-and-justice,

accessed 23 April 2017. In April 2017, Marine Le Pen, presidential candidate for the right-wing populist Front National, crowed the same call, saying that pupils in France only learned the darkest parts of their history, which she, at any rate, did not find to be so dark, and that she wanted the French 'to be proud to be French again', Editorial Board, 'Marine Le Pen's Denial of French Guilt', *The New York Times*, 12 April 2017, https://www.nytimes.com/2017/04/12/opinion/marine-le-pens-denial-of-french-guilt.html, accessed 23 April 2017.

188. Douglas Jehl, 'The President's Inclination: No, It Wasn't a Bow-Bow', *The New York Times*, 19 June 1994, http://www.nytimes.com/1994/06/19/weekinreview/the-world-the-president-s-inclination-no-it-wasn-t-a-bow-bow.html; Editorial, 'Barack Takes a Bow', *The Washington Times*, 7 April 2009, http://www.washingtontimes.com/news/2009/apr/07/barack-takes-a-bow/, all accessed 17 December 2016.

189. Hevia, 'Sovereignty', gives in footnote 3 numerous examples from political speeches between 1989 and 1992.

190. Adcock Kaufman, 'Century'; Gries, *Nationalism*; Moïsi, *Geopolitics*, ch. 3; Lilia Shevtsova, 'Humiliation as a Tool of Blackmail', *The American Interest*, 2 June 2015, http://www.the-american-interest.com/2015/06/02/humiliation-as-a-tool-of-blackmail/, accessed 7 July 2016; with more understanding towards Russia: Eppler, 'Demütigung'.

191. Pöschl and Kondylis, 'Würde', 654 ff.; Wahlberg, *Ehrenfolgen*, 36.

192. Wick, *Ehrenstrafen*, 7: 'Human dignity is nothing other than the universal human honour to which every human as such has a right.' Similarly, Noellner, *Verhältniss*, 4; Köstlin, *Abhandlungen*, 3, 5; Binding, *Lehrbuch*, 137 ff.

Conclusion

1. Hetzel, 'Schlosser', 107-8.

2. Staatsarchiv Detmold, M1 IE Nr 2487, Suggestion of the mayor of Bielefeld according to a regional parliamentary report, 27 June 1817.

3. Jason Webb, 'In Top Hat and Tails, Spanish Debt Agents Prosper', *Reuters*, 21 August 2008, www.reuters.com/article/us-spain-debtors-idUSLJ5525 1720080821; 'Administration of Justice Act 1970', www.legislation.gov.uk/ukpga/1970/31/section/40, both accessed 2 September 2017.

4. *Mittheilungen über die Verhandlungen des Landtags in Sachsen* (1883-4), 2nd chamber, i. (1884), quotes 256, 261-2, 819-21, 826-7; ibid. (1887-8), 2nd chamber, ii. 966; ibid. (1897-8), 2nd chamber, ii. 784; ibid. (1899-1900), 2nd chamber, ii. (1900), 1424.

5. On the case, see Lorenz and Bollmann, *Hamburg*, 88. I would like to thank Benno Gammerl for drawing my attention to this example. On the case's legal foundations, see Grapengeter, *Kultusrecht*, C III 2; *Mitteilungsblatt der Schulbehörde der Freien und Hansestadt Hamburg* 10 (1965), 44–9; 'Anordnung über Mitteilungen in Strafsachen' (1961), esp. 162; 'Anordnung über Mitteilungen in Strafsachen' (1956).

6. Rummel, 'Motive'; Banks, *Informal Justice*. On the Bavarian practice of shaming through the public reading of defamatory poems and police efforts to stop the practice, see Kaltenstadler, *Haberfeldtreiben*. On the prohibition against guilds discrediting members, see §153 of the commercial law of the German Reich, in *Deutsches Reichsgesetzblatt 1883*, 239.

7. Gorsky, 'Tuckfield's "Ride"'; Frank, 'Popular Justice'; Favretto and Itcaina, *Protest*.

8. Multiple examples can be found in Zhensheng, *Red-Color News Soldier*, esp. 102–13.

9. Berg and Ellger-Rüttgardt, '*Du bist nichts*'.

10. Wierling, *Geboren*, 149–53; Dikötter, *Mao's Great Famine*, 36–7, 303–4; Greiner, *Schamverlust*, 38. Greiner's claim that totalitarian regimes sought to do away with shame overlooks their widespread practice of shaming.

11. Braithwaite, *Crime*; Jacquet, *Shame*. Jon Ronson describes his personal conversion from a proponent of shaming to critic in Ronson, *Publicly Shamed*.

12. Bettina Vestring, 'Alle Sünder an den Pranger!', *Frankfurter Rundschau*, 13 November 2012, http://www.fr.de/politik/meinung/linkspartei-alle-suender-an-den-pranger-a-774404, accessed 11 April 2017.

13. Bloch, *Jewish Ethical Concepts*, 104; Wurmser, *Mask*, epigram.

14. *The New York Times*, 11 November 1971, 1, 17; Patrick Carville, 'Ulster Girl, 19, Tarred by Crowd', *Chicago Tribune*, 11 November 1971, sect. 2, 17.

15. Kühne, 'Soldat', esp. 348–51, on the 'Grinder of Nagold,' who was taken to court for 'constantly mistreating subordinates in a demeaning way' in 1963.

16. See the young adult novel by P. G. Wodehouse, *The White Feather*, printed in 1907.

17. Woolf, *Room*, 248. Woolf spoke of 'fifty or sixty feathers', but Nicoletta F. Gullace believes the number was much greater. See Gullace, 'White Feathers'; Ellsworth-Jones, *We Will Not Fight*, 46–9; Francis Beckett, 'The Men Who Would Not Fight', *The Guardian*, 11 November 2008, https://www.theguardian.com/world/2008/nov/11/first-world-war-white-feather-cowardice, accessed 12 April 2017. As to female opposition to the campaign, see Crozier-De Rosa, *Shame*, 172–3.

18. Rickards, *Posters*, 21, 39; Timmers, *Power*, 111.

19. Pence, 'Herr Schimpf'; Lemke, *Mauer*, 357–61.
20. Neckel, *Status*, 200–1. On advertisements and public service announcements that use shaming and the limits of their effectiveness, see Kama and Barak-Brandes, 'Taming'; Rutherford, *Propaganda*, 139–43.
21. 'Außergerichtliche Justiz', *Frankfurter Allgemeine Zeitung*, 18 March 1959, 2; Dobson, *Khrushchev's Cold Summer*, 138, 161.
22. Wiede, 'Von Zetteln', quotes from George Orwell and Siegfried Kracauer.
23. Bednarek-Gilland, *Fragiler Alltag*, 37, 55 on the long-term unemployed. The centres tasked with administering unemployment benefits in Germany give clients food stamps either in acute situations or to sanction them. The 'Tafel' has been around in Germany since 1993; the USA has had food banks since the 1960s. On loss of status as an occasion to feel shame, see Neckel, *Status*, 193 ff.
24. Sachße and Tennstedt, *Armenfürsorge*, 307–8, *passim*.
25. Crew, 'Gewalt'.
26. Munt, *Queer Attachments*; Halperin and Traub, *Gay Shame*; on the high significance of honour in patriarchal societies, see Petersen, *Ehre*, 21; Lebra, 'Social Mechanism'; Bourdieu, 'Dialektik'.
27. Massaro, 'Shame', here above all 1922–5; Hoffer, Eric, 'Long Live Shame', *The New York Times*, 18 October 1974; Lowenfeld, 'Notes'.
28. On the semantics of respect, see Assmann, 'Höflichkeit und Respekt', 179 ff.
29. See also Braithwaite, 'Shame and Modernity'.
30. Court ruling, 25 September 1952 (BGH-Urteil v. 25.9.1952–3 StR 742/51, margin number 10).
31. Peschel-Gutzeit, 'Recht'.
32. Court ruling, 23 October 1957 (BGH-Urteil v. 23.10.1957). See p. 94.
33. Court ruling, 25 November 1986 (BGH-Urteil v. 25.11.1986–4 StR 605/86, margin number 2); Salgo, 'Sterben'; Göbel, *Züchtigungsrecht*; Priester, *Ende*, 57–99.
34. Cretney, 'Children', 154–5.
35. Bates, *Evolution*, 326–30, 332–3; Mowbray, *Cases*, 223–31; Gibson, *English Vice*, 178–93. Article 3 of the 1950 European Convention on Human Rights forbids denigrating punishments and treatment (Webster, 'Degradation').
36. Laura McDaid, 'NI Primary School Sends Moving Letter with Children's Results', *BBC News*, 2 February 2016, http://www.bbc.com/news/uk-northern-ireland-35449405, accessed 11 April 2017.
37. www.bullypolice.org, accessed 8 February 2017. On the differences between US and continental European anti-bullying laws (which are not limited to

schools and also encompass the workplace), see Friedman and Whitman, 'European Transformation'.

38. Wildt, *Hitler's Volksgemeinschaft*, 181–2.

39. Forrest Hanson, 'From Crawling through the Snow to Eating Live Worms: Bizarre Public Humiliations in Chinese Workplaces', *Daily Mail Online*, 30 December 2016, http://www.dailymail.co.uk/news/article-4012956/Public-humiliations-Chinese-workplaces-live-worms-crawling-people.html; Frank Frang and Leo Timm, 'To Motivate Employees, Chinese Companies Try Public Humiliation', https://www.theepochtimes.com/to-motivate-employees-chinese-companies-try-public-humiliation_2132730.html, accessed 20 August 2018.

40. Ebhardt, *Ton*, 3rd edn, 326; Schrott, *Korsett*, 225 ff.

41. Sulzer, 'Gebehrden', 428; Claudius, *Anweisung*, 117; Darwin, *Expression*, 367; Wundt, 'Ausdruck'. See also Wundt, *Language of Gestures*.

42. 'The Queen Receives the Chancellor of Germany Angela Merkel at Buckingham Palace', https://www.youtube.com/watch?v=q4_yzwoy8Xc, accessed 11 April 2017; Schmidt, *Teppich*, 158.

43. Lee Edwards, 'Obama in Japan: Not a Bow but a Kowtow', *The Daily Signal*, 16 November 2009, http://dailysignal.com/2009/11/16/obama-in-japan-not-a-bow-but-a-kowtow/, accessed 11 April 2017; 'Conservatives Slam Obama for Bow in Japan', *CBS News*, 17 November 2009, http://www.cbsnews.com/news/conservatives-slam-obama-for-bow-in-japan/, accessed 11 April 2017.

44. Bourgeois behaviour guides started thematizing 'apologizing' in the 1870s. They claimed that when one had done injury to another, one should ask for forgiveness in person or even in writing (Ebhardt, *Ton*, 3rd edn, 707). People of 'education and tact' would certainly make things easier by 'empathically receiving' the person apologizing, since they would sense 'how much it cost him to make such a gesture of apology' (Schramm, *Ton*, 360; Kistner, *Schicklichkeitsregeln*, 93, 98–9).

45. Robert Kagan and William Kristol, 'A National Humiliation', *The Weekly Standard*, 15 April 2001, www.weeklystandard.com/article/12603, accessed 11 April 2017; Gries and Peng, 'Culture Clash?'; Avruch and Wang, 'Culture'.

46. Kagan and Kristol, 'A National Humiliation' (see note 45); Weidemann, *Lernen*, 83–105; Jentsch, *'Gesichts'-Konzept*.

47. Brown and Levinson, *Politeness*, 13, 62.

48. Gadamer, 'Hegel's Dialectic', 64.

49. Mel Leonor, 'Trump Proclaims "We Are Not Going to Apologize for America"', *Politico*, 25 May 2018, https://www.politico.com/story/2018/05/25/trump-no-apologies-america-608713, accessed 12 August 2018.

50. In 1936, the NSDAP held a National Party Convention of 'honour' to celebrate what it thought was the renewed honour of Germany after the occupation of the Rhineland. Thus, it associated honour with the restitution of state sovereignty. At the National Party Convention of 1935, the Reichstag ratified the 'Law for the Protection of German Blood and German Honour', which was supposed to guard the honour of the Aryan people and separate them from 'foreign races'.

51. This is the argument laid out in Rorty, *Contingency*, 89, where Rorty defines humiliation as an act that causes long-lasting pain. See also Shklar, *Ordinary Vices*, 37, who defines 'moral cruelty' as 'deliberate and persistent humiliation'. On torture as physical violence and psychic humiliation, see Améry, *Mind's Limits*, 21–40; Hunt, *Inventing*, 70–112. For a recent philosophical critique of this idea, see Sangiovanni, *Humanity without Dignity*.

52. Czeguhn, 'Verhältnis', 18–19.

53. Nussbaum, *Anger*, 137 ff.; Lewis, 'Shame', 113; Scheff and Retzinger, *Emotions*, 66; Wurmser, *Mask*, 137 and 198.

54. Lunbeck, *Americanization*, 110. For a criticism of the task force, see Christopher Lasch, 'For Shame', *The New Republic*, 10 August 1992, 29–34; Lasch, *Narcissism*. See also Nathanson, 'Timetable', esp. 5–7; Lewis, 'Shame'.

BIBLIOGRAPHY

Newspaper articles, court decisions, and internet sources are fully cited in the endnotes and are not listed separately here.

Abb, Edmund, *Erziehungskunde* (1915), 3rd edn (Nuremberg, 1928).

Abb, Edmund, *Lehrbuch der allgemeinen Erziehungs- und Bildungslehre* (1932), ed. Theodor Schwerdt, 2nd edn (Paderborn, 1957).

Adcock Kaufman, Alison, 'The "Century of Humiliation", Then and Now: Chinese Perceptions of the International Order', *Pacific Focus*, 25 (2010), 1–33.

Adelung, Friedrich, *Augustin Freiherr von Meyerberg und seine Reise nach Russland* (St Petersburg, 1827).

Adenauer, Konrad, *Memoirs: 1945–1953*, trans. Beate Ruhm von Oppen, 2 vols (London, 1966).

Ahmed, Sara, *The Cultural Politics of Emotion*, 2nd edn (Edinburgh, 2014).

Alberti, J. J. (ed.), *Neuestes Complimentirbuch*, 16th edn (Quedlinburg, 1848).

Alberts, Carol L., *Coaching Issues and Dilemmas: Character Building through Sport Participation* (Oxon Hill, Md., 2003).

Aleya-Sghaier, Amira, 'The Tunisian Revolution: The Revolution of Dignity', *The Journal of the Middle East and Africa*, 3 (2012), 18–45.

Allfrey, Katherine, *Golden Island*, trans. Edelgard von Heydemampf Bruehl (Garden City, NY, 1966).

Allgemeines Landrecht für die Preußischen Staaten von 1794 (ALR), ed. Hans Hatten-hauer, 2nd edn (Neuwied, 1994).

Althoff, Gerd, '"Compositio": Wiederherstellung verletzter Ehre im Rahmen gütlicher Konfliktbeendigung', in Klaus Schreiner and Gerd Schwerhoff (eds), *Verletzte Ehre: Ehrkonflikte in Gesellschaften des Mittelalters und der Frühen Neuzeit* (Cologne, 1995), 63–76.

Althoff, Gerd, 'Das Grundvokabular der Rituale: Knien, Küssen, Thronen, Schwören', in Barbara Stollberg-Rilinger et al. (eds), *Spektakel der Macht: Rituale im alten Europa 800–1800* (Darmstadt, 2008), 149–80.

Althoff, Gerd, *Die Macht der Rituale: Symbolik und Herrschaft im Mittelalter*, 2nd edn (Darmstadt, 2013).

Améry, Jean, *At the Mind's Limits: Contemplations by a Survivor on Auschwitz and Its Realities* (Bloomington, 1980).

Ammerer, Gerhard, '"durch Strafen (. . .) zu neuen Lastern gereizt". Schandstrafe, Brandmarkung und Landesverweisung—Überlegungen zur Korrelation und Kritik von kriminalisierenden Sanktionen und Armutskarrieren im späten 18. Jahrhundert', in Sebastian Schmidt (ed.), *Arme und ihre Lebensperspektiven in der Frühen Neuzeit* (Frankfurt, 2008), 311–39.

Andrews, Donna T., 'The Press and Public Apologies in Eighteenth-Century London', in Norma Landau (ed.), *Law, Crime and English Society, 1660–1830* (Cambridge, 2002), 208–29.

'Anordnung über Mitteilungen in Strafsachen', in *Strafvollstreckung— Strafregister—Gnadenwesen*, 3rd edn (Munich, 1956), 235–66.

'Anordnung über Mitteilungen in Strafsachen', in *Strafvollstreckung— Strafregister—Gnadenwesen*, 4th edn (Munich, 1961), 146–77.

Arnold, [Friedrich Christian], 'Erfahrungen aus dem bayerischen Strafgesetzbuche vom Jahr 1813, und Betrachtungen hierüber', *Archiv des Criminalrechts*, new ser. (1843), 96–112, 240–80, 377–411, 512–39, and ibid., new ser. (1844), 190–212.

Arnold, David, 'Salutation and Subversion: Gestural Politics in Nineteenth-Century India', *Past and Present*, 203 (2009), suppl. 4, 191–211.

Aschmann, Birgit, 'Ehre—das verletzte Gefühl als Grund für den Krieg. Der Kriegsausbruch 1870', in Birgit Aschmann (ed.), *Gefühl und Kalkül: Der Einfluss von Emotionen auf die Politik des 19. und 20. Jahrhunderts* (Stuttgart, 2005), 151–74.

Aschmann, Birgit, *Preußens Ruhm und Deutschlands Ehre: Zum nationalen Ehrdiskurs im Vorfeld der preußisch-französischen Kriege des 19. Jahrhunderts* (Munich, 2013).

Askin, Kelly D., 'Prosecuting Wartime Rape and Other Gender-Related Crimes under International Law', *Berkeley Journal of International Law*, 21 (2003), 288–349.

Assmann, Aleida, 'Höflichkeit und Respekt', in Gisela Engel et al. (eds), *Konjunkturen der Höflichkeit in der Frühen Neuzeit* (Frankfurt, 2009), 173–89.

Assmann, Aleida, and Ute Frevert, *Geschichtsvergessenheit—Geschichtsversessenheit. Vom Umgang mit deutschen Vergangenheiten nach 1945* (Stuttgart, 1999).

Avruch, Kevin, and Zheng Wang, 'Culture, Apology, and International Negotiation', *International Negotiation*, 10 (2005), 337–53.

Bach, Jakob, et al. (eds), *Das Volksschulwesen im Volksstaat Hessen* (Gießen, 1931).

Bader-Weiß, Grete, and Karl Siegfried Bader, *Der Pranger: Ein Strafwerkzeug und Rechtswahrzeichen des Mittelalters* (Freiburg, 1935).

Badie, Bertrand, *Humiliation in International Relations: A Pathology of Contemporary International Systems*, trans. Jeff Lewis (Oxford, 2017).

Baets, Antoon De, 'A Successful Utopia: The Doctrine of Human Dignity', *Historein*, 7 (2007), 71–85.

Bahr, Egon, *Zu meiner Zeit* (Munich, 1996).

Baier, Dirk, et al., *Kinder und Jugendliche in Deutschland—Gewalterfahrungen, Integration, Medienkonsum* (Hannover, 2010).

Bailey, Paul J. (ed.), *Strengthen the Country and Enrich the People: The Reform Writings of Ma Jianzhong (1845–1900)* (Richmond, 1998).

Banks, Stephen, *Informal Justice in England and Wales 1760–1914: The Courts of Popular Opinion* (Woodbridge, 2014).

Bar, Ludwig von, 'Zur Lehre von der Beleidigung mit besonderer Rücksicht auf die Presse', *Der Gerichtssaal*, 52 (1896), 81–208.

Barkan, Elazar, *The Guilt of Nations: Restitution and Negotiating Historical Injustices* (New York, 2000).

Barros, James, *The Corfu Incident of 1923: Mussolini and the League of Nations* (Princeton, 1965).

Bartlett, Peter, 'Sodomites in the Pillory in Eighteenth-Century London', *Social and Legal Studies*, 6 (1997), 553–72.

Baske, Siegfried, and Martha Engelbert (eds), *Zwei Jahrzehnte Bildungspolitik in der Sowjetzone Deutschlands. Dokumente*, ii: 1959 bis 1965 (Berlin/East, 1966).

Bates, Ed, *The Evolution of the European Convention on Human Rights: From Its Inception to the Creation of a Permanent Court of Human Rights* (Oxford, 2010).

Bayefsky, Rachel, 'Dignity, Honour, and Human Rights: Kant's Perspective', *Political Theory*, 41 (2013), 809–37.

Beales, Derek, *Joseph II, ii: Against the World: 1780–1790* (Cambridge, 2009).

Beattie, J. M., *Crime and the Courts in England 1660–1800* (Princeton, 1986).

Bednarek-Gilland, Antje, *Fragiler Alltag: Lebensbewältigung in der Langzeitarbeitslosigkeit* (Hannover, 2015).

Behrens, Alexander (ed.), *'Durfte Brandt knien?' Der Kniefall in Warschau und der deutsch-polnische Vertrag. Eine Dokumentation der Meinungen* (Bonn, 2010).

Behrens, Katharina, *Scham—zur sozialen Bedeutung eines Gefühls im spätmittelalterlichen England* (Göttingen, 2014).

Benjamin, Michael, *Konfliktkommissionen—Strafrecht—Demokratie* (Berlin/East, 1968).

Benthall, Jonathan, 'Invisible Wounds: Corporal Punishment in British Schools as a Form of Ritual', *Child Abuse and Neglect*, 15 (1991), 377–88.

Berchem, Verena, *Das Oberlandesgericht Köln in der Weimarer Republik* (Cologne, 2004).

Berg, Christa, '"Rat geben". Ein Dilemma pädagogischer Praxis und Wirkungsgeschichte', *Zeitschrift für Pädagogik*, 37 (1991), 709–34.

Berg, Christa, and Sieglind Ellger-Rüttgardt (eds), *'Du bist nichts, Dein Volk ist alles': Forschungen zum Verhältnis von Pädagogik und Nationalsozialismus* (Weinheim, 1991).

Berg, Ilse, *Theorie der Strafe in der sozialistischen Schule* (Berlin/East, 1961).

Bergk, J[ohann] A[dam] (ed.), *Des Marchese Beccaria's Abhandlung über Verbrechen und Strafen*, i (Leipzig, 1798).

Betts, Paul, 'Property, Peace and Honour: Neighbourhood Justice in Communist Berlin', *Past and Present*, 201 (2008), 215–54.

Biddiscombe, Perry, 'Dangerous Liaisons: The Anti-Fraternization Movement in the US Occupation Zones of Germany and Austria, 1945–1948', *Journal of Social History*, 34 (2001), 611–47.

Bieri, Peter, *Eine Art zu leben. Über die Vielfalt menschlicher Würde* (Munich, 2013).

Biggerstaff, Knight, 'The Ch'ung Hou Mission to France, 1870–1871', *Nankai Social and Economic Quarterly*, 8 (1935), 633–47.

Binding, Karl, *Lehrbuch des Gemeinen Deutschen Strafrechts: Besonderer Teil*, 2nd edn, i (Leipzig, 1902).

Bissonnette, Pierre André, *La satisfaction comme mode de réparation en droit international* (Annemasse, 1952).

Bitter, Albrecht von, *Das Strafrecht des Preußischen Allgemeinen Landrechts von 1794 vor dem ideengeschichtlichen Hintergrund seiner Zeit* (Baden-Baden, 2013).

Bjørnlund, Matthias, '"A Fate Worse than Dying": Sexual Violence during the Armenian Genocide', in Dagmar Herzog (ed.), *Brutality and Desire: War and Sexuality in Europe's Twentieth Century* (New York, 2009), 16–58.

Blattmann, Lynn, '"Laßt uns den Eid des neuen Bundes schwören...": Schweizerische Studentenverbindungen als Männerbünde 1870–1914', in Thomas Kühne (ed.), *Männergeschichte—Geschlechtergeschichte: Männlichkeit im Wandel der Moderne* (Frankfurt, 1996), 119–35.

Bloch, Abraham P., *A Book of Jewish Ethical Concepts* (New York, 1984).

Blume, Judy, *Blubber* (New York, 1974).

Bluntschli, Johann Caspar, *Das moderne Völkerrecht der civilisirten Staaten* (Nördlingen, 1868).

Blussé, Leonard, 'Peeking into the Empires: Dutch Embassies to the Courts of China and Japan', *Itinerario*, 37 (2013), no. 3, 14–29.

Boiter, Albert L., *Trotsky at the Moscow Treason Trials* (Louisville, 1947), electronic dissertation, https://doi.org/10.18297/etd/1870.

Böll, Heinrich, *The Lost Honour of Katharina Blum* (German original: 1972) (New Brunswick, 2000).

Bömer, Karl, *Das Dritte Reich im Spiegel der Weltpresse* (Leipzig, 1934).

Bootz, Margret R. I., *Die Hamburger Rechtsprechung zum Arbeitsrecht im Nationalsozialismus bis zum Beginn des 2. Weltkriegs* (Frankfurt, 2012).

Bors, Marc, 'Abbitte, Widerruf und Ehrenerklärung: Zur Geschichte der Privatgenugtuung im Ehrverletzungsrecht des 19. Jahrhunderts', in Sylvia Kesper-Biermann et al. (eds), *Ehre und Recht: Ehrkonzepte, Ehrverletzungen und Ehrverteidigungen vom späten Mittelalter bis zur Moderne* (Magdeburg, 2011), 133–41.

Bösch, Frank, 'Politische Skandale in Deutschland und Großbritannien', *Aus Politik und Zeitgeschichte*, 7 (2006), 25–32.

Bösch, Frank, *Öffentliche Geheimnisse: Skandale, Politik und Medien in Deutschland und Großbritannien 1880–1914* (Munich, 2009).

Boswell, James, *The Life of Samuel Johnson*, iii (Boston, 1807).

Botz, Gerhard, *Nationalsozialismus in Wien: Machtübernahme und Herrschaftssicherung 1938/39*, 3rd edn (Vienna, 1988).

Bourdieu, Pierre, 'Die Dialektik von Herausforderung und Erwiderung der Herausforderung', in Steffen K. Herrmann et al. (eds), *Verletzende Worte: Die Grammatik sprachlicher Missachtung* (Bielefeld, 2007), 89–105.

Braithwaite, John, *Crime, Shame, and Reintegration* (Cambridge, 1989).

Braithwaite, John, 'Shame and Modernity', *The British Journal of Criminology*, 33 (1993), 1–18.

Brandt, Max von, *Dreiunddreißig Jahre in Ost-Asien: Erinnerungen eines deutschen Diplomaten*, 3 vols (Leipzig, 1901).

Brandt, Willy, *My Life in Politics* (London, 1992).

Brezina, Markus, *Ehre und Ehrenschutz im nationalsozialistischen Recht* (Augsburg, 1987).

Brockhaus' Kleines Konversations-Lexikon, 5th edn, 2 vols (Leipzig, 1911).

Brockhaus' Konversations-Lexikon, 14th rev. anniversary edn, 17 vols (Leipzig, 1898).

Brockhaus' Konversations-Lexikon, 14th newly rev. anniversary edn, 16 vols (Leipzig, 1901–4).

Brown, James Baldwin, *Memoirs of the Public and Private Life of John Howard, the Philanthropist*, 2nd edn (London, 1923).

Brown, Penelope, and Stephen C. Levinson, *Politeness: Some Universals in Language Usage* (Cambridge, 1987).

Brownmiller, Susan, *Against Our Will: Men, Women and Rape* (New York, 1975).

Bruckner, Pascal, *The Tyranny of Guilt: An Essay on Western Masochism*, trans. Steven Rendall (Princeton, 2010).

Brzezinski, Zbigniew, *Power and Principle: Memoirs of the National Security Adviser 1977–1981* (New York, 1983).

Bücker, Vera, et al. (eds), *Nikolaus Groß: Arbeiterführer—Widerstandskämpfer—Glaubenszeuge. Wie sollen wir vor Gott und unserem Volk bestehen? Der politische und soziale Katholizismus im Ruhrgebiet 1927 bis 1949* (Münster, 2001).

Budde, Gunilla-Friederike, *Auf dem Weg ins Bürgerleben: Kindheit und Erziehung in deutschen und englischen Bürgerfamilien 1840–1914* (Göttingen, 1994).

Buddeus, [Johann Karl Immanuel], 'Ehrenstrafen', in *Allgemeine Encyclopädie der Wissenschaften und Künste*, ed. Johann Samuel Ersch and Johann Gottfried Gruber, sec. 1, xxxi (Leipzig, 1838), 453–7.

Burghartz, Susanna, 'Geschlecht—Körper—Ehre: Überlegungen zur weibliche Ehre in der Frühen Neuzeit am Beispiel der Basler Ehegerichtsprotokolle', in Klaus Schreiner and Gerd Schwerhoff (eds), *Verletzte Ehre: Ehrkonflikte in Gesellschaften des Mittelalters und der Frühen Neuzeit* (Cologne, 1995), 214–34.

Burke, Edmund, *The Speeches of the Right Honourable Edmund Burke in the House of Commons and in Westminster Hall*, ii (London, 1816).

Callahan, William A., 'National Insecurities: Humiliation, Salvation, and Chinese Nationalism', *Alternatives*, 29 (2004), 199–218.

Callahan, William A., *China: The Pessoptimist Nation* (Oxford, 2010).

Carranza, Ruben, et al., *More than Words: Apologies as a Form of Reparation*, International Center for Transitional Justice (December 2015), https://www.ictj.org/publication/more-than-words-apologies-form-reparation, accessed 18 April 2017.

Cassell's Household Guide to Every Department of Practical Life, rev. edn, 2 vols (London, 1884).

Ceremonial-Buch für den Königlich Preussischen Hof, i–xii (Berlin, 1877).

Cesarani, David, *Final Solution: The Fate of the Jews 1933–49* (London, 2016).

Chang, Fêng chên, *The Diplomatic Relations between China and Germany since 1898* (Shanghai, 1936).

[Chesterfield, Philip Dormer Stanhope of,] *The Works of Lord Chesterfield Including His Letter to His Son etc.* (New York 1845).

Chinese School (Documentary originally broadcast on BBC 4, 2 DVD) (Milton Keynes, 2008).

Christiansen, Hans, *Die Beleidigung* (Diss. Kiel, 1965).

'Chun qinvang shi De riji (Prince Chun's Diary of His Voyage to Germany)', *Jindaishi ziliao*, 73 (1989), 138–68.

Claudius, G[eorg] C[arl], *Kurze Anweisung zur wahren feinen Lebensart nebst den nöthigsten Regeln der Etikette und des Wohlverhaltens in Gesellschaften für Jünglinge, die mit Glück in die Welt treten wollen* (Leipzig, 1800).

Cohen, Colleen Balerino, et al. (eds), *Beauty Queens on the Global Stage: Gender, Contests, and Power* (New York, 1996).

Cohen, Jerome A., *The Criminal Process in the People's Republic of China, 1949–1963* (Cambridge, Mass., 1968).

Cohn, Bernard S., *An Anthropologist among the Historians and other Essays* (1987), 4th edn (Delhi, 1996).

Cohn, Bernard S., *Colonialism and its Forms of Knowledge: The British in India* (Princeton, 1996).

Collar, Peter, *The Propaganda War in the Rhineland: Weimar Germany, Race and Occupation after World War I* (London, 2013).

Collection Complète des Lois, Décrets, Ordonannances, Réglements, et Avis du Conseil-d'État, ed. J. B. Duvergier, xxxii (Paris, 1833).

Conradi, Elisabeth, and Frans Vosman (eds), *Praxis der Achtsamkeit: Schlüsselbegriffe der Care-Ethik* (Frankfurt, 2016).

Coppard, George, *With a Machine Gun to Cambrai: The Tale of a Young Tommy in Kitchener's Army 1914–1918* (London, 1969).

Cordingly, David, *Cochrane the Dauntless: The Life and Adventures of Admiral Thomas Cochrane, 1775–1860* (London, 2007).

Cox, David J., *Crime in England 1688–1815* (New York, 2014).

Cranmer-Byng, J[ohn] L[ancelot] (ed.), *An Embassy to China: Lord Macartney's Journal, 1793–1794* (reprint London, 2000).

Cranmer-Byng, J[ohn] L[ancelot], 'Lord Macartney's Embassy to Peking in 1793: From Official Chinese Documents', *Journal of Oriental Studies*, 4 (1957/8), 117–83.

Cretney, Stephen, 'Children, Cruelty and Corporal Punishment in Twentieth-Century England: The Legal Framework', in Laurence Brockliss and Heather Montgomery (eds), *Childhood and Violence in the Western Tradition* (Oxford, 2010), 151–8.

Crew, David, 'Gewalt "auf dem Amt": Wohlfahrtsbehörden und ihre Klienten in der Weimarer Republik', in Thomas Lindenberger and Alf Lüdtke (eds), *Physische Gewalt* (Frankfurt, 1995), 213–37.

Croll, Andy, 'Street Disorder, Surveillance and Shame: Regulating Behaviour in the Public Spaces of the Late Victorian British Town', *Social History*, 24 (1999), 250–68.

Crosby, Eileen H., 'Fighting for Honor: Legal Adversaries and the Complaint for Ehrverletzung in Early Modern Saxony', in Harriet Rudolph and Helga Schnabel-Schüle (eds), *Justiz = Justice = Justicia? Rahmenbedingungen von Strafjustiz im frühneuzeitlichen Europa* (Trier, 2003).

Crozier-De Rosa, Sharon, *Shame and the Anti-Feminist Backlash: Britain, Ireland and Australia, 1890–1920* (New York, 2018).

Czeguhn, Ignacio, 'Das Verhältnis von Menschenwürde und Menschenrechten in historischer Perspektive', in Eric Hilgendorf (ed.), *Menschenwürde und Demütigung: Die Menschenwürdekonzeption Avishai Margalits* (Baden-Baden, 2013).

Dabhoiwala, Faramerz, 'Sex and Societies for Moral Reform, 1688–1800', *Journal of British Studies*, 46 (2007), 290–319.

Dahm, Georg, 'Die Erneuerung der Ehrenstrafe', *Deutsche Juristen-Zeitung*, 39 (1934), 821–32.

Dahm, Georg, 'Der strafrechtliche Ehrenschutz der Familie', *Juristische Wochenschrift*, 65 (1936), 2497–503.

Dahs (jun.), Hans, 'Referat', in *Verhandlungen des 54. Deutschen Juristentages*, ii (Munich, 1982), K 7–26.

Dahs (sen.), Hans, *Handbuch des Strafverteidigers* (Cologne, 1969).

Dalrymple, William, *White Mughals: Love and Betrayal in Eighteenth-Century India* (London, 2002).

D'Artagnan, Liliane, 'Le Rituel Punitif du Pilori au Moyen Age', *Francia*, 44 (2017), 99–121.

Darwall, Stephen, 'Kant on Respect, Dignity, and the Duty of Respect', in Stephen Darwall, *Honor, History, and Relationship: Essays in Second-Personal Ethics II* (Oxford, 2014), 247–70.

Darwin, Charles, *The Expression of the Emotions in Man and Animals* (London, 1872).

Davidoff, Leonore, 'Class and Gender in Victorian England: The Diaries of Arthur J. Munby and Hannah Cullwick', *Feminist Studies*, 5 (1979), 86–141.

Davis, Michael T., '"I Can Bear Punishment": Daniel Isaac Eaton, Radical Culture and the Rule of Law, 1793–1812', in Louis A. Knafla (ed.), *Crime, Punishment, and Reform in Europe* (Westport, 2003), 89–106.

Davis, Natalie Zemon, *Society and Modern Culture in Early Modern France* (Stanford, 1975).

Delbrück, Hans, 'Rezension zu Ludwig Diemer, Von der Schulbank gegen die Franzosen', *Preußische Jahrbücher*, 148 (1912), 515–19.

Denkschrift des Zentralausschusses der Strafrechtsabteilung der Akademie für Deutsches Recht über die Grundzüge eines Allgemeinen Deutschen Strafrechts (Berlin, 1934).

Denney, John, *Respect and Consideration: Britain in Japan 1853–1868 and Beyond* (Leicester, 2011).

Deonna, Julien A., et al., *In Defense of Shame: The Faces of an Emotion* (Oxford, 2012).

Der Auswärtige Ausschuß des Deutschen Bundestages: Sitzungsprotokolle 1949–1953, ed. Wolfgang Hölscher (Düsseldorf, 1998).

Desnoyers, Charles A., 'Self-Strengthening in the New World: A Chinese Envoy's Travels in America', *Pacific Historical Review*, 60 (1991), 195–219.

Deuchler, Martina, *Confucian Gentlemen and Barbarian Envoys: The Opening of Korea, 1875–1885* (Seattle, 1977).

Die Grosse Politik der Europäischen Kabinette 1871–1914, ed. Johannes Lepsius et al., 40 vols (Berlin, 1922–27).

Die Ursachen des Deutschen Zusammenbruches im Jahre 1918, Abt. 2, ed. Albrecht Philipp, ii.i: Soziale Heeresmißstände als Teilursache des deutschen Zusammenbruchs von 1918 (Berlin, 1929).

Dikötter, Frank, *Mao's Great Famine: The History of China's Most Devastating Catastrophe, 1958–1962* (New York, 2010).

Dikötter, Frank, *The Tragedy of Liberation: A History of the Chinese Revolution, 1945–57* (London, 2013).

Dikötter, Frank, *The Cultural Revolution: A People's History, 1962–1976* (New York, 2016).

Dinges, Martin, *Der Maurermeister und der Finanzrichter: Ehre, Geld und soziale Kontrolle im Paris des 18. Jahrhunderts* (Göttingen, 1994).

Dirks, Nicholas B., *The Hollow Crown: Ethnohistory of an Indian Kingdom* (Cambridge, 1987).

Dixon, Simon (ed.), *Britain and Russia in the Age of Peter the Great: Historical Documents* (London, 1998).

Dobson, Miriam, *Khrushchev's Cold Summer: Gulag Returnees, Crime, and the Fate of Reform after Stalin* (Ithaca, 2009).

Dodd, Martha, *My Years in Germany* (London, 1939).

Doerner, [Karl], 'Gerichtsberichterstattung und Ehrenschutz', in Roland Freisler et al., *Der Ehrenschutz im neuen deutschen Strafverfahren* (Berlin, 1937), 138–50.

Domentat, Tamara, 'Hallo Fräulein': Deutsche Frauen und amerikanische Soldaten (Berlin, 1998).

Dorn, E., 'Zur Geschichte der Kniebeugungsfrage und der Prozeß des Pfarrers Volkert in Ingolstadt', in *Beiträge zur bayerischen Kirchengeschichte*, ed. Theodor Kolde, v (Erlangen, 1899), 1–37, 53–75.

Duchhardt, Heinz, 'Das "Westfälische System". Realität und Mythos', in Hillard von Thiessen and Christian Windler (eds), *Akteure der Außenbeziehungen: Netzwerke und Interkulturalität im historischen Wandel* (Cologne, 2010), 393–401.

Dufriche de Valazé, Charles, *Loix Pénales* (Alençon, 1784).

Dülmen, Richard van, *Der ehrlose Mensch: Unehrlichkeit und soziale Ausgrenzung in der Frühen Neuzeit* (Cologne, 1999).

Dundes, Alan, and Lauren Dundes, 'The Elephant Walk and Other Amazing Hazing: Male Fraternity Initiation through Infantilization and Feminization', in Alan Dundes (ed.), *Bloody Mary in the Mirror* (Jackson, 2002), 95–121.

Duyvendak, J[an] J. L., 'The Last Dutch Embassy to the Chinese Court (1794–1795)', *T'oung Pao*, 34 (1938), 1–137.

Easton, Laird McLeod, *The Red Count: The Life and Times of Harry Kessler* (Berkeley, 2002).

Eben von Racknitz, Ines, *Die Plünderung des Yuanmingyuan: Imperiale Beutenahme im britisch-französischen Chinafeldzug von 1860* (Stuttgart, 2012).

Ebert, Friedrich, *Schriften, Aufzeichnungen, Reden*, 2 vols (Dresden, 1926).

Ebhardt, Franz (ed.), *Der gute Ton in allen Lebenslagen: Ein Handbuch für den Verkehr in der Familie, in der Gesellschaft und im öffentlichen Leben*, 3rd edn (Berlin, 1878).

Ebhardt, Franz (ed.), *Der gute Ton in allen Lebenslagen: Ein Handbuch für den Verkehr in der Familie, in der Gesellschaft und im öffentlichen Leben*, 13th edn (Leipzig, 1896).

Eckel, Jan, *Die Ambivalenz des Guten: Menschenrechte in der internationalen Politik seit den 1940ern* (Göttingen, 2014).

Eckel, Jan, and Samuel Moyn (eds), *Moral für die Welt? Menschenrechtspolitik in den 1970er Jahren* (Göttingen, 2012).

Edgeworth, Maria, *Early Lessons* (1801), 4th edn, iii (London, 1821).

Edinburgh Annual Register for 1815, viii (Edinburgh, 1817).

Edwards, Jason A., 'Apologizing for the Past for a Better Future: Collective Apologies in the United States, Australia, and Canada', *Southern Communication Journal*, 75 (2010), 57–75.

Eitler, Pascal, 'Übertragungsgefahr: Zur Emotionalisierung und Verwissenschaftlichung des Mensch-Tier-Verhältnisses im Deutschen Kaiserreich', in Uffa Jensen and Daniel Morat (eds), *Rationalisierungen des Gefühls: Zum Verhältnis von Wissenschaft und Emotionen 1880–1930* (Munich, 2008), 171–87.

Eitz, Thomas, and Georg Stötzel, *Wörterbuch der 'Vergangenheitsbewältigung': Die NS-Vergangenheit im öffentlichen Sprachgebrauch*, i (Hildesheim, 2007).

El Edroos, Syed Fakhruddin Aboobaker, *Modern Indian Etiquette* (Surat 1921).

Elias, Norbert, *The Civilizing Process: Sociogenetic and Psychogenetic Investigations*, trans. Edmund Jephcott, rev. edn (Malden, Mass., 2010).

Ellis, Heather, 'Corporal Punishment in the English Public School in the Nineteenth Century', in Laurence Brockliss and Heather Montgomery (eds), *Childhood and Violence in the Western Tradition* (Oxford, 2010), 141–51.

Ellsworth-Jones, Will, *We Will Not Fight: The Untold Story of the First World War's Conscientious Objectors* (London, 2007).

Emsley, Clive, *Crime and Society in England, 1750–1900*, 4th edn (Harlow, 2010).

Encyclopaedia Britannica; or, A Dictionary of Arts and Sciences, Compiled upon a New Plan, 3 vols (Edinburgh, 1768–71).

Encyklopädisches Handbuch der Pädagogik, ed. W[ilhelm] Rein, 2nd edn, 10 vols (Langensalza, 1903–10).

Englmann, Johann Anton, *Das bairische Volksschulwesen* (Munich, 1871).

Entscheidungen des Bundesgerichtshofs in Zivilsachen, ed. Mitgliedern des Bundesgerichtshofes und der Bundesanwaltschaft (Cologne).

Entscheidungen des Reichsgerichts in Strafsachen, 77 vols (Berlin, 1880–1944).

Eppler, Erhard, 'Demütigung als Gefahr', *Blätter für deutsche und internationale Politik*, 7 (2015), 69–77.

Erman, Adolf, *Mein Werden und Wirken* (Leipzig, 1929).

Etzioni, Amitai, 'Back to the Pillory?', *The American Scholar*, 68 (1999), 43–50.

Evans, Richard J., *Rituals of Retribution: Capital Punishment in Germany, 1600–1987* (Oxford, 1996).

Evans, Richard J., *Tales from the German Underworld: Crime and Punishment in the Nineteenth Century* (New Haven, 1998).

Fahne, A., *Etwas über Ehrenkränkungen mit besonderer Berücksichtigung der exceptio veri, der Beleidigung durch Denunciation und im Amt nach gemeinem französischem und preußischem Rechte* (Düsseldorf, 1838).

Fanon, Frantz, *The Wretched of the Earth*, trans. Constance Farrington (New York, 1963).

Fassbender, Bardo, 'Westphalia Peace of (1648)', in Rüdiger Wolfrum (ed.), Max Planck Encyclopedia of Public International Law [MPEPIL] (Oxford, 2012), http://www.mpepil.com.

Favretto, Ilaria, 'Rough Music and Factory Protest in Post-1945 Italy', *Past and Present*, 228 (2015), 207–47.

Favretto, Ilaria, and Xabier Itçaina (eds), *Protest, Popular Culture and Tradition in Modern and Contemporary Western Europe* (London, 2017).

Feindt, Gregor, 'Semantiken der Versöhnung: Theologische Hintergründe der Versöhnung mit Polen am Beispiel des Briefwechsels der deutschen und polnischen Bischöfe und des Polen-Memorandums des Bensberger Kreises', *Kirchliche Zeitgeschichte*, 24 (2011), 396–414.

Feuerbach, Anselm Ritter von, *Betrachtungen über die Oeffentlichkeit und Mündlichkeit der Gerechtigkeitspflege*, i (Gießen, 1821).

Fisher, Michael H., 'The Resident in Court Ritual, 1764–1858', *Modern Asian Studies*, 24 (1990), 419–58.

Fitzpatrick, Matthew P., 'Kowtowing before the Kaiser? Sino-German Relations in the Aftermath of the Boxer Uprising', *The International History Review* (Advanced online publication 2018), DOI: 10.1080/07075332.2018.1441892.

Flüchter, Antje, 'Diplomatic Ceremonial and Greeting Practices at the Mughal Court', in Wolfram Drews and Christian Scholl (eds), *Transkulturelle Verflechtungsprozesse in der Vormoderne* (Berlin, 2016), 89–120.

Foerster, Friedrich Wilhelm, *Lebenskunde: Ein Buch für Knaben und Mädchen* (Berlin, 1904).

Foerster, Friedrich Wilhelm, *Lebensführung* (1909), new edn (Berlin, 1914).

Foerster, Friedrich Wilhelm, *Jugendlehre* (1904) (Erlenbach, 1929).

Ford, Richard, 'Fraternal Order: Rules of the House', *Esquire*, 105 (June 1986), 231–4.

Fortescue, John, *Narrative of the Visit to India of Their Majesties King George V and Queen Mary and of the Coronation Durbar Held at Delhi 12th December 1911* (London, 1912).

Förtsch, Folker, '"... eine erhebliche Empörung über das Verhalten solcher Personen vorhanden...". Verbotener Umgang zwischen Hallerinnen und

Kriegsgefangenen/Fremdarbeitern', in Folker Förtsch and Andreas Maisch (eds), *Frauenleben in Schwäbisch Hall 1933–1945: Realitäten und Ideologien* (Schwäbisch Hall, 1997), 275–85.

Foster, William (ed.), *The Embassy of Sir Thomas Roe to the Court of the Great Mogul 1615–1619*, 2 vols (London, 1899).

Foucault, Michel, *Discipline and Punish: The Birth of the Prison* (New York, 1995).

Frank, Michael, *Dörfliche Gesellschaft und Kriminalität: Das Fallbeispiel Lippe 1650–1800* (Paderborn, 1995).

Frank, Michael, 'Ehre und Gewalt im Dorf der Frühen Neuzeit: Das Beispiel Heiden (Grafschaft Lippe) im 17. und 18. Jahrhundert', in Klaus Schreiner and Gerd Schwerhoff (eds), *Verletzte Ehre: Ehrkonflikte in Gesellschaften des Mittelalters und der Frühen Neuzeit* (Cologne, 1995), 320–38.

Frank, Reinhard, *Das Strafgesetzbuch für das Deutsche Reich nebst dem Einführungsgesetze* (Leipzig, 1901).

Frank, Stephen P., 'Popular Justice, Community and Culture among the Russian Peasantry 1870–1900', *Russian Review*, 46 (1987), 239–65.

Franke, Otto, *Erinnerungen aus zwei Welten* (Berlin, 1954).

Franz, A., *Der gute Ton oder wie man sich in guter Gesellschaft bewegt* (Berlin, [1897]).

Freisler, Roland, 'Allgemeines zur Ehrenwahrung im Strafverfahren', in Roland Freisler et al., *Der Ehrenschutz im neuen deutschen Strafverfahren* (Berlin, 1937), 9–25.

Frese, Matthias, *Betriebspolitik im 'Dritten Reich': Deutsche Arbeitsfront, Unternehmer und Staatsbürokratie in der westdeutschen Großindustrie 1933–1939* (Paderborn, 1991).

Frevert, Ute, *Men of Honour: A Social and Cultural History of the Duel* (Cambridge, 1995).

Frevert, Ute, *A Nation in Barracks: Modern Germany, Military Conscription and Civil Society* (Oxford, 2004).

Frevert, Ute, *Emotions in History—Lost and Found* (Budapest, 2011).

Frevert, Ute, et al., *Learning How to Feel: Children's Literature and Emotional Socialization, 1870–1970* (Oxford, 2014).

Frey, Linda, and Marsha Frey, '"The Reign of the Charlatans is Over": The French Revolutionary Attacks on Diplomatic Practice', *Journal of Modern History*, 65 (1993), 706–44.

Friedland, Paul, *Seeing Justice Done: The Age of Spectacular Capital Punishment in France* Oxford, 2012).

Friedman, Gabrielle S., and James Q. Whitman, 'The European Transformation of Harassment Law: Discrimination versus Dignity', *The Columbia Journal of European Law*, 9 (2003), 241–74.

Frodsham, John D. (ed.), *The First Chinese Embassy to the West: The Journals of Kuo Sung-T'ao, Liu Hsi-Hung and Chang Te-Yi* (Oxford, 1974).

Frodsham, John D., 'The Record of an Envoy's Voyage to the West', *Asian Studies*, 3 (December 1967), 409–36.

Fröhling, Mareike, *Der moderne Pranger: Von den Ehrenstrafen des Mittelalters bis zur Prangerwirkung der medialen Berichterstattung im heutigen Strafverfahren* (Marburg, 2014).

Frommer, Benjamin, 'Denouncers and Fraternizers: Gender, Collaboration, and Retribution in Bohemia and Moravia during World War II and After', in Nancy M. Wingfield and Maria Bucur (eds), *Gender and War in Twentieth-Century Eastern Europe* (Bloomington, 2006), 111–32.

Frötschel, Ruth, 'Mit Handkuss: Die Hand als Gegenstand des Zeremoniells am Wiener Hof im 17. und 18. Jahrhundert', in Irmgard Pangerl et al. (eds), *Der Wiener Hof im Spiegel der Zeremonialprotokolle (1652–1800)* (Innsbruck, 2007), 337–56.

Fuchs, [Carl], 'Kritische Erörterung von Entscheidungen des Reichsgerichts in Strafsachen', *Archiv für Strafrecht*, 29 (1881), 422–34.

Fuchs, Ralf-Peter, *Um die Ehre: Westfälische Beleidigungsprozesse vor dem Reichskammergericht (1525–1805)* (Paderborn, 1999).

Füssel, Marian, 'Riten der Gewalt: Zur Geschichte der akademischen Deposition und des Pennalismus in der frühen Neuzeit', *Zeitschrift für Historische Forschung*, 32 (2005), 605–48.

Fureix, Emmanuel, 'Le charivari politique: Un rite de surveillance civique dans les années 1830', in Adeline Beaurepaire-Hernandez et Jérémy Guedj (eds), *L'entre-deux électoral: Une autre histoire de la représentation politique en France (XIXe–XXe siècle)* (Rennes, 2015), 53–70.

Gadamer, Hans-Georg, 'Hegel's Dialectic of Self-Consciousness', in *Hegel's Dialectic: Five Hermeneutical Studies*, trans. P. Christopher Smith (New Haven, 1976), 54–74.

Gao, Hao, 'The "Inner Kowtow Controversy" during the Amherst Embassy to China, 1816–1817', *Diplomacy and Statecraft*, 27 (2016), 595–614.

Garrioch, David, 'Verbal Insult in Eighteenth-Century Paris', in Peter Burke and Roy Porter (eds), *The Social History of Language* (Cambridge, 1987), 104–19.

Gass-Bolm, Torsten, 'Das Ende der Schulzucht', in Ulrich Herbert (ed.), *Wandlungsprozesse in Westdeutschland: Belastung, Integration, Liberalisierung 1945–1980*, 2nd edn (Göttingen, 2003), 436–66.

Gass-Bolm, Torsten, *Das Gymnasium 1945–1980: Bildungsreform und gesellschaftlicher Wandel in Westdeutschland* (Göttingen, 2005).

Gebhardt, Miriam, *Die Angst vor dem kindlichen Tyrannen: Eine Geschichte der Erziehung im 20. Jahrhundert* (Munich, 2009).

Gebhardt, Miriam, 'Eltern zwischen Norm und Gefühl: Wertewandel in der bürgerlichen Familiensozialisation im 20. Jahrhundert', in Gunilla Budde et al. (eds), *Bürgertum nach dem bürgerlichen Zeitalter: Leitbilder und Praxis seit 1945* (Göttingen, 2010), 187–204.

Gebhardt, Miriam, *Crimes Unspoken: The Rape of German Women at the End of the Second World War*, trans. Nick Somers (Cambridge, 2017).

Gedye, G[eorge] E[ric] R[owe], *Die Bastionen fielen: Wie der Faschismus Wien und Prag überrannte* (Vienna, 1947).

Geißler, Gert, *Geschichte des Schulwesens in der Sowjetischen Besatzungszone und in der Deutschen Demokratischen Republik 1945 bis 1962* (Frankfurt, 2000).

Geppert, Klaus, 'Straftaten gegen die Ehre', *Jura*, 5 (1983), 530–44, 580–92.

Gershoff, Elizabeth T., et al., *Corporal Punishment in US Public Schools: Legal Precedents, Current Practices, and Future Policy* (Heidelberg, 2015).

Gervais, Joe, 'In the Name of Obedience: Overcoming the Damaging Myths about Hazing', in Sandra Spickard Prettyman and Brian Lampman (eds), *Learning Culture through Sports: Exploring the Role of Sports in Society* (Lanham, Md., 2006), 203–13.

Gesetzblatt der Deutschen Demokratischen Republik (Berlin, 1955–90).

Gesetze und Vorschriften für die Studirenden an den königlichen Studien-Anstalten des Unterdonau-Kreises (Passau, 1836).

Gesetzrevision (1825–1848): Quellen zur preußischen Gesetzgebung des 19. Jahrhunderts, Abt. I: Straf- und Strafprozessrecht, ed. Werner Schubert and Jürgen Regge (Vaduz, 1981–96).

Gesetz-Sammlung für die Königlich Preußischen Staaten (Berlin, n.d.).

Gibney, Mark, and Erik Roxstrom, 'The Status of State Apologies', *Human Rights Quarterly*, 23 (2001), 911–39.

Gibson, Ian, *The English Vice: Beating, Sex and Shame in Victorian England and After* (London, 1978).

Giglioli, Daniele, *Critica della vittima: un esperimento con l'etica* (Roma, 2014).

Gleixner, Ulrike, *'Das Mensch' und 'der Kerl': Die Konstruktion von Geschlecht in Unzuchtsverfahren der Frühen Neuzeit (1700–1760)* (Frankfurt, 1994).

Globig, Hans Ernst von, and Johann Georg Huster, *Abhandlung von der Criminal-Gesetzgebung* (Zurich 1783).

Göbel, Andreas, *Vom elterlichen Züchtigungsrecht zum Gewaltverbot* (Hamburg, 2005).

Goebbels, Joseph, *Goebbels-Reden 1932–1945*, ed. Helmut Heiber (Düsseldorf, 1971).

Goebbels, Joseph, *Die Tagebücher*, ed. Elke Fröhlich (Munich, 1993–2006).

Goffman, Erving, *Asylums: Essays on the Social Situation of Mental Patients and Other Inmates* (Garden City, NY, 1973).

Goldberg, Ann, *Honor, Politics, and the Law in Imperial Germany, 1871–1914* (Cambridge, 2010).

Golding, William, *Lord of the Flies* (London, 1954).

Goldstein, Moritz, *'Künden, was geschieht . . . ' Berlin in der Weimarer Republik: Feuilletons in der Weimarer Republik*, ed. Irmtraud Ubbens (Berlin, 2012).

Goltdammer, Theodor, *Die Materialien zum Straf-Gesetzbuche für die Preußischen Staaten*, 2 vols (Berlin, 1851–2).

Gorlizki, Yoram, 'Delegalization in Russia: Soviet Comrades' Courts in Retrospect', *American Journal of Comparative Law*, 46 (1998), 403–25.

Görner, Kurt, 'Erste Erfahrungen aus der Tätigkeit der Schiedskommissionen', *Neue Justiz*, 17 (1963), 712–7.

Gorsky, Martin, 'James Tuckfield's "Ride": Combination and Social Drama in Early Nineteenth-Century Bristol', *Social History*, 19 (1994), 319–38.

Gottschall, Terrell D., *By Order of the Kaiser: Otto von Diederichs and the Rise of the Imperial German Navy, 1865–1902* (Annapolis, 2003).

Govan, Dara Aquila, 'Old School Values and New School Methods: Preserving the Integrity of the Pledge Process and Defending against Hazing', in Matthew W. Hughey and Gregory S. Parks (eds), *Black Greek-Letter Organizations 2.0: New Directions in the Study of African American Fraternities and Sororities* (Jackson, 2011), 235–72.

Gowing, Laura, *Domestic Dangers: Women, Words, and Sex in Early Modern London* (Oxford 1996).

Gräff, H[einrich], et al. (eds), *Ergänzungen und Erläuterungen des Preußischen Criminal-Rechts durch Gesetzgebung und Wissenschaft*, sec. 1, ii (Breslau, 1838).

Grapengeter, Andrew (ed.), *Kultusrecht, ii: Hochschulwesen* (Hamburg, 1953).

Grass, Günter, 'Politisches Tagebuch: Betroffen sein', in Günter Grass, *Werkausgabe*, ed. Volker Neuhaus and Daniela Hermes, xv (Göttingen, 1997), 80–2.

Graves, Robert, *Goodbye to All That* (Harmondsworth, 1960).

Greenhill, Pauline, *Make the Night Hideous: Four English-Canadian Charivari, 1881–1940* (Toronto, 2010).

Greiner, Ulrich, *Schamverlust: Vom Wandel der Gefühlskultur* (Reinbek, 2014).

Greschat, Martin, 'Vom Tübinger Memorandum (1961) zur Ratifizierung der Ostverträge: Protestantische Beiträge zur Aussöhnung mit Polen', in Friedhelm Boll et al. (eds), *Versöhnung und Politik: Polnisch-deutsche Versöhnungsinitiativen der 1960er Jahre und die Entspannungspolitik* (Bonn, 2009), 29–51.

Gribbohm, Günter, 'Nahrung für Defätisten', *Publik*, 22 May 1970, 10.

Gries, Peter Hays, *China's New Nationalism: Pride, Politics and Diplomacy* (Berkeley, 2004).

Gries, Peter Hays, and Kaiping Peng, 'Culture Clash? Apologies East and West', *Journal of Contemporary China*, 11 (2002), 173–8.

Grimes, Dorothy A., *Like Dew before the Sun: Life and Language in Northamptonshire* (Northampton, 1991).

Grimm, Dieter, *Souveränität: Herkunft und Zukunft eines Schlüsselbegriffs* (Berlin, 2009).

Grolman, Karl, *Grundsätze der Criminalrechtswissenschaft*, 2nd edn (Gießen, 1805).

Gugglberger, Martina, 'Inszenierte Täterinnen: Geschorene Frauen als Opfer sexualisierter Gewalt', in Christine Künzel (ed.), *Täterinnen und/oder Opfer? Frauen in Gewaltstrukturen* (Hamburg, 2007), 88–102.

Gullace, Nicoletta F., 'White Feathers and Wounded Men: Female Patriotism and the Memory of the Great War', *Journal of British Studies*, 36 (1997), 178–206.

Gumpert, Thekla von (ed.), *Herzblättchens Zeitvertreib: Unterhaltungen für kleine Knaben und Mädchen zur Herzensbildung und Entwickelung der Begriffe*, xxix (Glogau, 1884).

Gusko, Kurt, 'Sinn und Ziel der Sozialen Ehrengerichtsbarkeit', *Monatsheft für NS-Sozialpolitik*, 3 (1936), 262–73.

Gustav Radbruchs Entwurf eines Allgemeinen Deutschen Strafgesetzbuches (1922) (Tübingen, 1952).

Haarer, Johanna, *Die deutsche Mutter und ihr erstes Kind* (Berlin, 1934).

Haarer, Johanna, *Unsere kleinen Kinder* (Munich, 1936).

Haarer, Johanna, *Unsere Schulkinder* (Munich, 1950).

Habermas, Rebekka, *Thieves in Court: The Making of the German Legal System in the Nineteenth Century*, trans. Kathleen Mitchell Dell'Orto (Washington, DC, 2016).

Haerendel, Holger, *Gesellschaftliche Gerichtsbarkeit in der Deutschen Demokratischen Republik* (Frankfurt, 1997).

Hagglund, Ryan, 'Constitutional Protections against the Harms to Suspects in Custody Stemming from Perp Walks', *Mississippi Law Journal*, 81 (2012), 1757–908.

Hahn, C[arl] (ed.), *Die gesammten Materialien zur Strafprozeßordnung*, sect. 1, 2nd edn (Berlin, 1885).

[Haken, Johann Christian Ludwig,] *Romantische Ausstellungen*, ii (Gdansk, 1798).

Hall, Alex, 'The Kaiser, the Wilhelmine State and Lèse-Majesté', *German Life and Letters*, 27 (1974), 101–15.

Halperin, David M., and Valerie Traub (eds), *Gay Shame* (Chicago, 2009).

Hamann, Steffen, *Die soziale Ehrengerichtsbarkeit und die Konfliktkommissionen: Ein rechtshistorischer Vergleich* (Göttingen, 2007).

Han, Seunghee, *Corporal Punishment in Rural Schools: Student Problem Behaviours, Academic Outcomes and School Safety Efforts* (Heidelberg, 2017).

Hardinge of Penshurst, Charles Lord, *Old Diplomacy* (London, 1947).

Harrison, Henrietta, 'The Qianlong Emperor's Letter to George III and the Early-Twentieth-Century Origins of Ideas about Traditional China's Foreign Relations', *The American Historical Review*, 122 (2017), 680–701.

Hartley, Janet, 'A Clash of Cultures? An Anglo-Russian Encounter in the Early Eighteenth Century', in Roger Bartlett and Lindsey Hughes (eds), *Russian Society and Cultures and the Long Eighteenth Century: Essays in Honour of Anthony G. Cross* (Münster, 2004), 48–61.

Hartley, Janet M., *Charles Whitworth: Diplomat in the Age of Peter the Great* (Aldershot, 2002).

Hartmann, Andrea, *Majestätsbeleidigung und Verunglimpfung des Staatsoberhauptes* (Berlin, 2006).

Hartmann, Stefan, *Martin Kippenberger und die Kunst der Persiflage* (Berlin, 2013).

Hashimoto, Mitsuru, 'Collision at Namamugi', *Representations*, 18 (1987), 69–90.

Hausen, Carl Renatus, *Historisches Portefeuille zur Kenntnis der gegenwärtigen und vergangenen Zeit*, ii (Vienna, 1783).

Hazlitt, William Carew, *Faiths and Folklore: A Dictionary*, ii (London, 1905).

Heber, Fritz, 'Über Sinnhaftigkeit und Sinnlosigkeit der Strafe im Alltag der höheren Schule', *Die Höhere Schule*, 14 (1961), 113–16.

Heiber, Beatrice, and Helmut Heiber (eds), *Die Rückseite des Hakenkreuzes: Absonderliches aus den Akten des Dritten Reiches* (Munich, 1993).

Heim, Ernst Ludwig, *Tagebücher und Erinnerungen*, ed. Wolfram Körner (Leipzig, 1989).

Helfer, Christian, 'Denkmäler des Vollzugs von Ehrenstrafen am unteren Mittelrhein', *Rheinisches Jahrbuch für Volkskunde*, 15/16 (1965), 56–75.

Helm, Clementine, *Backfischchen's Leiden und Freuden: Eine Erzählung für junge Mädchen* (1863) (Munich, 1981).

Hennings, Jan, *Russia and Courtly Europe: Ritual and the Cultures of Diplomacy, 1648–1725* (Cambridge, 2016).

Hentig, Hans von, 'Der Pranger', *Schweizerische Juristen-Zeitung*, 32 (1935/6), 342–6.

Hentig, Hans von, *Die Strafe*, 2 vols (Berlin, 1954–5).

Herbert, Ulrich, *Fremdarbeiter: Politik und Praxis des 'Ausländer-Einsatzes' in der Kriegswirtschaft des Dritten Reiches* (Bonn, 1985).

Herold, Heiko, *Reichsgewalt bedeutet Seegewalt: Die Kreuzergeschwader der Kaiserlichen Marine als Instrument der deutschen Kolonial- und Weltpolitik 1885 bis 1901* (Munich, 2013).

Herzog, Dagmar, *Sex After Fascism: Memory and Morality in Twentieth-Century Germany* (Princeton, 2005).

Hetze, Stefanie, 'Feindbild und Exotik: Prinz Chun zur "Sühnemission" in Berlin', in Kuo Heng-Yü (ed.), *Berlin und China* (Berlin, 1987), 79–88.

Hetzel, Ernst, 'Johann Georg Schlosser und die "Stadt Emmendingen"', in *Johann Georg Schlosser (1739–1799): Eine Ausstellung der Badischen Landesbibliothek und des Generallandesarchivs Karlsruhe* (Karlsruhe, 1989), 103–13.

Hetzer, Hildegard, *Seelische Hygiene!—Lebenstüchtige Kinder! Richtlinien für die Erziehung im Kleinkindalter* (1930), 5th edn (Lindau, 1940).

Heusinger, Johann Heinrich Gottlieb (ed.), *Die Familie Werthheim: Eine theoretisch-praktische Anleitung zu einer regelmäßigen Erziehung der Kinder*, ii (Gotha, 1800).

Heusler, Andreas, '"Straftatbestand" Liebe: Verbotene Kontakte zwischen Münchnerinnen und ausländischen Kriegsgefangenen', in Sybille Krafft (ed.), *Zwischen den Fronten: Münchner Frauen in Krieg und Frieden 1900–1950* (Munich, 1995), 324–41.

Hevia, James L., 'Making China "Perfectly Equal"', *Journal of Historical Sociology*, 3 (1990), 379–400.

Hevia, James L., 'Sovereignty and Subject: Constituting Relations of Power in Qing Guest Ritual', in Angela Zito and Tani E. Barlow (eds), *Body, Subject and Power in China* (Chicago, 1994), 181–200.

Hevia, James L., *Cherishing Men from Afar: Qing Guest Ritual and the Macartney Embassy of 1793* (Durham, 1995).

Heyking, Elisabeth von, *Tagebücher aus vier Weltteilen 1886–1904*, ed. Grete Litzmann (Leipzig, 1926).

Hilgendorf, Eric, 'Beleidigung: Grundlagen, interdisziplinäre Bezüge und neue Herausforderungen', *Erwägen Wissen Ethik*, 19 (2008), 403–13.

Hilgers, Judith, *Inszenierte und dokumentierte Gewalt Jugendlicher: Eine qualitative Untersuchung von 'Happy slapping'-Phänomenen* (Wiesbaden, 2011).

Hitler, Adolf, *Mein Kampf*, complete and unabridged, fully annotated (New York, 1941).

Hofer, Walter (ed.), *Der Nationalsozialismus: Dokumente 1933–1945* (Frankfurt, 1982).

Hoffmann, Stefan-Ludwig (ed.), *Human Rights in the Twentieth Century* (Cambridge, 2011).

Hörnle, Tatjana, 'Warum sich das Würdekonzept Margalits zur Präzisierung von "Menschenwürde als geschütztes Rechtsgut eignet"', in Eric Hilgendorf (ed.), *Menschenwürde und Demütigung: Die Menschenwürdekonzeption Avishai Margalits* (Baden-Baden, 2013), 91–108.

Horowitz, Helen L., *Campus Life: Undergraduate Cultures from the End of the Eighteenth Century to the Present* (New York, 1987).

Houghton, David Patrick, *US Foreign Policy and the Iran Hostage Crisis* (Cambridge, 2001).

House, Edward, *The Intimate Papers of Colonel House*, ed. Charles Seymour, 4 vols (London, 1926–8).

Hsü, Immanuel C. Y., *The Rise of Modern China*, 6th edn (New York, 2000).

Hu, Kai, 'Das frühe offizielle Preußenbild Chinas: Zur Aufnahme diplomatischer Kontakte zwischen Preußen und China', *Forschungen zur Brandenburgischen und Preußischen Geschichte*, new ser. 17 (2007), 233–49.

Hudtwalcker, [Martin Hieronymus], 'Noch ein Wort über die körperlichen Züchtigungen als Strafe', *Archiv des Criminalrechts*, new ser. (1842), 163–187.

Humphrey, Heman, 'Duties of the filial relation', *The Mother's Assistant and Young Lady's Friend*, part II (Boston, 1853), 42–50.

Hunt, Lynn, *Inventing Human Rights: A History* (New York, 2007).

Hurrelbrink, Peter, *Der 8. Mai 1945—Befreiung durch Erinnerung: Ein Gedenktag und seine Bedeutung für das politisch-kulturelle Selbstverständnis in Deutschland* (Bonn, 2005).

Hüttel, Gustav, *Die öffentliche Bekanntmachung des Strafurteils in ihrer Entwicklung seit 1870 bis zum Strafgesetzbuch von 1925* (Diss. Göttingen, 1926).

Hüttner, Johann Christian, *Nachricht von der britischen Gesandtschaftsreise nach China 1792–94*, ed. Sabine Dabringhaus (Sigmaringen, 1996).

Iacobelli, Teresa, 'The "Sum of Such Actions": Investigating Mass Rape in Bosnia-Herzegovina through a Case Study of Foca', in Dagmar Herzog (ed.), *Brutality and Desire: War and Sexuality in Europe's Twentieth Century* (New York, 2009), 261–83.

Ilan, Amitzur, *Bernadotte in Palestine, 1948* (Houndmills, 1989).

Ingram, Martin, 'Shame Punishments, Penance and Charivari in Early Modern England', in Bénédicte Sère and Jörg Wettlaufer (eds), *Shame between Punishment and Penance* (Florence, 2013), 285–308.

In Their Own Words: Letters from History (London, 2016).

Irvin, Benjamin H., 'Tar, Feathers, and the Enemies of American Liberties, 1768–1776', *The New England Quarterly*, 76 (2003), 197–238.

Jacquet, Jennifer, *Is Shame Necessary? New Uses for an Old Tool* (New York, 2015).

Jagemann, Ludwig von, 'Die Strafe der körperlichen Züchtigung vor dem Forum der Wissenschaft und der Erfahrung', *Archiv des Criminalrechts*, new ser. (1841), 230–68.

James, Barbara, 'Frauenstrafen des 18. Jahrhunderts in Lied, Bild und Redensart', *Jahrbuch für Volksliedforschung*, 27/8 (1982/3), 307–15.

Japanische Etikette: Ein Handbuch aus dem Jahre 1887, ed. Hartmut Lamparth (Hamburg 1998).

Jensen, Wiebke, 'Chicaneur, Dieb und Hure: Beleidigungsklagen vor dem Göttinger Universitätsgericht (1814–1852)', in Sylvia Kesper-Biermann et al. (eds), *Ehre und Recht: Ehrkonzepte, Ehrverletzungen und Ehrverteidigungen vom späten Mittelalter bis zur Moderne* (Magdeburg, 2011), 161–76.

Jentsch, Markus, *Das 'Gesichts'-Konzept in China* (Baden-Baden, 2015).

Jochim, Christian, 'The Imperial Audience Ceremonies of the Ch'ing Dynasty', *Bulletin of the Society for the Study of Chinese Religion*, 7 (1979), 88–103.

John, Michael, 'Das "Haarabschneiderkommando" von Linz: Männlicher Chauvinismus oder nationalsozialistische Wiederbetätigung? Ein Fallbeispiel aus den Jahren 1945–1948', in Fritz Mayrhofer (ed.), *Entnazifizierung und Wiederaufbau in Linz* (Linz, 1996), 335–59.

Johnson, Jay, and Margery Holman (eds), *Making the Team: Inside the World of Sport Initiations and Hazing* (Toronto, 2004).

Johnson, Samuel, *Dictionary of the English Language*, 2 vols (London, 1755).

Jones, Dorothy V., *Splendid Encounters: The Thought and Conduct of Diplomacy* (Chicago, 1984).

Joseph des Zweyten Römischen Kaisers Gesetze und Verfassungen im Justiz-Fache (1786–1787) (Vienna, 1817).

Kabisch, Richard, *Das neue Geschlecht: Ein Erziehungsbuch* (1913), 2nd edn (Göttingen, 1916).

Kaempfer, Engelbertus, *The History of Japan*, trans. J. G. Scheuzer, 2 vols (London, 1727).

Kahan, Dan M., 'What Do Alternative Sanctions Mean?', *University of Chicago Law Review*, 63 (1996), 591–653.

Kaltenstadler, Wilhelm, *Das Haberfeldtreiben: Theorie, Entwicklung, Sexualität und Moral, sozialer Wandel und soziale Konflikte, staatliche Bürokratie, Niedergang, Organisation* (Munich, 1999).

Kama, Amit, and Sigal Barak-Brandes, 'Taming the Shame: Policing Excretions and Body Fluids in Advertisements for Hygienic Products', *European Journal for Cultural Studies*, 16 (2013), 582–97.

Kamachi, Noriko, 'The Chinese in Meiji Japan: Their Interactions with the Japanese before the Sino-Japanese War', in Akira Iriye (ed.), *The Chinese and the Japanese: Essays in Political and Cultural Interactions* (Princeton, 1980), 58–73.

Kämper, Heidrun, *Der Schulddiskurs in der frühen Nachkriegszeit: Ein Beitrag zur Geschichte des sprachlichen Umbruchs nach 1945* (Berlin, 2005).

Kansteiner, Wulf, *In Persuit of German Memory: History, Television, and Politics after Auschwitz* (Athens, Oh., 2006).

Kant, Immanuel, *Groundwork of the Metaphysics of Morals*, trans. Mary Gregor and Jens Timmermann, rev. edn (Cambridge, 2012).

Kant, Immanuel, *The Metaphysics of Morals*, ed. Lara Denis and trans. Mary Gregor, rev. edn (Cambridge, 2017).

Kästner, Erich, *The Flying Classroom*, trans. Cyrus Brooks (Harmondsworth, 1967).

Kay, Carolyn, 'How Should We Raise Our Son Benjamin? Advice Literature for Mothers in Early Twentieth-Century Germany', in Dirk Schumann (ed.), *Raising Citizens in the Century of the Child: The United States and German Central Europe in Comparative Perspective* (New York, 2010), 105–21.

Keating, Caroline F., et al., 'Going to College and Unpacking Hazing: A Functional Approach to Decrypting Initiation Practices among Undergraduates', *Group Dynamics*, 9 (2005), 104–26.

Keene, Donald, *Emperor of Japan: Meiji and His World, 1852–1912* (New York, 2002).

Keller, Nicole, *Pädagogische Ratgeber in Buchform. Leserschaft eines Erziehungsmediums* (Bern, 2008).

Kelly, Michael, 'The Reconstruction of Masculinity at the Liberation', in H. R. Kedward and Nancy Wood (eds), *The Liberation of France* (Oxford, 1995), 117–28.

Kemmerich, Dieterich Hermann, *Grund-Sätze des Völcker-Rechts von der Unverletzlichkeit der Gesandten* (Erlangen, 1710).

Kerbs, Diethart, et al. (eds), *Die Gleichschaltung der Bilder: Zur Geschichte der Pressefotografie 1930–36* (Berlin, 1983).

Kershaw, Ian, *Hitler 1936–1945: Nemesis* (London, 2000).

Kerski, Basil, et al., *'Wir vergeben und bitten um Vergebung': Der Briefwechsel der polnischen und deutschen Bischöfe von 1965 und seine Wirkung* (Osnabrück, 2006).

Kesper-Biermann, Sylvia, '"Nothwendige Gleichheit der Strafen bey aller Verschiedenheit der Stände im Staat?" (Un)gleichheit im Kriminalrecht der ersten Hälfte des 19. Jahrhunderts', *Geschichte und Gesellschaft*, 35 (2009), 603–28.

Kessler, Harry, *Gesichter und Zeiten: Erinnerungen* (1935) (Frankfurt, 1988).

Kießling, Friedrich, 'Täter repräsentieren: Willy Brandts Kniefall in Warschau', in Johannes Paulmann (ed.), *Auswärtige Repräsentationen: Deutsche Kulturdiplomatie nach 1945* (Cologne, 2005), 205–24.

Kipling, Rudyard, *Stalky & Co* (London, 1899).

Kippenberger, Susanne, *Kippenberger: The Artist and His Families*, trans. Damion Searls (New York, 2011).

Kirchliches Handlexikon, ed. Carl Meusel, 7 vols (Leipzig 1887–1902).

Kistner, Anna, *Schicklichkeitsregeln für das bürgerliche Leben* (Guben, 1886).

Kitchen, Ruth, *A Legacy of Shame: French Narratives of War and Occupation* (Oxford, 2013).

Kleensang, Michael, *Das Konzept der bürgerlichen Gesellschaft bei Ernst Ferdinand Klein* (Frankfurt, 1998).

Klein, Donald C., 'The Humiliation Dynamic: An Overview', *Journal of Primary Prevention*, 12 (1991), 93–121.

Klein, Ernst Ferdinand, 'Kurze Darstellung meiner Meinung über den Werth und Unwerth der körperlichen Züchtigungen als Strafmittel', *Archiv des Criminalrechts*, 1 (1799), no. 3, 113–18.

Klein, Thoralf, 'Sühnegeschenke: Der Boxerkrieg', in Ulrich van der Heyden and Joachim Zeller (eds), '... Macht und Anteil an der Weltherrschaft': Berlin und der deutsche Kolonialismus (Münster, 2005), 208–14.

Klencke, Hermann, Die Mutter als Erzieherin ihrer Töchter und Söhne zur physischen und sittlichen Gesundheit vom ersten Kindesalter bis zur Reife (1870), 10th edn (Leipzig, 1895).

Kluetz, Alfred, Volksschädlinge am Pranger (Berlin, 1940).

Kluger, A[lfons] (Ed.), Die deutsche Volksschule im Großdeutschen Reich (Breslau, 1940).

Koch, Hannsjoachim W., In the Name of the Volk: Political Justice in Hitler's Germany (London, 1997).

Köhler, Andrea, 'Am Online-Pranger: Scham und Beschämung in Zeiten des Internet', in Daniel Tyradellis (ed.), Scham (Göttingen, 2016), 112–19.

Köhler, Matthias, 'No Punctilios of Ceremony? Völkerrechtliche Anerkennung, diplomatisches Zeremoniell und symbolische Kommunikation im Amerikanischen Unabhängigkeitskonflikt', in Hillard von Thiessen and Christian Windler (eds), Akteure der Außenbeziehungen: Netzwerke und Interkulturalität im historischen Wandel (Cologne, 2010), 427–43.

König, Martin, 'Die "deutsche Frau und Mutter": Ideologie und Wirklichkeit', in Hans Eugen Specker (ed.), Ulm im Zweiten Weltkrieg (Ulm, 1995), 99–127.

Kooistra, J[etje], Sittliche Erziehung (Leipzig, 1899).

Kopp, Werner von, 'Zu dem Urteil des BGH über das Züchtigungsrecht der Lehrer', JuristenZeitung, 10 (1955), 319–20.

Kornetis, Kostis, Children of the Dictatorship: Student Resistance, Cultural Politics and the 'Long 1960s' in Greece (New York, 2013).

Koselleck, Reinhard, Preußen zwischen Reform und Revolution: Allgemeines Landrecht, Verwaltung und soziale Bewegung von 1791 bis 1848 (Stuttgart, 1967).

Köstlin, Reinhold, Abhandlungen aus dem Strafrechte (Tübingen, 1858).

Koziol, Geoffrey, Begging Pardon and Favor: Ritual and Political Order in Early Medieval France (Ithaca, 1992).

Krüger, Gerd, 'Straffreie Selbstjustiz: Öffentliche Denunzierungen im Ruhrgebiet 1923–1926', Sowi. Sozialwissenschaftliche Information, 27 (1998), 119–25.

Krünitz, Johann Georg, Oekonomische Encyklopädie, oder allgemeines System der Staats-Stadt- Haus- und Landwirthschaft, 242 vols (Berlin, 1773–1858).

Krutzki, Gottfried, '"Verunglimpfung des Staates und seiner Symbole": Eine Dokumentation zu § 90a StGB', Kritische Justiz, 13 (1980), 294–314.

Krzemiński, Adam, 'Der Kniefall: Warschau als Erinnerungsort deutsch-polnischer Geschichte', Merkur, 54 (2000), 1077–88.

Kübler, Friedrich, 'Ehrenschutz, Selbstbestimmung und Demokratie', Neue Juristische Wochenschrift, 52 (1999), 1281–7.

Kuhlman, Erika, Reconstructing Patriarchy after the Great War: Women, Gender and Postwar Reconciliation between Nations (New York, 2008).

Kuhn, Bruno, Die öffentliche Bekanntmachung des Urteils nach schweizerischem Strafrecht mit spezieller Berücksichtigung des Vorentwurfes von 1918 (Diss. Zurich, 1919).

Kühne, Thomas, 'Der Soldat', in Ute Frevert and Heinz-Gerhard Haupt (eds), *Der Mensch des 20. Jahrhunderts* (Frankfurt, 1999), 344–72.

Kühne, Thomas, *Kameradschaft: Die Soldaten des nationalsozialistischen Krieges und das 20. Jahrhundert* (Göttingen, 2006).

Kundrus, Birthe, '"Verbotener Umgang": Liebesbeziehungen zwischen Ausländern und Deutschen 1939–1945', in Katharina Hoffmann and Andreas Lembeck (eds), *Nationalsozialismus und Zwangsarbeit in der Region Oldenburg* (Oldenburg, 1999), 149–70.

Kürschner, Joseph (ed.), *China: Schilderungen aus Leben und Geschichte, Krieg und Sieg* (Leipzig, 1901).

Lamberty, Guillaume de, *Mémoires pour servir à l'histoire du XVIII siècle*, 2nd edn, v (Amsterdam, 1735).

Land, Brad, *Goat: A Memoir* (New York, 2004).

Landsberg, Ernst, *Die Gutachten der Rheinischen Immediat-Justiz-Kommission und der Kampf um die rheinische Rechts- und Gerichtsverfassung 1814–1819* (Bonn, 1914).

Landweer, Hilge, 'Ist Sich-gedemütigt-Fühlen ein Rechtsgefühl?', in Hilge Landweer and Dirk Koppelberg (eds), *Recht und Emotion I* (Freiburg, 2016), 103–35.

Langhoff, Wolfgang, *Rubber Truncheon: Being an Account of Thirteen Months Spent in a Concentration Camp*, trans. Lilo Linke (London, 1935).

Lasch, Christopher, *The Culture of Narcissism: American Life in an Age of Diminishing Expectations* (New York, 1978).

Laurens, Corran, '"La Femme au Turban": Les Femmes tondues', in H. R. Kedward and Nancy Wood (eds), *The Liberation of France* (Oxford, 1995), 155–79.

Lebra, Takie Sugiyma, 'The Social Mechanism of Guilt and Shame: The Japanese Case', *Anthropological Quarterly*, 44 (1971), 241–55.

Lebzelter, Gisela, 'Die "Schwarze Schmach": Vorurteile—Propaganda—Mythos', *Geschichte und Gesellschaft*, 11 (1985), 37–58.

Lehmann, Friedrich, *Wir von der Infanterie: Tagebuchblätter eines bayerischen Infanteristen aus fünfjähriger Front- und Lazarettzeit* (Munich, 1929).

Leibetseder, Mathis, *Die Hostie im Hals: Eine 'schröckliche Bluttat' und der Dresdner Tumult des Jahres 1726* (Konstanz, 2009).

Leitner, F. W. (ed.), *Sammlung der für die Königl. Preuß. Rheinprovinz seit dem Jahre 1813 hinsichtlich der Rechts- und Gerichtsverfassung ergangenen Gesetze, Verordnungen, Ministerial-Rescripte etc.*, v (Berlin, 1838).

Lemke, Michael, *Vor der Mauer: Berlin in der Ost-West-Konkurrenz 1948–1961* (Cologne, 2011).

Lethen, Helmut, *Cool Conduct: The Culture of Distance in Weimar Germany* (Berkeley, 2002).

'Letters to a younger Brother No. XII: False shame', *Sunday School Journal and Advocate of Christian Education*, 28 May 1834, 88.

Leutner, Mechthild (ed.), *'Musterkolonie Kiautschou': Die Expansion des Deutschen Reiches in China. Deutsch-chinesische Beziehungen 1897 bis 1914* (Berlin, 1997).

Lewis, Helen Block, 'Shame and the Narcissistic Personality', in Donald L. Nathanson (ed.), *The Many Faces of Shame* (New York, 1987), 93–132.

Lexikon der Pädagogik, ed. Ernst M. Roloff, 5 vols (Freiburg, 1913–17).

Leys, Ruth, *From Guilt to Shame: Auschwitz and After* (Princeton, 2007).

Lhotzky, Heinrich, *The Soul of Your Child*, trans. Anna Barwell (London, 1924).

Lidman, Satu, *Zum Spektakel und Abscheu: Schand- und Ehrenstrafen als Mittel öffentlicher Disziplinierung in München um 1600* (Frankfurt, 2008).

Lidman, Satu, 'Um Schande: Profil eines frühneuzeitlichen Strafsystems', in Sylvia Kesper-Biermann et al. (eds), *Ehre und Recht: Ehrkonzepte, Ehrverletzungen und Ehrverteidigungen vom späten Mittelalter bis zur Moderne* (Magdeburg, 2011), 197–216.

Liepmann, Max, *Die Beleidigung* (Berlin, 1909).

Lindgren, Astrid, *Pippi in the South Seas*, trans. Gerry Bothmer (New York, 1959).

Lindner, Evelin, *Making Enemies: Humiliation and International Conflict* (Westport, 2006).

Lindner, Gustav Adolf, *Encyklopädisches Handbuch der Erziehungskunde* (Vienna, 1884).

Liszt, Franz von, *Lehrbuch des Deutschen Strafrechts*, 16th/17th edn (Berlin, 1908).

Liu Hai-kwan, *Gēngzi hǎiwài jìshì* [Overseas Chronicles of the Boxer Rebellion, 4 vols] (Shanghai, 1902).

Lohmann, Ulrich, 'Die Gesellschaftlichen Gerichte in der DDR', *Informationsbrief der Sektion Rechtssoziologie in der Deutschen Gesellschaft für Soziologie*, no. 12 (1976), 43–55.

Lorenz, Gottfried, and Ulf Bollmann, *Liberales Hamburg? Homosexuellenverfolgung durch Polizei und Justiz nach 1946* (Hamburg, 2013).

Lottner, F[riedrich] A[ugust] (ed.), *Sammlung der für die Königl. Preuß. Rheinprovinz seit dem Jahre 1813 hinsichtlich der Rechts- und Gerichtsverfassung ergangenen Gesetze, Verordnungen, Ministerial-Rescripte etc.*, i (Berlin, 1834).

Lowenfeld, Henry, 'Notes on Shamelessness', *The Psychoanalytic Quarterly*, 45 (1976), 62–72.

Łuczak, Czeslaw (Ed.), *Położenie polskich robotników przymusowych w Rzeszy 1939–1945*. Documenta Occupationis, ed. Instytut Zachodni, ix (Posen 1975).

Lumumba Speaks: The Speeches and Writings of Patrice Lumumba, 1958–1961, ed. Jean Van Lierde (Boston, 1972).

Lunbeck, Elizabeth, *The Americanization of Narcissism* (Cambridge, Mass., 2014).

Lunceford, Brett, 'The Walk of Shame: A Normative Description', *ETC. A Review of General Semantics*, 65 (2008), 319–329.

Lüngen, [Wilhelm], 'Allgemeine Charaktererziehung', in Adele Schreiber (ed.), *Das Buch vom Kinde: Ein Sammelwerk für die wichtigsten Fragen der Kindheit*, i.ii (Leipzig, 1907), 192–202.

Luo, Zhitian, 'National Humiliation and National Assertion: The Chinese Response to the Twenty-One Demands', *Modern Asian Studies*, 27 (1993), 297–319.

Mackeprang, Rudolf, *Ehrenschutz im Verfassungsstaat: Zugleich ein Beitrag zu den Grenzen der Freiheiten des Art. 5 Abs. 1 GG* (Berlin, 1990).

MacMillan, Margaret, *Paris 1919: Six Months that Changed the World* (New York, 2003).

MacMurray, John V. A. (ed.), *Treaties and Agreements with and concerning China 1894–1919*, 2 vols (New York, 1921).

Malcolm, John, *The Political History of India from 1784 to 1823*, 2 vols (London, 1826).

Malfèr, Stefan, 'Die Abschaffung der Prügelstrafe in Österreich unter besonderer Berücksichtigung der Militärgrenze', *Zeitschrift der Savigny-Stiftung für Rechtsgeschichte, Germanistische Abteilung*, 102 (1985), 206–38.

Mallmann, Klaus-Michael, and Horst Steffens, *Lohn der Mühen: Geschichte der Bergarbeiter an der Saar* (Munich, 1989).

Mann, Viktor, *Wir waren fünf: Bildnis der Familie Mann* (Konstanz, 1949).

Manual of Indian Etiquette: For the Use of European Officers Coming to India (Allahabad, 1910).

Manual of Military Law, 6th edn (London, 1914).

Margalit, Avishai, *The Decent Society* (Cambridge, Mass., 1996).

Marrus, Michael R., 'Official Apologies and the Quest for Historical Justice', *Journal of Human Rights*, 6 (2007), 75–105.

Martens, Kurt, *Schonungslose Lebenschronik 1870–1900* (Vienna, 1921).

Martin, Peter, and Christine Alonzo (eds), *Zwischen Charleston und Stechschritt: Schwarze im Nationalsozialismus* (Cologne, 2004).

Marton, Kati, *A Death in Jerusalem* (New York, 1994).

Marx, Karl, 'Letters from the Deutsch-Französische Jahrbücher', in *Karl Marx and Frederick Engels, Collected Works, iii: Marx and Engels, 1843–44* (Moscow, 1975), 133–45.

Marx, Karl, 'The Eighteenth Brumaire of Louis Bonaparte', in *Karl Marx and Frederick Engels, Collected Works, ii: Marx and Engels, 1851–53* (Moscow, 1979), 99–197.

Maß, Sandra, 'The "Volkskörper" in Fear: Gender, Race and Sexuality in the Weimar Republic', in Luisa Passerini et al. (eds), *New Dangerous Liaisons: Discourses on Europe and Love in the Twentieth Century* (New York, 2010), 233–50.

Massaro, Toni M., 'Shame, Culture, and American Criminal Law', *Michigan Law Review*, 89 (1991), 1880–944.

Massie, Robert, *Peter the Great: His Life and World* (New York, 2012).

Matthias, Adolph, *Wie erziehen wir unsern Sohn Benjamin? Ein Buch für deutsche Väter und Mütter* (Munich, 1897).

McCloy, John J., 'Adenauer und die Hohe Kommission', in Dieter Blumenwitz et al. (eds), *Konrad Adenauer und seine Zeit: Politik und Persönlichkeit des ersten Bundeskanzlers* (Stuttgart, 1976), 421–6.

McCrudden, Christopher, 'Human Dignity and Judicial Interpretation of Human Rights', *The European Journal of International Law*, 19 (2008), 655–724.

McWilliams, Wayne C., 'East Meets East: The Soejima Mission to China, 1873', *Monumenta Nipponica*, 30 (1975), 237–75.

Mechling, Jay, *On My Honor: Boy Scouts and the Making of American Youth* (Chicago, 2001).

Mechling, Jay, 'Paddling and the Repression of the Feminine in Male Hazing', *Thymos. Journal of Boyhood Studies*, 2 (2008), 60–75.

Mechling, Jay, 'Is Hazing Play?', in Cindy Dell Clark (ed.), *Transactions at Play* (Lanham, Md., 2009), 45–61.

Meister, Leonhard, 'Ueber die Schamhaftigkeit', in Leonard Meister, *Fliegende Blätter größtentheils historischen und politischen Inhalt* (Basel, 1783), 112–39.

Memoirs of Father Ripa during Thirteen Years' Residence at the Court of Peking in the Service of the Emperor of China, ed. Fortunato Prandi (New York, 1846).

Messenger, Charles, *Call-To-Arms: The British Army 1914–18* (London, 2005).

Meulenbelt, Anja, *The Shame is Over: A Political Life Story* (London, 1980).

Meyers Großes Konversations-Lexikon, 6th edn, 20 vols (Leipzig, 1905–9).

Meyers neues Lexikon, 8 vols (Leipzig, 1961–4).

Middleton, Jacob, 'The Experience of Corporal Punishment in Schools, 1890–1940', *History of Education*, 37 (2008), 253–75.

Miller, William Ian, *Humiliation and Other Essays on Honor, Social Discomfort, and Violence* (Ithaca, 1993).

Millett, Kate, 'The Shame is Over', *Ms.* (January 1975), 26–9.

Mittelstädt, Otto, *Gegen die Freiheitsstrafen: Ein Beitrag zur Kritik des heutigen Strafsystems*, 2nd edn (Leipzig, 1879).

Mittermaier, [Carl Joseph Anton], 'Die körperliche Züchtigung als Strafart', *Neues Archiv des Criminalrechts*, 12 (1832), 650–67.

Mittermaier, Carl Joseph Anton, *Die Strafgesetzgebung in ihrer Fortbildung*, 2 vols (Heidelberg, 1841–3).

Mittheilungen über die Verhandlungen des Ordentlichen Landtags im Königreiche Sachsen (Dresden, 1837 ff.).

Mohr, Friedrich Wilhelm, *Gedanken zur neudeutschen Chinapolitik* (Neuwied, 1920).

Moisey, Andrew, *The American Fraternity: Psi Rho Ritual Book* (Hillsborough, NC, 2018).

Moïsi, Dominique, *The Geopolitics of Emotion: How Cultures of Fear, Humiliation, and Hope are Reshaping the World* (London, 2008).

Möller, Silke, *Zwischen Wissenschaft und 'Burschenherrlichkeit': Studentische Sozialisation im deutschen Kaiserreich 1871–1914* (Stuttgart, 2001).

Mommsen, Theodor, *Die Grundrechte des deutschen Volkes mit Belehrungen und Erläuterungen* (1849) (Frankfurt, 1969).

Monroe, Paul (ed.), *A Cyclopedia of Education*, 5 vols (New York, 1911–13).

Montgomery, Lucy Maud, *Anne of Green Gables* (Boston, 1908).

Moore, John Robert, *Defoe in the Pillory and Other Studies* (New York, 1973).

Moosheimer, Thomas, *Die actio injuriarum aestimatoria im 18. und 19. Jahrhundert: Eine Untersuchung zu den Gründen ihrer Abschaffung* (Tübingen, 1997).

Morat, Daniel, *Von der Tat zur Gelassenheit: Konservatives Denken bei Martin Heidegger, Ernst Jünger und Friedrich Georg Jünger 1920–1960* (Göttingen, 2007).

Morley, Henry (ed.), *The Earlier Life and the Chief Earlier Works of Daniel Defoe* (London, 1889).

Möser, Justus, *Patriotische Phantasien*, i (Berlin, 1775).

Motive zu dem Entwurfe eines Strafgesetzbuches für den Norddeutschen Bund (Berlin, 1869).

Mowbray, Alastair, *Cases, Materials, and Commentary on the European Convention on Human Rights*, 3rd edn (Oxford, 2012).

Moyn, Samuel, *The Last Utopia: Human Rights in History* (Cambridge, Mass., 2010).

Mühlen, Bengt von zur (ed.), *Die Angeklagten des 20. Juli vor dem Volksgerichtshof* (Berlin, 2001).

Mühlhausen, Walter, *Friedrich Ebert 1871–1925: Reichspräsident der Weimarer Republik* (Bonn, 2006).

Mühlhausen, Walter, 'Die Weimarer Republik entblößt: Das Badehosen-Foto von Friedrich Ebert und Gustav Noske', in Gerhard Paul (ed.), *Das Jahrhundert der Bilder 1900 bis 1949* (Göttingen, 2009), 236–43.

Mühlhäuser, Regina, *Eroberungen: Sexuelle Gewalttaten und intime Beziehungen deutscher Soldaten in der Sowjetunion, 1941–1945* (Hamburg, 2010).

Müller, Alfred von, *Die Wirren in China und die Kämpfe der verbündeten Truppen*, 2 vols (Berlin, 1902).

Müller, Philipp, *Auf der Suche nach dem Täter: Die öffentliche Dramatisierung von Verbrechen im Berlin des Kaiserreichs* (Frankfurt, 2005).

Münster, Peter Maria, 'Wiederentdeckung von Scham und Beschämung in der strafrechtlichen Sozialkontrolle: Das Konzept des reintegrative shaming', in Bénédicte Sère and Jörg Wettlaufer (eds), *Shame between Punishment and Penance* (Florence, 2013), 349–67.

Munt, Sally, *Queer Attachments: The Cultural Politics of Shame* (Aldershot, 2008).

Muyart de Vouglans, Pierre-Francois, *Les loix criminelles de France, dans leur ordre naturel* (Paris, 1780).

Nash, David, and Anne-Marie Kilday, *Cultures of Shame: Exploring Crime and Morality in Britain, 1600–1900* (Basingstoke, 2010).

Nathanson, Donald L., 'A Timetable for Shame', in Donald L. Nathanson (ed.), *The Many Faces of Shame* (New York, 1987), 1–63.

Neckel, Sighard, *Status und Scham: Zur symbolischen Reproduktion sozialer Ungleichheit* (Frankfurt, 1991).

Nelson, Camille, 'Honor and Criminal Law in the United States of America', in Silvia Tellenbach (ed.), *Die Rolle der Ehre im Strafrecht* (Berlin, 2007), 663–99.

Neuhof, Werner, and Helmut Schmidt, 'Anwendung von Zusatzstrafen', *Neue Justiz*, 23 (1969), 171–5.

Neumann, Friederike, 'Beschämung durch öffentliche Kirchenbuße? Beispiele aus dem Bistum Konstanz und der Stadt Freiburg im 15.–18. Jahrhundert', in Bénédicte Sère and Jörg Wettlaufer (eds), *Shame between Punishment and Penance* (Florence, 2013), 263–84.

Neumann, Stephanie, 'Gang Rape: Examining Peer Support and Alcohol in Fraternities', in Eric W. Hickey (ed.), *Sex Crimes and Paraphilia* (London, 2005), 397–407.

Newell, Peter, *A Last Resort? Corporal Punishment in Schools* (Harmondsworth, 1972).

Nicolson, Harold, *Peacemaking 1919* (New York, 1965).

Nietzsche, Friedrich, *Beyond Good and Evil*, trans. Judith Norman, ed. Rolf-Peter Horstmann and Judith Norman (Cambridge, 2002).

Nobes, Gavin, and Marjorie Smith, 'Physical Punishment of Children in Two-Parent Families', *Clinical Child Psychology and Psychiatry*, 2 (1997), 271–81.

Nobles, Melissa, *The Politics of Official Apologies* (Cambridge, Mass., 2008).

Noellner, [Friedrich], 'Bemerkungen über die Strafart der körperlichen Züchtigung', *Archiv des Criminalrechts*, new ser. (1843), 184–204.

Noellner, Friedrich, *Das Verhältniss der Strafgesetzgebung zur Ehre der Staatsbürger* (Frankfurt, 1846).

Nolte, Georg, *Beleidigungsschutz in der freiheitlichen Demokratie* (Berlin, 1992).

Nöstlinger, Christine, *The Cucumber King* (German original: 1972) (London, 1975).

Novum Corpus Constitutionum Prussico-Brandenburgensium Praecipue Marchicarum (NCC), Oder Neue Sammlung Königl. Preußl. und Churfürstl. Brandenburgischer, sonderlich in der Chur- und Marck-Brandenburg, Wie auch andern Provintzien, publicirten und ergangenen Ordnungen, Edicten, Mandaten, Rescripten, ed. Samuel von Coccejus (Berlin, 1753–1822).

Nuckolls, Charles W., 'The Durbar Incident', *Modern Asian Studies*, 24 (1990), 529–59.

Nussbaum, Martha C., *Hiding from Humanity: Disgust, Shame, and the Law* (Princeton, 2004).

Nussbaum, Martha C., *Anger and Forgiveness: Resentment, Generosity, Justice* (New York, 2016).

Nuwer, Hank (ed.), *The Hazing Reader* (Bloomington, 2004).

O'Meara, Barry, *Napoleon in Exile; Or, A Voice from St Helena*, 2 vols (London, 1822).

O'Neill, Barry, *Honor, Symbols, and War* (Ann Arbor, 1999).

Oeffentlichkeit, Mündlichkeit, Anklageproceß, Geschwornengerichte: Eine systematische Zusammenstellung der Verhandlungen der Sächsischen Ständeversammlung hierüber (Grimma, 1843).

Offenberger, Ilana F., *The Jews of Nazi Vienna, 1938–1945* (Cham, 2017).

Olick, Jeffrey K., *In the House of the Hangman: The Agonies of German Defeat, 1943–1949* (Chicago, 2005).

Ortmann, Alexandra, *Machtvolle Verhandlungen: Zur Kulturgeschichte der deutschen Strafjustiz 1879–1924* (Göttingen, 2014).

Pädagogische Real-Encyclopädie oder Encyclopädisches Wörterbuch des Erziehungs- und Unterrichtswesens und seiner Geschichte, ed. Karl Gottlob Hergang, 2nd edn, 2 vols (Grimma, 1851–2).

Pädagogisches Real-Lexicon oder Repertorium für Erziehungs- und Unterrichtskunde und ihre Literatur, ed. D. Reuter (Nuremberg, 1811).

Paine, S[arah] C. M., *The Sino-Japanese War of 1894–1895: Perceptions, Power and Primacy* (Cambridge, 2003).

Pape, H. M. M., *Ueber die Wiedereinführung der Prügelstrafe und die Züchtigung des Gesindes* (Insterburg, 1853).

Papers Relating to the Foreign Relations of the United States, Transmitted to Congress, With the Annual Message of the President, December 9, 1891 (Washington, 1892).

Pascal, [Blaise], 'Pensées', in *Œuvres complètes*, ed. Jacques Chevalier (Paris 1954), 1081–1345.

Patterson, David S., et al. (eds), *Foreign Relations of the United States, 1961–1963*, v: The Soviet Union (Washington, 1998).

Paulmann, Johannes, *Pomp und Politik: Monarchenbegegnungen in Europa zwischen Ancien Régime und Erstem Weltkrieg* (Paderborn, 2000).

Paulmann, Johannes, 'Searching for a "Royal International": The Mechanics of Monarchical Relations in Nineteenth-Century Europe', in Martin H. Geyer and Johannes Paulmann (eds), *The Mechanics of Internationalism: Culture, Society, and the Politics from the 1840s to the First World War* (Oxford, 2001), 145–76.

Paulsen, Hermann Christian, *Die Regierung der Morgenländer* (Altona, 1755).

Peitsch, Helmut, '"Verordneter Antifaschismus": 1949 "in die Scham gezwungen" (Heuss), 1989 von der Scham befreit?', in Clare Flanagan and Stuart Taberner (eds), *1949/1989: Cultural Perspectives on Division and Unity in East and West* (Amsterdam, 2000), 1–26.

Pence, Katherine, 'Herr Schimpf und Frau Schande: Grenzgänger des Konsums im geteilten Berlin und die Politik des Kalten Krieges', in Burghard Ciesla et al. (eds), *Sterben für Berlin? Die Berliner Krisen 1948–1958* (Berlin, 2000), 185–202.

Pergaud, Louis, *The War of the Buttons* (French Original: 1912), trans. Stanley and Eleanor Hochman (New York, 1968).

Pertz, G[eorg] H[einrich], *Das Leben des Feldmarschalls Grafen Neithardt von Gneisenau*, i (Berlin, 1864).

Peschel-Gutzeit, Lore Maria, 'Das Recht auf gewaltfreie Erziehung: Was hat sich seit seiner Einführung im Jahr 2000 geändert?', *Familie Partnerschaft Recht*, 18 (2012), 195–9.

Petersen, Andrea, *Ehre und Scham: Das Verhältnis der Geschlechter in der Türkei* (Berlin, 1985).

Petley, Julian (ed.), *Media and Public Shaming: Drawing the Boundaries of Disclosure* (London, 2013).

Pfordten, Dietmar von der, *Menschenwürde* (Munich, 2016).

Pierer's Universal-Lexikon der Vergangenheit und Gegenwart, 4th edn, 19 vols (Altenburg 1857–65).

Pin, Xavier, 'L'honneur et le droit pénal en France', in Silvia Tellenbach (ed.), *Die Rolle der Ehre im Strafrecht* (Berlin, 2007), 149–219.

Pollack, Martin, *Topographie der Erinnerung* (Vienna, 2016).

Pommerin, Reiner, '*Sterilisierung der Rheinlandbastarde*': Das Schicksal einer farbigen deutschen Minderheit 1918–1937 (Düsseldorf 1979).

Pörksen, Bernhard, and Hanne Detel, *Der entfesselte Skandal: Das Ende der Kontrolle im Digitalen Zeitalter* (Cologne, 2012).

Pöschl, Viktor, and Panajotis Kondylis, 'Würde', in Otto Brunner et al. (eds), *Geschichtliche Grundbegriffe. Historisches Lexikon zur politisch-sozialen Sprache in Deutschland*, vii (Stuttgart, 1992), 637–77.

Preuß, Horst Dietrich, et al., 'Demut', in *Theologische Realenzyklopädie*, viii (Berlin, 1981), 459–88.

Priester, Jens-Michael, *Das Ende des Züchtigungsrechts* (Baden-Baden, 1999).

Pritchard, Earl H., 'The Kotow in the Macartney Embassy to China in 1793', *The Far Eastern Quarterly*, 2 (1943), 163–203.

Przetacznik, Franciszek, *Protection of Officials of Foreign States according to International Law* (Den Haag, 1983).

Przyrembel, Alexandra, *'Rassenschande'. Reinheitsmythos und Vernichtungslegitimation im Nationalsozialismus* (Göttingen, 2003).

Przyrembel, Alexandra, 'Ambivalente Gefühle: Sexualität und Antisemitismus während des Nationalsozialismus', *Geschichte und Gesellschaft*, 39 (2013), 527–54.

Quanter, Rudolf, *Die Schand- und Ehrenstrafen in der deutschen Rechtspflege* (Dresden 1901; reprint Aalen 1970).

Quellen zur Geschichte des Parlamentarismus und der politischen Parteien, ser. I, ix: Der Hauptausschuß des Deutschen Reichstags 1915–1918 (Düsseldorf, 1981).

Rachlin, Robert D., 'Roland Freisler and the Volksgerichtshof', in Alan E. Steinweis and Robert D. Rachlin (eds), *The Law in Nazi Germany: Ideology, Opportunism, and the Perversion of Justice* (New York, 2013), 63–87.

Ramm, Arnim, *Der 20. Juli vor dem Volksgerichtshof* (Berlin, 2007).

Ratzinger, Joseph Cardinal, *The Spirit of the Liturgy*, trans. John Saward (San Francisco, 2000).

Rauer, Valentin, 'Geste der Schuld: Die mediale Rezeption von Willy Brandts Kniefall in den neunziger Jahren', in Bernhard Giesen and Christoph Schneider (eds), *Tätertrauma: Nationale Erinnerungen im öffentlichen Diskurs* (Konstanz, 2004), 133–56.

Rauer, Valentin, 'Symbols in Action: Willy Brandt's Kneefall at the Warsaw Memorial', in Jeffrey C. Alexander et al. (eds.), *Social Performance: Symbolic Action, Cultural Pragmatics, and Ritual* (Cambridge, 2006), 257–82.

Rawski, Evelyn S., *The Last Emperors: A Social History of Qing Imperial Institutions* (Berkeley, 1998).

Reif, Sieglinde, 'Das "Recht des Siegers". Vergewaltigungen in München 1945', in Sybille Krafft (ed.), *Zwischen den Fronten: Münchner Frauen in Krieg und Frieden 1900–1950* (Munich, 1995), 360–71.

Reiland, Werner, *Die gesellschaftlichen Gerichte der DDR* (Tübingen, 1971).

Reinders, Eric, *Buddhist and Christian Responses to the Kowtow Problem in China* (London, 2015).

Remarque, Erich Maria, *Three Comrades*, trans. A. W. Wheen (Boston, 1937).

Rexroth, Frank, *Deviance and Power in Late Medieval London*, trans. Pamela E. Selwyn (New York, 2007).

Rhoden, Emmy von, *Der Trotzkopf* (1885) (Menden, n.d.).

Rhoden, Emmy von, *Taming a Tomboy*, trans. and adapted for American readers by Felix L. Oswald (Chicago, 1898).

Rickards, Maurice, *Posters of the First World War* (New York, 1968).

Riegel, Klaus-Georg, 'Rituals of Confession Within Communities of Virtuosi: An Interpretation of the Stalinist Criticism and Self-Criticism in the Perspective of Max Weber's Sociology of Religion', *Totalitarian Movements and Political Religions*, 1 (2000), 16–42.

Rietzsch, Otto, 'Die Strafen und Maßregeln der Sicherung, Besserung und Heilung', in Franz Gürtner (ed.), *Das kommende deutsche Strafrecht. Allgem. Teil. Bericht über die Arbeit der amtlichen Strafrechtskommission*, 2nd edn (Berlin, 1935), 118–62.

Rittner, C. H., *Dr Mittelstädt's Broschüre: 'Gegen die Freiheitsstrafen'* (Hamburg, 1880).

Robbins, Alexandra, *Pledged: The Secret Life of Sororities* (New York, 2004).

Roberts, Mary Louise, *What Soldiers Do: Sex and the American GI in World War II France* (Chicago, 2013).

Rockhill, William Woodville, 'Diplomatic Missions to the Court of China: The Kowtow Question', *American Historical Review*, 2 (1897), 427–42, 627–43.

Rockhill, William Woodville, *Diplomatic Audiences at the Court of China* (London, 1905).

Röger, Maren, *Kriegsbeziehungen: Intimität, Gewalt und Prostitution im besetzten Polen 1939 bis 1945* (Frankfurt, 2015).

Rohr, Julius Bernhard von, *Einleitung zur Ceremoniel-Wissenschafft der Grossen Herren* (Berlin, 1733).

Ronson, Jon, *So You've Been Publicly Shamed* (London, 2015).

Rorty, Richard, *Contingency, Irony, and Solidarity* (Cambridge, 1989).

Rosenblum, Warren, *Beyond the Prison Gates: Punishment and Welfare in Germany, 1850–1933* (Chapel Hill, 2008).

Rossner, Meredith, 'Reintegrative Ritual: Restorative Justice and Micro-Sociology', in Susanne Karstedt et al. (eds), *Emotions, Crime and Justice* (Oxford, 2011), 169–91.

Rothstein, Andrew, *Peter the Great and Marlborough: Politics and Diplomacy in Converging Wars* (Houndmills, 1986).

Rousseau, Jean-Jacques, *Emil, or On Education* (French original: 1762) (New York, 1979).

Rowbotham, Judith, 'When to Spare the Rod? Legal Reactions and Popular Attitudes towards the (In)appropriate Chastisement of Children, 1850–1910', *Law, Crime and History*, 7 (2017), 98–125.

Rublack, Ulinka, 'Anschläge auf die Ehre: Schmähschriften und -zeichen in der städtischen Kultur des Ancien Régime', in Klaus Schreiner and Gerd

Schwerhoff (eds), *Verletzte Ehre: Ehrkonflikte in Gesellschaften des Mittelalters und der Frühen Neuzeit* (Cologne, 1995), 381–411.

Rudolph, Hartmut, *Evangelische Kirche und Vertriebene 1945–1972*, ii (Göttingen, 1985).

Rummel, Walter, 'Motive staatlicher und dörflicher Gewaltanwendung im 19. Jahrhundert: Eine Skizze zum Ende der frühneuzeitlichen Sozialkultur in der preußischen Rheinprovinz', in Magnus Eriksson and Barbara Krug-Richter (eds), *Streitkulturen: Gewalt, Konflikt und Kommunikation in der ländlichen Gesellschaft (16.–19. Jahrhundert)* (Cologne, 2003), 157–78.

Rush, Benjamin, *An Enquiry into the Effects of Public Punishments upon Criminals, and upon Society* (Philadelphia, 1787).

Rutherford, Paul, *Endless Propaganda: The Advertising of Public Goods* (Toronto, 2000).

Rutz, Willi, *Die Genugtuung für den Verletzten in der strafrechtlichen Reformbewegung und in den Entwürfen* (Diss. Göttingen, 1928).

Ruxton, Ian C. (ed.), *The Diaries of Sir Ernest Satow, British Envoy in Peking (1900–1906)*, 2 vols (Morrisville, 2011).

Sabatier, Gérard, 'Les itinéraires des ambassadeurs pour les audiences à Versailles au temps de Louis XIV', in Ralph Kauz et al. (eds), *Diplomatisches Zeremoniell in Europa und im Mittleren Osten in der Frühen Neuzeit* (Vienna, 2009), 187–211.

Sachße, Christoph, and Florian Tennstedt, *Geschichte der Armenfürsorge in Deutschland: Vom Spätmittelalter bis zum Ersten Weltkrieg* (Stuttgart, 1980).

Saint Augustine, 'Miscellany of Questions in Response to Simplician', in *The Works of Saint Augustine, part I, xii: Responses to Miscellaneous Questions*, trans. Boniface Ramsey (New York, 2008), 159–232.

Salgo, Ludwig, 'Vom langsamen Sterben des elterlichen Züchtigungsrechts', *Recht der Jugend und des Bildungswesens*, 49 (2001), 283–94.

Sanday, Peggy Reeves, *Fraternity Gang Rape: Sex, Brotherhood, and Privilege on Campus* (New York, 1990).

Sander, Helke, and Barbara Johr (eds), *BeFreier und Befreite: Krieg, Vergewaltigungen, Kinder* (Munich, 1992).

Sangiovanni, Andrea, *Humanity without Dignity: Moral Equality, Respect, and Human Rights* (Cambridge, Mass., 2017).

Satow, Ernest, *A Diplomat in Japan* (Tokio 1968).

Saurette, Paul, 'You Dissin Me? Humiliation and Post 9/11 Global Politics', *Review of International Studies*, 32 (2006), 495–522.

Sayer, Derek, 'British Reaction to the Amritsar Massacre 1919–1920', *Past and Present*, 131 (1991), 130–64.

Schaffstein, Friedrich, 'Die Bedeutung der Ehrenstrafe im nationalsozialistischen Strafrecht', *Deutsches Recht*, 5 (1935), 269–71.

Scheff, Thomas J., and Suzanne M. Retzinger, *Emotions and Violence: Shame and Rage in Destructive Conflicts* (Lexington, 1991).

Scheidler, [Konrad], 'Dürfen in der Schule entehrende Strafen vorkommen? Und wenn ja: wie müssen sie beschaffen seyn, damit sie nicht erbittern?', Der Deutsche Schulbote, 10 (1851), 137–40.

Schejnin, Lew, 'Kriminalität und Gesellschaft', Neue Justiz, 14 (1960), 220–7.

Schivelbusch, Wolfgang, The Culture of Defeat: On National Trauma, Mourning, and Recovery, trans. Jefferson Chase (New York, 2004).

Schlabrendorff, Fabian von, The Secret War against Hitler, trans. Hilda Simon (London, 1966).

Schmidt, Loki, Auf dem roten Teppich und fest auf der Erde (Hamburg, 2010).

Schmitt, Jean-Claude, La raison des gestes dans l'Occident médiéval (Paris, 1990).

Schneider, Christoph, 'Der Warschauer Kniefall: Zur Geschichte einer Charismatisierung', in Bernhard Giesen and Christoph Schneider (eds), Tätertrauma: Nationale Erinnerungen im öffentlichen Diskurs (Konstanz, 2004), 195–235.

Schneider, Wolfgang Ludwig, 'Brandts Kniefall in Warschau: Politische und ikonographische Bedeutungsaspekte', in Bernhard Giesen and Christoph Schneider (eds), Tätertrauma: Nationale Erinnerungen im öffentlichen Diskurs (Konstanz, 2004), 157–94.

Schnell, Heinrich, Ich und meine Jungens: Zufällige Gespräche über allerhand Erziehungsfragen von heute für die Eltern unserer Gymnasiasten (Leipzig, 1914).

Schomburg, Wolfgang, 'Die öffentliche Bekanntmachung einer strafrechtlichen Verurteilung: Rechtslage und Rechtstatsachen unter besonderer Berücksichtigung von §200 StGB', Zeitschrift für Rechtspolitik, 19 (1986), 65–8.

Schönburg-Waldenburg, Heinrich Prinz von, Erinnerungen aus kaiserlicher Zeit (Leipzig, 1929).

Schönfeldt, Hans-Andreas, Vom Schiedsmann zur Schiedskommission: Normdurchsetzung durch territoriale gesellschaftliche Gerichte in der DDR (Frankfurt, 2002).

Schönke, Adolf, Strafgesetzbuch für das Deutsche Reich. Kommentar (Munich, 1942).

Schönke, Adolf, Strafgesetzbuch (Munich, 1947).

Schönke, Adolf, u.a., Strafgesetzbuch. Kommentar, 28th edn (Munich, 2010).

Schramm, Hermine, Der gute Ton oder das richtige Benehmen in der Familie, in der Gesellschaft und im öffentlichen Leben (Berlin, 1892).

Schreiner, Klaus, 'Verletzte Ehre', in Dietmar Willoweit (ed.), Die Entstehung des öffentlichen Strafrechts (Cologne, 1999), 263–320.

Schröder, Martin, Prügelstrafe und Züchtigungsrecht in den deutschen Schutzgebieten Schwarzafrikas (Münster, 1997).

Schroeder, Paul W., The Transformation of European Politics 1763–1848 (Oxford, 1994).

Schrott, Karin, Das normative Korsett: Reglementierungen für Frauen in Gesellschaft und Öffentlichkeit in der deutschsprachigen Anstands- und Benimmliteratur zwischen 1871 und 1914 (Würzburg, 2005).

Schulte, Nikos, Öffentliche Strafe und Privatgenugtuung bei Ehrverletzungen (Breslau, 1913).

Schultze-Pfaelzer, Gerhard, Kampf um den Kopf: Meine Erlebnisse als Gefangener des Volksgerichtshofes 1943–1945 (Berlin, 1948).

Schulz, Heinrich, *Die Mutter als Erzieherin: Kleine Beiträge zur Praxis der proletarischen Hauserziehung* (1907), 4th edn (Stuttgart, 1919).

Schulz, Peter-Bernd, 'Gruppensoziologische und psychologische Elemente der Tätigkeit der Konfliktkommissionen', *Strafe und Recht*, 16 (1967), 40–53.

Schumann, Dirk, 'Schläge als Strafe? Erziehungsmethoden nach 1945 und ihr Einfluss auf die "Friedenskultur" in beiden Deutschlands', in Thomas Kühne (ed.), *Von der Kriegskultur zur Friedenskultur? Zum Mentalitätswandel in Deutschland seit 1945* (Hamburg, 2000), 34–48.

Schumann, Dirk, 'Legislation and Liberalization: The Debate about Corporal Punishment in Schools in Postwar West Germany, 1945–1975', *German History*, 25 (2007), 192–218.

Schumann, Dirk, 'Asserting their "Natural Right": Parents and Public Schooling in Post-1945 Germany', in Dirk Schumann (ed.), *Raising Citizens in the 'Century of the Child': The United States and German Central Europe in Comparative Perspective* (New York, 2010), 206–25.

Schürmann, Thomas, *Tisch- und Grußsitten im Zivilisationsprozeß* (Münster, 1994).

Schwarze, Friedrich Oskar, *Commentar zum Strafgesetzbuch für das Deutsche Reich*, 3rd edn (Leipzig, 1873).

Schwarze, Friedrich Oskar von, *Die Freiheitsstrafe* (Leipzig, 1880).

Schwarzer, Alice, *PorNo* (Cologne, 1994).

Schwerhoff, Gerd, 'Verordnete Schande? Spätmittelalterliche und frühneuzeitliche Ehrenstrafen zwischen Rechtsakt und sozialer Sanktion', in Andreas Blauert and Gerd Schwerhoff (eds), *Mit den Waffen der Justiz: Zur Kriminalitätsgeschichte des Spätmittelalters und der Frühen Neuzeit* (Frankfurt, 1993), 158–88.

Sellert, Wolfgang, and Hinrich Rüping, *Studien- und Quellenbuch zur Geschichte der deutschen Strafrechtspflege*, 2 vols (Aalen, 1989–94).

Sen, Satadru, *Disciplining Punishment: Colonialism and Convict Society in the Andaman Islands* (Delhi, 2000).

Sharpe, James A., 'The Decline of Public Punishment in England, Sixteenth to Nineteenth Centuries', in Reiner Schulze et al. (eds), *Strafzweck und Strafform zwischen religiöser und weltlicher Wertevermittlung* (Münster, 2008), 73–87.

Sheffield, G. D., *Leadership in the Trenches: Officer–Man Relations, Morale and Discipline in the British Army in the Era of the First World War* (Houndmills, 2000).

Shklar, Judith N., *Ordinary Vices* (Cambridge, Mass., 1984).

Shoemaker, Robert B., 'The Decline of Public Insult in London 1660–1800', *Past and Present*, 169 (2000), 97–131.

Shoemaker, Robert, 'Streets of Shame? The Crowd and Public Punishments in London, 1700–1820', in Simon Devereaux and Paul Griffiths (eds), *Penal Practice and Culture, 1500–1900: Punishing the English* (Basingstoke, 2004), 232–57.

Siemens, Daniel, *Metropole und Verbrechen: Die Gerichtsreportage in Berlin, Paris und Chicago 1919–1933* (Stuttgart, 2007).

Simmel, Georg, 'Zur Psychologie der Scham (1901)', in Georg Simmel, *Schriften zur Soziologie*, ed. Heinz-Jürgen Dahme and Otthein Rammstedt (Frankfurt, 1983), 140–50.

Singer, Kurt, *Die Würde des Schülers ist antastbar: Vom Alltag in unseren Schulen und wie wir ihn verändern können* (Reinbek, 1998).

Singha, Radhika, 'The "Rare Infliction": The Abolition of Flogging in the Indian Army, circa 1835–1920', *Law and History Review*, 34 (2016), 783–818.

Smirra, Nikolas, *Entwicklung der Strafzwecklehre in Frankreich: vom Vorabend der Revolution bis zum Ende des 1. Weltkrieges* (Regensburg, 2014).

Smith, Greg T., 'Civilized People Don't Want to See That Kind of Thing: The Decline of Public Physical Punishment in London, 1760–1840', in Carolyn Strange (ed.), *Qualities of Mercy: Justice, Punishment, and Discretion* (Vancouver, 1996), 21–51.

Sohn, Louis B. (ed.), *Cases on United Nations Law* (Brooklyn, 1956).

Solberg, Winton U., 'Harmless Pranks or Brutal Practices? Hazing at the University of Illinois, 1868–1913', *Journal of the Illinois State Historical Society*, 91 (1998), 233–59.

Sonnenfels, Joseph von, *Grundsätze der Polizey-, Handlung- und Finanzwissenschaft*, part 1, 3rd edn (Vienna, 1777).

Sources of Chinese Tradition, ed. William Theodore de Bary and Richard Lufrano, 2nd edn, ii (New York, 2000).

Speitkamp, Winfried, *Ohrfeige, Duell und Ehrenmord: Eine Geschichte der Ehre* (Stuttgart, 2010).

Spence, Jonathan, *The Memory Palace of Matteo Ricci* (London, 1985).

Spencer, Herbert, *The Principles of Sociology*, 3 vols (New York, 1898).

Sperlich, Peter W., *The East German Social Courts: Law and Popular Justice in a Marxist-Leninist Society* (Westport, 2007).

Spierenburg, Pieter, *The Spectacle of Suffering: Executions and the Evolution of Repression: From a Preindustrial Metropolis to the European Experience* (Cambridge, 1984).

Spock, Benjamin, *The Common Sense Book of Baby and Child Care* (New York, 1946).

Staunton, George, *An Authentic Account of an Embassy from the King of Great Britain to the Emperor of China*, i (Philadelphia, 1799).

Stearns, Peter N., *Shame: A Brief History* (Urbana, Ill., 2017).

Steen, Andreas, 'From Resistance to International Diplomacy: Unwelcome Prussia and the Signing of the First Sino-German Treaty in Tianjin, 1859–1861', in Klaus Mühlhahn (ed.), *The Limits of Empire: New Perspectives on Imperialism in Modern China* (Berlin, 2008), 9–33.

Steinbacher, Sybille, *Wie der Sex nach Deutschland kam: Der Kampf um Sittlichkeit und Anstand in der frühen Bundesrepublik* (Munich, 2011).

Steller, Verena, *Diplomatie von Angesicht zu Angesicht: Diplomatische Handlungsformen in den deutsch-französischen Beziehungen 1870–1919* (Paderborn, 2011).

Stevenson, Robert Louis, *The Letters of Robert Louis Stevenson*, ed. Sidney Colvin, i (New York, 1917).

Stollberg-Rilinger, Barbara, 'Honores regii. Die Königswürde im zeremoniellen Zeichensystem der Frühen Neuzeit', in Johannes Kunisch (ed.), *Dreihundert Jahre Preußische Königskrönung* (Berlin, 2002), 1–26.

Stollberg-Rilinger, Barbara, 'Kneeling before God—Kneeling before the Emperor: The Transformation of a Ritual during the Confessional Conflict in Germany', in Nils Holger Petersen et al. (eds), *Resonances: Historical Essays on Continuity and Change* (Turnhout, 2011), 149–72.

Stollberg-Rilinger, Barbara, *The Emperor's Old Clothes: Constitutional History and the Symbolic Language of the Holy Roman Empire*, trans. Thomas Dunlap (New York, 2015).

Storr, Matthias, *Zwangsarbeit: 'Ausländereinsatz' in Göppingen 1939 bis 1945* (Göppingen, 1993).

Streit, Josef, 'Einige Gedanken zur Vorbereitung der Richterwahl', *Neue Justiz*, 13 (1959), 37–9.

Streng, Adolf, *Studien über Entwicklung, Ergebnisse und Gestaltung des Vollzugs der Freiheitsstrafe in Deutschland* (Stuttgart, 1886).

Strittmatter, Erwin, *Nachrichten aus meinem Leben: Aus den Tagebüchern 1954–1973*, ed. Almut Giesecke (Berlin, 2012).

Stürner, Rolf, 'Die verlorene Ehre des Bundesbürgers', *JuristenZeitung*, 49 (1994), 865–77.

Sulzer, Johann Georg, 'Gebehrden', in Johann Georg Sulzer, *Allgemeine Theorie der schönen Künste*, i (Leipzig, 1771), 427–30.

Sulzer, Johann Georg, *Versuch von der Erziehung und Unterweisung der Kinder* (1745), reprint of the edn Zurich 1748, ed. Olaf Breidbach (Hildesheim, 2012).

Svarez, Carl Gottlieb, *Vorträge über Recht und Staat*, ed. Hermann Conrad and Gerd Kleinheyer (Cologne, 1960).

Svarverud, Rune, *International Law as World Order in Late Imperial China: Translation, Reception and Discourse, 1847–1911* (Leiden, 2007).

Tändler, Maik, 'Erziehung der Erzieher. Lehrer als problematische Subjekte zwischen Bildungsreform und antiautoritärer Pädagogik', in Pascal Eitler and Jens Elberfeld (eds), *Zeitgeschichte des Selbst: Therapeutisierung—Politisierung—Emotionalisierung* (Bielefeld, 2015), 85–112.

Tangney, June Price, 'The Self-Conscious Emotions: Shame, Guilt, Embarrassment and Pride', in Tim Dalgleish and Mick J. Power (eds), *Handbook of Cognition and Emotion* (Chichester, 1999), 541–68.

Taschenbuch für teutsche Schulmeister auf das Jahr 1789, ed. Christoph Ferdinand Moser (Ulm, 1789).

Taylor, Gabriele, *Pride, Shame and Guilt: Emotions of Self-Assessment* (Oxford, 1985).

Teitel, Ruti, 'The Transitional Apology', in Elazar Barkan and Alexander Karn (eds), *Taking Wrongs Seriously: Apologies and Reconciliation* (Stanford, 2006), 101–14.

Teng, Ssu-yü, and John K. Fairbank, *China's Response to the West: A Documentary Survey 1839–1923* (Cambridge, Mass., 1979).

Tettinger, Peter J., *Die Ehre—ein ungeschütztes Verfassungsgut?* (Cologne, 1995).

The Historical Record of the Imperial Visit to India 1911 (London, 1914), ⟨http://www. empire.amdigital.co.uk/contents/document-detail.aspx?sectionid=277, accessed 18 April 2017⟩.

The Paris Covenant for a League of Nations: Text of the Plan Adopted by the Paris Peace Conference April 28, 1919, New York [1919].

The Penal Code of France, trans. into English; with a Preliminary Dissertation, and Notes (London, 1819).

The Summa Theologica of St Thomas Aquinas, trans. Fathers of the English Dominican Province (London, 1922).

Tholander, Christa, *Fremdarbeiter 1939 bis 1945: Ausländische Arbeitskräfte in der Zeppelin-Stadt Friedrichshafen* (Essen, 2001).

Thom, Deborah, '"Beating Children is Wrong": Domestic Life, Psychological Thinking and the Permissive Turn,' in Lucy Delap et al. (eds), *The Politics of Domestic Authority in Britain since 1800* (Houndmills, 2009), 261–83.

Thompson, E. P., 'Rough Music', in E. P. Thompson, *Customs in Common* (London, 1991), 467–538.

Tilly, Charles, *The Contentious French* (Cambridge, Mass., 1986).

Timmers, Margaret (ed.), *The Power of the Poster* (London, 1998).

Toeche-Mittler, Theodor, 'Die Kaiserproklamation in Versailles am 18. Januar 1871', *Beihefte zum Militär-Wochenblatt* (1896), 1–50.

Tsiang, T. F., 'Sino-Japanese Diplomatic Relations, 1870–1894', *Chinese Social and Political Science Review*, 17 (1933), 1–106.

Tsipursky, Gleb, 'Coercion and Consumption: The Khrushchev Leadership's Ruling Style in the Campaign against "Westernized" Youth, 1954–1964', in William Jay Risch (ed.), *Youth and Rock in the Soviet Bloc: Youth Cultures, Music, and the State in Russia and Eastern Europe* (Lanham, Md., 2015), 55–79.

Tuchel, Johannes, 'Vor dem "Volksgerichtshof": Schauprozesse vor laufender Kamera', in Gerhard Paul (ed.), *Das Jahrhundert der Bilder 1900 bis 1949* (Göttingen, 2009), 648–57.

Turner, Victor, *Vom Ritual zum Theater: Der Ernst des menschlichen Spiels* (Frankfurt, 1989).

Twain, Mark, *The Adventures of Huckleberry Finn* (New York, 1885).

'Über Dorfschulen und ihre Verbesserung', *Allgemeines Magazin für Prediger, Seelsorger und Katecheten*, 9 (1796), 18–38.

Uhland, Robert, *Geschichte der Hohen Karlsschule in Stuttgart* (Stuttgart, 1953).

Uhlig, Gottfried (ed.), *Dokumente zur Geschichte des Schulwesens in der Deutschen Demokratischen Republik, i: 1945–1955* (Berlin/East, 1970).

Unfried, Berthold, 'Foreign Communists and the Mechanisms of Soviet Cadre Formation in the USSR', in Barry McLoughlin and Kevin McDermott (eds), *Stalin's Terror* (Basingstoke, 2004), 175–93.

Vaksberg, Arkady, *The Prosecutor and the Prey: Vyshinsky and the 1930s' Moscow Show Trials*, trans. Jan Butler (London, 1990).

Van Braam, André Everard, *An Authentic Account of the Embassy of the Dutch East-India Company, to the Court of the Emperor of China, in the Years 1794 and 1795*, i (London, 1798).

Van Gennep, Arnold, *The Rites of Passages* (French original: 1909), trans. Monika B. Vizedom and Gabriele L. Caffee (London, 1960).

van Guido Meersbergen, 'The Diplomatic Repertoires of the East India Companies in Mughal South Asia, 1608–1717', *The Historical Journal*, 62 (2019), 875–898.

Vattel, Emer de, *The Law of Nations: Or, Principles of the Law of Nature, Applied to the Conduct and Affairs of National and Sovereigns. From the New Edition by Joseph Chitty* (Philadelphia, 1852).

Vec, Miloš, *Zeremonialwissenschaft im Fürstenstaat: Studien zur juristischen und politischen Theorie absolutistischer Herrschaftsrepräsentationen* (Frankfurt, 1998).

Verhandlungen der deutschen verfassunggebenden Reichsversammlung zu Frankfurt am Main, 6 vols (Frankfurt, 1848/9).

Verhandlungen des Deutschen Reichstags (Berlin, 1871 ff.).

Vervenioti, Tassoula, 'Left-Wing Women between Politics and Family', in Mark Mazower (ed.), *After the War Was Over: Reconstructing the Family, Nation, and State in Greece, 1943–1960* (Princeton, 2000), 105–21.

Virgili, Fabrice, *Shorn Women: Gender and Punishment in Liberation France* (Oxford, 2002).

Voigt, Erik Nils, *Die Gesetzgebungsgeschichte der militärischen Ehrenstrafen und der Offizierehrengerichtsbarkeit im preußischen und deutschen Heer von 1806 bis 1918* (Frankfurt, 2004).

Wahlberg, W[ilhelm] E[mil], *Die Ehrenfolgen der strafgerichtlichen Verurtheilung: Ein Beitrag zur Reform des Strafensystems* (Vienna, 1864).

Wahrhold and Antistiani, 'Soll der sogenannte gemeine Diebstahl jederzeit mit Fustigation und Zuchthaus bestraft werden? Ist eine die Schaamhaftigkeit verletzende körperliche Züchtigung gesetzlich erlaubt? Muß eine Privatperson, welcher gesetzlich zusteht, ein Vergehen oder Verbrechen zu verzeihen, diese Verzeihung gerichtlich erklären?', *Zeitschrift für die Criminal-Rechts-Pflege in den Preußischen Staaten*, 18/35 (1831), 145–58.

Waldow, Jörg Ernst August, *Der strafrechtliche Ehrenschutz in der NS-Zeit* (Baden-Baden, 2000).

Walter, Natasha, *Living Dolls: The Return of Sexism* (London, 2010).

Walton, Charles, *Policing Public Opinion in the French Revolution: The Culture of Calumny and the Problem of Free Speech* (Oxford, 2009).

Walz, Rainer, 'Schimpfende Weiber: Frauen in lippischen Beleidigungsprozessen des 17. Jahrhunderts', in Heide Wunder and Christine Vanja (eds), *Weiber, Menschen, Frauenzimmer* (Göttingen, 1996), 175–98.

Wang, S[hen-Tsu], *The Margary Affair and the Chefoo Agreement* (London, 1940).

Wang, Tseng-Tsai, 'The Audience Question: Foreign Representatives and the Emperor of China, 1858–1873', *Historical Journal*, 14 (1971), 617–26.

Wang, Zheng, *Never Forget National Humiliation: Historial Memory in Chinese Politics and Foreign Relations* (New York, 2012).

Warring, Anette, 'Intimate and Sexual Relations', in Robert Gildea et al. (eds), *Surviving Hitler and Mussolini: Daily Life in Occupied Europe* (Oxford, 2006), 88–128.

Weber, [Heinrich Benedikt von], 'Von den Hauptforderungen an eine zeitgemäße Straf-Prozeßordnung', *Neues Archiv des Criminalrechts*, 4 (1821), 596–631.

Weber, Adolph Dieterich, *Ueber Injurien und Schmähschriften*, i (Schwerin, 1793).

Weber, Max, *Economy and Society: An Outline of Interpretive Sociology*, ed. Guenther Roth and Claus Wittich (Berkeley, 1968).

Weber, Petra, *Carlo Schmid 1896–1979* (Munich, 1996).

Weber-Guskar, Eva, *Würde als Haltung: Eine philosophische Untersuchung zum Begriff der Menschenwürde* (Münster, 2016).

Webster, Elaine, 'Degradation: A Human Rights Law Perspective', in Paulus Kaufmann et al. (eds), *Humiliation, Degradation, Dehumanization: Human Dignity Violated* (Dordrecht, 2011), 67–84.

Weckel, Ulrike, 'Disappointed Hopes for Spontaneous Mass Conversions: German Responses to Allied Atrocity Film Screenings, 1945–46', *Bulletin of the German Historical Institute*, 51 (2012), 39–53.

Weckel, Ulrike, 'Shamed by Nazi Crimes: The First Step Towards Germans' Reeducation or a Catalyst for Their Wish to Forget?', in Mary Fulbrook et al. (eds), *Reverberations of Nazi Violence in Germany and Beyond: Disturbing Pasts* (London, 2016), 33–46.

Weidemann, Doris, *Interkulturelles Lernen: Erfahrungen mit dem chinesischen 'Gesicht'. Deutsche in Taiwan* (Bielefeld, 2004).

Welcker, Carl, 'Infamie, Ehre, Ehrenstrafen', in Carl von Rotteck and Carl Welcker (eds), *Das Staats-Lexikon*, 2nd edn, vii (Altona, 1847), 377–404.

Welcker, Carl, 'Injurie', in Carl von Rotteck and Carl Welcker (eds), *Das Staats-Lexikon*, 2nd edn, vii (Altona, 1847), 404–422.

Wentker, Sibylle, 'Besuch aus Persien: Die Gesandtschaft von 1819 an den Wiener Hof', in Ralph Kauz et al. (eds), *Diplomatisches Zeremoniell in Europa und im Mittleren Osten in der Frühen Neuzeit* (Vienna, 2009), 131–53.

Wetherell, Elisabeth, *The Wide, Wide World* (Leipzig, 1854).

Wettlaufer, Jörg, 'Schand- und Ehrenstrafen des Spätmittelalters und der Frühneuzeit', in Andreas Deutsch (ed.), *Das Deutsche Rechtswörterbuch—Perspektiven* (Heidelberg, 2010), 265–80.

Wettlaufer, Jörg, and Yasuhiro Nishimura, 'The History of Shaming Punishments and Public Exposure in Penal Law in Comparative Perspective: Western Europe and East Asia', in Bénédicte Sère and Jörg Wettlaufer (eds), *Shame between Punishment and Penance* (Florence, 2013), 197–228.

Whaley, Deborah Elizabeth, *Disciplining Women: Alpha Kappa Alpha, Black Counterpublics, and the Cultural Politics of Black Sororities* (Albany, 2010).

Wheaton, Henry, *Elements of International Law* (1836), 6th edn (Boston, 1855).

Whitman, James Q., 'What is Wrong with Inflicting Shame Sanctions?', *The Yale Law Journal*, 107 (1998), 1055–92.

Whitman, James Q., 'Enforcing Civility and Respect: Three Societies', *The Yale Law Journal*, 109 (2000), 1279–398.

Whitman, James Q., *Harsh Justice: Criminal Punishment and the Widening Divide between America and Europe* (Oxford, 2003).

Wick, Adolf von, *Ueber Ehrenstrafen und Ehrenfolgen der Verbrechen und Strafen* (Rostock, 1845).

Wiede, Wiebke, 'Von Zetteln und Apparaten. Subjektivierung in bundesdeutschen und britischen Arbeitsämtern der 1970er- und 1980er-Jahre', *Zeithistorische Forschungen/Studies in Contemporary History*, online edition, 13/3 (2016), URL: http://www.zeithistorische-forschungen.de/3-2016/id=5398, print edition: 466–87.

Wiedner, Hartmut, 'Soldatenmißhandlungen im Wilhelminischen Kaiserreich (1890–1914)', *Archiv für Sozialgeschichte*, 22 (1982), 159–99.

Wierling, Dorothee, *Geboren im Jahr Eins: Der Jahrgang 1949 in der DDR* (Berlin, 2002).

Wigger, Iris, '"Against the Laws of Civilization": Race, Gender and Nation in the International Racist Campaign against the 'Black Shame', *Berkeley Journal of Sociology* 46 (2002), 113–31.

Wigger, Iris, *Die 'Schwarze Schmach' am Rhein: Rassistische Diskriminierung zwischen Geschlecht, Klasse, Nation und Rasse* (Münster, 2007).

Wildeblood, Joan, and Peter Brinson, *The Polite World: A Guide to English Manners and Deportment from the Thirteenth Century to the Nineteenth Century* (London, 1965).

Wildt, Michael, *Hitler's Volksgemeinschaft and the Dynamics of Racial Exclusion: Violence against Jews in Provincial Germany, 1919–1939*, trans. Bernard Heise (New York, 2007).

Wilhelm, Th. [i.e. Therese Proßl], *Ist die körperliche Züchtigung ein Erziehungsfaktor?* (Warendorf, 1911).

Wilkens, Andreas, 'Kniefall vor der Geschichte: Willy Brandt in Warschau 1970', in Corine Defrance and Ulrich Pfeil (eds), *Verständigung und Versöhnung nach dem 'Zivilisationsbruch? Deutschland in Europa nach 1945* (Brussels, 2016), 83–102.

Wilkinson, Endymion, *Chinese History: A Manual* (Cambridge, Mass., 2000).

Williams, Bernard, *Shame and Necessity* (Berkeley, 2008).

Williams, Samuel Wells, *The Middle Kingdom: A Survey of the Geography, Government, Literature, Social Life, Arts, and History of the Chinese Empire and its Inhabitants* (1848), rev. edn, 2 vols (New York, 1900).

Windler, Christian, 'Diplomatic History as a Field for Cultural Analysis: Muslim–Christian Relations in Tunis, 1700–1840', *Historical Journal*, 44 (2001), 79–106.

Windler, Christian, *La diplomatie comme expérience de l'autre: Consuls français au Maghreb (1700–1840)* (Genf, 2002).

Wodehouse, P. G., *The White Feather* (London, 1907).

Wolf, Eugen, *Meine Wanderungen, i: Im Innern Chinas* (Stuttgart, 1901).

Wölfel, Ursula, *Tim Fireshoe*, trans. E. M. Prince (London, 1963).

Wolffsohn, Michael, and Thomas Brechenmacher, *Denkmalsturz? Brandts Kniefall* (Munich, 2005).

Wong, J. Y., *Deadly Dreams: Opium, Imperialism, and the Arrow War (1856–1860) in China* (Cambridge, 1998).

Woolf, Virginia, *A Room of One's Own and Three Guineas*, ed. Anna Snaith (Oxford, 2015).

Wundt, Wilhelm, 'Ueber den Ausdruck der Gemüthsbewegungen', *Deutsche Rundschau*, 11 (1877), 120–33.

Wundt, Wilhelm, *The Language of Gestures* (The Hague, 1973).

Wurmser, Léon, *The Mask of Shame* (Baltimore, 1981).

Xiaomin, Zhang, and Xu Chunfeng, 'The Late Qing Dynasty Diplomatic Transformation', *Chinese Journal of International Politics*, 1 (2007), 405–55.

Zeit- und Handbüchlein für Freunde der theologischen Lektüre auf das Jahr 1781 (Bayreuth, 1781).

Zedler, Johann Heinrich (ed.), *Grosses vollständiges Universal-Lexikon aller Wissenschafften und Künste*, 64 vols (Leipzig 1731–54).

Zhensheng, Li, *Red-Color News Soldier: A Chinese Photographer's Odyssey through the Cultural Revolution* (London, 2003).

Ziemann, Benjamin, *Front und Heimat: Ländliche Kriegserfahrungen im südlichen Bayern 1914–1923* (Essen, 1997).

Zink, Michel, *L'humiliation, le moyen âge et nous* (Paris, 2017).

Zur Nieden, Susanne, 'Erotische Fraternisierung: Der Mythos der schnellen Kapitulation der deutschen Frauen im Mai 1945', in Karen Hagemann and Stefanie Schüler-Springorum (eds), *Heimat-Front: Militär und Geschlechterverhältnisse im Zeitalter der Weltkriege* (Frankfurt, 2002), 313–25.

Żurek, Robert, 'Bolesław Kominek—Autor der Versöhnungsbotschaft der polnischen Bischöfe', in Friedhelm Boll et al. (eds), *Versöhnung und Politik: Polnisch-deutsche Versöhnungsinitiativen der 1960er Jahre und die Entspannungspolitik* (Bonn, 2009), 52–66.

Żurek, Robert, 'Der Briefwechsel der katholischen Bischöfe von 1965', in Friedhelm Boll et al. (eds), *Versöhnung und Politik: Polnisch-deutsche Versöhnungsinitiativen der 1960er Jahre und die Entspannungspolitik* (Bonn, 2009), 67–76.

'Zwey merkwürdige Verordnungen, welche wegen Bestrafung der Diebstähle zu Berlin d.d. 26. Febr. 1799 erlassen worden, nebst Anmerkungen von Klein', *Archiv des Criminalrechts*, 2 (1799), no. 1, 32–73.

ILLUSTRATION CREDITS

akg-images: **12**; Musée d'Histoire de l'Education, Paris/akg-images: **11**; © British Library Board. All Rights Reserved/Bridgeman Images: **24**; Bettmann/Getty Images: **15**; Santi Burgos/Bloomberg/Getty Images: **23**; Carl Mydans/The LIFE Picture Collection via Getty Images: **2**; ullstein bild/Getty Images: **16**; Heidelberg University Library G 5442-3 Folio RES (copyright status unknown): **21**; Herder Institute, Marburg, Image Archive: **6**; *Hohenzollernjahrbuch* 14 (1910), p. 101: **20**; *Punch*, 10 October 1900. Internet Archive: **18**; *Martin, ab in die Ecke und schäm dich (Martin, into the Corner, You Should Be Ashamed of Yourself)*, 1989/90. Hard foam, cast resin, latex, acrylic, metal, styrofoam, foam rubber, clothing. 178 × 67 × 47 cm. © Estate of Martin Kippenberger, Galerie Gisela Capitain, Cologne. Photo: Lothar Schnepf, Cologne, courtesy Estate of Martin Kippenberger, Galerie Gisela Capitain, Cologne: **10**; © Kreismuseum Bitterfeld: **5**; Landesarchiv Thüringen— State Archives Altenburg, picture collection, no. 5109 (the humiliation of Martha Vollrath in Altenburg, February 1941): **8**; © Ingrid Vang Nyman/The Astrid Lindgren Company: **13**; Robert Capa © International Center of Photography/ Magnum Photos: **9**; Metropolitan Museum of Art, New York. Harris Brisbane Dick Fund, 1932: **3**; *National-Zeitung* (Essen, Germany), 12 September 1933: **7**; Courtesy of Robert Ostermeyer (www.otto-reutter.de): **19**; Tony Dejak/AP/ Shutterstock: **1**; © *DER SPIEGEL* 51/1970: **22**; Wellcome Collection (CC BY): **4**; Wikimedia Commons: **14**; Beinecke Rare Book and Manuscript Library, Yale University: **17**.

INDEX

Places